AFTER AFRICA

AFTER AFRICA

Extracts from British Travel Accounts and Journals of the Seventeenth, Eighteenth, and Nineteenth Centuries concerning the Slaves, their Manners, and Customs in the British West Indies

Introduced and edited by

ROGER D. ABRAHAMS and JOHN F. SZWED,

assisted by

LESLIE BAKER *and* ADRIAN STACKHOUSE

YALE UNIVERSITY PRESS

NEW HAVEN AND LONDON

Portions of the introduction first appeared in different form in Szwed and Abrahams, "After the Myth: Studying Afro-American Culture Patterns in the Plantation Literature," *Research in African Literatures*, 7 (1976), 211–29, and in Abrahams, "The West Indian Tea Meeting: An Essay in Creolization," in *Old Roots in New Lands*, ed. Ann M. Pescatello (Westport, Ct.: Greenwood Press, 1977), pp. 173–208.

Figure 1 (p. 15) is from David Kunzle, *The Early Comic Strip* (Berkeley and Los Angeles, 1973), p. 374. Figures 2–19 follow p. 76. Figures 2–4 and 7–19 are from R. Bridgens, *Sketches of West India Scenery with Illustrations of Negro Character . . . from sketches taken during a voyage to, and residence of 7 years in, the Island of Trinidad* (London, 1836?). Figures 5 and 6 are from I. M. Belisario, *Sketches of Character in Illustration of the Habits, Occupations and Costume of the Negro Population in the Island of Jamaica*, 3 parts (Kingston, 1837–38).

Published with the assistance of the A. Whitney Griswold Publication Fund.

Designed by James J. Johnson and set in Caledonia Roman type. Printed in the United States of America by Vail-Ballou Press, Binghamton, N.Y.

Library of Congress Cataloging in Publication Data
Main entry under title:

After Africa.

   Bibliography: p.
   Includes index.
   1. Blacks—West Indies, British—History—Sources.
   2. Blacks—West Indies, British—Social life and customs—Sources. 3. Slaves—West Indies, British—History—Sources. I. Abrahams, Roger D. II. Szwed, John F., 1936–.
F2131.A47   1983   972.9'00497   82–20110
ISBN 0–300–02748–6

10 9 8 7 6 5 4 3 2 1

TO
EDWARD KAMAU BRATHWAITE

Contents

Acknowledgments

This work was first begun under the sponsorship of the Center for Urban Ethnography at the University of Pennsylvania, supported by Public Health Grant no. MH-17216 of the National Institute of Mental Health. It was also aided by a travel grant from the American Philosophical Society. Some of the library research was done by then graduate students Richard Raichelson and Robert Ulle, and much of the organization and editing were carried out by Leslie Baker and Adrian Stackhouse. Throughout we were aided and guided by the staffs of the libraries of the British Museum, Harvard University, the Institute of Jamaica, the University of Pennsylvania, the University of Texas at Austin, and Yale University. It is also a pleasure to recognize here the fine editorial work of Charles Grench and Alexander Metro of Yale University Press. And last, we wish to acknowledge the counsel given us by three extraordinary scholars of Afro-American life and culture, Edward Kamau Brathwaite, William A. Stewart, and Robert Farris Thompson. Their help can be acknowledged, but never repaid.

Introduction

When we began this project some ten years ago we had a goal which was easy to state if difficult to achieve. It seemed to us that existing knowledge of the history of the culture of African-derived peoples in the New World was woefully inadequate and generally wrong, and we wanted to make a contribution to its improvement. Perhaps the most succinct statement of what we thought to be wrong is found in Nathan Glazer and Daniel P. Moynihan's *Beyond the Melting Pot:* "The Negro is only an American, and nothing else. He has no values and culture to guard and protect."[1] On the contrary, we thought, Afro-Americans had guarded, protected, used, and kept intact a remarkably distinct culture, and this maintenance had been accomplished more fully than among most other peoples who had come from the Old World to the New. It is more complicated than this, of course, as much of what might be identified as Afro-American culture was newly developed in the Americas in response to the peculiar circumstances of New World development. But even these new forms of culture, these Afro-American innovations, have gone unrecognized.

In the 1960s there had been the beginnings of a new Afro-American culture history which had catalogued the contributions of outstanding Afro-American individuals, and the list was impressive. But there were still very few scholars of the mundane, the everyday, of the folk; very few chroniclers of black cultural contributions to the root facts of daily existence in America. It seemed amazing to us as folklorists and ethnographers that such black cultural innovations as baton twirling, cheerleading, jug bands, broken field running in football, the North American cultivation of rice, okra, yams, and sweet po-

1. Nathan Glazer and Daniel P. Moynihan, *Beyond the Melting Pot* (Cambridge, Mass.: MIT Press), p. 53.

1

tatoes, the terms *OK, wow, uh-huh* and *unh-unh, daddy* (as a term of endearment and respect between unrelated males), and *buddy* were not recognized as such.

So what? (some might ask). Who wants to play pop trivia games? But this was precisely the point. Far from being trivial, the very fundamentalness and everydayness of these elements make acknowledging their sources seem odd; their common, taken-for-granted quality has put them beyond history and thus beyond examination. Yet it is at this elemental level that real culture change occurs, and at which the Americas became the creolized societies which Europe had long thought them to be.

If we neglect the basic elements of a culture we get a very peculiar vision of it; but in the case of a dominated and an excluded people the result is grotesque. If we accept Glazer and Moynihan's vision of blacks as ciphers, as being "only" Americans, when we encounter ways in which they differ from other Americans, we are likely to see them as deviants, as pathological. Indeed, this was exactly the conclusion reached by the most influential of all studies of black Americans, Gunnar Myrdal's *An American Dilemma.*

This, then, is the task of our book: to seek out in the oldest documents available the encounter of Africans and Europeans in the New World, toward the discovery of what was and is distinctly Afro-American in the cultures of the Americas.

I

The difficulties of describing the cultural relationships between Afro-American peoples and their African progenitors is not due to any lack of data. *Any* argument of culture flow is difficult to wage, to be sure, and needs as much bolstering from ethnographic study as possible. But the problems that attend describing the forced dispersal of African peoples in the New World in its sociocultural dimension is made all the more difficult because of the inadequacy of the models of culture contact and resultant change which have been employed in any situation involving such a massive dispersal of peoples. Though there have been many such major movements analogous to the coming together of Europeans and Africans in the New World, we do not even have a clear statement of the important variables which operate in such situations. Rather, the casual and the anecdotal approach has prevailed; the forced encounter is viewed almost solely in terms of who is politically or economically the dominant people and who are subordinate, with the assumption that such subordination will lead to cultural as well as political and economic dominance.

No case undercuts this model of acculturation and its assumptions so clearly as that of Afro-Americans, for many of the most basic features of plantation and modern New World life have been strongly influenced by Afro-American cultural practices. What seems central to an understanding of the Afro-American situations from our culture-centered point of view is: the ways in which subordination was asserted and rationalized through the operation of a stereotypical notion directed at the slaves; and the fact that the Africans often came from groups with a developed agricultural technology and were brought together with Europeans who lacked experience in tropical gardening.

There were certain areas of culture in which the planters found it convenient not only not to attempt to eliminate African-style practices but in fact to encourage them. This was especially so in such noninstitutional dimensions of culture as work practices, ways of playing, and systems of magical practices and curing. These carryovers of African life assisted in a direct or an indirect way in the maintenance of the plantation (or some other unit of production). Further, there was little problem in accommodating such features within the stereotypical portrayal of blacks as perpetual children or as animals. In this view, then, active and self-conscious deculturation arose in plantation America only in those domains of life in which continuing the African forms of sociopolitical organization would threaten the status and power arrangements of the plantations. Thus, the various types of extended families of the Old World were indeed discouraged, as were the larger political and social units of African societies. From our perspective, this resulted more in a desocietalization than a deculturation, and even here there was not and could not have been a total brainwashing.

Wherever Afro-Americans could interact with one another (whether or not in the presence of Euro-Americans) there emerged a set of expectations, attitudes, and feelings which in great part derived from past practices. These encounters would naturally draw upon the shared experiences in Africa and the New World. We need not posit, then, wholesale carryovers of community-based culture to argue that African cultural continuities are obvious and long-lasting. Furthermore, many Euro-Americans recognized this cultural persistence from the earliest plantation days and give us a large—if selective—record of African and Afro-American cultural practices as filtered through the stereotypical rationalizing practice. We do not argue with the view that the plantation experience was, in great part, a European invention and arose in the wake of European markets for products of tropical gardening. But to ignore the African and Afro-American cultural inheritance in the development of life in these New World communities would be folly indeed. We will look, then, at Afro-American life through the documents of the planters and travelers.

II

Although this anthropological perspective seems self-evident to us, it is instructive before looking at the documents concerning Afro-America, to detail why it has been so difficult to wage such an argument or develop such a common-sense model in the past. Roger Bastide begins his book, *African Civilizations in the New World:* "The current vogue for the study of African civilization in America is a comparatively recent phenomenon. Before the abolition of slavery such a thing was inconceivable, since up till then the Negro had simply been regarded as a source of labour, not as the bearer of a culture."[2] In the sense that Afro-American communities are now studied in a methodical and holistic manner, Bastide is undoubtedly right but this is true of all such study, for the techniques for analysis of cultural continuities and discontinuities are comparatively recent developments. But with regard to the question of whether Afro-Americans might exhibit those patterned and predictable behaviors we call culture, this subject has been debated for at least two centuries.

To anthropologists, the idea that a group could be forcibly divested of culture, yet maintain itself and even proliferate, seems like a strange argument indeed. Yet this is just what social scientists (including some anthropologists) have been agreeing to agree upon for many years; even today, with the growing literature on the integrity of Afro-American culture the deculturation argument remains an article of faith for most writers dealing with the subject of Afro-Americans. And most anthropologists have acquiesced in this judgment. Just why this should be is certainly due in some part to the unwillingness of Euro-Americans to call the ways of black peoples manifestations of culture—except when these ways are sufficiently close to some European practice or another to register those black ways as misunderstandings or corruptions.

To most social scientists, the deculturation argument was a *given,*

2. Roger Bastide, *African Civilizations in the New World* (New York: Harper & Row, 1971), p. 1.

an unexamined set of assumptions paralleling similar arguments concerning other immigrant groups living in capitalist countries. This loss of culture, it is implicitly argued, happens to all traditional peoples when they are forced off the land in search of wages. Such divested groups, and their divestment, provided the raison d'être for sociological study and can be seen as a constant rationalizing thread of argument from Tönnies and Durkheim through Parsons and Merton, even Fredrick Barth.

This is not to say that anthropologists were blameless in such treatments of "the dispossessed." Redfield's folk–urban continuum is an obvious extension of Tönnies's *Gesellschaft–Gemeinschaft* distinction, as is Oscar Lewis's conception of a "culture of poverty" directly related to such "negative pastoral" commonplaces of argument as are found in Durkheim and even Marx. (We use this term because the pastoral is the literary form castigating city life while extolling simple country existence.[3])

But perhaps the most frustrating line of argument against the distinct features of Afro-American cultures arose in response to the work of Melville J. Herskovits, especially his *The Myth of the Negro Past* of 1941. Herskovits there details numerous directions in which cultural relationships between Africa and Afro-America might be explored; in the process he offers a barrage of illustrations of "Africanisms." At that point in American history, almost no one found it convenient to conceive of blacks as culturally distinct in any defining way, and so two types of counterarguments arose. On the one hand, specific Africanisms noted by Herskovits and his students were debated and rejected (bringing about a classic baby-and-bathwater problem). On the other, such African elements were not situated in community studies so that the whole way of life of communities might be demonstrated to be developed or retained from a specific African group; therefore the Africanness of the traits so designated were not so much rejected as ignored for being data unworthy of anthropological attention.

The frustrations of attempting to pursue the cultural continuities argument have not diminished since the famous Melville Herskovits–E. Franklin Frazier face-off carried on after the publication of *The Myth of the Negro Past*. In fact the lines of argument have not altered very much since the early 1940s, as we (and many other Afro-Americanists) have found to our sorrow. Listen to one recorded conversation

3. Cf. Raymond Williams, *The Country and the City* (London: Chatto and Windus, 1973).

between Frazier and Herskovits to catch the direction of the arguments and the sense of frustration:

> *Mr. Frazier:* I have not found anyone who could show any evidence of survival of African social organization in this country. I may cite a concrete case. You will recall that in reviewing my book, *The Negro Family in the United States,* in *The Nation,* you said that the description I gave of the reunion of a Negro family group could, with the change of a few words, be regarded as a description of a West African institution. But it also happens to be equally adequate as a description of a Pennsylvania Dutch family reunion. What are we to do in a case like that? Are we to say that it is African?
>
> *Mr. Herskovits:* Methodologically, it seems to me that if in studying a family whose ancestry in part, at least, came from Africa I found that something they do resembles a very deep-seated African custom, I should not look to Pennsylvania Dutch folk, with whom this family has not been in contact, for an explanation of such a custom. I may be wrong but that seems elementary.
>
> *Mr. Frazier:* But where did the Pennsylvania Dutch get their custom that resembles the one I described? Did they get it from Africa too?
>
> *Mr. Herskovits:* May I ask if the methodological point at issue is this: is it maintained that if we find anything done by Negroes in this country that resembles anything done in Europe, we must therefore conclude that the Negroes' behavior is derived from the European customs, the inference then being that the traditions of their African ancestors were not strong enough to stand against the impact of European ways?
>
> *Mr. Frazier:* No I wouldn't say that, but I believe it should be the aim of the scholar to establish an unmistakable historical connection between the African background and present behavior of Negroes, rather than to rely on *a priori* arguments.
>
> *Mr. Herskovits:* We will be in agreement, if you will add to your statement that neither should the scholar deny any such connection on *a priori* grounds.[4]

Even when such arguments emerge today among social scientists, one still hears a call for the tracing of specific elements of cultural practices directly back to Africa. Never mind that there may be highly cognate forms of practice throughout West Africa and the New World.[5]

4. Melville J. Herskovits, ed., *The Interdisciplinary Aspects of Negro Studies,* American Council of Learned Societies Bulletin no. 32 (Washington, D.C., 1941), p. 85.

5. Cf. M. G. Smith, "The African Heritage in the Caribbean," in *Caribbean Studies: A Symposium,* ed. Vera Rubin (Seattle: University of Washington Press, 1960), pp. 34–36.

There *are*, of course, some evidences of such direct and specific retentions. Sea Island basketry, for instance, can be shown to be made with the same technique and similar materials as those from Senegambia.[6] Similarly, William Bascom has surveyed the wide range of retentions of Yoruba and Dahomean deity names in various New World cult religions like *Vodû, Candomblé,* and *Shango,* even while he demonstrates why such continuities in different parts of the New World have been maintained.[7] In many of the documents which we draw upon in this study, many practices (such as dancing, drumming, funeral behaviors, and so on) are obviously close to some African antecedent, many of which are still to be observed in various communities in Afro-America.

However, in this kind of debate we are inclined to the position expressed by Richard Price when he noted that there are richer areas of cultural investigation in looking for such "development within historically related and overlapping sets of . . . ideas" than to restrict ourselves to a search for "direct retentions or survivals."[8] Or as two of the few followers of Herskovits, George E. Simpson and Peter Hammond, commented:

> Both past records and an examination of the contemporary situation in the New World indicate that beneath the relative superficial level of form there is a significant, non-conscious level of psychological function. On this level there is an important basic similarity [for instance], between varieties of religious practices both throughout West Africa and in the various New World Negro communities.[9]

They go on to discuss the means and style of spirit possession, accounting for the cultural tenacity of the practices by citing the basic commonality in this dimension of West African religious behavior. Finally, rejecting those (here specifically referring to M. G. Smith's argument) who assert that continuities from Africa can be established only through commonality of form from one specific place in the Old World to one in the New, Simpson and Hammond respond as follows:

6. Robert Farris Thompson, "African Influence on the Art of the United States," in *Black Studies in the University: A Symposium,* ed. Armstead L. Robinson et al. (New Haven: Yale University Press, 1969), pp. 122–70; Robert E. Perdue, Jr., "African Baskets in South Carolina," *Economic Botany,* 22 (1968), 289–92.

7. William R. Bascom, *Shango in the New World* (Austin: African and Afro-American Research Institute Occasional Publication, University of Texas, 1972).

8. Richard Price, "Saramaka Woodcarving: The Development of an Afro-American Art," *Man,* new ser. 5 (1970), 375.

9. George E. Simpson and Peter B. Hammond, "Discussion," in *Caribbean Studies: A Symposium,* p. 48.

Form is the most superficial level of cultural reality. Since it is consciously realized, it is often much quicker to change than the profounder philosophic principles and psychological attitudes which are frequently more persistent and tenacious because they exist beneath the level of consciousness.[10]

But such voices are to be encountered only rarely in the Afro-American anthropological scholarship. Though making less pointed objections than E. Franklin Frazier or M. G. Smith, a number of recent commentators have continued to maintain the deculturation argument even while carrying out some impressive ethnographic reporting. These scholars, by diverting focus from African continuities in the New World setting and by assuming the intent of the slavers to culturally strip the slaves, argue rather that if there are New World Negro cultures, they must arise for the most part from the common black experiences of enslavement and social exclusion. For instance, Sidney Mintz argues that

enslaved Africans were quite systematically prevented ... with few exceptions ... from bringing with them the personnel who maintained their homeland institutions: the complex social structures of the ancestral societies, with their kings and courts, guilds and cult-groups, markets and armies were not, and could not be transferred. Cultures are linked as continuing patterns of and for behavior in such social groupings; since the groupings themselves could not be maintained or readily reconstituted, the capacities or random representatives of these societies to perpetuate or to recreate the cultural contents of the past were seriously impaired. Again, the slaves were not usually able to regroup themselves in the New World settings in terms of their origins; the cultural heterogeneity of any slave group normally meant that what was shared culturally was likely to be minimal.... [However] the slaves could and did create viable patterns of life, for which their pasts were pools of available symbolic and material resources.[11]

We certainly agree that African institutions were vulnerable to elimination in the New World, at least where they were incompatible with those of slavery. Still, there is simply too much contrary evidence for us to accept Mintz's argument without some real qualifications. One thinks, for instance, of the important West African practice of *susu* (sharing group), which has not only been encountered under that very name in several places in Afro-America, but which should

10. Ibid., p. 50.
11. Sidney Mintz, in *Afro-American Anthropology: Contemporary Perspectives*, ed. Norman E. Whitten, Jr. and John F. Szwed (New York: Free Press, 1970), pp. 7–8.

also give us insight into the importance of many Afro-American group activities such as Friendly Societies, lodges, burial societies, rent parties, and the like.[12] In the religious domain, too, institutional arrangements were continued in modified form in a variety of cults in Brazil, Cuba, and elsewhere.[13] There are also the numerous expressions of apparent African nationalities in such practices as the Nation Dance of Carriacou,[14] "the dance in Place Congo" in New Orleans,[15] the "jubilee" in Washington Square in eighteenth-century Philadelphia,[16] Pinkster Day in Albany, New York,[17] and many other celebrations. In the same way, although the intricate African kinship organizations certainly were not widely maintained in the Americas, should not the relatively independent and complementary position of men and women observed widely in the slaving areas of Africa be considered as one possible formative force in the development of the "matrifocal" household system?[18] This is a sample of what we mean by our appeal to the deeper forms of culture that seem to bind together Afro-Americans.

It is just such expressive continuities then which are crucial to an understanding of the institutions developed by blacks in their various New World situations. The great diversity of settings in which Africans found themselves (plantations, cities, mining areas, escaped slave outposts, and so forth) makes it impossible to explain parallel developments in such areas as religious practice, community governance, economics, even the concepts of the family, simply in terms of

12. Daniel J. Crowley, "American Credit Institutions of Yoruba Type," *Man*, 53 (1953), 80; William R. Bascom, "Acculturation Among the Gullah Negroes," *American Anthropologist*, 43 (1941), 43–50; Ira De A. Reid, "Mrs. Bailey Pays the Rent," in *Ebony and Topaz*, ed. Charles S. Johnson (New York: National Urban League, 1927), pp. 144–48.

13. Ruth Landes, "Review of *Afro-American Anthropology*," *American Anthropologist*, 73 (1971), 1310; Melville J. Herskovits, "The Social Organization of the Candomblé," *Anaais do XXXI Congresso Internacional de Americanistas* (Sao Paulo, 1954), vol. 1, pp. 505–32; Lydia Cabrera, *El Monte*, 2d ed. (Miami: Rema Press, 1968); William R. Bascom, "The Focus of Cuban Santeria," *Southwestern Journal of Anthropology*, 6 (1952), 64–68.

14. M. G. Smith, *Kinship and Community on Carriacou* (New Haven: Yale University Press, 1962).

15. Benjamin Henry Latrobe, *The Journals of Benjamin Henry Latrobe*, ed. Edward C. Carter II, John Van Horne, and Lee W. Formwalt, vol. 3, *1799–1820: From Philadelphia to New Orleans* (New Haven: Yale University Press, 1980), pp. 203–05.

16. John F. Watson, *Annals of Philadelphia and Pennsylvania, in the Olden Times* (Philadelphia: Edwin S. Stuart, 1857), vol. 2, p. 261.

17. James Eights, "Pinkster Festivities in Albany Sixty Years Ago," *Collections on the History of Albany* (Albany: 1867), vol. 2, pp. 323–27.

18. Melville J. Herskovits, *The Myth of the Negro Past* (New York: Harper, 1941), pp. 167–86.

the shared plantation and slavery experience. These similarities almost certainly arose because there were shared perspectives and a
common conceptual and affective system of which the slave could not
be stripped, and shared practices and beliefs and behavioral patterns
which not only survived but were enlarged upon in the New World
setting. The importance of performance in the stylization of individual
and group relationships cannot be overemphasized. These patterns of
performance, models of social organization in the Old World, provided the basic groundwork on which African-like community interactions would be generated despite the loss of the details of their institutional superstructure, and indeed mythic rationalization.

III

In attempting to gain a common-sense view of the cultural dimension
of the dispersal of African peoples, we confront the long history of
those who argue the deculturation of the slave. It is difficult to decide
which is the more insidious argument: that of the racist denigrating
anything black as noncultural in order to maintain the rationale for ex-
ploitation by reaffirming the animal nature of blacks; or the enlightened liberal, ignoring expressions of the black cultural presence so
that the finger may be pointed at stultifying and delimiting displays of
the Euro-American sociocultural system. We must agree with the African Afro-Americanist Okon Uya that these decriers of various European systems and practices create just as great a distortion of Afro-
American life as the racists.

> Perhaps the most subtle distortion of the Afro-American experi-
> ence occurs from postulating that experience as a function of some
> white European or colonial first cause. Whether the first cause is white
> national character ... or white moral perceptions and institutional
> mechanisms ... , or white economic drives ... , or white racial mythol-
> ogy ... , the result is the same—the slave experience is pictured as a
> black response to a white impulse ... without serious analysis of the
> internal determinants in the slave world, the image of the Afro-Ameri-
> can ... will continue to be distorted by the white filter.[19]

But to view Afro-American culture only from the perspective of what
was going on only *within* the black communities would be equally
foolish. Peoples cannot live side-by-side, even in the most extremely

19. Okon E. Uya, "The Culture of Slavery: Black Experience Through a Filter,"
Afro-American Studies, 1 (1971), 209.

restricted situations, and not affect each other culturally. This is especially so in black–white communities, for we have witnessed the wholesale acceptance by both groups of central cultural forms, styles, and techniques wherever Europeans and Africans came together in the New World.

One of the problems in developing a common-sense perspective with regard to black–white cultural relations is that we have not adequately considered how stereotypes operate in monitoring behavior between and among groups. This is especially crucial in the present case, for it is evident that not only did the white stereotype of blacks have an important effect upon what areas of African practices were overtly or covertly encouraged, but that the Euro-Americans in the New World operated in the knowledge that they too were being stereotyped in much the same way by their European cousins. Just how much effect this had on the virulency of the Euro-American plantocracy's actual interactions with their slaves is difficult to ascertain, but ought not be ignored in an evaluation of black–white relations.

A further problem relating to the white stereotype of blacks is that much of our knowledge of what happened culturally before the twentieth century comes from the biased accounts of slavers, travelers, and the planters themselves. In using observers' accounts, one must always bear in mind that the practices which came to the notice of these Euro-American observers were selected by them not just because they were different but also because they often confirmed the white stereotype of blacks. There may then be an over-focus on the kinds of events which confirmed this convenient European ethnocentric perspective.

But this stereotypical dimension can be seen in certain regards as a positive aspect of the history of Africans in the New World, for once such typing is acknowledged, it is also possible to calculate its effects. If one is to understand the nature of the Negro practices which were and are observed by Europeans, one must consider at all times the possibility that some characteristics of these occasions may have arisen in response to this Western value system in its stereotype dimension. Furthermore, as noted, these observers were often operating with regard to the two closely related stereotypes—the one of blacks, the other of West Indians. Especially in the travel literature, the European visitors came not only to see whether or not blacks were human (and thus should or should not be freed) but also whether living away from Europe had made savages of their white brethren.

The travelers, already on edge culturally because of the exigencies of travel, were observing with critical eyes Europeans and Afri-

cans who had been thrown together by the promise of this new agricultural system of the plantation. What a fearsome experience for a
European man or woman of the seventeenth or eighteenth century to
be faced with the possibility of travel with all its sense of adventure
and ultimate discomfort. How disquieting to have been reared in the
European belief system in which life was envisaged as a trip, a pilgrimage, yet where one's reflexes and one's common sense said stay
at home. And how awful must have been the transplantation of self in
search of material gain into a social system in which one's subordi-
nates were transplanted as well, and in which enslavement was the
primary means by which subservience was maintained. Add to this
the ambivalence existing toward the exotic dark-skinned savage, and
some of the anxieties of the plantation adventure become more immediate and real.[20]

Certainly the European observers' prime motive in making cultural notes arose from the ambivalence of exoticism, the strange attraction and repulsion on confronting what they imagined was man's
past lived in a state of nature. And for "nature," read "energy and fertility," but also read "chaos." It was this constant incipiency of chaos,
a promise of contamination by some exotic mad disease brought about
simply by placing oneself outside civilization, which was the dark
rendering of the enthusiastic and fanatic argument over the edenic innocence of the newly encountered worlds. European civilization, it
was clearly felt, had been too recently and dearly bought. Clashes
with the heathens and the barbarians were, after all, a recent memory.
One need listen only to Ned Ward's shrill lampoonery in his description of the character and people of the newly colonized Jamaica in
1698 to reverberate to the fears of a reversion of Europeans to their
own savage past:

A CHARACTER OF JAMAICA

The Dunghill of the Universe, the Refuse of the whole Creation,
the Clippings of the Elements, a shapeless Pile of Rubbish confusd'ly
jumbl'd into an Emblem of the *Chaos*, neglected by Omnipotence when
he form'd the World into its admirable Order. The Nursery of Heavens
Judgments, where the Malignant Seeds of all Pestilence were first
gather'd and scatter'd thro' the Regions of the Earth, to Punish Mankind
for their Offences. The Place where *Pandora* fill'd her Box, where *Vul-*

20. Carl and Roberta Bridenbaugh's *No Peace Beyond the Line* (New York: Oxford
University Press, 1972), chaps. 4–6, brings out these fears and the real basis for them in
a profusion of detail.
    21. Ibid., pp. 193–94.

can Forg'd *Joves* Thunder-bolts, and that Phaeton, by his rash misguid-
ance of the Sun, scorched into a Cinder. The Receptacle of Vagabonds,
the Sanctuary of Bankrupts, and a Close-stool for the Purges of our Pris-
ons. As Sickly as an Hospital, as Dangerous as the Plague, as Hot as
Hell, and as Wicked as the Devil. Subject to Turnadoes, Hurricanes and
Earthquakes, as if the Island, like the People, were troubled with the
*Dry Belly-Ach.**

OF THE PEOPLE

The generality of the Men look as if they had just knock'd off their
Fetters, and by an unexpected Providence, escap'd the danger of a near
Mis-fortune; the dread of which, hath imprinted that in their *Looks,*
which they can no more alter than an *Ethiopian* can his *Colour.*

They are all *Colonels, Majors, Captains, Lieutenants,* and *Ensigns;*
the two last being held in such disdain, that they are look'd upon as a
Bungling Diver amongst a Gang of *Expert Pick-Pockets; Pride* being
their *Greatness,* and *Impudence* their *Virtue.*

They regard nothing but Money, and value not how they get it;
there being no other Felicity to be enjoy'd but purely Riches. They are
very Civil to Strangers who bring over considerable Effects; and will
try a great many ways to Kill him fairly, for the Lucre of his Cargo: And
many have been made Rich by such Windfalls.

A Broken *Apothecary* will make there a Topping *Physician;* a *Barbers Prentice,* a good *Surgeon;* a *Bailiffs Follower,* a passable *Lawyer;*
and an *English Knave,* a very *Honest Fellow.*

They have so great a veneration for *Religion,* That *Bibles*
and *Common-Prayer-Books* are as good a Commodity amongst them, as
Muffs and *Warming-Pans.*

A little Reputation among the *Women,* goes a great way; and if
their Actions be answerable to their Looks, they may vie *Wickedness*
with the *Devil:* An *Impudent Act,* being the only *Charms* of their *Countenance,* and a *Lewd Carriage,* the *Study'd Grace* of their *Deportment.*
They are such who have been *Scandalous* in *England* to the utmost degree, either *Transported* by the *State,* or led by their *Vicious Inclinations;* where they may be *Wicked* without *Shame,* and *Whore* on without
Punishment.

They are Stigmatiz'd with *Nick-Names,* which they bear, not with
Patience only, but with *Pride,* as *Unconscionable Nan, Salt-Beef Peg,
Buttock-de-Clink Jenny,* &c. *Swearing, Drinking,* and *Obscene Talk,* are
the Principal Qualifications that render them acceptable to *Male Conversation;* and she that wants a perfection in these admirable acquire-

---

*A complaint caused by drinking rum with too much lead in it.

ments, shall be as much Ridicul'd for her *Modesty,* as a *Plain-Dealing Man* amongst a Gang of *Knaves,* for his *Honesty.*

In short, *Virtue* is so *Despis'd,* and all sorts of *Vice Encourag'd* by both *Sexes,* that the Town of *Port-Royal* is the very *Sodom* of the Universe.[22]

It was this social dissolution which brought on these fears—and if one could be corrupted by the environment through being thrust back into the margins of the Earth in this way, what about the potential for contamination from the heathen blacks? One must read these documents remembering that there was still a real question in the minds of Europeans whether Africans (or any of the darker peoples) were really human, and whether they had the kind of shared order of their lives which today we call *culture.* If not, they might indeed be agents of the devil who could corrupt simply by their presence.

Just such fears are illustrated in another (and later) lampoon concerning the West Indian adventure, "Johnny Newcome in Love in the West Indies." Johnny is infected with all the germs of savage life: sexual passion which leads him to consort with black sorcerers, leading further to polygamy and the breeding of a bastard race—a bastardization emphasized by the combination names, half-African, half-European, given to the offspring of this interracial union. The artist-author, William Holland, also sees such offspring as being the source of the contagion of revolution, for Hector Sammy Newcome "promises to be the TOUSSAINT of his country."[23]

One can hypothesize that many of these perceptions were forced upon the observers' consciousness because of deep embarrassments and failures in social expectations in interactions between blacks and whites. In the process of reachieving order in the New World, the social process becomes much more self-conscious than usual and thus we have these recurring subjects of observation.

Nearly all the travel accounts spend much time exploring just such disruptions (or lack of them), not only in the social order but in the decorum of the European creoles. Lady Nugent, for instance, was uncommonly interested in the disruptions of English customs in Jamaican Euro-American society, especially with regard to the strange dietary, health, and sexual habits developed in the New World—the

22. Ned Ward, *A Trip to Jamaica: With a True Character of the People and the Island,* 1698 (Reprinted in *Five Travel Scripts* [New York: Columbia University Press, 1933]).

23. See David Kunzle, *The Early Comic Strip* (Berkeley and Los Angeles: University of California Press, 1973), pp. 374–76, for a discussion of this series of prints.

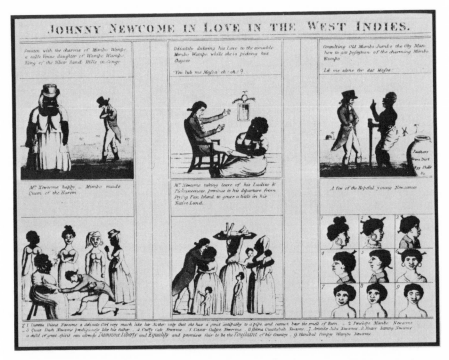

Figure 1. William Holland, *Johnny Newcome in Love in the West Indies*.

same subjects, we beg to point out, which recur in the stereotyping of the slaves (and any other marginalized group). As Silvia Wynter noted of Lady Nugent's journal, it seemed that Jamaicans "lived to eat. Yet they seemed perpetually hungry."[24] Lady Nugent records many conversations, mainly those concerned with gossip about the black and brown women with whom the men were consorting. The good lady is shocked at the wide variety of household and *keeping* relationships she observed and heard talk about. But life there, to her, was totally corrupt and the inhabitants were to be regarded as scarcely human because not only were they given to such excesses in eating, drinking, and sexual activities but they kept themselves in a filthy condition. Of one Lord Balcarres, she notes:

> I wish Lord B. would wash his hands and use a nailbrush, for the black edges of his nails really make me sick. He has besides an extraordinary propensity to dip his finger into every dish. Yesterday he absolutely helped himself to some fricasee with his dirty finger and thumb.[25]

24. Sylvia Wynter, "Lady Nugent's Journal," *Jamaica Journal*, 1, no. 1 (1967), 26.
25. Ibid., p. 27.

Little surprise then that the lady should exclaim, "This is indeed a sad im-moral country, but no use worrying myself."[26] She attributes this to the influence not only of the climate and the distance from the centers of culture but to the contaminating presence of blacks. She says, for instance, of Jamaican language habits, "The Creole language is not confined to the negroes. Many of the ladies, who have not been educated in England, speak a sort of broken English, with an indolent drawing out of their words, that is very tiresome and disgusting."[27] Habits concerning eating, sex, language, cleanliness, the major features of culture which distinguish man from animal, all are in question then from this European perspective, the very same concerns that whites demonstrate in looking at blacks to determine if they are human.

Throughout the plantation literature there is, then, a constant preoccupation with descriptions of "manners and customs" which extend far beyond the attractions of the exotic. The fortunes being made in the New World demanded that the young less well-to-do members of the genteel class consider emigration, and this meant the necessity of doing more than just observing these outlandish creatures who might become their slaves. Furthermore, the question of whether blacks were human determined the morality of enslavement, and humanity was determined by whether blacks were capable of having culture or "civilization." *Civilization* commonly meant simply an acceptance of European practices and behavior systems; therefore any variation from these Western ways was regarded as uncivilized, animalistic, or childlike, and often morally offensive. Most of these travel accounts or journals contained a list of these traits, usually under the title: *The Character of the Negros*. Generally, this enumeration of characteristics employed the same attributions of stupidity and laziness and filthiness, of strange eating, family, sexual, work habits. Defenders of slavery naturally stressed traits of black behavior which could be interpreted as being less than human. This subhuman image changes from one moment to another, of course, ranging from depicting them as happy children to uncontrollable wild beasts.

Many, such as Alexander Barclay in his *A Practical View of the Present State of Slavery*, rhapsodize on the pastoral aspects of plantation life in much the same tone as American southerners:

26. Ibid., p. 29.
27. Ibid., p. 28.

Let a stranger but visit such a scene; let him contemplate the abundance they possess: see their laughing faces, and listen to their careless song, under the sunshine of a perpetual summer, and say if these are the people who, amidst the whole race of mankind, stand most in need of his commiseration; or let him witness, as the writer has often done, a group of little negro children running to meet their master on his return home after a few days' absence, clinging to the skirts of his coat, and vociferating the endearing expression, *Tata come, Tata come,* and say if here, of all places on earth, there is a want of sympathy between the master and servants.

That they are ignorant is true, but they possess many virtues, especially kindness to one another, from which more civilized life might take a useful lesson. They are slaves, but this happily gives them no concern, as they have never known any other condition. Strangers to hunger and cold, the scourges of the poor in England, and equally so to the cares and anxieties which often perplex their masters, they are thoughtless, contented, and Mr. Dallas, of Jamaica, must have seen and felt this when he wrote the following verses so truly descriptive of the negro:—

What are the joys of white man here?
　What are his pleasures? say;
Me want no joys, no ill me fear,
　But on my bonja play.

Me sing all day, me sleep all night,
Me hab no care, my heart is light;
Me tink not what to-morrow bring,
Me happy, so me sing.

But white man's joys are not like mine,
　Dho' he look smart and gay;
He proud, he jealous, haughty, fine,
　While I my bonja play.

He sleep all day, he wake all night,
He full of care, his heart no light,
He great deal want, he little get,
He sorry, so he fret.

Me envy not dhe white man dhen,
　Me poor but me is gay;

Me glad at heart, me happy when
Me on my bonja play.

Me sing all day, me sleep all night,
Me hab no care, my heart is light;
Me tink not what to-morrow bring,
Me happy, so me sing.[28]

On the other side, and spelling out his discomfort and prejudice in far greater detail was one like Thomas Atwood in his *The History of the Island of Dominica*.

The characters of negros are not so various as one would imagine they would be, from the difference of the country they are brought from, to the West Indies; as very few of them on their arrival in the islands have the least appearance of having been civilized, or possessed of any endowments but such as are merely natural. For the generality of them, on their first introduction, appear as wild as the brute beasts; are indolent and stupid to a degree, so that they hardly know the use of the most common utensil of husbandry, much less the methods of cultivating the ground.

Every thing appears to them as entirely new, as to the infant just come to a moderate degree of vision; but, at the same time, they seem to be so very unconcerned at the sight of the most novel objects, that the bare recollection is not a moment in their minds. They appear insensible to every thing but hunger and thirst, which however, to satisfy, they have no more nicety than a hog; as any thing, either raw or dressed, is equally acceptable when given to them.

This stupidity of theirs continues a length of time after their arrival in the islands, before most of them can be brought to any degree of proper comprehension; and with many of them, it is entirely unconquerable.

The Creole negros, that is to say, those who are born in the West Indies, having been brought up among white people, and paid some attention to from their infancy, lose much of that uncommon stupidity so conspicuous in their new negro parents; and are in general tolerably sensible, sharp, and sagacious. But there is actually something so very unaccountable in the genius of all negros, so very different from that of white people in general, that there is not to be produced an instance in the West Indies, of any of them ever arriving to any degree of perfection in the liberal arts or sciences, notwithstanding the greatest pains

28. Alexander Barclay, *A Practical View of the Present State of Slavery in the West Indies* (London, 1826), pp. 206–08.

taken with them; and the only thing they are remarkable for attaining to any degree of perfections, is Musick.

Negros are in general much addicted to witchcraft and idolatry, both of which seem to be inherent in them, so that though many of them profess the Christian Religion, especially that of the Roman Catholicks, and some of them pay great attention thereto, yet, in all matters which concern themselves, they have recourse to their superstitious confidence in the power of the dead, of the sun and moon; nay, even of sticks, stones and earth from graves hung in bottles in their gardens. . . .

Negros are in general much addicted to drunkenness, thievery, incontinency, and idleness. The first vice very few of them will refrain from when they can get liquor, and in their fits of this kind, many of them are very mischievous.

Thieving from their owners they look upon as no crime, nor have they any dread of being punished for it, if they do it without detection; and so general is this crime, that there goes a proverb current in all the islands, "Shew me a negro, and I will shew you a thief," . . .

So little are the sexes attached to each other, or constant in connubial connections, that it is common for the men to have several wives at a time, besides transcient mistresses; and the women to leave their husbands for others, and to submit to the embraces of white men for money or fine clothes. Mothers will dispose of their virgin daughters to white men for a moderate sum, nor do they look upon it as any crime, but an honour to the damsel, who is thereby better qualified for being afterwards taken to wife by one of her own colour.

Idleness is so very predominant in negros, especially those brought to the island immediately from Africa, and their dislike of labour is so great, that it is very difficult to make them work; it is sometimes absolutely necessary to have recourse to measures that appear cruel, in order to oblige them to labour. Nay, very often the same means must be used to make them work for themselves, to dress their own victuals, or to keep themselves free from vermine. This vice is so very remarkable in many negros, that they will actually very often, under some tree, sleep out the hours allowed them to get their victuals in, rather than be at the pains of going home to dress them. . . .[29]

Today it is easy to recognize these stereotyped arguments, typical of one group attempting to stigmatize another and thus establish social boundaries. But although most of the traits pointed to will be

29. Thomas Atwood, *The History of the Island of Dominica* (London, 1791), pp. 265–68, 272–74.

part of the deep reservoir of stigmatizing features, they also may, at the same time, arise out of a real recognition of differences in cultural practices. We can disregard the attributions of venery, thievery, idleness, and incontinency as being simply negative reflections of the values of the stereotyping person and his group. But the description of how idleness is *practiced* (sleeping in the fields, eating food carried there) sketches the beginning of a real picture of one practice which may still be observed among West Indian gardening peoples. Buried in the midst of these descriptions of character are many such reports of actual practices, even though they are often misconstrued and misunderstood.

This is true, for instance, of our vitriolic commentator Atwood, who follows his diatribe with some of his remarkable notes on witchcraft and diablerie and an accurate description of the hanging of containers of earth, sticks, and stones in the gardens. He also provides a full, true description of burial customs and the practice of *obeah* curing and conjuring:

> Their superstitious notions with respect to their dead are truly ridiculous, for they suppose that the deceased both eat and drink in their coffins; and for that purpose, they put therein articles for both, together with a pipe and tobacco, and such things as they know the deceased was fond of in his life time. Moreover, at their funerals they believe the dead body has the power of compelling them to carry it to the grave, in which road it likes, to shew its resentment to those who have offended it; by the coffin's tumbling off the shoulders of the bearer, making them stand stock still, or running therewith with speed, now one way, then another, and sometimes throwing down and trampling on the people who stand in the way.
>
> They have their necromancers and conjurors of both sexes, whom they call "Obeah men and women," to whom they apply for spells and charms against sickness, to prevent their being robbed, or to find out the thief, and to punish those who do them any injury. These Obeah people are very artful in their way, and have a great ascendancy over the other negroes, whom they persuade that they are able to do many miracles by means of their art; and very often get good sums of money for their imaginary charms.
>
> The method of treating such as apply to these conjurors for curing any imaginary disorder, excited by lowness of spirits or fearful dreams, is very laughable; they persuade them that they are possessed by the devil, as a punishment for some hidden crime; but if not well paid for it, besides promising to submit to every direction of the Obeah master, he will not undertake the cure. Every preliminary being settled be-

tween the patient and the operator, the latter begins his work with mumbling over a few strange words, and having every thing ready, the patient so placed in a dark room, that he cannot discover the cheat, he pinches and pulls him till the other cries out with the pain; after which, the conjuror produces sticks, knives, pieces of glass, and even whole bottles, which he persuades the other that he actually took out of the place he complained of; and then rubbing it over with grease and soot, or some such thing, the simple patient believes himself to be perfectly cured.[30]

It is hardly difficult to sort out what is based on actual observed (or reported) behavior in works such as Atwood's and biased comments on the morality of such practices. His mode of argument reveals its own insufficiencies today—but it also forces us to see that such a reaction was engendered by a confrontation with cultural practices differing from those of the European observer. In fact these very apologists for the plantocracy, because they were apologists and were attuned to finding evidence for inferiority based on a lack of civilized life patterns, provide us with the evidence that an African conceptual and interactional system ran very deep and was not totally disrupted by the imposition of slavery.

The attitudes and indeed the rhetoric of these reports are still very much with us. For example, the writings of V. S. Naipaul[31] often resemble those of Anthony Trollope (whom, in fact, Naipaul often quotes), who had observed West Indian life over one hundred years before, and are aimed at the same kind of English audience.[32] Indeed, the most pedestrian of British newspaper accounts dealing with West Indian subjects resound with much the same vocabulary and social perspectives.

It strains credulity to recognize in these accounts even a thread of what we would today see as humanistic anthropology, but there is a peculiar sense in which similar concerns are present. For even in those accounts which modern sensibilities would reject as profoundly ethnocentric there is a consciousness of the nature and limits of humanness; there is a measuring of human similarities and differences behind these travelers' writings, such that a personal transformation

30. Ibid., pp. 268–70.
31. V. S. Naipaul, *The Middle Passage: The Caribbean Revisited* (London: André Deutsch, 1962); *The Overcrowded Baracoon* (London: André Deutsch, 1972).
32. Linda Rabben, "Transgressed Limits: British Representations of West Indian Song and Dance, 1840–1960," MA thesis, Division of Social Anthropology, Sussex University, 1976.

takes place, a transformation which K. O. L. Burridge speaks of as "the articulate distillation of an experience born of a union between observer and observed—which represents additions to knowledge and which are distinctive of anthropology whether professional or amateur."[33] In addition, these personal confrontations with different realities parallel European ideological constructions which emerged from such data:

> The point is simply that within the European ambience these travellers' accounts have become the raw data for constructions of varieties of social order which, drawn from the pragmatic or imaginative experience, pop from our shelves like snowdrops in January. The utopias of More and dozens of others; Rousseau's noble savage; Defoe's Crusoe; Lafiteau's Iroquois; Sagard's Hurons; Swift's Gulliver—a few landmarks at random from among the scores of descriptions, analyses, satires, histories and novels which have striven not only to impart information, but to distill an essence of man [by] on the one hand placing the given individual in different kinds of social situations, and on the other hand measuring the social order against different kinds of individuals.[34]

There is another sense, too, in which these travel accounts anticipate contemporary thought and concern. The fact that their posture toward their subjects was so often blatantly biased does not gainsay the fact that they were engaged, situated (as today's rhetoric would have it) in the events they describe. And it is this very *lack* of detachment or pseudo-objectivity that in part allows a modern reader critical of the methods of social science and history to approach these books with less than revulsion. The fact that we may find uses for these works not originally intended by their authors should not surprise us, for Wylie Sypher has shown that these books were also used by British abolitionists in the eighteenth century.[35] What seemed like a savage practice to one generation became evidence for a capacity for refinement in another.

IV

If one were to use only the literature of the white journalist and traveler, the area of black life which could be most fully documented for

33. K. O. L. Burridge, "Claude Lévi-Strauss: Fieldwork, Explanation and Experience," unpublished paper, pp. 11–12.

34. Ibid., p. 12.

35. Wylie Sypher, *Guinea's Captive Kings* (Chapel Hill: University of North Carolina Press, 1942).

continuities from the African past would be folk beliefs and practices and ghost lore. In the United States under the name of "hants," or "hags," and "root work," "conjuring," or "hoodoo," and in the West Indies as "duppies" or "jumbies" (among many others) and "obeah men" or "wanga," there were few accounts of plantation life that did not include large sections devoted to the depth and persistence of such "superstitious" beliefs and practices.

The reasons for this fixation are various. Obviously, such practices were used as evidence for maintaining that facet of the stereotype configuration that holds that blacks are either simple-minded heathen nature-worshipers or, even worse, in league with the devil. But with each type of observer there would be different reasons why this subject was of interest. These practices were sometimes a threat to the planters' operations and sporadically they tried to militate against them—though one suspects that most of the time the folk medical practices and ceremonies were encouraged (or overlooked) as a way of keeping the slaves alive and happy. Undoubtably, some came to believe in them or fear them. With abolitionists or their foes, the strange practices would be used as examples of the presence or lack of human feeling and culture. And with missionaries they provided evidences of what had to be fought.

For whatever reason the observations were made, this material forms a large base of data that has not yet been used effectively in discussion of cultural continuities. The literature contains many extensive descriptions, such as the one provided by Atwood above, of expressive ceremonies, especially funerals.

But for our present purposes, there are three other areas in the plantation literature that are of even greater interest, the materials on work, play, and religion. These we will survey in hopes of showing how complex the sociocultural situation was, and how we might gain further insights from some features of black culture that tell us something of how African ways were transformed into Afro-American ways.

As noted, the Africans brought to the New World were often master tropical gardeners and animal husbanders. The journal-keepers reported again and again on the remarkable abilities of the slaves not only in working the cane fields and melting-houses but in providing their own foodstuffs (even to the point of marketing the excess on their one day off, Sunday). John Luffman's account of Antigua life of 1788 is typical of such often begrudging descriptions:

> Every slave on a plantation, whether male or female, when they attained their 14th or 15th year, has a piece of ground, from twenty five,

to thirty feet square, allotted to them, which by some is industriously and advantageously cultivated, and by others totally neglected. These patches are found to be of material benefit to the country, their produce principally supplying the "sunday market" . . . with vegetables. They are also allowed to raise pigs, goats, and fowls, and it is by their attention to these articles, that whites are prevented from starving, during such times of the year as vessels cannot come to these coasts with safety.[36]

Just how extensive the contribution of the slaves was to the development and operation of the plantation is yet to be studied widely. But Peter H. Wood has done suggestive work on South Carolina in which he shows Africans to be the source of rice agriculture, new forms of cattle breeding and herding, boat building, inland water navigation, hunting and trapping, medicine, and other innovations. Indeed, the agricultural success of South Carolina seems more a function of the slaves' knowledge and technology that it was of the masters'.[37]

The slaves often found themselves in a position to teach their masters much and, more important, to carry out agricultural tasks in agricultural time or tempo. Numerous European observers recount with amazement the coordination of activities in Afro-American work gangs, many of them becoming so interested that they recorded the songs that were being sung while carrying out the work-task. Many such observers were especially taken with the coordination of the black's work activities. "Their different instruments of husbandry, particularly their gleaming hoes, when uplifted to the sun, and which, particularly, when they are digging cane-holes, they frequently raise all together, and in as exact time as can be observed, in a well-conducted orchestra, in the bowing of the fiddles, occasion the light to break in momentary flashes around them."[38]

This work, many observers noted, was carried out through the use of songs which were in classic African call-and-response pattern, through which the work gangs both coordinated movements and created and maintained a sense of common purpose. Such descriptions,

---

36. John Luffman, *A Brief Account of the Island of Antigua* (London, 1789), p. 94.

37. Peter H. Wood, " 'It Was a Negro Taught Them,' A New Look at African Labor in Early South Carolina," in *Discovering Afro-America*, ed. Roger D. Abrahams and John F. Szwed (Leiden: E. J. Brill, 1975), pp. 26–45. See also Henry Glassie, "The Nature of the New World Artefact: The Instance of the Canoe," in *Festschrift für Robert Wildhaber* (Basel: Schweizerische Gesellschaft für Volkskunde, 1973), pp. 153–70, on canoes and canoeing.

38. William Beckford, *A Descriptive Account of the Island of Jamaica* (London, 1790), p. 255.

as this from J. B. Moreton's *West Indian Customs and Manners,* are a commonplace of the genre:

> When working, though at the hardest labour, they are commonly singing; and though their songs have neither rime nor measure, yet many are witty and pathetic. I have often laughed heartily, and have been as often struck with deep melancholy at their songs:—for instance, when singing of the overseer's barbarity to them:
>
>> Tink dere is a God in a top,
>> No use we ill, Obisha!
>> Me no horse, me no mare, me no mule,
>> No use me ill, Obisha.[39]

Such activities, of course, were given as indications that the slaves were a happy, childlike people who loved their work. As one especially lighthearted observer describes it, the harvest provided "a scene of animation and cheerfulness" in which the ear and eye are suffused with evidences of "the light-hearted hilarity of the negroes" in which "the confused clamour of voices in dialogue and song, present a singular contrast to that calm repose which nature seems to claim for herself in these clear and ardent climes."[40]

However, it was not only working styles which made Africans the ideal slaves in the plantation system. As a gardening people, they already measured time and apportioned energy by the cycles of the crops. Thus, they understood the necessity of working long and hard hours during planting and harvesting seasons, but they also were used to working considerably less hard during the other seasons. This disparity was often noticed from one perspective to another, but without much comprehension as to the system of time and energy allocation which lay behind it.[41]

From the perspective of the stereotyping rationale, this cycle was at any rate convenient. When blacks were working very hard in the sun or the heat of the house in which the sugar was boiled, they might be portrayed in brute work-animal terms. But during the other seasons, when they resisted what they obviously regarded as senseless work, they could be accused of being lazy. One way or another, the mechanism of stereotype was bound to be applied.

Continuities of African work practices are then relatively easily accounted for, as they both fit the needs of the planters and in no way

39. J. B. Moreton, *West Indian Customs and Manners* (London, 1793), p. 152.

40. Trelawney Wentworth, *A West Indian Sketch Book* (London, 1834), vol. 1, p. 66.

41. Eugene Genovese, *Roll Jordan Roll* (New York: Pantheon, 1974), book 2, pt. 2.

challenge the European image of blacks. More problematic is the area of play, for here there is a longer history of black–white relations (and imaginings) and here too we are involved with a range of behaviors viewed by some as anathema to enterprise. Nevertheless, for some time before colonization Europeans had associated Africans with festival entertainments. Further, music, dance, and other public performance types were fit subjects for those onlookers who were concerned with the problem of whether blacks had or might acquire culture. For whatever reason, we have a great many detailed descriptions of black festive activities. These data enable us to explore the deeper levels of cultural continuity and may thus help in understanding the dynamic involved in the creation of Afro-American culture. Festive and ludic materials tell us a good deal about patterns of behavior far beyond the realm of play because playing involves a selective stylization of motives also found in other domains of activity. For instance, see Alan Lomax and his associates' studies in choreometrics (Lomax has demonstrated the high level of correlation between work and dance movements within specific groups and culture areas[42]). Equally important, however, in discovering deeper cultural patterns, is how and with what play activities are contrasted.

V

Even before there was direct contact between Europeans and Africans, black peoples to the south held a special symbolic importance for Europeans. As Henri Baudet pointed out, this interest was occasioned by a pre-Rousseauean primitivism which included all non-Europeans, who were envisaged as simpler people living closer to nature and therefore closer to a state of primal innocence and harmony. As travel increased, the black African was contrasted, positively, with the Muslim, who had become a feared enemy during the times of the Crusades.

However, with the beginning of the Renaissance, Europeans became more knowledgeable of Muslims and came to admire them and their old high culture. Baudet describes the consequences of this change:

---

42. Alan Lomax, *Folk Song Style and Culture* (Washington, D.C.: American Association for the Advancement of Science, 1968).

Unlucky Negro: our culture has always presented him in unequivocal opposition to the Muslim. But now, quite suddenly, Islam is found to merit admiration. Rapidly and unexpectedly, its star moves into a new orbit and the traditional contrast between Negro and Muslim is reversed. For a century or more Islam, and not the Negro, has been the subject of scientific interest. . . . A new reputation for the unfortunate Negro has its origins here, and he approaches the next two centuries as typifying the lowest stage of human development . . . an altogether inferior creature, a slave by nature, lacking all historical background.[43]

Of course, during these "next two centuries" Africans and Europeans are brought together in huge numbers, and at a time when the negative dimensions of the image of the primitive are convenient in rationalizing enslavement.

However, during the earlier period the fascination with Africans had created a pattern of practice in Europe in which blacks become central both as performers and as embodying alternative performance styles. "Moors," "Blacks," and "Negroes" were especially associated in the Western mind with parades and other kinds of festival behaviors. Eldred D. Jones's *The Elizabethan Image of Africa* brings together a number of illustrations of this fascination: blackface characters identified with Africa appeared in the medieval mummers plays or in the courtly "disguises" of the sixteenth century; Henry VIII and the Earl of Essex marched with such "Moors" in 1510; blackface figures led the pageants and cleared away crowds during the same period; Edward VI took part in a Shrovetide masque in 1548 in which the marchers' legs, arms, and faces were all blackened; and Queen Anne appeared as a Negro in Ben Jonson's *The Masque of Blackness*.[44] Numerous other Elizabethan dramas—most notably *Othello*—also contained important black roles.

Later, after the beginning of the slave trade and following the increasing presence of "real" Africans in Europe, the cultural impact became even greater. For example, black drummers were popular in European military and court bands in the late eighteenth and early nineteenth centuries.[45] Their music, style of performance, and cos-

43. Henri Baudet, *Paradise on Earth: Some Thoughts on European Images of Non-European Man* (New Haven: Yale University Press, 1965), p. 47.

44. Eldred D. Jones, *The Elizabethan Image of Africa* (Charlottesville: University of Virginia Press, 1971).

45. Robert Pierpoint, "Negro, or Coloured, Bandsmen in the Army," *Notes and Queries*, 2 (1916), 303–04; W. B. H., "Negro, or Coloured, Bandsmen in the Army," *Notes and Queries*, 2 (1916), 378; Leigh Hunt, *Wishing Cap Papers* (London, 1873), p. 72.

tumes had significant and lasting consequences for Europeans and Euro-Americans. To offer just one case, though it has been recognized that African and Turkish drum corps were the inspirations for compositions by Glück, Mozart, and Haydn, it is not so well known that the source of the "Turkish music" (seventh) variation of the "Ode to Joy" theme of Beethoven's Ninth Symphony was not very likely Turkish drummers,[46] but rather the African drum corps active in Germany at that time who played what was called "Turkish music."[47] Surely, part of the shock value of Beethoven's last movement for Europeans lay in presenting images of African drums and drummers gathering with the heavenly hosts around the throne of Heaven![48]

Despite this association of blacks with such public entertainments, there is nothing here which undermines the stereotypical set of traits. One of the few roles available to outsiders in European culture (and many others) is that of the performer. Therefore one of the few ways the members of such a group can survive economically is by capitalizing upon their performance abilities. (In the case of Gypsies in Europe this performer role has been developed into an entire way of life, as it has with the Bauls in Bengal and the Arioi society in Melanesia.)

In any case, whether it was due to such expectations on the part of the European plantocrats or because it represented an inherited cultural focus, black parades and festivals were encouraged by the plantocracy and used by them as one of the most important times for celebration. But Euro-American interest and occasional participation simply place an unofficial stamp of approval for practices which came to fill a central role in Afro-American communities throughout the New World. In Bahia, Rio de Janeiro, Havana, Port of Spain, New Orleans, and elsewhere (and, in past times, in Mexico City, Philadelphia, Wilmington, North Carolina, Albany, Hartford, and other cities), Afro-American carnivals, processions, and street parades have been performed annually for many years. Although such events have often been dismissed by puritanical members of Euro-American societies as mob scenes or simple bacchanals, they are in fact highly structured performances tied to a firmly established social base of cults and clubs, many of which have a strong sense of continuity and histories

46. Martin Cooper, *Beethoven: The Last Decade 1817–1827* (London: Oxford University Press, 1970), p. 33.

47. Pierpoint, p. 303.

48. We are indebted to Dell Hymes, who drew our attention to this connection between Beethoven and black drummers.

of more than three hundred years. The characteristics of these events are well known. Clubs of maskers organize around a variety of religious, dramatic, or exotic themes, elect kings and queens, make banners, and focus on such special performances as stick fighting, baton twirling, *JonKanoo*, group dancing, and singing on the streets and roads. In some areas sacred and secret Afro-American symbols are displayed on this day; in others group spirit possession occurs before and during the clubs' appearances. More important is the fact that on these days groups, social roles, and their associated symbols are moved from the privacy of *favelas, barrios,* or ghetto neighborhoods (where they have been part of their life throughout the year) into the public areas where Euro- and Afro-Americans come together. The significance of these events is noted well by the guardians of public order, the police, who have always viewed these affairs with considerable fear: for these "back-street" social organizations are recognized for what they are, the organizations who rule their streets "after dark," as the Havana police once put it.

Some have dismissed these obvious displays of arcane and "African"-like institutions as the results of partial and incomplete acculturation, as way-stations on the road to national homogeneousness—in other words, blacks attempting to join in Euro-American festivities with whatever cultural resources they can muster. We might better take our lead from the studies of sociolinguists who speak of multiple codes in language systems. In the case of festivals the codes are not linguistic ones alone but are also musical, motor, and religious traditions governed by performance rules which are the legacy of a wide variety of African people brought to Spanish-, Portuguese-, French- and English-America. These Afro-American processions and carnivals might best be described as rites of passage, not between social positions in single societies but between the performance rules and the social hierarchies belonging to different segments in single societies. These festivities exist because of the cultural dualities present in New World societies and have survived within the context of the distinctions made between public and private areas of urban life. During these festivities these boundaries are broken down and the performances become more creole, more "country," more "African" as the effects of license take hold.[49]

49. Morton Marks and John F. Szwed, "Afro-American Cultures on Parade," paper read at the American Anthropological Association's Annual Meeting, New York City, 1971; Morton Marks, "Performance Rules and Ritual Structure in Afro-American Music" (Diss., University of California, Berkeley, 1971).

Certainly the organizations which support and give life to these Afro-American events in no way approximate the full complex of institutional arrangements that characterized West African societies, but the fact of their existence must modify our thinking about the ways in which identification with the African homeland was maintained or broken, and where maintained, how this contributed to a sense of ethnicity and cultural identity in these various Afro-American societies.

Thus, carnival, JonKanoo, and other such festivities are regarded as the most public and the most unrestrained, "primitive," and often most African of all Afro-American performance occasions (with the exception of Shango, Vodû, and some other religious practices). It is easy for the Euro-American to be carried into the spirit of such occasions and whites have a long history of participation. But to understand how very differently these performances function for Afro-Americans, it is necessary to understand the world order of black communities, especially in terms of their contrasts between *serious* and *play*, and between *private* and *public*. To relegate such expressive behaviors as represented in JonKanoo to the periphery of culture is to ignore the centrality of interpersonal performance in the prosecution of life in black communities, and to ignore the importance of such expression as a countervailing force against enslavement. Furthermore, to do so is to retain an institution-centered definition of culture at the expense of the microbehaviors and the larger interactional systems which provide the formal and informal rules by which groups live on a day-to-day, minute-to-minute basis.

To get at what we mean here, it is necessary to look at some basic cultural differences between what we view Euro- and Afro-American attitudes and behaviors to be in the domains of play and work (or seriousness). Since playing calls for a departure from these everyday behaviors (especially from the intensity and self-consciousness of stylization), it is crucial to note what play is contrasted with.

Play generally has been employed by Euro-Americans to refer to a mode of activity identified in terms of its freedom from the need to be productive within the so-called real or serious world. Often this freedom to be unproductive is confused with freedom from rule-governed constraints; but even the most casual observer of play knows that the opposite is true—that to play is to act in accord with a self-consciously articulated and tightly circumscribed set of rules. Although this is less apparent in contest games where winning comes to take precedence, the rule-governed and stylistic dimensions nonetheless remain paramount. This concept of play is probably characteristic of all groups, not just Euro-Americans. But a group's play behavior, its serious behavior, and the manner in which play departs from serious behavior will be specific to that culture, and it is in this realm that we can most clearly distinguish the differences between Euro- and Afro-Americans in their use of the term and in their practices.

Euro-Americans employ the term *play* primarily in contrast to *work.* This is true to a certain extent in Afro-America, but what is meant by work and play often seems to differ among the groups. Work is what one does in Euro-America (and elsewhere in the Western world) to distinguish oneself as an individual. One learns to work successfully by most fully employing one's individual talents on a presented task. One proves one's worth by one's works—or so it has been voiced until recently. Play, on the other hand, has been the activity by which one progressively learns how to coordinate with others. Our values emphasize that the older we get, the more we must learn the importance of team play. In an admittedly oversimplified rendering then, working comes to mean, as one grows up, developing one's individual abilities, while playing during the same period comes to refer to the individual's attempt to subordinate individuality and to coordinate with others, to cooperate. However, work becomes one's most *public* set of behaviors, and playing remains as *private* as one can maintain—unless one chooses to enact that most deviant of all our acceptable roles, the entertainer or the athlete: those who *play* in *public.* But even in this case we attempt to redefine their behavior as work. Thus, the most individuating of all our behaviors—work—is also the most public.

Almost exactly the reverse seems to characterize Afro-Americans. Work tends to be identified with family and, by extension, with home and its relative privacy. Work is learned within the home as the most important feature of (extended) family living and is identified with the maintenance of the familial order of the household. Commonly under the direction of *Momma,* children learn to work from older children in the household. Furthermore, in the West Indies it is regarded as appropriate for mothers to pay for a child's apprenticing to get a trade. Finally, it is to Momma that the now-working offspring gives money or sends remittances.

Conversely, play is something which is learned from one's peers, and commonly outside the home and comes to be *the* activity by which Afro-American individuality is asserted and maintained. Thus, *playing* performing comes to be associated with public places, as work begins in the home and remains, in the main, as a kind of private (or, at least, guarded) range of behaviors. This accounts in part for the common negative and often uncomprehending reaction of blacks to requests to discuss their work, especially in the kind of public circumstances in which verbal playing would be regarded by them as appropriate.

A recent series of studies is concerned with the means by which the different worlds, values, and norms of women and men in Afro-American communities throughout the New World are given articulation. The primary social differentiation has been carried out along sexual lines, the distinction being made between the female-dominated household world and the essentially male streetcorner or crossroads way of life. This distinction is pursued in terms of the differences of orientation, activity, and value systems between the female system of respectability and the male valuation of reputation maintenance.[50] In the anglophonic Afro-American sense of the term, *play* is not commonly allowed in the house because it is generally used to refer to some of the central practices by which masculine, crossroads, reputation-centered values are enacted. *Play* in this sense means highly unruly behavior, engaging in noisy verbal dueling, but also the use of a variety of speaking which is dramatically black, known in the West Indies as *talking bad* or *broken*. When the noise, unruliness, and speaking variety are brought together, the result is called *nonsense* or *foolishness*, valuation terms from the perspective of the household values but usually readily accepted by the speakers themselves. Being public- and individual-centered, playing will be regarded as inappropriate most of the time within those areas dominated by values of respectability, especially the house.[51]

Undoubtedly the term *play* is used by Afro-Americans with many of the same meanings that other speakers of English use it for. But in black communities in the United States and the West Indies it has developed another range of meanings which seem significant because they point to an important social feature of Afro-American be-

50. Peter J. Wilson, "Reputation and Respectability: Suggestions for Caribbean Ethnology," *Man*, 4 (1969), 70–84.
51. Roger D. Abrahams and Richard Bauman, "Sense and Nonsense on St. Vincent: Speech Behavior and Decorum in a Caribbean Community," *American Anthropologist*, 73 (1971), 262–72; Roger D. Abrahams, "Talking My Talk: Black English and Social Segmentation in Black Communities," *Florida FL Reporter*, 10 (1972), 29–38; idem, "Negotiating Respect: Patterns of Presentation Among Black Women," *Journal of American Folklore*, 88 (1975), 58–80; idem, *Talking Black* (Rowley, Mass.: Newbury House, 1976).

havioral style. Specifically, *play* is used to focus on situations of style- and code-switching, changes which have consequences reaching far beyond the merely stylistic and aesthetic dimension of culture and which have to do with the assertion of value- and culture-differences in performance terms.

Though we make these generalizations from contemporary ethnographic study, the travel literature indicates that these differences have existed, both with regard to the use of the word *play* and the concept of what playing is and how it should be properly carried out. As early as 1729, A. Holt mentioned that the slaves on Barbados have gatherings on Sunday "which they call their plays . . . in which with their various instruments of horrid music howling and dancing about the graves of the dead, they [give] victuals and strong liquor to the souls of the deceased."[52] In 1788 Peter Marsden wrote similarly of the slaves' weekly entertainments: "Every Saturday night many divert themselves with dancing and singing, *which they style plays;* and notwithstanding their week's labour, continue this violent exercize all night."[53] But such festivities were more commonly associated with the major holidays, especially Christmas. Another commentator, William Beckford, noticed:

> Some negroes will sing and dance, and some will be in a constant state of intoxication, during the whole period that their festival at Christmas shall continue; and what is more extraordinary, several of them will go ten or twelve miles to *what is called a play,* will sit up and drink all night, and yet return in time to the plantation for their work the ensuing morning.[54]

It is this different approach to time, this all-night and unrestrained performance of play that seems to have most troubled these spectators, for almost formulaically when they mention the term they discuss the nocturnal aspects of the practice.

> The dance, or play as it is sometimes called, commences about eight o'clock . . . and . . . continues to day-break with scarcely an intermission.[55]

52. Cited in Jerome C. Handler and Charlotte J. Frisbie, "Aspects of Slave Life in Barbados: Music and Its Cultural Context," *Caribbean Quarterly*, 11 (1972), 14.
53. Peter Marsden, *An Account of the Island of Jamaica* (Newcastle, 1788), p. 33. Our italics.
54. Beckford, *Descriptive Account of Jamaica*, vol. 1, p. 392. Our italics.
55. H. T. De La Beche, *Notes on the Present Conditions of the Negroes in Jamaica* (London, 1825), p. 40.

Nothing troubled the plantocrats more than the association of their slaves with nighttime activities. This equation, of course, fits in well with the whole group of stereotype traits: nighttime, diablerie, hypersexuality, and so forth. Throughout the area attempts were made to reduce these excessive nocturnal ceremonials, the night burials and wakes, the practice of obeah, and, of course, these *plays*. Yet, as anyone knows who has spent much time in the West Indies, the value placed on playing any celebration all night has remained evident to this day. Whether it is wake, Christmas, carnival, tea meeting, or thanksgiving, it is felt that if the celebration cannot be sustained all night, it is a sad commentary on the performers, and the community.

Furthermore, the designation of these all-night performances as *plays* was only one of the black uses for the term, fastened onto by whites because it departed so fully from their usage, it would seem. James Stewart in his book *A View of Jamaica* gives us some glimmer of the Afro-American domain of the term, when he not only mentions that "Plays, or dances, very frequently take place on Saturday nights," but also suggests that *play* is their term for any of a range of licensed nonsense occasions.[56] Any holiday was called a *play-day*,[57] as was a wake.[58]

Thus, this set of practices, persistently defined as bad (and often illegal), has been maintained and even recently intensified. Significantly, the most licentious of these celebrations are still referred to in play terms: One "plays" wake, Carnival *mas'*, Christmas sports, or any of that range of performances—generally termed *nonsense* or *foolishness* events throughout the anglophonic West Indies.

Playing, then, has meant for some time the range of activities which elicit the acting out of behaviors regarded as *bad,* and yet which have provided a means of usefully channeling the energies of all those in the performance environment. This kind of acceptance of negative self-image (by at least one sector of black communities) during these licentious occasions has been widely noted by ethnographers recently. Karl Reisman has pointed out that there is a "duality of cultural patterning" between positive (usually European) forms and negative (usually old-fashioned, "country," or "African") forms.[59] It is

56. James Stewart, *A View of the Past and Present State of the Island of Jamaica* (Edinburgh, 1823), pp. 269–70.

57. Matthew G. Lewis, *Journal of a West India Proprietor* (London, 1834), pp. 45, 97.

58. Michael Scott, *Tom Cringle's Log* (Edinburgh, 1833), p. 204.

59. Karl Reisman, "Cultural and Linguistic Ambiguity in a West Indian Village," in *Afro-American Anthropology: Contemporary Perspectives*, ed. Norman E. Whitten, Jr. and John F. Szwed (New York: Free Press, 1970), pp. 129–44.

an integral part of this performance system to accept the power inherent in the playing out of negative roles and performances in public. These *bad* performances are regarded as appropriately masculine and embody male reputation values. This kind of nonsense behavior is performed constantly in such communities by the *sporty fellows*, the *bad-johns*, and *rude boys*. But it is only on those occasions when *playing* is sanctioned that the *sporty* ones are permitted to perform to the community as a whole, and only then by dressing up or dressing down, taking on unaccustomed roles into which they channel these *nonsense*, antinormative (i.e., antihousehold) motives.

The point of all this is that *playing* in anglophonic Afro-America means not only the switching of styles and codes characteristic of all types of play, but the switching downward to roles and behaviors regarded from the household (and the Euro-American) perspectives as ridiculous. Furthermore, as Morton Marks has noted of this style switching in other parts of Afro-America, it is always from a "white" to a "black" style, and in music and dance at least, from a "European" to an "African" one. It is in the juxtaposition of the implicitly good household-based norms of the black community with the negative alternatives that we have the kind of mass release of energies reported by all observers of Afro-American celebrations. *Playing* then means among other things playing bad, playing black. It is not coincidental then that playing Christmas often led to insurrection, as often was noted by the planter-journalists and travelers. The play world with its nonsense, masculine, defensive, and regressive black motives at such points simply began to break down the boundaries and rules of play, spreading from the roads, over the fences, into the yards of the great houses.

Play is used in an analogous but somewhat more restricted way in black talk in the United States. Here *playing, playing the dozens,* and other similar locutions refer to code switching into *baaad* varieties of speaking and acting calling for the same kind of performative acceptance of the negative role for the power inherent in such behaviors. Thus, throughout Afro-America, playing comes to be equated with a powerful but negative image of the performer. The power which resides in the liminal world is drawn upon as a means of *getting into it,* setting up *the action;* but such playing provides a continued threat to the household world.

This speaking frame of reference acts both positively (in establishing the street environment as an appropriate place for witty and inverted performances) and negatively (in restricting speaking behavior within the household and other places dominated by respectability values).[60] Of importance for this present argument is the demonstration that in the Afro-American order of behaviors, "play" is not distinguished from "real" or "work" but from "respectable" behavior. Play is thus situated in a very different way in Afro-American communities than in Euro-America. It is an important element of public performance in black communities, and one by which black men-of-words are able to establish and maintain their "reputations."

These descriptions of West Indian *plays* give an indication of the depth of interest given such entertainments. Through these accounts we can gain insight not only into the alternative attitude to playing, but also into the ambivalence of Euro-Americans to such energetic practices and the ways in which the slaves gradually incorporated European play occasions and in the process developed an Afro-American creole culture.

With *plays*, as with the majority of performance events introduced into Afro-American life from Europe, the focus and uses of the ceremony were changed along with some aspects of the pattern of performance, and these changes were in accord with the ethical and esthetic demands of a conceptual system shared by Africans and Afro-Americans. This process can be understood to a degree by reference to the "Creole language hypothesis," which seeks to demonstrate that English, French, and other New World Negro Creole languages are all developments from a West African Creole tongue used by traders and which is perhaps built of an amalgam of Portuguese and West African features.[61] Those who pursue this line of argument point to the large number of underlying similarities among the various New World creole systems, accounting for the major differences in vocabulary by relexification, the substitution of foreign words into the phonological and morphological structure of the West African-based language. This word (and phrase) substitution does not necessarily mean that the vocabulary substituted is used with the same system of reference. Indeed, there is good evidence that the process of relexification cannot be understood without taking into account the *calque* (or "loan translation") words which are translated into their nearest Western equiv-

60. Roger D. Abrahams, *Positively Black* (Englewood Cliffs: Prentice-Hall, 1970).

61. Keith Whinnom, "The Origin of European-based Creoles and Pidgins," *Orbis*, 14 (1965), 511–26; William A. Stewart, "Continuity and Change in American Negro Dialects," *Florida FL Reporter*, 6, no. 1 (1968), 3–14; idem, "Sociolinguistic Factors in the History of American Negro Dialects," ibid., 5, no. 2 (1967), 11–29; J. L. Dillard, *Black English* (New York: Random House, 1972).

alent but which continue to be used in the same system of reference as in Africa. This process of vocabulary substitution has ramifications, then, in the entire semantic realm, especially in the area of joking and oratory, as well as song and dance.[62]

Whether or not the Creole language hypothesis proves valid, something like relexification seems to have operated on this larger communication level; among other things one can observe in speech-making events throughout English-speaking Afro-America the utilization of the oratorical variety of Standard English, but in contexts which demand a different performer–audience relationship than would be found in British usage and for purposes which are in many ways diametrically opposite the British practices. This is also true of song and dance in the adaptation of the "sentimental song" and European formal dances, like quadrilles, for marking formal, more respectable public occasions.

Many of these features (such as the oratorical variety of Standard English) were introduced into ceremonial proceedings as a substitution for similar prestige varieties used for oratory in West Africa. Of course, this was no one-way cultural interplay, as we well know from white imitations of blacks. Rather, it is the inevitable by-product of cultural fascination and renewal that occurs when different groups encounter each other. Early observers noted just such a cultural mix and in the process demonstrate the plantocracies' ambivalence on the subject. From our earliest documents on the slave populations and their social ways, it is evident that Europeans were fascinated by the tremendous energies devoted to these recreations by the slaves. For instance, in his wonderfully open-eyed description of Negro life on Barbados very early in the slave period, Richard Ligon discusses the black aptitude for making music and dancing and describes their Sunday afternoon entertainments:

> On Sundayes in the afternoon, their musick playes, and to dancing they go, the men by themselves, and the women by themselves, no mixt dancing. Their motions are rather what they aim at, than what they do; and by that means, transgress the less upon the Sunday; their hands having more of motion than their feet, and their heads more than their hands. They may dance a whole day, and ne'r heat themselves; yet, now and then, one of the activest amongst them will leap bolt upright, and fall in his place again, but without cutting a capre. When they have

62. Roger D. Abrahams, "Traditions of Eloquence in the West Indies," *Journal of Inter-American Studies and World Affairs,* 12 (1970), 505–27; "Talking My Talk"; *Talking Black.*

danc'd an hour or two, the men fall to wrestle, (the musick playing all the while).[63]

Ligon's fascination was shared by almost every British observer of slave life throughout the plantation period, but subsequent descriptions did not share his delight and open-mindedness. Instead, the others often saw the dances and singing as evidence of all the worst attributes of Africans, and thus these descriptions were often flavored heavily with stereotypical responses to the retention of these "savage practices." In another very early account (1707), Sir Hans Sloane observed: "The Negroes are much given to Venery, and although hard wrought, will at nights, or on Feast days Dance and Sing; their Songs are all bawdy, and leading that way.... Their Dances consist in great activity and strength of Body, and keeping time, if it can be."[64]

Not only was this kind of activity seen as indicative of the continuing depravity of the slaves but it also was viewed as something of a threat to the morality of white Creoles. William Beckford so saw it: "I have often been surprised to observe how infinitely more the negro appears to be affected by music and dancing, than the white children ..., and for this fact I know not how in any manner to account. The same customs are daily before the eyes of both; nay, the Creole [white] infants are suffered to associate too much with those of the negroes: they converse and play together, and are too apt, as they grow up, to copy their manners and to imitate their vices."[65]

On the other hand, there were a number of such observers who saw the acculturative stream flowing the other way. They noted, with mixed feelings, that there was an attempt on the part of native-born slaves to imitate (without understanding) the entertainments of the plantocracy. Thus, they were able to use these entertainments as an index of the degree of "civilization" of the resident blacks. Mrs. Carmichael, one of the great Creole journal keepers, observed a division between the types of entertainments given by the African slaves and those of the native born, the latter of which were imitations of the more genteel European practices.[66] Further, this kind of cultural recognition on the part of performing blacks is still very much with us.

63. Richard Ligon, *A True and Exact Description of the Island of Barbados* (London, 1673), p. 50.
64. Sir Hans Sloane, *A Voyage to the Islands, Madera, Barbados, Nieves, St. Christophers, and Jamaica* (London, 1707), vol. 1, p. xl.
65. Beckford, *Descriptive Account of Jamaica*, p. 391.
66. Mrs. Carmichael, *Domestic Manners and Social Conditions of the White, Coloured, and Negro Population of the West Indies* (London, 1833), vol. 1, p. 292.

With the growing economic and social intercourse among various modern Afro-American countries as well as with Africa, not only have folk recognitions of stylistic and behavioral differences been maintained but actually intensified. Nothing puts the lie to the Afro-American deculturation argument more fully than the commentary of those living in (or near) Afro-American communities.

VI

As one may easily imagine, it was "venial" practices like the West Indian *play* sort which missionaries sought to counteract with their strongest weapons. As usual they reached into their British armory of devices and came up with the meeting featuring tea and testimonials, in which the proceeds go to the church. The tea meeting seems to have been introduced into West Indian life in the nineteenth century by Methodist missionaries. Indeed, the tea meeting as we know it today seems to have developed in the nineteenth century. The OED, for instance, notes its use as denoting "a public social meeting (usually in connexion with a religious organization) at which tea is taken" and their only reference to the term is late in the century.

The earliest, but in many ways the fullest, report we have of this ceremony was given us by Mrs. Lanigan in her *Antigua and the Antiguans* of 1844:

> The place of all others where the greatest display of colored beaux and belles are to be found is at the tea-parties given at the Methodist chapel for charitable purposes.
>
> It being a beautiful moonlight evening upon the last occasion of the kind, we determined to avail ourselves of it, and attend the party whose gastronomic performance was to commence at seven o'clock. Upon gaining the outer wall of the chapel, we found the gate guarded by a few of the "new police," and the porter appointed to receive the tickets of admission, for which the sum of 2s.6d sterling was demanded.
>
> Passing across the court-yard, we stopped for a few moments at an open window, to view the interior. The entertainment was held in the school-room, a large apartment, forming the ground floor of the chapel; the walls of which were hung round with various pictorial embellishments, seen to advantage by the aid of numerous lamps. We entered at that auspicious moment when nearly the whole of the company were assembled, and before the actual business of the evening commenced. The effect was really very picturesque, and the scene would have been worthy of the painter's pencil. The whole of the interior, with the ex-

ception of a space all round the apartment, reserved for a promenade, was laid out with tables, placed breadthwise, surrounded by well-dressed groups, and covered with all those delicate "cakes and confections," . . . .

After the prayer, a few hymns were played and sung; during which period, I took the opportunity of walking with my companion around the space already mentioned, in order to obtain a full view of the assembled guests; and then followed some speeches by the missionaries and one or two of the leading members, which afforded much interest to the assembled group.

One old gentleman—a very excellent man, by the way, but rather too much given to prosing while on the pulpit—spoke in favour of the tea-meetings and of the chapel debt, (to pay off which these entertainments were given as one means of raising money). Another preacher gave us a long rambling account of a bowie-knife; paid his compliments to the ladies, which were received with a grin of applause; said how much better it was to have these agreeable parties, and thus raise money, instead of the old way of trudging from house to house, begging to inmates to put down their names for certain sums, and attributing the happy change to the fertile genius of the "tender sex"; and concluded by remarking, that in the course of a week or two there would be a bazaar held at the court-house for the purpose of raising more cash to liquidate the chapel debt, at which he understood there was to be a *solid lunchtable* spread besides one for confectionary; and although he liked *tea* very well, he liked *lunch* a great deal better.

After Mr. _____ had concluded, a mild, quiet-looking man rose who spoke of social intercourse, referred to Job's sons and daughters; talked of heaven and heavenly enjoyments; and then after a few more speeches, more compliments to the ladies, a few more hymns, and a concluding prayer, came the cloaking, shawling and bonneting, we returned home.[67]

Subsequent reportings indicate that the practice caught on but became immediately secularized in a number of ways. Like the "grand balls," the tea meetings in certain places came to be a resource for the entrepreneur who made the arrangements and who charged for them. The proceedings also came to be lengthened into the all-night and sometimes licentious ceremonials characteristic of these previous Afro-American celebrations. Only the name seems to have changed from *play* to *tea*. Greville John Chester for one notes in his *Transatlantic Sketches:* "Sometimes a cottager in want of money will give a tea, charging a shilling entrance, and the entertainment lasts till sun-

67. Mrs. Lanigan, *Antigua and the Antiguans* (London, 1844), vol. 2, pp. 171–75.

rise next morning. These teas lead to a great deal of immorality, and the evil is rather increased than lessened by the vociferous singing of the most sacred hymns throughout the whole night."[68]

In a similar vein, the Reverend H. V. P. Bronkhurst somewhat later describes his Guyanese parishioners:

> There is another institution, of a pseudo-religious character, which is largely patronized by the natives especially in country districts, and that is the "tea meeting." Instrumental music is allowed in these tea meeting gatherings; the people sing heartily and lustily enough to the sound of the music. Only sacred (or, as some are pleased to call it, "secret") music is allowed, and every thing goes on well for a time, but bye and bye the musicians ("musicianers") play a sacred march, and the friends take up the musical strain by keeping time with their feet or by marching round with a limitation of the number of hops in each bar of the music.[69]

This type of dancing, however, is not common to tea meeting practices elsewhere.

The element of the tea meeting which seems to have persevered in spite of the numerous changes was the alternation of speeches and songs. That the songs and speeches were secularized in some places is also clear, though when secular performance pieces were introduced, this seems to have necessitated a distinction between *tea meeting* and *service of song,* the latter then conforming more or less to the tea parties as described by Mrs. Lanigan.

The tea meeting developed as the major form of entertainment for the community in the last generation of the nineteenth century and flourished until World War II. By the 1960s everyone judged it moribund although it is still given on a number of islands. It accrued a number of different kinds of performances on each island but it became known primarily for the fine, eloquent speeches which were elicited as a result of the occasion. Certainly developing out of the preacher–congregation distinction and testimonial tradition, these speeches became the keynote to the ceremony. There are a number of twentieth-century reportings from the farthest reaches of the British West Indies, most notably a pair of sentimental discussions concerning the practice on Barbados (where, though the practice still goes on in the countryside, it is reported to be dead by Bridgetown reporters), and another two from observers on Jamaica.

68. Greville John Chester, *Transatlantic Sketches* (London, 1869), p. 80.
69. H. V. P. Bronkhurst, *The Colony of British Guiana and its Labouring Population* (London, 1883), pp. 387–88.

The local tea meeting . . . was a sort of prolonged concern whose main features were songs, both solo and choral, an abundance of refreshments, and a type of oratory that delighted in the display of resounding polysyllabic words (some of them specially coined for the occasion), and elaborate alliterative allusions to the great names of history and literature. Preparations for the tea-meeting were begun several months before the event, and admission was by ticket: one shilling. The tea-meeting, usually held in a school hall or in the lodge of a friendly society, adorned with evergreen branches and flowers, began at nine o'clock with an oration by the vice-chairman, although for an hour previously the choir-master and his carefully rehearsed choir would have been welcoming the in-coming audience with a selection from their repertoire. The vice-chairman would then address the gathering reminding them that he was no great orator "such as Plato or Dido, Demosthenes or Socrates," but only the forerunner of the "man of gladness" who was now to entertain them. Amid great cheering the chairman would then take his seat, and the vice would introduce him, exhorting him as being "fundamental and groundamental enough to take and hold his place the Mark Anthony or Cicero, or Blake or Drake, or Wordsworth or Tennyson." etc., etc. "Take it and hold it," he would conclude "until the cock says *Claro Clarum* pronouncing or announcing the break of day." The chairman would then address the audience at some length, after which the vice would introduce to the chairman those who would provide the various items of the programme: There would be solos, choruses, monologues, dialogues, and "trialogues." The chairman would comment on each item until the stroke of midnight, when there would be an intermission of two hours for refreshment: large quantities of bread, biscuits, sponge cakes and puddings, with large pots of boiling hot tea and chocolate. Afterwards the songs and speeches would be resumed and continue until daybreak.[70]

Martha Warren Beckwith briefly reports tea meetings from Jamaica from the same period. She too notes the importance of speeches but the details she describes indicate that the ceremony had developed in a somewhat different direction in Jamaica: with an election of king and queen and much storytelling, riddling, and other secular forms of announcement.[71]

Finally, David DeCamp briefly describes tea meetings on Jamaica in the 1950s and 1960s in his discussion of the practice of mock-bidding. He reports:

70. Frank C. Collymore, *Notes for a Glossary of Words and Phrases of Barbadian Dialect*, 3d ed., rev. and enlarged (Bridgetown, Barbados: Advocate Co., 1965), pp. 110–11. See also Louis Lynch, *The Barbados Book* (London: André Deutsch, 1964).

71. Martha Warren Beckwith, *Black Roadways: A Study of Jamaican Folk Life* (Chapel Hill: University of North Carolina Press, 1929), p. 104.

The tea meeting . . . is simply a fund-raising event, which may be sponsored by any organization. . . . Inside the meeting the crowd can buy food and drink, including tea, of course, but beer and rum are more popular. A program is provided, which can be brought to a halt at any moment by a bid to "mek him stop" and can be got under way again only by the inevitable final bid to "mek him go on." It is this mock bidding which is the real source of revenue, and a successful tea meeting may net more than a hundred pounds. People of all classes attend. . . .

The program is a matter of local tradition and varies from district to district, though very little from decade to decade. . . . The orations and other set pieces in the program . . . are . . . reminiscent of traditional school graduation exercises, and a few features of the program echo considerable antiquity. There is always a veiled queen, for example, and in some communities she is seated in a fishing boat on the stage or is surrounded by farm produce. . . .

The crowd participates during these performances in two ways. First, of course, they bid to stop or resume the bidding. Second they applaud and encourage their favorite performers. Applause may take the form of whistling or hand-clapping but most characteristically consists of the shouted syllable "gee!" This is shouted in unison at the end of each couplet or quatrain of a song or poem and at each rhetorical pause in orations and other prose recitations. I have no idea of the origin of the word, not even whether it represents the injection *gee* (from *Jesus*) or, as is claimed by some participants, the alphabetic letter G. It is very effective, however, in accentuating the progressively accelerating rhythm of the speaker, comparable to the cries of "Amen! Yes, Lord!" etc. which punctuate the sermon of the revivalist preacher. Booing and hissing sometimes occur but only as good-natured ribbing among friends, not as serious heckling. Only once did I see a performer really disgruntled at being forced to step down because of negative bidding.

Third, the crowd "play the sticks." That is, many of them bring with them . . . a piece of thick bamboo . . . a small stick to beat against the bamboo or to scrape along its side. A few may bring along a large and a small piece of steel pipe for the same purpose. . . . The players match the chanted rhythm of the orator, and the effect is hypnotic. A few skilled stick players can effectively support their favorite speaker by creating such an irresistable rhythm that people jump to their feet and start dancing to the recitation.[72]

Quite clearly, the focal element of the tea meeting is the oratory. Just as clearly, the reason this ceremony caught on throughout the West Indies was that it provided the occasion for a public demonstra-

72. David DeCamp, "Mock Bidding in Jamaica," in *Tire Shrinker to Dragster*, ed. William M. Hudson (Austin, Texas: Encino Press, 1968), pp. 150–53.

tion of speechmaking abilities. But from the speeches given by these observers, as well as those noted in a number of other communities, the style of oratory seems to have been derived primarily from the Afro-American's imitation of British patterns, an imitation that has been viewed as often ludicrous.

The attribution of imitation almost certainly arises because the variety which is used is, on its face, the "formal style" of Standard English apparently learned from British sources. This style is characterized, as Martin Joos points out, by detachment of speaker from audience and cohesion of text so that the psychically removed audience may easily follow it. Virtually each key word defines the speaker's removal from the audience; the speaker effects this removal by using predominately elaborate sentence constructions, precise pronunciations, and a self-consciously ornamental diction. He does this in order to state implicitly that he is there not to interact so much as to inform his audience.[73] This sense of removal also makes the audience focus on the content and form of the text, forcing "the text to fight its own battles. Form becomes its dominant character,"[74] but other stylistic and content features must be consistent with the form.

There is little doubt that, in most regards, both the content and the form of the text of the speeches given in tea meetings are derived from this British tradition. But to see this as an evidence of total acculturation to the British model is hardly warranted, as there are numerous other facets of this eloquence tradition that differ greatly from British practices. The most obvious of these is the ways in which there is a failure of imitation as pointed out by the observers quoted above. These include certain hypercorrections in pronunciation and in diction, and severe "misunderstandings" in the meanings of certain of the most elaborate words and phrases (especially those in Latin and other foreign tongues). But just as clearly, on closer examination, these "mistakes" do not occur because of failures of understanding by the speakers or their audience but rather a different expectation and attitude toward the ongoing speech event. Certain attributes of formal style are employed, to be sure, but for purposes and effects that differ in crucial respects from British practices.

The basis of the failure to understand this performance lies in the stereotypical assumption that Africans brought no culture with them (or that they became deculturated early on) and this lack ex-

73. Martin Joos, *The Five Clocks* (New York: Harcourt, Brace and World, 1967), pp. 33–34.
74. Ibid., p. 37.

cluded the possibilities of traditions of eloquence.[75] However, there are similar eloquence traditions throughout Africa, ones in which effective oratory is regarded as central to the prosecution of life there, and these patterns of performance were transplanted and acclimatized to the new plantation environment.[76] But in certain regards, the African and European speechmaking traditions differed, and where the differences were greatest the African style of performance prevailed and it was this that often lead to the attribution of the "bad imitation" on the part of the Afro-American orators.

Perhaps the most important of these differences lies in the fundamental expectations surrounding these speeches. As Martin Joos points out, formal style emphasizes the imparting of information or wisdom and is text oriented. Therefore, the use of formal style creates a distance between performer and audience which the performer then capitalizes upon in his teaching; his expectation is that the audience will listen in silence, judging the aptness and validity of his argument. But this kind of distancing strategy is not the norm in New World black performances. Rather, any Afro-American performance is expected to elicit verbal and kinesthetic audience participation. An orator must therefore not only inform but he must contend successfully with those elements in the environment which would eliminate the coordination of the group—forces like rudeness, noise, others vying for the spotlight, and so on. A performance is judged in terms of how well it brings about this coordination, this participation. The West Indian orator is judged not only in terms of the information he imparts and the copiousness of his delivery but also by his ability to convert the noise of the audience into a guided, effective, appropriate response to his words.

This means that part of the expectation pattern of these eloquence performances is that noise will occur, so that the effective speaker can demonstrate his abilities at bringing about decorum, at guiding the response in a competitive manner. This provides "the basis of the symbolism of most [West Indian] village rituals. Meetings begin with a call for Conduct, and descend into 'noise' and Creole via argument."[77] The opposition between the speaker and the audience in such cases is seen as a creative and an expected one, and as Karl Reisman indicates, it also may be viewed as a clash of codes, between

75. Abrahams, "Traditions of Eloquence."
76. See especially Ruth Finnegan, *Oral Literature in Africa* (Oxford: Oxford University Press, 1970).
77. Reisman, "Cultural and Linguistic Ambiguity," p. 141.

household-based manners and public rudeness, and between formal
Standard English and Creole, the latter identified in the West Indian
mind with noise and contentiousness and most gatherings of men in
public.

The configuration of features characteristic of the tea meeting,
the eloquent speechmaking, the competition, the all-night duration of
the performance, and the alternation between speeches and songs are
not unique to this ceremony. Indeed, this is the modal pattern for the
whole series of festive ceremonies which surround rites of passage
and other person-centered rituals. Wedding feasts, first night wakes,
send-offs, thanksgivings (to celebrate the end of an illness or the return from a trip or some other ending to a transitional event) all share
these characteristics of performance. In the most formal of these ritual
occasions (such as the wedding feast and the wake), moreover, a person is designated to keep the proceedings going. Just as in the tea
meeting, this man of words may be called "chairman" (or "master of
ceremonies"). Keeping the proceedings going means maintaining
some sense of decorum in the midst of noise, making sure that everyone who wants to speak or sing is given the opportunity, and perhaps
most important, if no competitive element has been introduced into
the proceedings, he will make sure that this is done.

These competitive elements are a matter of ritual, having nothing to do with hostility between individuals. Rather, they are crucial
to both the interactional and the aesthetic systems of the group. David
DeCamp's article on mock-bidding gives an example of one of these
play–competition devices used by Jamaicans on virtually every public
occasion, as does Reisman's study of Antiguan speech. There are numerous other contrived mock-arguments, such as the Vincentian wedding feast in which the bride and groom are chastised and defended
for "sticking" the cake with a knife and fork; and the Herskovitses recorded their experience of culture shock in viewing a first-night wake
in Toco, Trinidad, in which the two chairmen had a fight over which
hymns were to be sung and in what order—a proceeding which they
were informed was "a matter of usage."[78] This competitive pattern can
go far beyond simply engineering a mock-argument. In their description of the wake, for instance, the Herskovitses go on to detail the
competition which arose during this hymn singing, between the
group in the yard and those in the house. This opposition, often ex-

78. Melville J. Herskovits and Frances S. Herskovits, *Trinidad Village* (New
York: Knopf, 1947).

pressed simply by noise in the yard, is to be observed in familial ceremonies of this sort throughout this culture area.

VI

This lengthy discussion on tea meeting, then, is a sample of what can be learned from travel accounts and how this knowledge can be used. This exercise should illustrate at least this: that contemporary studies of black peoples are misleading or at least painfully one-dimensional without historical and comparative perspective; but it is equally true that the travelers' records are of only limited use unless accompanied by what we can know through modern ethnographies.

We have not provided a bibliography with this volume simply because it would necessarily be book length itself. In fact the authors have published a two-volume bibliography of Afro-American folk culture,[79] and we recommend its use with this book as a guide to further materials, both historical and contemporary.

We have provided an appendix of selected parallel travel and plantation observations in the United States. Although not so eloquent as the material for the Caribbean, the accounts of the United States are rich and barely explored. For North America the student can also draw upon the resources of the ex-slave autobiographies, a literature almost totally lacking in the West Indies.

In the process of exploring Afro-American cultures through material such as appears in this book the object should not be simply to search out "Africanisms" as survivals of African traditions—instead, the idea is to use Africa as a baseline, in order to have a perspective from which to look. In the same way, the other Afro-American cultures of contemporary North and South America provide significant points of comparison. Instead of simply searching out the *sources* of this or that pattern of behavior, we should concern ourselves with finding parallel *processes* and *functions* in Africa and Afro-America after European colonial and slavery contact. It is also worth remembering what Hortense Powdermaker pointed out long ago in *After Freedom*,[80] her study of a Mississippi community: that in taking on

79. John F. Szwed and Roger D. Abrahams, eds., *Afro-American Folk Culture: An Annotated Bibliography of Materials from North, Central and South America and the West Indies*, 2 vols., Bibliography and Special Series, American Folklore Society (Philadelphia: ISHI, 1978).

80. Hortense Powdermaker, *After Freedom: A Cultural Study in the Deep South* (New York: Viking, 1939).

new cultural values from the whites, blacks did not simply replace older "African" values but rather added newer patterns to older ones. This is what Paul Radin meant when he suggested that the "Negro was not converted to [the white Christian] God. He converted God to himself."[81] Both implied that African sensibilities were the starting place and that European values were selectively adapted to the specialized needs of Afro-Americans. All this is elementary anthropology, but in taking up the politically charged subject of the roots and nature of Afro-American culture it is best to remind ourselves of the universal principles which operate in the most diverse groups of the Earth's peoples.

The insistence of contemporary Afro-American students on a cultural history that is relevant to black people—that is, one which includes both the past and present of black people and speaks to the future—has often been dismissed as lacking substance. But such dismissals depend entirely on the view that there is no unique Afro-American cultural past as such, only that of Africa and the plantation's institutional requirements, and the connection between the two is at best more discontinuous than continuous, or at worst nothing more than (to use Ralph Ellison's phrase) the sum of a people's brutalization.

Melville J. Herskovits recognized this view for what it was, the myth of the Negro past. We would add that it also constitutes the myth of the Negro present, and it is to this myth and its debunking that we address these travelers' accounts, cultural shards of a complex history though they be.

---

81. Paul Radin, *God Struck Me Dead*, ed. Clifton H. Johnson (Philadelphia: Pilgrim Press, 1968), p. ix (originally published in 1945 by Fisk University).

1

The Slave Accounts in Context:
Two Extracts

Most of the accounts included here offer brief glimpses of one dimension or another of slave or ex-slave life. There are a few of these documents, however, which are fuller in coverage and illustrate the wide range of matters of interest to the traveler and observer of locale. It seems useful to present, almost in toto, the jottings of two of the most congenial and sprightliest observers, Richard Ligon and Bryan Edwards. Though there are differences—there is over a hundred years' gap between the two, and Ligon writes of Barbados and Edwards of Jamaica—both writers were responsive to many aspects of the experience.

Ligon came to Barbados in 1647, only twenty years after its settlement by the British. Barbados was the first British island to receive slaves from Dutch and Brazilian slavers, and was the island on which the idea of the plantation in the British apotheosis caught on. Because of its geographical place it rapidly became a key point of contact between England and New England, and part of the triangle of trade that included Africa. Ligon then is writing of an as-yet-strange world to the eager reader at home. His tone of deep fascination has the appearance of the truly open-minded observer. He presents himself as an outcast, a failure in search of a way out of his embarrassment. Thus, this early account is less defensively ethnocentric than those to come and includes ethnographic observations of both slaveholder *and* slave. Every aspect of the business was new to the Europeans—climate, geography, crops, the Africans—so Ligon approaches the subject with an ethnographer's eye for detail: His book contains the most mundane of material descriptions and was accompanied by illustrations of plants, fields, buildings, and technology.

There is included in this excerpt a remarkable account of a slave's reaction to European culture, in which the slave Macow learns how to build a European musical instrument after first exposure, and then appears to adapt the European instrument to an African or perhaps even new form of playing. There are also some examples of a European's reactions to the changes which his countrymen had undergone within the slaving experience.

Ligon is concerned with the categories of African slave culture which we soon learn obsessed all Europeans: their physiques, skills, dances, music, their "invisible" institution of religion. See, for example, his comments on slaves' expertise at sword-fighting and other sports, something which continued to be remarked upon through the late nineteenth century and even today for the United States.[1]

Remarkable, too, is Ligon's alertness to slaves as *people*, as individual *human beings*, something which was to be remarked upon less and less as slavery took hold and established itself as a norm.

Bryan Edwards was, like Ligon, English born, but he inherited considerable property in Jamaica, emigrated there, and became a member of the Jamaican Assembly and later the Council. Though he was caught up in the politics and interests of the slaveholders, he nonetheless was not a Creole and thus maintained some perspective between himself and the island.

Edwards is a student of the details of differences among slaves, but unlike Ligon his interests are more practical in form. The practicality is, in fact, the result of an accumulation of functional experiences with slaves and the slave trade. Thus it is that he sets out generalizations about African "nations." Still, he is aware of the effects of slavery and the consequent difficulties of assessing the relative influences of African national culture and the developments under slavery. In this he is very modern. And in another respect (his acknowledgment of slaves' ties to fellow Africans from the same region or to "shipmates," slaves transported on the same boats) he is still ahead of most modern writers, who have yet to notice such things.

There *are* other documents as rich in detail as these, and as wide ranging. We think of Monk Lewis's account of his slaves and Hesketh Bell's later discussion of black life under emancipation. Yet there are none with the economy of means and felicity of Ligon and Edwards.

1. Lafcadio Hearn, "The Last of the New Orleans Fencing Masters," in *An American Miscellany,* ed. Albert Mordell (New York: Dodd, Mead, 1924), vol. 2, pp. 185–200; Norman Mailer, *Existential Errands* (Boston: Little, Brown, 1972), pp. 3–36, 305–16.

RICHARD LIGON, *A True and Exact History of the Island of
Barbadoes* (London, 1673), 43–54.

It were somewhat difficult, to give you an exact account, of the number of persons upon the Island; there being such store of shipping that
brings passengers daily to the place, but it has been conjectur'd, by
those that are long acquainted, and best seen in the knowledge of the
Island, that there are not lesse then 50 thousand souls, besides *Negroes;* and some of them who began upon small fortunes, are now
risen to very great and vast estates.

The Island is divided into three sorts of men, *viz.* Masters, Servants, and slaves. The slaves and their posterity, being subject to their
Masters for ever, are kept and preserv'd with greater care then the
servants, who are theirs but for five years, according to the law of the
Island. So that for the time, the servants have the worser lives, for
they are put to very hard labour, ill lodging, and their diet very
sleight. When we came first on the Island, some Planters themselves
did not eat bone meat, above twice a week: the rest of the seven
dayes, Potatoes, Loblolly, and Bonavist. But the servants no bone
meat at all; unless an Oxe died: and then they were feasted, as long
as that lasted. And till they had planted good store of Plantines, the
Negroes were fed with this kind of food; but most of it Bonavist, and
Loblolly, with some eares of Mayes toasted, which food (especially
Loblolly,) gave them much discontent: But when they had Plantines
enough to serve them, they were heard no more to complain; for 'tis
a food they take great delight in, and their manner of dressing, and
eating it, is this: 'tis gathered for them (somewhat before it be ripe, for
so they desire to have it,) upon *Saturday,* by the keeper of the Plantine grove; who is an able *Negro,* and knowes well the number of
those that are to be fed with this fruit; and as he gathers, layes them
all together, till they fetch them away, which is about five a clock in
the afternoon, for that day they break off work sooner by an hour:
partly for this purpose, and partly for that the fire in the furnaces is to
be put out, and the Ingenio and the roomes made clean; besides they
are to wash, shave and trim themselves against *Sunday.* But 'tis a
lovely sight to see a hundred handsome *Negroes,* men and women,
with every one a grasse-green bunch of these fruits on their heads,
every bunch twice as big as their heads, all coming in a train one after
another, the black and green so well becoming one another. Having
brought this fruit home to their own houses, and pulling off the skin
of so much as they will use, they boil it in water, making it into balls,

and so they eat it. One bunch a week is a *Negroe's* allowance. To this, no bread nor drink, but water. Their lodging at night a board, with nothing under, nor any thing a top of them. They are happy people, whom so little contents. Very good servants, if they be not spoiled by the *English*. But more of them hereafter.

As for the usage of the Servants, it is much as the Master is, merciful or cruel; Those that are mercifull, treat their Servants well, both in their meat, drink, and lodging, and give them such work, as is not unfit for Christians to do. But if the Masters be cruel, the Servants have very wearisome and miserable lives. Upon the arrival of any ship, that brings servants to the Island, the Planters go aboard; and having bought such of them as they like, send them with a guid to his Plantation; and being come, commands them instantly to make their Cabins, which they not knowing how to do, are to be advised by other of their servants, that are their Seniors; but, if they be churlish, and will not shew them, or if materials be wanting, to make them Cabins, then they are to lye on the ground that night. These Cabins are to be made of sticks, withs, and Plantine leaves, under some little shade that may keep the rain off; Their suppers being a few Potatoes for meat, and water or Mobbie for drink. The next day they are rung out with a Bell to work, at six a clock in the morning, with a severe Overseer to command them, till the Bell ring again, which is at eleven a clock; and then they return, and are set to dinner, either with a messe of Lob-lolly, Bonavist, or Potatoes. At one a clock, they are rung out again to the field, there to work till six, and then home again, to a supper of the same. And if it chance to rain, and wet them through, they have no shift, but must lye so all night. If they put off their cloaths, the cold of the night will strike into them; and if they be not strong men, this ill lodging will put them into a sickness: if they complain, they are beaten by the Overseer; if they resist, their time is doubled. I have seen an Overseer beat a Servant with a cane about the head, till the blood has followed, for a fault that is not worth the speaking of; and yet he must have patience, or worse will follow. Truly, I have seen such cruelty there done to Servants, as I did not think one Christian could have done to another. But as discreeter and better natur'd men have come to rule there, the servants lives have been much bettered; for now, most of the servants lie in Hamocks, and in warm rooms, and when they come in wet, have shift of shirts and drawers, which is all the cloths they were, and are fed with *bone meat* twice or thrice a week. Collonel *Walrond* seeing his servants when they came home, toyled with their labour, and wet through with their sweating, thought that shifting of their linnen not sufficient refreshing, nor

warmth for their bodies, their pores being much opened by their
sweating; and therefore resolved to send into *England* for rug Gowns,
such as poor people wear in Hospitals, that so when they had shifted
themselves, they might put on those Gowns, and lye down and rest
them in their Hamocks: For the Hamocks being but thin, and they
having nothing on but Shirts and Drawers, when they awak'd out of
their sleeps, they found themselves very cold; and a cold taken there,
is harder to be recovered, than in *England,* by how much the body is
infeebled by the great toyl, and the Sun's heat, which cannot but very
much exhaust the spirits of bodies unaccustomed to it. But this care
and charity of Collonel *Walrond*'s, lost him nothing in the conclusion;
for, he got such love of his servants, as they thought all too little they
could do for him; and the love of the servants there, is of much con-
cernment to the Masters, not only in their diligent and painful labour,
but in fore-seeing and preventing mischiefs that often happen, by the
carelessness and slothfulness of retchless servants; sometimes by laying fire so negligently, as whole lands of Canes and Houses too, are
burnt down and consumed, to the utter ruine and undoing of their
Masters: For, the materials there being all combustible, and apt to
take fire, a little oversight, as the fire of a Tobacco-pipe, being knockt
out against a dry stump of a tree, has set it on fire, and the wind fanning that fire, if a land of Canes be but near, and they once take fire,
all that are down the wind will be burnt up. Water there is none to
quench it, or if it were, a hundred *Negroes* with buckets were not able
to do it; so violent and spreading a fire this is, and such a noise it
makes, as if two Armies, with a thousand shot of either side, were continually giving fire, every knot of every Cane, giving as great a report
as a Pistol. So that there is no way to stop the going on of this flame,
but by cutting down and removing all the Canes that grow before it,
for the breadth of twenty or thirty foot down the wind, and there the
Negroes to stand and beat out the fire, as it creeps upon the ground,
where the Canes are cut down. And I have seen some *Negroes* so earnest to stop this fire, as with their naked feet to tread, and with their
naked bodies to tumble, and roll upon it; so little they regard their
own smart or safety, in respect of their Masters benefit. The year before I came away, there were two eminent Planters in the Island, that
with such an accident as this, lost at least 10000 £. sterling, in the
value of the Canes that were burnt; the one, Mr. *James Holduppe,* the
other, Mr. *Constantine Silvester:* And the latter had not only his
Canes, but his house burnt down to the ground. This, and much more
mischiefe has been done, by the negligence and wilfulness of servants. And yet some cruel Masters will provoke their Servants so, by

extream ill usage, and often and cruel beating them, as they grow desperate, and so join together to revenge themselves upon them.

A little before I came from thence, there was such a combination amongst them, as the like was never seen there before. Their sufferings being grown to a great height, and their daily complainings to one another (of the intolerable burdens they labour'd under) being spread throughout the Island; at the last, some amongst them, whose spirits were not able to endure such slavery, resolved to break through it, or dye in the act; and so conspired with some others of their acquaintance, whose sufferings were equal, if not above theirs; and their spirits no way inferiour, resolved to draw as many of the discontented party into this plot, as possibly they could; and those of this perswasion, were the greatest numbers of Servants in the Island. So that a day was appointed to fall upon their Masters, and cut all their throats, and by that means, to make themselves not only freemen, but Masters of the Island. And so closely was this plot carried, as no discovery was made, till the day before they were to put it in act: And then one of them, either by the failing of his courage, or some new obligation from the love of his Master, revealed this long plotted conspiracy; and so by this timely advertisement, the Masters were saved: Justice *Hethersall* (whose servant this was) sending Letters to all his friends and they to theirs, and so one to another, till they were all secured; and, by examination, found out the greatest part of them; whereof eighteen of the principal men in the conspiracy, and they the first leaders and contrivers of the plot, were put to death, for example to the rest. And the reason why they made examples of so many, was, they found these so haughty in their resolutions, and so incorrigible, as they were like enough to become Actors in a second plot, and so they thought good to secure them; and for the rest, to have a special eye over them.

It has been accounted a strange thing, that the *Negroes*, being more than double the numbers of the Christians that are there, and they accounted a bloody people, where they think they have power or advantages; and the more bloody, by how much they are more fearful than others: that these should not commit some horrid massacre upon the Christians, thereby to enfranchise themselves, and become Masters of the Island. But there are three reasons that take away this wonder; the one is, They are not suffered to touch or handle any weapons: The other, That they are held in such awe and slavery, as they are fearful to appear in any daring act; and seeing the mustering of our men, and hearing their Gun-shot, (than which nothing is more terrible to them) their spirits are subjugated to so low a condition, as they dare not look up to any bold attempt. Besides these, there is a third reason, which stops all designs of that kind, and that is, They are fetch'd from several parts of *Africa,* who speake several languages, and by that means, one of them understands not another: For, some of them are fetch'd from *Guinny* and *Binny,* some from *Cutchew,* some from *Angola,* and some from the River of *Gambia.* And in some of these places where petty Kingdomes are, they sell their Subjects, and such as they take in Battle, whom they make slaves; and some mean men sell their Servants, their Children, and sometimes their Wives; and think all good traffick, for such commodities as our Merchants send them.

When they are brought to us, the Planters buy them out of the Ship, where they find them stark naked, and therefore cannot be deceived in any outward infirmity. They choose them as they do Horses in a Market; the strongest, youthfullest, and most beautiful, yield the greatest prices. Thirty pound sterling is a price for the best man Negroe; and twenty five, twenty six, or twenty seven pound for a Woman; the Children are at easier rates. And we buy them so, as the sexes may be equall; for, if they have more Men than Women, the men who are unmarried will come to their Masters, and complain, that they cannot live without Wives, and desire him, they may have Wives. And he tells them, that the next ship that comes, he will buy them Wives, which satisfies them for the present; and so they expect the good time: which the Master performing with them, the bravest fellow is to choose first, and so in order, as they are in place; and every one of them knows his better, and gives him the precedence, as Cows do one another, in passing through a narrow gate; for, the most of them are as near beasts as may be, setting their souls aside. Religion they know none; yet most of them acknowledge a God, as appears by their motions and gestures: For, if one of them do another wrong, and he cannot revenge himself, he looks up to Heaven for vengeance, and holds up both his hands, as if the power must come from thence, that must do him right. Chast they are as any people under the Sun; for, when the men and women are together naked, they never cast their eyes towards the parts that ought to be covered; and those amongst us, that have Breeches and Petticoats, I never saw so much as a kiss, or embrace, or a wanton glance with their eyes between them. Jealous they are of their Wives, and hold it for a great injury and scorn, if another man make the least courtship to his Wife. And if any of their Wives have two Children at a birth, they conclude her false to his Bed, and so no more adoe but hang her. We had an excellent *Negro* in the Plantation, whose name was *Macow,* and was our chief Musician; a very valiant man, and was keeper of our Plantine-Grove. The *Negroe's* Wife was brought to bed of two Children, and her Husband, as their manner is, had provided a cord to hang her. But the Overseer finding what he was about to do, enformed the Master of it, who sent for *Macow*, to disswade him from this cruell act, of murdering his Wife, and used all persuasions that possible he could, to let him see, that such double births are in Nature, and that divers presidents were to be found amongst us of the like; so that we rather praised our Wives, for their fertility, than blamed them for their falseness. But this prevailed little with him, upon whom custom had taken so deep an impression; but resolved, the next thing he did, should be to hang her. Which when the Master perceived, and that the ignorance of the man, should take away the life of the woman, who was innocent of the crime her Husband condemned her for, told him plainly, that if he hang'd her, he himself should be hang'd by her, upon the same bough; and therefore wish'd him to consider what he did. This threatening wrought more with him, than all the reasons of Philosophy that could be given him; and so let her alone; but he never car'd much for her afterward, but chose another which he lik'd better. For the Planters there deny not a slave, that is a brave fellow, and one that has extraordinary qualities, two or three Wives, and above that number they seldom go: But no woman is allowed above one Husband.

At the time the wife is to be brought a bed, her husband removes his board (which is his bed), to another room (for many several divisions they have, in their little houses, and none above six foot square). And leaves his wife to God, and her good fortune, in the room, and upon the board alone, and calls a neighbour to come to her, who gives little help to her delivery, but when the child is borne, (which she calls her Pickaninny) she helps to make a little fire near her feet and that serves instead of Possets, Broaths, and Caudles. In a fortnight, this woman is at worke with her Pickaninny at her back, as merry a soul as any is there: If the Overseer be discreet, she is suffer'd to rest her self a little more than ordinary; but if not, she is compelled to do as others do. Times they have of suckling their Children in the fields, and refreshing themselves; and good reason, for they carry burthens on their backs; and yet work too. Some women, whose Pickaninnies are three years old, will, as they work at weeding which is a stooping work, suffer the wee Pickaninny, to sit a stride upon their backs, like St. *George* a Horse-back; and there Spur his mother with his heels, and sings and crows on her back, clapping his hands, as if he meant to flye; which the mother is so pleas'd with, as she continues her painful stooping posture, longer then she would do, rather

than discompose her Joviall Pickaninny of his pleasure, so glad she is
to see him merry. The work which the women do, is most of it weeding, a stooping and painful worke; at noon and night they are call'd
home by the ring of a Bell, where they have two hours time for their
repast at noone; and at night, they rest from six, till six a Clock next
morning.

On *Sunday* they rest, and have the whole day at their pleasure;
and the most of them use it as a day of rest and pleasure; but some of
them who will make benefit of that dayes liberty, go where the Man-
grave trees grow, and gather the bark, of which they make ropes,
which they truck away for other Commodoties, as Shirts and Drawers.

In the afternoons on *Sundayes*, they have their Musick, which is
of kettle drums, and those of several sizes; upon the smallest the best
Musician playes, and the other come in as Chorasses: the drum all
men know, has but one tone; and therefore variety of tunes have little
to do in this musick; and yet so strangely they varie their time, as 'tis
a pleasure to the most curious ears, and it was to me one of the strangest noises that ever I heard made of one tone; and if they had the variety of tune, which gives the greater scope in Musick, as they have of
time, they would do wonders in that Art. And if I had not faln sick
before my coming away, at least seven months in one sickness, I had
given them some hints of tunes, which being understood, would have
serv'd as a great addition to their harmony; for time without tune, is
not an eighth part of the Science of Musick.

I found *Macow* very apt for it of himself, and one day coming
into the house, (which none of the *Negroes* use to do, unless an Officer, as he was,) he found me playing on a Theorbo, and singing to it
which he hearkened very attentively to; and when I had done, he took
the Theorbo in his hand, and strook one string, stopping it by degrees
upon every fret, and finding the notes to varie, till it came to the body
of the instrument; and that the nearer the body of the instrument he
stopt, the smaller or higher the sound was, which he found was by the
shortning of the string, considered with himself, how he might make
some tryl of this experiment upon such an instrument as he could
come by; having no hope ever to have any instrument of this kind to
practise on. In a day or two after, walking in the Plantine grove, to
refresh me in that cool shade, and to delight my self with the sight of
those plants, which are so beautiful, as though they left a fresh
impression in me when I parted with them, yet upon a review, something is discern'd in their beauty more than I remembered at parting:
which caused me to make often repair thither, I found this *Negro*
(whose office it was to attend there) being the keeper of that grove,

sitting on the ground, and before him a piece of large timber, upon
which he had laid cross, six Billets, and having a handsaw and a
hatchet by him, would cut the billets by little and little, till he had
brought them to the tunes, he would fit them to; for the shorter they
were, the higher the Notes, which he tryed by knocking upon the
ends of them with a stick, which he had in his hand. When I found
him at it, I took the stick out of his hand, and tryed the sound, finding
the six billets to have six distinct notes, one above another, which put
me in a wonder, how he of himself, should without teaching do so
much. I then shewed him the difference between flats and sharps,
which he presently apprehended, as between *Fa,* and *Mi:* and he
would have cut two more billets to those tones, but I had then no time
to see it done, and so left him to his own enquiries. I say this much to
let you see that some of these people are capable of learning Arts.

Another, of another kind of speculation I found; but more ingenious then he: and this man with three or four more, were to attend me
into the woods, to cut Church wayes, for I was imployed sometimes
upon publick works; and those men were excellent Axe-men, and because there were many gullies in the way, which were impassable,
and by that means I was compell'd to make traverses, up and down in
the wood; and was by that in danger to miss of the point, to which I
was to make my passage to the Church, and therefore was fain to take
a Compasse with me, which was a Circumferenter, to make my traverses the more exact, and indeed without which, it could not be done,
setting up the Circumferenter, and observing the Needle: This *Negre
Sambo* comes to me, and seeing the needle wag, desired to know the
reason of its stirring, and whether it were alive: I told him no, but it
stood upon a point, and for a while it would stir, but by and by stand
still, which he observ'd and found it to be true.

The next question was, why it stood one way; and would not remove to any other point, I told him that it would stand no way but
North and South, and upon that shew'd him the four Cardinal points
of the compass, East, West, North, South, which he presently learnt
by heart, and promis'd me never to forget it. His last question was,
why it would stand North, I gave this reason, because of the huge
Rocks of Loadstone that were in the North part of the world, which
had a quality to draw Iron to it; and this Needle being of Iron, and
touch'd with a Loadstone, it would always stand that way.

This point of Philosophy as a little too hard for him, and so he
stood in a strange muse; which to put him out of, I bad him reach his
axe, and put it near to the Compass, and remove it about; and as he

did so, the Needle turned with it, which put him in the greatest admiration that ever I saw a man, and so quite gave over his questions, and desired me, that he might be made a Christian; for, he thought to be a Christian, was to be endued with all those knowledges he wanted.

I promised to do my best endeavour; and when I came home, spoke to the Master of the Plantation, and told him, that poor *Sambo* desired much to be a Christian. But his answer was, That the people of that Island were governed by the Lawes of *England,* and by those Lawes, we could not make a Christian a Slave. I told him, my request was far different from that, for I desired him to make a Slave a Christian. His answer was, That it was true, there was a great difference in that: But, being once a Christian, he could no more account him a Slave, and so lose the hold they had of them as Slaves, by making them Christians; and by that means should open such a gap, as all the Planters in the Island would curse him. So I was struck mute, and poor *Sambo* kept out of the Church; as ingenious, as honest, and as good a natur'd poor soul, as ever wore black, or eat green.

On *Sundayes* in the afternoon, their Musick plays, and to dancing they go, the men by themselves, and the women by themselves, no mixt dancing. Their motions are rather what they aim at, than what they do; and by that means, transgress the less upon the *Sunday;* their hands having more of motion than their feet, and their heads more than their hands. They may dance a whole day, and ne'r heat themselves; yet, now and then, one of the activest amongst them will leap bolt upright, and fall in his place again, but without cutting a capre. When they have danc'd an houre or two, the men fall to wrestle, (the Musick playing all the while) and their manner of wrestling is, to stand like two Cocks, with heads as low as their hips; and thrusting their heads one against another, hoping to catch one another by the leg, which sometimes they do: But if both parties be weary, and that they cannot get that advantage, then they raise their heads, by pressing hard one against another, and so having nothing to take hold of but their bare flesh, they close, and grasp one another about the middle, and have one another in the hug, and then a fair fall is given on the back. And thus two or three couples of them are engaged at once, for an houre together, the women looking on: for when the men begin to wrestle, the women leave of their dancing, and come to be spectatours of the sport.

When any of them dye, they dig a grave, and at evening they bury him, clapping and wringing their hands, and making a doleful sound with their voices. They are a people of a timerous and fearful disposition, and consequently bloody, when they find advantages. If any of them commit a fault, give him present punishment, but do not threaten him; for if you do, it is an even lay, he will go and hang himself, to avoid the punishment.

What their other opinions are in matter of Religion, I know not; but certainly, they are not altogether of the sect of the *Sadduces:* For, they believe a Resurrection, and that they shall go into their own Countrey again, and have their youth renewed. And lodging this opinion in their hearts, they make it an ordinary practice, upon any great fright, or threatening of their Masters, to hang themselves.

But Collonell *Walrond* having lost three or foure of his best Negroes this way, and in a very little time, caused one of their heads to be cut off, and set upon a pole a dozen foot high; and having done that, caused all his Negreș to come forth, and march round about this head, and bid them look on it, whether this were not the head of such an one that hang'd himself. Which they acknowledging, he then told them, That they were in a main errour, in thinking they went into their own Countreys, after they were dead; for, this mans head was here, as they all were witnesses of; and how was it possible, the body could go without a head. Being convinc'd by this sad, yet lively spectacle, they changed their opinions; and after that, no more hanged themselves.

When they are sick, there are two remedies that cure them; the one, an outward, the other, an inward medicine. The outward medicine is a thing they call *Negro-oyle,* and 'tis made in *Barbary,* yellow it is as Bees wax, but soft as butter. When they feel themselves ill, they call for some of that, and annoint their bodies, as their breasts, bellies, and sides, and in two dayes they are perfectly well. But this does the greatest cures upon such, as have bruises or strains in their bodies. The inward medicine is taken, when they find any weakness or decay in their spirits and stomachs, and then a dram or two of *kill-devil* revives and comforts them much.

I have been very strict, in observing the shapes of these people; and for the men, they are very well limber'd, that is, broad between the shoulders, full breasted, well filleted, and clean leg'd, and may hold good with *Albert Durers* rules, who allowes *twice the length of the head,* to the breadth of the shoulders; and twice the *length of the face,* to the breadth of the hips, and according to this rule these men are shap'd. But the women not; for the same great Master of Proportions, allowes to each woman, twice the length of the face to the breadth of the shoulders, and twice the length of her own head to the breadth of the hips. And in that, these women are faulty; for I have seen very few of them, whose hips have been broader then their shoulders, unless they have been very fat. The young Maids have ordinarily very large breasts, which stand strutting out so hard and firm, as no leaping, jumping, or stirring, will cause them to shake any more, then the brawns of their arms. But when they come to be old, and have had five or six Children, their breasts hang down below their navels, so that when they stoop at their common work of weeding, they hang almost down to the ground, that at a distance, you would think they had six legs: And the reason of this is, they tie the cloaths about their Children's backs, which comes upon their breasts, which by pressing very hard, causes them to hang down to that length. Their Children, when they are first born, have the palms of their hands and soles of their feet, of a whitish colour, and the sight of their eyes of a blewish colour, not unlike the eyes of a young Kitling; but, as they grow older, they become black.

Their way of reckoning their ages, or any other notable accident they would remember, is by the Moon; and so accounting from the time of their Childrens births, the time they were brought out of their own Countrey, or the time of their being taken Prisoners, by some Prince or Potentate of their own Country, or any other notorious accidents, that they are resolved to remember, they account by the Moon; as, so many Moons since one of these, and so many Moons since another; and this account they keep as long as they can: But if any of them live long, their Arithmetick fails them, and then they are at a dead fault, and so give over the chase, wanting the skill to hunt counter. For what can poor people do, that are without Letters and Numbers, which is the soul of all business that is acted by Mortals, upon the Globe of this World.

Some of them, who have been bred up amongst the *Portugals*, have some extraordinary qualities, which the others have not; as singing and fencing. I have seen some of these *Portugal Negroes*, at Collonel *James Draxes*, play at Rapier and Dagger very skilfully, with their Stookados, their Imbrocados, and their Passes: And at single Rapier too, after the manner of *Charanza*, with such comeliness; as, if the skill had been wanting, the motions would have pleased you; but they were skilful too, which I perceived by their binding with their points, and nimble and subtle avoidings with their bodies, and the advantages the strongest man had in the close, which the other avoided by the nimbleness and skilfulness of his motion. For, in this Science,

I had been so well vers'd in my youth, as I was now able to be a competent Judge. Upon their first appearance upon the Stage, they march towards one another, with a slow majestick pace, and a bold commanding look, as if they meant both to conquer; and coming near together, they shake hands, and embrace one another, with a cheerful look. But their retreat is much quicker then their advance, and, being at first distance, change their countenance, and put themselves into their posture; and so after a pass or two, retire, and then to't again: And when they have done their play, they embrace, shake hands, and putting on their smoother countenances, give their respects to their Master, and so go off. For their Singing, I cannot much commend that, having heard so good in *Europe;* but for their voices, I have heard many of them very loud and sweet.

Excellent Swimmers and Divers they are, both men and women. Collonel *Drax (who was not so strict an observer of Sundayes,* as to deny himself lawful recreations) would sometimes, to shew me sport, upon that day in the afternoon, send for one of the *Muscavia* Ducks, and have her put into his largest Pond, and calling for some of his best swimming Negroes, commanded them to swim and take this Duck; but forbad them to dive, for if they were not bar'd that play, they would rise up under the Duck, and take her as she swome, or meet her in her diving, and so the sport would have too quick an end. But that play being forbidden, the duck would make them good sport for they are stronger ducks, and better Divers by far then ours: and in this chase, there was much of pleasure, to see the various swimmings of the *Negroes;* some the ordinary wayes, upon their bellies, some on their backs, some by striking out their right leg and left arm, and then turning on the other side, and changing both their leg and arm, which is a stronger and swifter way of swimming, than any of the others: and while we were seeing this sport, and observing the diversities, of their swimmings, a *Negro* maid, who was not there at the beginning of the sport, and therefore heard nothing of the forbidding them to dive, put off her peticoat behind a bush, that was at one end of the Pond, and closely sunk down into the water, and at one diving got to the Duck, pul'd her under water, and went back again the same way she came to the bush, all at one dive. We all thought the Duck had div'd: and expected her appearance above water, but nothing could be seen, till the subtilty was discovered, by a Christian that saw her go in, and so the duck was taken from her. But the trick being so finely and so closely done, I begg'd that the Duck might be given her again, which was granted, and the young girle much pleased.

Though there be a marke set upon these people, which will hardly ever be wip'd off, as of their cruelties when they have advantages, and of their fearfulness and falsness; yet no rule so general but hath his acception: for I believe, and I have strong motives to cause me to see of that persuasion, that there are as honest, faithfull, and conscionable people amongst them, as amongst those of *Europe,* or any other part of the world.

A hint of this, I will give you in a lively example; and it was in a time when Victuals were scarce, and Plantins were not then so frequently planted, as to afford them enough. So that some of the high spirited and turbulent amongst them, began to mutiny, and had a plot, secretly to be reveng'd on their Master, and one or two of these were Firemen that made the fires in the furnaces, who were never without store of dry wood by them. These villains, were resolved to make fire to such part of the boyling-house, as they were sure would fire the rest, and so burn all, and yet seem ignorant of the fact, as a thing done by accident. But this plot was discovered, by some of the others who hated mischief, as much as they lov'd it; and so traduc'd them to their Master, and brought in so many witnesses against them, as they were forc'd to confess, what they meant should have been put in act the next night: so giving them condign punishment, the Master gave order to the overseer that the rest should have a dayes liberty to themselves and their wives, to do what they would; and with all to allow them a double proportion of vitual for three dayes, both which they refus'd: which we all wonder'd at, knowing well how much they lov'd their liberties, and their meat, having been lately pinch'd of the one, and not having overmuch of the other; and therefore being doubtful what their meaning was in this, suspecting some discontent amongst them, sent for three or four of the best of them, and desir'd to know why they refus'd this favour that was offer'd them, but receiv'd such an answer: as we little expected; for they told us, it was not sullenness, of slighting the gratuity their Master bestow'd on them, but they would not accept any thing as a recompence for doing that which became them in their duties to do, nor would they have him think, it was hope of reward, that made them to accuse their fellow servants, but an act of Justice, which they thought themselves bound in duty to do, and they thought themselves sufficiently rewarded in the Act. The substance of this, in such language, as they had, they delivered, and poor *Sambo* was the Orator; by whose example the others were led both in the discovery of the Plot, and refused all of the gratuity. And withall they said, that if it pleas'd their Master, at any time, to bestow a voluntary boon upon them, be it never so sleight, they would willingly and thankfully accept it: and this act might have beseem'd the best Christians, though some of them were denyed Christianity; when they earnestly sought it. Let others have what opinion they please, yet I am of this belief; that there are to be found amongst them, some who are as morally honest, as Conscionable, as humble, as loving to their friends, and as loyall to their Masters, as any that live under the Sun, and one reason they have to be so, is, they set no great value upon their lives: And this is all I can remember concerning the *Negroes,* except of their games, which I could never learn, because they wanted language to teach me.

BRYAN EDWARDS, *The History, Civil and Commercial, of the British Colonies in the West Indies* (Dublin, 1793), vol. II, 56–77.

Most, if not all, the nations that inhabit that part of Africa which lies to the northward and eastward of Sierra Leone, are Mahometans; and following the means of conversion prescribed by their prophet, are, as we are told, perpetually at war with such of the surrounding nations as refuse to adopt their religious tenets. The prisoners taken in these religious wars furnish, I doubt not, great part of the slaves which are exported from the factories on the Windward coast; and it is probable that death would be the fate of most of the captives, if purchasers were not to be met with.

But the Mandingoes have frequent wars with each other, as well as with such nations as they consider enemies of their faith; and I am afraid that some of these wars arise from motives even less justifiable than religious zeal. An old and faithful Mandingo servant, who stands at my elbow while I write this, relates that being sent by his father to visit a distant relation in a country wherein the Portuguese had a settlement, a fray happened in the village in which he resided; that many people were killed, and others taken prisoners, and he himself was seized and carried off in the skirmish; not, as he conceives, by a foreign enemy, but by some of the natives of the place; and being sent down a river in a canoe, was sold to the captain of the ship that brought him to Jamaica. Of his national customs and manners he remembers but little, being, at the time of his captivity, but a youth. He relates, that the natives practice circumcision, and that he himself has undergone that operation; and he has not forgot the morning and evening prayer which his father taught him; in proof of this assertion, he chants, in an audible and shrill tone, a sentence that I conceive to be part of the Alcoran, *La illa, ill lilla!*,* which he says they sing aloud at the first appearance of the new moon. He relates, moreover, that in his own country Friday was constantly made a day of strict fasting. It was almost a sin, he observes, on that day, *to swallow his spittle,*— such is his expression.

Besides this man, I had once another Mandingo servant, who could write with great beauty and exactness, the Arabic alphabet, and some passages from the Alcoran. Whether his learning extended any further, I had no opportunity of being informed, as he died soon after he came into my possession.

The advantage possessed by a few of these people, of being able to read and write, is a circumstance on which the Mandingo Negroes in the West Indies pride themselves greatly among the rest of the slaves; over whom they consider that they possess a marked superiority; and in truth they display such gentleness of disposition and demeanour, as would seem the result of early education and discipline, were it not that, generally speaking, they are more prone to theft than any of the African tribes. It has been supposed that this propensity, among other vices, is natural to a state of slavery, which degrades and corrupts the human mind in a deplorable manner; but why the Mandingoes should have become more vicious in this respect than the rest of the Natives of Africa in the same condition of life, is a question I cannot answer.

In their complexions and persons, the Mandingoes are easily to be distinguished from such of the Africans as are born nearer to the equator; but they consist nevertheless of very distinct tribes, some of which are remarkably tall and black, and there is one tribe among them (called also the Phulies) that seems to me to constitute the link between the Moors and Negroes properly so called. They are of a less glossy black than the Gold Coast Negroes; and their hair, though bushy and crisped, is not woolly, but soft and silky to the touch. Neither have the Mandingoes, in common, the thick lips and flat noses of the more southern Natives; and they are, in a great degree, exempt from that strong and fetid odour, which exhales from the skin of most of the latter; but in general they are not well adapted for hard labour.

After all, they differ less in their persons, than in the qualities of the mind, from the Natives of the Gold Coast; who may be said to constitute the genuine and original unmixed Negro, both in person and character. The circumstances that distinguish the Koromantyn, or

*There is no God, but God.

Gold Coast, Negroes, from all others, are firmness both of body and mind; a ferociousness of disposition; but withal, activity, courage, and a stubbornness, or what an ancient Roman would have deemed an elevation, of soul, which prompts them to enterprizes of difficulty and danger; and enables them to meet death, in its most horrible shape, with fortitude or indifference. They sometimes take to labour with great promptitude and alacrity, and have constitutions well adapted for it; for many of them have undoubtedly been slaves in their own country, and were sold either to pay the debts, or to expiate the crimes, of their owners. On the other hand, the Gold Coast being inhabited by various different tribes which are engaged in perpetual warfare and hostility with each other, there cannot be a doubt that many of the captives taken in battle, and sold in the European settlements, were of free condition in their native country, and perhaps the owners of slaves themselves. It is not wonderful that such men should endeavour, even by means the most desperate, to regain the freedom of which they have been deprived; nor do I conceive that any further circumstances are necessary to prompt them to action, than that of being sold into captivity in a different country. I mean only to state facts as I find them. Such I well know was the origin of the Negro rebellion which happened in Jamaica in 1760. It arose at the instigation of a Koromantyn Negro of the name of Tacky, who had been a chief in Guiney; and it broke out on the Frontier plantation in St. Mary's parish, belonging to the late Ballard Beckford, and the adjoining estate of Trinity, the property of my deceased relation and benefactor Zachery Beyly. On those plantations were upwards of 100 Gold Coast Negroes newly imported, and I do not believe that an individual amongst them had received the least shadow of ill treatment from the time of their arrival there. Concerning those on the Trinity estate, I can pronounce of my own knowledge that they were under the government of an overseer of singular tenderness and humanity. His name was Abraham Fletcher, and let it be remembered, in justice even to the rebels, and as a lesson to other overseers, that his life was spared from respect to his virtues. The insurgents had heard of his character from the other Negroes, and suffered him to pass through them unmolested—this fact appeared in evidence. Having collected themselves into a body about one o'clock in the morning, they proceeded to the fort at Port Maria; killed the sentinel, and provided themselves with as great a quantity of arms and ammunition as they could conveniently dispose of. Being by this time joined by a number of their countrymen from the neighbouring plantations, they marched up the high road that led to the interior parts of the country, carrying death and desolation as they went. At Ballard's Valley they surrounded the overseer's house about four in the morning, in which eight or ten White people were in bed, everyone of whom they butchered in the most savage manner, and literally drank their blood mixed with rum. At Esher, and other estates, they exhibited the same tragedy; and then set fire to the buildings and canes. In one morning they murdered between thirty and forty Whites, not sparing even infants at the breast, before their progress was stopped. Tacky, the chief, was killed in the woods, by one of the parties that went in pursuit of them; but some others of the ringleaders being taken, and a general inclination to revolt appearing among all the Koromantyn Negroes in the island, it was thought necessary to make a few terrible examples of some of the most guilty. Of three who were clearly proved to have been concerned in the murders committed at Ballard's Valley, one was condemned to be burned, and the other two to be hung up alive in irons, and left to perish in that dreadful situation. The wretch that was burned was made to sit on the ground, and his body being chained to an iron stake, the fire was applied to his feet. He uttered not a groan, and saw his legs reduced to ashes with the utmost firmness and composure; after which one of his arms by some means getting loose, he snatched a brand from the fire that was consuming him, and flung it in the face of the executioner. The two that were hung up alive were indulged, at their own request, with a hearty meal immediately before they were suspended on the gibbet, which was erected in the parade of the town of Kingston. From that time, until they expired, they never uttered the least complaint, except only of cold in the night, but diverted themselves all day long in discourse with their countrymen, who were permitted, very improperly, to surround the gibbet. On the seventh day a notion prevailed among the spectators, that one of them wished to communicate an important secret to his master, my near relation; who being in St. Mary's parish, the commanding officer sent for me. I endeavoured, by means of an interpretor, to let him know that I was present; but I could not understand what he said in return. I remember that both he and his fellow sufferer laughed immoderately at something that occurred—I know not what. The next morning one of them silently expired, as did the other the morning of the ninth day.

Even the children brought from the Gold Coast manifest an evident superiority, both in hardiness of frame, and vigour of mind, over all the young people of the same age that are imported from other parts of Africa. The like firmness and intrepidity which are distinguishable in adults of this nation, are visible in their boys at an age which might be thought too tender to receive any lasting impression, either from precept or example.—I have been myself an eyewitness to the truth of this remark, in the circumstance I am about to relate. A gentleman of my acquaintance, who had purchased at the same time ten Koromantyn boys, and the like number of Eboes (the eldest of the whole apparently not more than thirteen years of age) caused them all to be collected and brought before him in my presence, to be marked on the breast. This operation is performed by heating a small silver brand, composed of one or two letters, in the flame of spirits of wine, and applying it to the skin, which is previously anointed with sweet oil. The application is instantaneous, and the pain momentary. Nevertheless it may be easily supposed that the apparatus must have a frightful appearance to a child. Accordingly, when the first boy, who happened to be one of the Eboes, and the stoutest of the whole, was led forward to receive the mark, he screamed dreadfully, while his companions of the same nation manifested strong emotions of sympathetic terror. The gentleman stopt his hand; but the Koromantyn boys, laughing aloud, and, immediately coming forward of their own accord, offered their bosoms undauntedly to the brand, and receiving its impression without flinching in the least, snapt their fingers in exultation over the poor Eboes.

One cannot surely but lament, that a people thus naturally emulous and intrepid, should be sunk into so deplorable a state of barbarity and superstition; and that their spirits should ever be broken down by the yoke of slavery. Whatever may be alledged concerning their ferociousness and implacability in their present notions of right and wrong, I am persuaded that they possess qualities, which are capable of, and well deserve cultivation and improvement.—But it is time to conclude my observations on this nation, which I shall do, with some account of their religion; for which my readers are indebted to the researches of an ingenious gentleman of Jamaica, who is well acquainted with their language and manners. Its authenticity has been frequently confirmed to me, on my own inquiries among the Koramantyn Negroes themselves.

They believe that *Accompong*, the God of the heavens, is the creator of all things; a Deity of infinite goodness; to whom however they never offer sacrifices, thinking it sufficient to adore him with praises and thanksgiving.

Assarci is the god of the earth; to him they offer the first fruits of the ground, and pour out libations of the liquors they drink to his honour.

Ipboa is the god of the sea; if the arrival of ships which trade upon their coast is delayed, they sacrifice a hog to deprecate the wrath of *Ipboa.*

Obboney is a malicious deity, who pervades heaven, earth, and sea; he is the author of all evil, and when his displeasure is signified by the infliction of pestilential disorders, or otherwise, nothing will divert his anger but human sacrifices; which are selected from captives taken in war, or, if there be none present, then from their slaves.

Besides the above deities, every family has a peculiar tutelar saint, who is supposed to have been originally a human being like one of themselves, and the first founder of their family; upon the anniversary of whose burial, the whole number of his descendants assemble round his grave, and the oldest man, after offering up praises to Accompong, Assarci, Ipboa, and their tutelar deity, sacrifices a cock or goat, by cutting its throat, and shedding the blood upon the grave. Every head of an household of the family, next sacrifices a cock, or other animal in like manner, and as soon as all those who are able to bring sacrifices have made the oblations, the animals which have been killed, are dressed, and a great festival follows.

Among their other superstitions also, must not be omitted their mode of administering an oath of secrecy or purgation.—Human blood, and earth taken from the grave of some near relation, are mixed with water, and given to the party to be sworn, who is compelled to drink the mixture, with a horrid imprecation, that it may cause the belly to burst, and the bones to rot, if the truth be not spoken. This test is frequently administered to their wives, on the suspicion of infidelity, and the resemblance which it bears to the trial of jealousy by the *bitter water* described in the book of Numbers (chap. v.) is a curious and striking circumstance.

I now proceed to the people of Whidah, or Fida. The Negroes of this country are called generally in the West Indies *Papaws*, and are unquestionably the most docile and best disposed Slaves that are imported from any part of Africa. Without the fierce and savage manners of the Koromantyn Negroes, they are also happily exempt from the timid and desponding temper of the Eboes, who will presently be mentioned.—The cheerful acquiescence with which these people apply to the labours of the field, and their constitutional aptitude for such employment, arise, without doubt, from the great attention paid to agriculture in their native country. Bosman speaks with rapture of the improved state of the soil, the number of villages, and the industry, riches, and obliging manners of the Natives. He observes, however, that they are much greater thieves than those of the Gold Coast, and very unlike them in another respect, namely—in the dread of pain, and the apprehension of death.—"They are," says he, "so very apprehensive of death, that they are unwilling to hear it mentioned, for fear *that* alone should hasten their end; and no man dares to speak of death in the presence of the king, or any great man, under the penalty of suffering it himself, as a punishment for his presumption." He relates further, that they are addicted to gaming beyond any people of Africa. All these propensities, if I am rightly informed, are observable in the character of the Papaws in a state of slavery in the West Indies. That punishment which excites the Koromantyn to rebel, and drives the Ebo Negro to suicide, is received by the Papaws as the chastisement of legal authority, to which it is their duty to submit patiently. The case seems to be, that the generality of these people are in a state of absolute slavery in Africa, and, having been habituated to a life of labour, they submit to a change of situation with little reluctance.

Many of the Whidah Negroes are found to be circumcised. Whether it be a religious ceremony common to all the tribes that go under the appellation of Papaws, I know not. It is practised universally by the *Nagoes;* a people that speak the Whidah language; but I have met with Negroes from this part of the coast that disavow the practice.

We are now come to the Bight of Benin, comprehending an extent of coast of near 300 English leagues, of which the interior countries are unknown, even by name, to the people of Europe. All the Negroes imported from these vast and unexplored regions, except a tribe which are distinguished by the name of *Mocoes*, are called in the West Indies *Eboes;* and in general they appear to be the lowest and most wretched of all the nations of Africa. In complexion they are much yellower than the Gold Coast and Whidah Negroes; but it is a sickly hue, and their eyes appear as if suffused with bile, even when they are in perfect health. I cannot help observing too, that the conformation of the face, in a great majority of them, very much resembles that of the baboon. I believe indeed there is, in most of the nations of Africa, a greater elongation of the lower jaw, than among the people of Europe; but this distinction I think is more visible among the Eboes, than in any other Africans. I mean not however to draw any conclusion of natural inferiority in these people to the rest of the human race, from a circumstance which perhaps is purely accidental, and no more to be considered as a proof of degradation, than the red hair and high cheek bones of the Natives of the North of Europe.

The great objection to the Eboes as slaves, is their constitutional timidity, and despondency of mind; which are so great as to occasion them very frequently to seek, in a voluntary death, a refuge from their own melancholy reflections. They require therefore the gentlest and mildest treatment to reconcile them to their situation; but if their confidence be once obtained, they manifest as great fidelity, affection, and gratitude, as can reasonably be expected from men in a state of slavery. The females of this nation are better labourers than the men, probably from having been more hardly treated in Africa.

The depression of spirits which these people seem to be under, on their first arrival in the West Indies, gives them an air of softness and submission, which forms a striking contrast to the frank and fearless temper of the Koromantyn Negroes. Nevertheless, the Eboes are in fact more truly savage than any nation of the Gold Coast; inasmuch as many tribes among them, especially the Moco tribe, have been, without doubt, accustomed to the shocking practice of feeding on human flesh. This circumstance I have had attested beyond the possibility of dispute, by an intelligent trustworthy domestic of the Ebo nation, who acknowledged to me, though with evident shame and reluctance (having lived many years among the Whites) that he had himself, in his youth, frequently regaled on this horrid banquet: and his account received a shocking confirmation from a circumstance which occurred in the year 1770 in Antigua, where two Negroes of the same country were tried for killing and devouring one of their fellow-slaves in the island. They were purchased, a short time before, by a gentleman of the name of Christian, out of a ship from Old Calabar, and I am told were convicted on the clearest evidence.

Of the religious opinions and modes of worship of the Eboes, we know but little; except that, like the inhabitants of Whidah, they pay adoration to certain reptiles, of which the guana (a species of lizard) is in the highest estimation.[†] They universally practise circumcision,

---

†I have been assured by an intelligent person who had visited many parts of Africa, that the Eboes frequently offer up human sacrifices in their worship of this animal. Perhaps the certainty of this may be questioned; but the following anecdote is undoubtedly true. In the year 1787, two of the seamen of a Liverpool ship trading at Bonny, being ashore watering, had the misfortune to kill a guana, as they were rolling a cask to the beach. An outcry was immediately raised among the Natives, and the boat's crew were surrounded and seized, and all trade interdicted, until public justice should be satisfied and appeased. The offenders being carried before the king, or chief man of the place,

"which with some other of their superstitions (says Purchas) may seem Mahometan, but are more likely to be ancient Ethnic rites; for many countries of Africa admit circumcision, and yet know not, or acknowledge not, Mahometism; but are either Christians, as the Cophti, Abissinians, or Gentiles. They (the people of Benin) cut or rase the skin with three lines drawn to the navel, esteeming it necessary to salvation."

Next in order to the Whidah Negroes, are those from Congo and Angola; whom I consider to have been originally the same people. I can say but little of them that is appropriate and particular; except that they are in general a slender and sightly race, of a deep and glossy black (a tribe of the Congoes excepted, who very nearly resemble the Eboes) and I believe of a disposition naturally mild and docile. They appear to me to be fitter for domestic service than for field-labour. They are said however to become expert mechanics; and, what is much to their honour, they are supposed to be more strictly honest than many other of the African tribes.

Having thus recited such observations as have occurred to me on contemplating the various African nations to the West Indies separately and distinct from each other, I shall now attempt an estimate of their general character and dispositions, influenced, as undoubtedly they are in a great degree, by their situation and condition in a state of slavery; circumstances that soon efface the native original impression which distinguishes one nation from another in Negroes newly imported, and create a similitude of manners, and a uniformity of character throughout the whole body.

Thus, notwithstanding what has been related of the firmness and courage of the natives of the Gold Coast, it is certain that the Negroes in general in our islands (such of them at least as have been any length of time in a state of servitude) are of a distrustful and cowardly disposition. So degrading is the nature of slavery, that fortitude of mind is lost as free agency is restrained. To the same cause probably must be imputed their propensity to conceal or violate the truth; which is so general, that I think the vice of falsehood is one of the most prominent features in their character. If a Negro is asked even

---

were adjudged to die. However, the severity of justice being softened by a bribe from the captain, the sentence was at length changed to the following, that they should pay a fine of 700 bars (about £175) and remain in the country as slaves to the king, until the money should be raised. The captain not being willing to advance so large a sum for the redemption of these poor wretches, sailed without them, and what became of them afterwards, I have not heard.

an indifferent question by his master, he seldom gives an immediate reply; but affecting not to understand what is said, compels a repetition of the question, that he may have time to consider, not what is the true answer, but, what is the most politic one for him to give. The proneness observable in many of them to the vice of theft, has already been noticed; and I am afraid that evil communication makes it almost general.

It is no easy matter, I confess, to discriminate those circumstances which are the result of proximate causes, from those which are the effects of national customs and early habits in savage life; but I am afraid that cowardice and dissimulation have been the properties of slavery in all ages, and will continue to be so, to the end of the world. It is a situation that necessarily suppresses many of the best affections of the human heart.—If it calls forth any latent virtues, they are those of sympathy and compassion towards persons in the same condition of life; and accordingly we find that the Negroes in general are strongly attached to their countrymen, but above all, to such of their companions as came in the same ship with them from Africa. This is a striking circumstance: the term shipmate is understood among them as signifying a relationship of the most endearing nature; perhaps as recalling the time when the sufferers were cut off together from their common country and kindred, and awakening reciprocal sympathy, from the remembrance of mutual affliction.

But their benevolence, with a very few exceptions, extends no further. The softer virtues are seldom found in the bosom of the enslaved African. Give him sufficient authority, and he becomes the most remorseless of tyrants. Of all the degrees of wretchedness endured by the sons of men, the greatest, assuredly, is the misery which is felt by those who are unhappily doomed to be the Slaves of Slaves; a most unnatural relation, which sometimes takes place in the sugar plantations, as for instance, when it is found necessary to instruct young Negroes in certain trades or handicraft employments. In those cases it is usual to place them in a sort of apprenticeship to such of the old Negroes as are competent to give them instruction; but the harshness with which these people enforce their authority, is extreme; and it serves in some degree to lessen the indignation which a good mind necessarily feels at the abuses of power by the Whites, to observe that the Negroes themselves, when invested with command, give full play to their revengeful passions; and exercise all the wantonness of cruelty without restraint or remorse.

The same observation may be made concerning their conduct towards the animal creation. Their treatment of cattle under their direction is brutal beyond belief. Even the useful and social qualities of the dog secure to him no kind usage from an African master. Although there is scarce a Negro that is not attended by one, they seem to maintain these poor animals solely for the purpose of having an object whereon to exercise their caprice and cruelty. And by the way, it is a singular circumstance, and not the less true of being somewhat ludicrous, that the animal itself, when the property of a Negro, betrays at first sight to whom he belongs; for, losing his playful propensities, he seems to feel the inferiority of his condition, and actually crouches before such of his own species, as are used to better company. With the manners, he acquires also the cowardly, thievish, and sullen disposition of African tyrant.

But, notwithstanding what has been related of the selfish and unrelenting temper of the enslaved Africans, they are said to be highly susceptible of the passion of love. It has even been supposed that they are more subject to, and sensible of its impression, than the natives of colder climates. "The Negro (says Dr. Robertson) glows with all the warmth of desire natural to his climate." "The tender passion (says another writer) is the most ardent one in the breast of the enslaved African.—It is the only source of his joys, and his only solace in affliction." Monsieur de Chanvalon (the historian of Martinico) expatiates on the same idea with great eloquence.—"Love, says he, the child of nature, to whom she entrusts her own preservation; whose progress no difficulties can retard, and who triumphs even in chains; that principle of life, as necessary to breathe, inspires and invigorates all the thoughts of his slavery. No perils can abate, nor impending punishments restrain, the ardour of his passion. He leaves his master's habitation, and traversing the wilderness by night, disregarding its noxious inhabitants, seeks a refuge from his sorrows, in the bosom of his faithful and affectionate mistress."

All this however is the language of poetry and the visions of romance. The poor Negro has no leisure in a state of slavery to indulge a passion, which, in civilized life is desire heightened by sentiment, and refined by delicacy, I doubt if it ever found a place in an African bosom.—The Negroes in the West Indies, both men and women, would consider it as the greatest exertion of tyranny, and the most cruel of all hardships, to be compelled to confine themselves to a single connection with the other sex; and I am persuaded that any attempt to restrain their present licentious and dissolute manners, by

introducing the marriage ceremony among them, as is strenuously rec-
ommended by many persons in Great Britain, would be utterly im-
practicable to any good purpose. Perhaps it may be thought that the
Negroes are not altogether reduced to so deplorable a state of slavery,
as is commonly presented, when it is known that they boldly claim
and exercise a right of disposing of themselves in this respect, according to their own will and pleasure, without any control from their
masters.

That passion therefore to which (dignified by the name of Love)
is ascribed the power of softening all the miseries of slavery, is mere
animal desire, implanted by the great Author of all things for the preservation of the species. This the Negroes, without doubt, possess in
common with the rest of animal creation, and they indulge it, as inclination prompts, in an almost promiscuous intercourse with the other
sex; or at least in temporary connections, which they form without
ceremony, and dissolve without reluctance. When age indeed begins
to mitigate the ardour, and lessen the fickleness of youth, many of
them form attachments, which, strengthened by habit, and endeared
by the consciousness of mutual imbecility, produce a union for life. It
is not uncommon to behold a venerable couple of this stamp, who, tot-
tering under the load of years, contribute to each other's comfort, with
a cheerful assiduity which is at once amiable and affecting.

The situation of the aged among the Negroes is indeed commonly such as to make them some amends for the hardships and sufferings of their youth. The labour required of the men is seldom any
thing more than to guard the provision grounds; and the women are
chiefly employed in attending the children, in nursing the sick, or in
other easy avocations; but their happiness chiefly arises from the high
veneration in which old age is held by the Negroes in general, and
this I consider as one of the few pleasing traits in their character. In
addressing such of their fellow servants as are any ways advanced in
years, they prefix to their names the appellation of Parent, as *Ta*
Quaco, and *Ma* Quasheba; *Ta* and *Ma*, signifying Father and Mother,
by which designation they mean to convey not only the idea of filial
reverence, but also that of esteem and fondness. Neither is the regard
thus displayed towards the aged, confined to outward ceremonies and
terms of respect alone. It is founded on an active principle of native
benevolence, furnishing one of the few exceptions to their general unrelenting and selfish character. The whole body of Negroes on a plantation must be reduced to a deplorable state of wretchedness, if, at

any time, they suffer their aged companions to want the common necessaries of life, or even many of its comforts, as far as they can procure them. They seem to me to be actuated on these occasions by a kind of involuntary impulse, operating as a primitive law of nature, which scorns to wait the cold dictates of reason: among them, it is the exercise of a common duty, which courts no observations, and looks for no applause.‡

‡The greatest affront (says Mr. Long) that can be offered to a Negro, is to curse his father and mother, or any of his progenitors.

Figure 2. R. Bridgens, *Negro Superstition, The Doo di Doo bush, or which is the Thief.*

Figure 3. Bridgens, *Negro Figuranti.*

Figure 4. Bridgens, *Negro Dance.*

Figure 5. A. Brunyas, *A Negro Festival drawn from Nature in the Island of St. Vincent.*

Figure 6. A. Brunyas, *Villagers merrymaking in the island of St. Vincent, with dancers and musicians; a landscape with huts on a hill.*

Figure 7. Bridgens, *Negro Mode of Nursing.* Figures 8–19 are also by Bridgens.

Figure 8. *Sunday Morning in the Country.*

Figure 9. *Sunday Morning in Town.*

Figure 10. *Field Negro.
Sugar Cane in the
Background.*

Figure 11. *Cutting Canes.*

Figure 12. *Planting the Sugar Cane.*

Figure 13. *Carting Sugar. Rose Hill the residence of Edward Jackson Esquire.*

Figure 14. *Carting Canes to the Mill.* Boiling house is on left, sugar mill on right.

Figure 15. *Interior of a Boiling-House.*

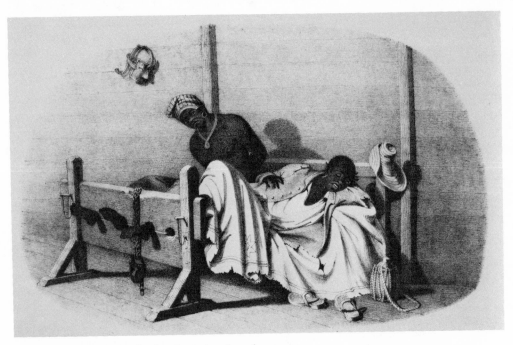

Figure 16. *Bed-Stocks for Intoxication, & c.*

Figure 17. *Stocks for Hands and Feet, with Bed and Hand Stocks (from the approved Models).*

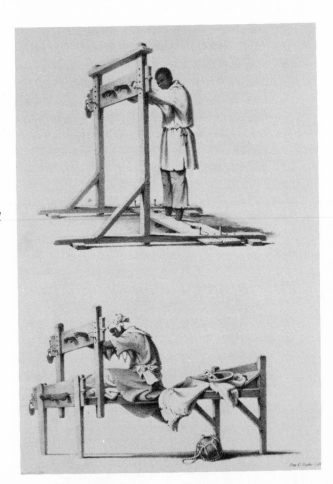

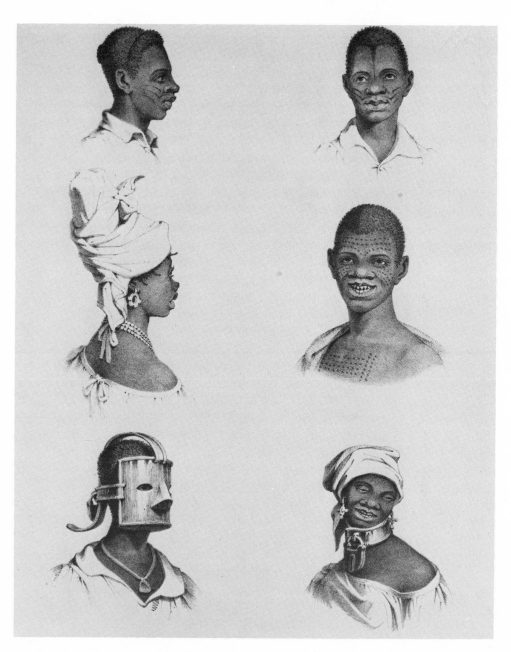

Figure 18. *Negro Heads, with punishments for Intoxication and Dirt-eating.*

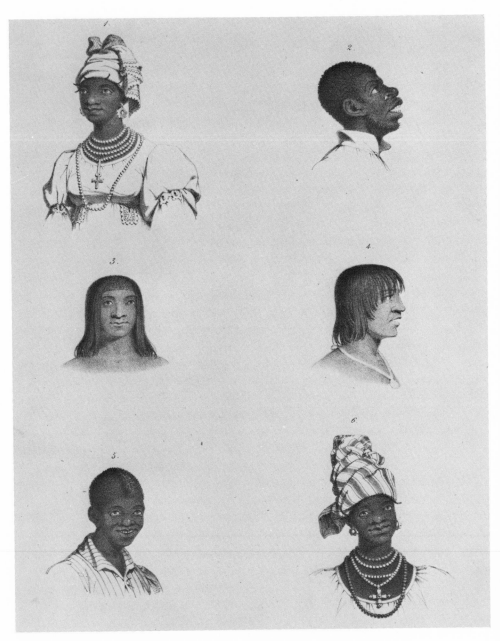

Figure 19. *No. 1, 2, 5 & 6, Negro, 3 & 4, Indian Characters.*

2

Ways of Speaking:
Speech, Letters, Names, Proverbs

Nothing fascinated the observer of slave life more than their constant "chattering" and their strange propensity for making speeches. Of course, such speaking behavior was used as evidence that the slave was a monkey-like imitator, on the one hand, and of limited acumen on the other. Cleverness was permitted in such a stereotypical view as long as it was somehow attached to laziness.

Though the deficit theory of black language behavior is comparatively new, Western Europeans, and especially the English, have long used linguistic deviation as a means for proclaiming cultural deficiencies, constructing a stereotype by which they have engineered and rationalized domination. One can see this stereotype operating in the numerous journals and travel accounts written by whites about plantation life, especially in the West Indies. As the movement toward emancipation developed, these visitors or part-time residents were actively seeking evidence as to whether Afro-Americans were human, with special interest in the presence or absence of black culture. Consequently, there was a good deal of note taken of the manners and social ways of the slaves, including these reports concerning Negro attitudes toward words and word usage.

These accounts, although viewed from a stereotypical point of view, are remarkably accurate in recording an important segment of the range of Afro-American speech activities. We see here the tremendous significance attached to speech in all its forms: the use of talk to proclaim presence of self, to assert oneself vocally in the most anxious and the most unguarded situations. We are shown the value of arguing in the daily prosecution of life, as one technique of dramatizing oneself. And we are permitted a view of the importance of a highly formal

77

and decorous approach to language in both intercultural exchanges and in intragroup activities.

This gives us a confused picture of Negroes, for they are presented as being both chaotic and overformal in their use of language. This confusion arises primarily because of cultural differences which existed between the European and the slave over the value of words and the way in which effective verbal performance was used in Negro groups for the attainment of status. Little did the white observer understand that blacks had brought with them a concern for maintaining a wide variety of rhetorical processes and speech activities as well as the highly systematic canons of appropriateness in content, formality, and diction during recurrent interactional situations.

Most books concerning the West Indies in the eighteenth and nineteenth centuries contain discussions of one aspect or another of the verbal behavior of the slaves. Most commonly noted were the "noisy" aspects of Negroes in public, their tendency toward "overdramatization," and the trait of talking to themselves.

But not all commentators were so deeply offended by this exhibition of a different attitude toward language (and noise). For instance, we have already seen that Bryan Edwards wrote perceptively of the difference in modes of address and petition. In the hands of such a spectator language usage was observed to be different but nevertheless artful. And it was observers like him who first noted the propensity of certain slaves to flavor their everyday discourse with set speeches, effusive patterns of movement, and proverbs. This led to the notation of proverb usage in other situations in further works by travelers.

The reason why attention was paid to this kind of elaborate speech behavior was certainly more than just shock at the existence of Afro-American oratorical ability. More important, this behavior elicited a sense of embarrassment on the part of those toward whom the speech was directed, for it seemed inappropriate to the hierarchy-bound occasion. These observers were recording, then, a recurrent interpersonal situation in which a failure of communication arose because the speaker and the hearer were operating in different systems of speech decorum. Speech of the sort recorded here is, in the European system, regarded as inappropriate to a person-to-person communication, no matter how great the social distance that existed between the two. Thus, the observer took note of the oration both because of its similarities to British practices and its inappropriateness to the restricted communication event defined by the observer as a casual conversation and by the slave as an appropriate encounter in which to make a formal appeal. The European can only fall back on his stereotyping habits to handle his sense of embarrassment by suggesting that these Afro-Americans were trying to copy their master's verbal practices but misunderstood and therefore imperfectly reproduced them. Once we recognize this dimension of embarrassment and accept that the orator was operating in terms of a behavioral system (albeit a different one) there is little difficulty in separating actual behavior from stereotypical judgment of it.

The problem of dealing with data of this sort extends beyond contending with its stereotypical presentation, however, as can be seen in our discussion of the history of the tea meeting in the introduction. We are told about the uses of oratory in these situations of contact between master and slave, but from the evidence given it is difficult to place such speeches in the total repertoire of speaking devices existing within Afro-American communities. With this limitation one tends to see such speechmaking not only as being imitative of white people's ways but also as being developed primarily to direct an appeal to the plantocrat. This kind of speech is regarded as a borrowing from British sources rather than as an adaptation of African style to New World language, setting, and occasion. For this reason it is important to survey the other existing speech occasions in which this type of elaborate and formal oratory arises.

Unfortunately, here the evidence from the travel and journal literature is somewhat meager. However, it was recognized that not all such ornamental and elevated speechmaking was (and is) directed toward *buckra man*. To the observers, nothing seemed quite as ludicrous as the Negroes using all these large words and elaborate formalities; this sense of absurdity was probably more the result of a feeling of non sequitur that these children were trying to act like adults and failing at it, just as children do in play situations, because of the hypercorrections and the overposturing. Exhibiting such a perspective, for instance, is Hesketh Bell, who wrote of the wedding customs of his Grenadian black neighbors in the West Indies:

> Everything having been pretty well cleared off the table, the moment for speeches and toasts has now arrived. The health of the married couple is proposed by one of the guests in certain set phrases which are never departed from. Allusions to the happy connubial state of turtle doves, and the well-known adventures of Isaac and Rebecca are never omitted, and this speech once over, the other more amusing and original toasts begin. One of the groomsmen will get up and propose the

health of the bridesmaids. The more polysyllables and high-sounding, senseless phrases he can remember, the more will he and the company be pleased. Passages from any book containing very long words, though having no earthly reference to the occasion, will be learnt by heart and retailed to the admiring guests, who would disdain to listen to a sensible speech made up of commonplace, every-day words. Verses from the Bible are frequently pressed into service, and seem to afford much satisfaction.[1]

Bell identifies these speeches with the epistolary style of blacks, thus giving us a comparative description of the two practices.

Quashie has an intense love for long words of which he does not know the meaning, and delights in using them on any occasion. In his love letters especially does he express his feelings in the longwinded polysyllables. Sense is a secondary consideration, and his position in the affection of his lady love very much depends on the number of jaw-breaking words he can cram into an epistle.[2]

The assumption by some of these observers that unions between blacks were so easily and quickly entered into and dissolved is one of the primary reasons for us to see a great discrepancy between performance and behavior, and thus regard these speeches and letters as ludicrous. Only those who are capable of living with some manner of decorum and discretion can be accorded the pleasure of ornate words, it would seem. But Bell and the others provide us with a record of the perseverance of an essentially oral and African attitude toward eloquence.

The oratorical practices noted here achieved some literate formulations early on. Recent ethnographic evidence indicates that speeches to be spoken by the young were written out as "lessons" for delivery in "sweet talk" household ceremonies, in tea meetings and service of song at church, and in the performance of plays, including Shakespearean scenes.

In addition we encounter a number of notices of letter writing among the slaves which involve the oratorical modes of address. The observers' interest in them was not surprising, for English culture placed great emphasis on eloquence and style in letter writing. In-

1. Hesketh Bell, *Obeah: Witchcraft in the West Indies* (London: Sampson Low, Marston, Garleand Rivington, Ltd., 1889), p. 139.
2. Ibid., p. 140. References to this courtship and love-letter tradition in the United States are conveniently brought together by Newbell Niles Puckett, *Folk Beliefs of the Southern Negro* (Chapel Hill: University of North Carolina Press, 1926), pp. 29–30. For other West Indian reportings, see [Charles Rampini] *Letters from Jamaica* (Edinburgh, 1873), pp. 103–10, and Winifred James, *The Mulberry Tree* (London, 1913), pp. 45–57.

deed, the earliest English novels incorporated letters wholesale. And despite the obvious selection of slave letters for their whimsical qualities, we can nonetheless value their survival as evidence of early developments in literacy.

There are two other aspects of Afro-American language practice that caught the attention of these observers: strange naming practices and the widespread employment of proverbs.

Slaves' names were a continuous source of fascination and confusion for whites, especially where naming appeared to be a very flexible and adaptive practice. The amused tone of the observers should not mislead us into believing that there was not also a considerable source of deeper wonder—especially as these naming practices seemed to have begun to influence the naming of whites.[3]

Proverbs were yet another point at which European and African cultures intersected on common ground. Both peoples valued proverbial expression as a source of wisdom and entertainment, even though there were some basic differences in the social setting and functions of proverbs. Here again is the same ambivalence one sees elsewhere in European accounts of Africans, but the care with which these proverbs were remembered and reproduced tells us something of the importance with which they were perceived by whites. Later observers of black life, indeed, came to make lists of proverbs as illustrations of the life of the ex-slave.

SPEECH

J. G. STEDMAN, *Narrative of a Five Years' Expedition against the Revolted Negroes of Surinam* (Amherst: University of Massachusetts Press, 1971 [1796]), vol. II, 361–62.

With the languages of the African negroes I am but little acquainted; as a specimen, however, I will insert a few sentences of that called the *Coromantyn*, upon the credit of my boy Quaco, who belonged to that nation, together with a translation in English; and only observe, that they break off their words very short, in a kind of guttural manner, which I cannot easily describe:—For instance, *"Co faansyo, na baramon bra,* Go to the river, and bring me some water."—*"Mee yeree, nacomeda mee,* My wife, I want some food."—So much for the

3. For the comments of a slaveholder's son on the influence of black naming practices on white in the United States, see B. Carradine, *Mississippi Stories* (Chicago: Christian Witness Co., 1904).

Coromantyn language, as spoken by the negroes on the coast of Guinea.

But as to that spoken by the black people in Surinam, I consider myself a perfect master, it being a compound of Dutch, French, Spanish, Portuguese, and English. The latter they like best, and consequently use the most. It has been already observed, that the English were the first Europeans who possessed this colony, hence probably the predilection for that language which they have still retained. In this mixed dialect, for which I have seen a printed grammar, the words end mostly with a vowel, like the Indian and Italian, and it is so sweet, so sonorous and soft, that the genteelest Europeans in Surinam speak little else; it is also wonderfully expressive and sentimental, such as, "Good eating, *sweety-muffo*."—"Gun-powder, *man sanny*." "I will love you, with all my heart, so long as I live, *Mee saloby you, langa alla mee hatty, so langa me leeby*."—"A pleasing tale, *ananassy tory*."—"I am very angry, *me hatty brun*."—"Live long, so long until your hair become white as cotton, *Lebee langa, tay, tay, tay you weeree weeree tan wity likee catoo*."—"Small, *peekeen*."— "Very small, *peekeeneenee*."—"Farewell! Good-bye! I am dying, and going to my God, *Adioso, cerroboay, mee de go dede, me de to na mee Gado*."—In this sample, many corrupt English words are perceptible, which however begin to grow out of use near the capital, but are still retained in the distant plantations; for instance, at the estate *Goet-Accoord*, in Cottica, I have heard an old negro woman say, *"We lobee fo leebee togeddere,"* by which she meant, we love to live together; and at Paramaribo to express the same sentence," *"Wee looka for tanna macandera."*

BRYAN EDWARDS, *The History, Civil and Commercial, of the British Colonies in the West Indies* (Dublin, 1793), vol. II, 77–78.

Among the propensities and qualities of the Negroes must not be omitted their loquaciousness. They are as fond of exhibiting set speeches, as orators by profession; but it requires a considerable share of patience to hear them throughout; for they commonly make a long preface before they come to the point; beginning with a tedious enumeration of their past services and hardships. They dwell with peculiar energy (if the fact admits it) on the number of children they have presented to *Massa (Master)* after which they recapitulate some of the instances of particular kindness shewn them by their owner or employer, adducing these also as proofs of their own merit; it being evident, they think that no such kindness can be gratuitous. This is their usual exordium, as well when they bring complaints against others, as when they are called upon to defend themselves; and it is vain to interrupt either plaintiff or defendant. Yet I have sometimes heard them convey much strong meaning in a narrow compass; I have been surprised by such figurative expressions and (notwithstanding their ignorance of abstract terms) such pointed sentences, as would reflect no disgrace on poets and philosophers.

ALEXANDER BARCLAY, *A Practical View of the Present State of Slavery in the West Indies . . .* , (London, 1826), 10.

. . . The day on which the last of the canes are cut down upon a sugar plantation, flags are displayed in the field, and all is merriment. A quart of sugar, and a quart of rum, are allowed to each Negro on the occasion, to hold what is called CROP-OVER, or harvest home. In the evening they assemble in their master's or manager's house, and as a matter of course, take possession of the largest room, bringing with them a fiddle and a tambourine. Here all authority and all distinction of colour ceases; black and white, overseer and book-keeper, mingle together in the dance. About twenty years ago, it was common on occasions of this kind, to see the different African tribes forming each a distinct party, singing and dancing to the *gumbay*, after the rude manners of their native Africa; but this custom is now extinct. The fiddle is now the leading instrument with them, as with the white people, whom they imitate; they dance Scotch reels, and some of the better sort (who have been house servants) country-dances. . . .

TRELAWNY WENTWORTH, *The West India Sketch Book* (London, 1834), vol. I, 44, 198.

Talk they will in despite of all consequences—they appear to be wound up for it; you might as well expect a clock to keep time without ticking, as for a negro to be awake and keep his tongue quiet, and should he happen to be solus, he will gratify the propensity by soliloquizing, something in this way, interrogatively and respondentively:—

"Daw hog aw bin mek fat, daw ranger him kirry he—he ugry granfarrar babboon—he hed tan lek dem ugry musmillen—nebber mine daw hum much he bin mek?—aw tay you, von foo quatter foo sissy bit an a haf—turrer foo quatter foo sissy bit an fower dog—put sissy bit an haf pun sissy bit an fower dog, ee no mek donner two bit and tre dog?—'t be sure, berry well. Turrer quatter foo sissy bit and a haf, long daw quatter he obeshay bin tek foo sissy bit law two dog—

ee no mek donner two bit law two dog?—'t be sure, berry well—put daw donner two bit an a haf pun da donner two bit la two dog, he no mek two donner fower bit la fi dog?—'t be sure—him mek two donner fower bit la fi dog—daw hed him goo fu notin!" It appeared that master Sambo had his pig killed by the ranger, for committing manifest and unlawful depredations upon the sugar-canes, an article of diet held in high estimation by the species, and its head was forfeited to the executioner by way of perquisite. Sambo naturally placed the body to the best account, and we behold him soliloquizing over the result in these terms:—"The hog I been make fat the ranger kill him— an ugly grandfather babboon, his head stands like them ugly musk-melons—never mind, how much he been make? I'll tell you—one four quarter for six bits and a half—'t other four quarter for six bits and four dogs—put six bits and a half upon six bits and four dogs, he no make a dollar two bits and three dogs?—to be sure, very well.—The other quarter for six bits and a half, along with the quarter the over-seer been take for six bits and two dogs—he no make a dollar two bits and two dogs—to be sure—very well—put the dollar two bits and a half upon the dollar two bits and two dogs, he no make two dollars four bits and five dogs?—To be sure—he make two dollars four bits and five dogs: the head, its good for nothing."

. . .

The principal, or weekly market, which was held at this time on Sundays, is near the southern entrance to Saint John's, where the slaves of every description assembled, and where the gratification of their vanity in the display of their finery was no inconsiderable incentive to their congregating, as well as the more ostensible motive of traffic—and what with the jabbering of their voices, the noise of pigs, goats, and poultry, and the compound animal and vegetable odours, the whole thing was enough to confound the senses of any man that had not become familiar with such an ordeal. And then their jeers and jokes upon those who happen to be better dressed than themselves, or whose pig is more sleek than their own—their semi-civilized proverbs and quaint sententious remarks, accompanied by gesticulations which seem appertinent to the same ideas, are all so exquisitely ludicrous, that we defy the most saturnine temper not to be tickled by risible emotion. "Eh, me Gad! look da!" they will say, upon seeing a negro wench who has exchanged her working attire for a muslin or cambric frock—"aw nebber see de like—aw really gran—cockaw-benny tun a yellah tail!"—and if the lady happens to evince more than ordinary pride, or contempt, she will probably hear, by way of reproach, "Nawngaw mek kraub no hab no head"—pride was the cause of crabs having no heads—a saying, which among themselves admits of this exposition: that when all animals were called together to receive their heads, the crabs were so proud of their walk, so different from other creatures, that they continued walking backward and forward to show those that were passing and repassing their elegant steps, and this they continued so long, that when they applied for their heads, they were all gone. And if, perchance, in barter among themselves, they imagine the proposed bargain to be against them, they will observe with peculiar archness of expression, "ĕh, ĕh, you tink me foōl?—aw sabbey berry well-dat time de cockroach hab dance, him no hax fowl fu cum da."*

H. H. BREEN, *St. Lucia: Historical, Statistical, and Descriptive* (London, 1844), 200–03.

Amongst the numerous peculiarities of the Negro character, as it is moulded or modified by French society, is their constant aping of their superiors in rank. During slavery the most venial offence, the most innocent familiarity was regarded as an "insolence"; and all the year round the din of "Je vous trouve bien insolent" resounded in the Negro's ear. From long habit this expression has now become a bye-word with the lower orders: it is, in fact, the staple of their abuse of each other, and the most opprobrious epithet in their Billingsgate vocabulary. *Canaille* is deemed too vulgar, and *négraille* too personal; while *"in-so-lent"* carries with it a pungency and privilege, which receive added zest from the recollections of the past.

But if to be deemed *insolent* is the lowest depth of degradation, to be held *respectable* is the highest step in the ladder of social distinctions. From Marigot to Mabouya, from Cape Maynard to the Mole-à-chiques, respectability is the aim and end of every pursuit. With the baker in his shop, as with the butcher in his stall, it is the one thing needful—the cornerstone of social existence; and though it may not, like charity, cover a multitude of sins, it will screen a vast amount of meanness and misery. Nothing can be more amusing than to observe the talismanic effect of this word upon the lower orders: even the common street-criers take advantage of it in the disposal of their

---

*"You think me a fool, eh?—I understand very well, that time the cockroaches have a dance, they don't ask fowls to come there"; for the obvious reason, that the fowls would devour the dancing gentry. The negroes have been known to make a more pertinent application of this proverb, which is worthy of becoming a standing maxim in more refined society, not to encourage or invite those persons, the sole object of whose visits is to eat and drink, and who would devour their host if they could.

wares. Some time ago a female servant, being commissioned to sell a quantity of biscuits of inferior quality, hawked them about to the cry of "Mi* biscuits pour les dames respectables." As she passed along the street the conceited recommendation did not fail to attract the attention of those for whom it was thrown out. The hawker was stopped at every door, and so great was the anxiety of the Negresses to test the quality of her biscuits as a patent of respectability, that before she reached the end of the street, she had disburdened herself of the contents of her tray.

A still more striking illustration of the charm of respectability is presented in the following circumstances which occurred in August 1842. A dispute had arisen between the queen of the Roses and a coloured woman—a warm advocate for the Marguerites. During the altercation the parties came to blows, and the queen, being a strong, lusty woman, inflicted a pair of black eyes upon her antagonist. The matter soon reached the ears of the Attorney-General, and both combatants were brought before Chief Justice Reddie in the Court of Police. As the quarrel had grown out of the previous dispute about the blue flag, the Court House was crowded to suffocation by the friends and supporters of the accused—each party anxiously expected a verdict against its antagonist. This feature of the case did not escape the penetration of the Judge, who, resolving not to give either any cause of triumph, dismissed them both with a severe admonition, expressing his surprise that two such "respectable demoiselles" should have so far forgotten what was due to themselves, as to have assaulted each other in the public streets. The word "respectable" shot like electricity through the audience. A thrill of exultation seized every breast: the Marguerite looked at the Rose; the Rose smiled at the Marguerite; and as they retired from the Court, pleased with themselves and proud of the Judge, a murmur of applause ran from mouth to mouth. Since that period nothing but harmony has prevailed between the rival societies; and it would now require no small amount of provocation to draw them down from the niche of respectability in which they are enshrined.

MRS. LANIGAN, *Antigua and the Antiguans* (London, 1844), 115–16.

The negroes are indefatigable talkers, at all times, and in all seasons. Whether in joy or grief, they ever find full employment for that little

---

*Mi is a negro word used instead of *voici* and *voila*.

member, the tongue. If none of their acquaintance are near at hand to enter into conversation with, they talk to themselves, maintaining different characters, and answering their own questions. I have often thought two persons were conversing, but upon inquiry, have found it to be only one. One peculiarity of expression among the negroes is, that if you have to find fault with them, and you express your dislike of what they have been doing in the mildest terms, they immediately say you have been *cursing* them. When speaking, their tongues are very vociferous, and prove extremely disagreeable to a stranger.

CHARLES WILLIAM DAY, *Five Years' Residence in the West Indies* (London, 1852), vol. I, 23; vol. II, 61–64, 111–14.

The negro is very fond of talking to himself or herself, or at least of publishing in the streets his private opinions on his own private affairs for the benefit of the public at large, and he goes stumbling along in sweet colloquy with himself, seeming every now and then to "put it to you" whether he has been fairly dealt with. The women are particularly prone to this. They appear to have no idea of keeping their thoughts to themselves, and in fact their character is the strangest *mélange* of childish simplicity and low cunning it is possible to imagine.

∎ ∎ ∎

Surely no fiends can be more clamorous than negroes. The whole place resounds with cries—no time is sacred to quiet—even Sunday is desecrated by the yells and screams of children chastised to a barbarous extreme by their *mothers*. As may be supposed, by such excessive cruelty—a cruelty absolutely inconceivable in Europe—the parental ties are severed at an early age. The child dreads its mother! Sometimes, when the whole neighborhood is disturbed, some old negress, having in her a trace of humanity, will come forward and ask "Are you going to *lick* your child to death?" For my own sake, I was often compelled to interfere. . . .

Negroes, and the coloured tribes generally, are given to immoderate bursts of laughter, without any sufficiently exciting cause; and by transient travellers through the Antilles this cachinnatory propensity has been most erroneously ascribed to good temper. Most writers on the tropics have erred on one of the two points: they have either not been long enough in these countries to form a just estimate of the negroes, or so long a time as to have been reconciled to, and to consider as natural characteristics which abstractedly are frightful; but all whites who have lived amongst the Africans agree in detesting the negro. . . .

Laughable as it may seem to cultivated ears, amongst the minor nuisances of a West India town, are whistling and singing. Negroes are very fond of both these execrable accomplishments—execrable as practiced by them; for as they have stentorian organs of noise, and only pick up their tunes by ear, from sources of extremely equivocal authority, the torture of being compelled to listen all the live-long day to our popular airs, sung, or whistled, out of all time and tune, and so excruciatingly *incorrect* in the air as would cause even St. Cecilia to curse them, is inconceivable. A negro never seems to be happy but when he is yelling and bawling, whistling and singing, and he cannot understand the advantages of quiet. Shrieks of laughter also, or of rage, as the case may be, (from the women), are all very well now and then, but when ringing in one's ears *sans cesse* the whole day, they absolutely become "wearing." From the systematic thieving, swindling, or quarrelling, in some shape common to the negroes, there was a "row" in our street every five minutes throughout the day; and our street was but an epitome of every other street. A congregated negro population come very near to Pandemonium, or rather the inhabitants of one. In North America the negroes have (by comparison with the harsh tones of the Yankees) soft voices, or perhaps the climate there does not permit the full development of their lungs; but in the West Indies the reverse is the case, and negroes of both sexes have voices so harsh, coarse and stunning, that they create unutterable disgust. At the same time, their language is horrible in the extreme.

■　■　■

A negro market place presents some droll scenes, and a stroll through one never fails to repay a looker on. Billingsgate must hide its diminished head, must be silent, at the vituperative vocabulary of a couple of infuriated negresses. So excitable are these people, that a fourth of an hour never elapses without a "scene." Such gesticulation, such pantomime, such a roll out of unintelligible phrases, making it difficult to recognize one's own language! When negroes quarrel, they seldom look each other in the face. Nay, generally they turn back to back and seem to appeal to the bystanders, who usually answer each speech made by the belligerents at each other with a shout of laughter, until it comes to: "I mash you up." "I cut your t'roat." When some friends, male and female, judiciously interfere, and lead the infuriated demons off. . . .

Negroes are very voluble. They will roll out a stream of thick-tongued gabble in one uninterrupted flood. In this case, the capacity to talk is in inverse proportion to their capability to reason. They are, at the same time, exceedingly emphatic; so as to be, from their noisiness, most disagreeable neighbors. Every second word is emphasized and jerked out with a vehemence almost distressing.

ANONYMOUS, "Sketches in the West Indies," *Dublin University Magazine*, 56 (Nov. 1860), 613.

The negroes have a very singular habit common to the race. They are fond of soliloquizing aloud on their private grievances as they stride along the streets, altogether regardless of eaves-droppers. "My God! Justice in Demarary! *Me* work? De dem raskil not gib him pay for he wife an' chile!" He then extemporized supposed replies to his certainly just demands and worked up gradually a highly dramatic scene, modulating his voice from tones of sarcastic wheedling to those of the loudest indignation, and so passed on fuming. Possibly it was more the love of idle talking than any actual sense of wrong which roused him.

REV. J. S. SCOLES, *Sketches of African and Indian Life in British Guiana* (Demerara, 1885), 38, 48–49, 52–53, 56–57.

It is amusing to hear him ventilating his thoughts by conversing with his friend, say, on that bright Sunday afternoon when his clothes give an extra importance to his person, and add force and dignity to his words. Thus he accosts his friend while removing the cigar from his lips and balancing it beautifully between thumb and finger: "Mr. JOHN NOVEMBER (Jack he would not use even on a week-day, much less drop the Mr. or handle to the name), Mr. NOVEMBER, it gives you and I collectively controllable facility (for *felicity*) to encounter ourselves together this Sabbath evening and undertake unmistakable friendship discourse together. I venture, Mr. NOVEMBER, to attribute to you and myself the *fortunatus* and convenient encounter to-day. Is LUCRETIA ALEXANDRINA your daughter recovering the strength of her consequition (constitution!)?" After a few more questions, all wrapped up in long unintelligible words, our friend warns Mr. NOVEMBER not "to be lated" on the morrow, but quickly "one time" perform the important commissions entrusted to *him,* emphatically reminding him that "prochristianization is the tief (thief) of time"; then with a self-satisfied smile he shakes hands with his companion and both depart in silence, our friend evidently feeling that his superior superiority shone out brilliantly in the last display of knowledge and of learning, as shown forth in that grand old proverb he had so distinctly uttered and so correctly delivered himself of.

■   ■   ■

One of their strange customs, and one which, while amusing in its way, is certainly characteristic of the poor African woman in these parts. It is, the very common custom they have of talking or chatting to themselves as they go moving along the very middle of the street quite careless and unconcerned as to whether or not their family secrets and domestic troubles are listened to or overheard by others, or caring one whit who the passers-by may be. Thus you will hear one good Lady speaking in broken English, all about "Massa broken pie-dish" and how "she picknie come to mash* he!"; or again how she sister JUDITH when she went to doctor shop, for have she tooth pull out, the mulatto man mash up de fence, and stole de fowl, and how she fret up too bad and then after a moment of quiet reflection you will hear her dilating on "de wickedness of de human race" leaving the bad tief in the good hand of God hoping the world may soon come to an end "for people live too bad—tief too much—too much, for true." Again if our poor friend is in a more merry mood and has lost neither fowl nor teeth, much less her tongue, she will without the slightest intention of being rude, for African women are not by nature rude much less are they impudent,—she will criticize in her own simple way, and from her own point of view (and be it said often reasonably enough) the costume or dress of others, say for instance, the very high heel boots of her much fairer European sisters, as they go past her tripping by so merrily and decked so gaily, with a false flower on one shoulder and none upon the other, and she wonders much how "Missy no fall to de ground and mash up she foot and break she head when she stand on rock stone, heel too high, Missy shoe heel too high," and she will go on uttering and muttering the honest truth till some other outré fashion strikes or astonishes her simple mind, or till something else in the street attracts her attention bringing fresh thoughts to her head, and droll or funny words to her lips.

It may seem a little rude, and let us honestly confess it is so, but certainly it is more than a little amusing quietly to follow within fair

---

*The word *mash* is almost universally used by the creole population to denote anything destroyed or much damaged; hence they do not hesitate to say, me fall down and mash up me clothes. He mash me kite. She mash up me prayer book.

hearing distance, one of Africa's simple daughters telling out her petty wants and grievances or expressing aloud every quaint thought as it comes uppermost in her mind, changing each moment the topic of talk as fresh distractions would crowd in upon her mind. Now you will hear her talk all about Diana and her wedding-day, and how nice she looked in Church with her feathered fan and fresh white flowers—how all looked, as their expression has it "too sweet for true," and then after a moment's pause, reflecting on her own less happy or unlucky lot softly and sadly you would hear her singing some fragment of a picked up song ending in these pathetic words—"When me poor girl am dead and gone and de green grass growing ober me"—or a moment or so later, when thinking of her poor orphan state and her corporal wants she would sing out again, "Fader dead, moder dead, got no one to give I bread"; and thus she will go on, now chatting, now singing, now quarreling within herself, unconsciously amusing you so much, till some tattered and shoeless lady friend stops her on the road and enters into conversation.

■   ■   ■

Again as African women are neither vulgar in their gait nor ungainly in their manners, so at times they are truly graceful in their movements, and in the many gesticulations they love so much to indulge in, especially when engaged in very lively conversation, or when they have become suddenly a little excited at the approach of some big band, or the running over of some little baby; but now for fear of being taxed with undue partiality towards our good dark African friends, let us for a change revert to some of their few failings and weaker points. Modest in her dress and polite in her manner, the African woman is not always under perfect religious control in her speech, like indeed to so many of her lively sex in all other parts of this wicked world. True the poor African has only *broken* English at her command, but certain it is she makes the most of the *broken pieces*, flinging them at you right and left in most offensive or hurtful form when her monkey is fairly up, or when her ire or indignation has been fairly roused; then her language becomes every bit as saucy and quite as savage as that of any of the wicked, wily, and unwashed ones in the nooks and miserable corners of our model *European* cities! But as remarked many pages past, an African's indignation and hot anger soon cools down without as a rule leaving behind it the ordinary residue of vindictive feeling or the wicked desire of seeking revenge.

Speaking here of the naughty language of the African ladies, reminds one of a very peculiar and unexpected kind of abuse in not unfrequent usage among the African gentlemen of the lower orders; for they too like their loving wives and graceful daughters (and like each and every one of us besides) have their tongues and their tempers too.

For instance, a couple of black men on whose noble brow a casual smudge or smear of printer's ink would cause but little colour contrast, will enter into an angry and noisy dispute all about nothing, or at most it might be about some mislaid tool or injured bradawl; angry and ugly words are freely and rapidly exchanged while from blows and bloodshed they wisely enough abstain on account of the strange antipathy they have of being hit or hurt. When however the stronger of the two disputants has well nigh exhausted his vocabulary of unsavoury sounding words, and many times sent his opponent to that place where evil spirits everlastingly do dwell, as a last resource or as a last hard hit, he calls his jet black counterpart a *nigger* qualifying the term with a wicked adjective of his own unhappy choice far more expressive than either parliamentary or polite: now, the other not content with the obvious answer or retort *"and you are another,"* flings back the sarcastic word of reproach with its qualifying adjective in double quick time and we may say in double force like a ball in an active game of lawn-tennis, till at length when both parties are well tired with mutual abuse, the noisy-quarrel, (all about nothing), comes to an end.

■   ■   ■

Again our *cries* out here are distinctly uttered, and intelligible enough and furthermore are most polite:—nice scale fish ladies, nice peppers ladies, nice ochroes ladies; everything nice and all for the ladies, even nice hot *sauce* for the ladies! But curious to remark, if a real white lady requiring something, says *"woman* with the hot pepper come," the notice is unheeded, for the crier is offended and must be called a lady too. Formerly when the African element here was stronger or less mixed, the street cries were more original and droll than nowadays, hence among other curious cries a quaint old one has died away and though quoted by the writer in a previous article seems to claim a more fitting place just here, it ran thus:

> Nice cassava bread ladies,
>   Nice cassava bread;
> He who want me call me,
>   He who no want me no call me,
> He who shame to call me, give me
>   The wink, wink, wink.

The polite addition of the word Lady, whilst it at once points to our high state of civilization, renders the meaning of a cry at times vague or puzzling, as the following amusing incident may help to illustrate.

An Englishman some years ago on his first arrival in Demerara, heard as he walked up a street the following cry, loudly and distinctly uttered:

> Nice black eye ladies
> Nice black eye ladies
> Who buy my nice black eye ladies.

The Englishman started, and of course shuddered at the sound, and called at once upon an old Colonist close by, and with extenuated face and saddened countenance indignantly enquired how was it, that the Anti-Slavery Emancipation laws were so utterly disregarded out here, right under the British flag, and that detestable slavery still flourished in the English Colonies? How is it possible that human creatures could be in the market for sale, even "nice black eye ladies," what a national shame, what a foul blot on England's fair name! "But ladies are not for sale" cried out the old Colonist indignantly and somewhat taken at the bold assertion. "But they are," replied the other impetuously, "I with my own ears heard the cry and saw with my own eyes the crier, heard him cry these words; 'Nice black eye ladies, who buy my nice black eye ladies,' though it is true he had no ladies in a cart, but only a wooden tray with a cloth laid loosely over it." "Listen" said the old Colonist recovering quite, and immensely amused, as the bright twinkling of the eye did unmistakably tell, "listen to me a moment, please be seated, recover breath my friend. Nice black eyes have nothing to do with *ladies*, but refer to dark or black specks upon some peas the poor man has in his tray under his cloth for sale; what the black man meant to say, was simply this; nice black eyed *peas* for *ladies* to buy, he did not intend to cry out, that he had live ladies with *black eyes* for sale."

JAMES ANTHONY FROUDE, *The English in the West Indies* (London, 1888), 153–55.

In Roseau, as in most other towns, the most interesting spot is the market. There you see the produce of the soil; there you see the people that produce it; and you see them, not on show, as in church on Sundays, but in their active working condition. The market place at

Roseau is a large square court close to the sea, well paved, surrounded by warehouses, and luxuriantly shaded by large overhanging
trees. Under these trees were hundreds of black women, young and
old, with their fish and fowls, and fruit and bread, their yams and
sweet potatoes, their oranges and limes and plantains. They had
walked in from the country five or ten miles before sunrise with their
loaded baskets on their heads. They would walk back at night with
flour or salt fish, or oil, or whatever they happened to want. I did not
see a single sullen face among them. Their figures were unconscious
of lacing, and their feet of the monstrosities which we call shoes.
They moved with the lightness and elasticity of leopards. I thought
that I had never seen in any drawing room in London so many perfectly graceful forms. They could not mend their faces, but even in
some of these there was a swarthy beauty. The hair was hopeless, and
they knew it, but they turn the defect into an ornament by the coloured handkerchief which they twist about their heads, leaving the
ends flowing. They chattered like jackdaws about a church tower.
Two or three of the best looking, seeing that I admired them a little,
used their eyes and made some laughing remarks. They spoke in their
French *patois*, clipping off the first and last syllables of the words. I
but half understood them, and could not return their shots. I can only
say that if their habits were as loose as white people say they are, I
did not see a single licentious expression either in face or manner.
They seemed to me light-hearted, merry, innocent young women, as
free from any thought of evil as the peasant girls in Brittany.

Two middle-aged dames were in a state of violent excitement
about some subject on which they differed in opinion. A ring gathered
about them, and they declaimed at one another with fiery volubility.
It did not go beyond words; but both were natural orators, throwing
their heads back, waving their arms, limbs and chest quivering with
emotion. There was no personal abuse, or disposition to claw each
other. On both sides it was a rhetorical outpouring of emotional argument. One of them, a tall pure blood negress, black as if she had just
landed from Guinea, began at last to get the best of it. Her gesticulations became more imposing. She shook her finger. *Mandez* this, she
said, and *mandez* that, till she bore her antagonist down and sent her
flying. The audience then melted away, and I left the conqueror
standing alone shooting a last volley at the retreating enemy and making passionate appeals to the universe. The subject of the discussion
was a curious one. It was on the merits of race. The defeated cham-

pion had a taint of white blood in her. The black woman insisted that blacks were of pure breed, and whites were of pure breed. Mulattoes were mongrels, not creatures of God at all, but creatures of human wickedness. I do not suppose that the mulatto was convinced, but she accepted her defeat. The conqueror, it was quite clear, was satisfied that she had the best of the discussion, and that the hearers were of the same opinion.

HENRY KIRKE, *Twenty-five Years in British Guiana* (London, 1898), 191.

Their speeches are as wonderful as their letters. At a black wedding one of the guests delivered an oration which he had carefully written down.

"My friends, it is with feelings of no ordinary nature which have actuated my inmost heart on this present occasion, for on such festivities so full of mirth and aggrandisement, when the Bridegroom and Bride in all their splendour repair to the house of reception, and there we find familiar friends and neighbours heralding the consummation of their enterprise, it fills me with that enthusiasm which otherwise would fail to draw out our congratulations. . . . And now I must close, and take the phrase *no quid nomis*—'too much of one thing is good for nothing.' Trusting these few remarks may be found *multum in parvo*, as I am now attacked with *cacoethes loquendi*. I shall resort to my *ex cathedra* asking the ladies present melodiously to sing for me a verse of the hymn—

> How welcome was the call,
> And sweet the fest day."

LETTERS

CHARLES RAMPINI, *Letters from Jamaica* (London, 1873), 103–10.

A Batch of Negro Love-Letters   Love letters have always constituted an important branch of epistolary literature. They have been the making of many a *cause célebre*, the source of many a law-suit, a fruitful spring of pleasure and pain to the young, and sometimes to those old enough to know better, in every generation of the human race. We are a little too much inclined to form our ideas of negro manners and character from the burlesque representations of Christy's Minstrels and others. We are too much disposed to look upon the typical "man and brother" as a boneless, restless, grotesque creature, who wears shirt collars which reach long past his ears, and a necktie of which the bows are at least half a yard in length,—who spends his time in playing on a banjo, occasionally diversifying his pleasing occupation by dancing a breakdown, or cying "Yah! yah!" at intervals. Many of us have yet to learn that the negroes in the West Indies are an earnest work-a-day peasantry, having their own characteristic faults and vices, it is true, and dissimilar to any other peasantry in the world, but none the less real and existent. To many a little thatch-covered hut, half-hidden among broad-leaved bananas and scarlet-foliaged Poinsettias, or over-shadowed with white-flowered coffee plants, or buried admist tangled "bush" and close-enlaced brushwood, the letters which follow have doubtless brought pleasure and happiness,— shadowing forth, in phrase uncouth, nay, even grotesque, to us, but intelligible and real enough to their recipients, "that long bright future of which lovers dream."

> "There is no pleasure like the pain
> Of being loved and loving."

Penned after the day's labour on the plantation or the penn, or amongst the yams and sweet potatoes of his provision ground, they are the honest expression of the negro's inmost heart, the exponents of his most sincere sentiments.

I

My deare Love, my dearest Dove,—I have taken the pleasur of righten [writing] these few lines to you, hopin when they comes to hand they may find you in a perfect state of health, as it leaves me at preasent. My deare, I have never felt the enjoyment of love as I feel with you. These few lines is to let you know that it is my intention of maryin you, if it agreeable with you. My Deare, my mind is so taking up with you, I cannot help from righting you. I am not able to go on at preasant, but in time to come I hope to be your man of business. Let her kiss me with the kisses of her mouth, for thy love is better than wine. As the apple-tree among the trees of the wood, so is my love with you. Please to say howdeas [how-d'ye-do] to all kind friends for me.—I remain, love, your most affectionate love, J. A. Wite [White]. Answer as quick as possible.

II

Dear Lov,—I is wrote you a letter to beg of you to make me your lover, but you is not wrote me again. I is dead of love every day, wen you look so hansom. I cane [cannot] sleep, cane eat. I dun no how I feel. I beg you to accep af me as your lover. The rose is not sweet as a kiss from you, my love. Do meet me to-night at the bottom gate, and give me your lov. Miss Lucy toots [teeth] so green I is like one ear of carn, an' her eye dem is so pretty. Lard! I wish I never been barn. Poor me, Garg! [George]. I love Miss Lucy to distraction.—Yours truly, GARG PLUMMER. Answer me sone, lov.

III

January 25, 1865.
My dear Love,—I have taken the pleasure of writing you in time, hopen when it reaches your hand it may find you at a perfect state of health, as it leaves me at the present time. I have seeing in your letter, my dear, that you wisch to know from me if it is true Love from my heart. Dearest love, if it is not true Love from the deepest part of my heart, whold [would] I set down to write you a letter, my Dear? When hear I see they lovely face, my heart within will burnt; when here I absent from thy face, I long for thy return. But one thing I did like to tell you again. Do not make it known to the Public before we began. The reason why I say that. I heard a certain boy was telling me all about it, and that only done by you tellin you feamale friends, whom cannot help; these one secret must be yours, for this thing is not known to a soul but I and you and your brother-in-law. Therefor the fault must be yours. Do not let me hear such thing again from anybody. My dear love, I will be truly wish that I could be married to you know [now], but if my life is spared we shall tark [talk] further about that. My dear, pray for me that the Lord will speared my life to become a man, for I truly wich [wish] that I and you should be one fleach and one blood. Will you not like it, my dear love? If you don't wich that, let me know by your letter. My dear girl, you don't know

my love wich I have for you. May the Lord touch your heart to know
these thing wich I now put before you in this letter. But I must say
that I am doing you arm [harm] for taken such liberty to write you
such a letter as this. If it is a liberty please to let me know by your
next letter. Do not send me a note again for a letter. I can not satisfy
when I see a letter wich I can not take me some time to reed. If you
had not paper let me know about in your next letter, and I will send
you some paper. My dear love, at preasant my love for you is so
strong, that I cannot express. So I even write that you may see it. It is
every man deauty [duty] to write a formil [formal] letter. My pen is
bad, and my ink is pale, but my love will never fail. King Solomon say
that Love is strong as death, and Jealousy is cruel than the grave.
Love me little, bear me longer. Hasty love is not love at all. This is
the first time I sat down to write you about it. I love my Dove. Your
love is black and ruby—the chefer of ten thousand. You head is much
fine gold. You lock are bushy and black as a raven. Your eyes was the
eyes in a river, by the rivers of warter. Your cheeks as a bead [bed] of
spices as sweet flowers. Your lips is like lilies. Your hand as gold
wring. Your legs as a pillar of marble set upon sockets of fine gold.
Your countenance as a Lebenon. Your mouth look to be more sweet.
Your sweet altogether. I have no more time to write as I am so tiard
and full time to go to bead. I will now close my letter with love. I
remain yours truly, _____ _____. To Ann Williams.

IV

My dearest dear,—It is with a perplexing heart of anxiety that I take
up my pen to address you this time, having propos marriage to you. I
am now anxious to know the full intention of your mind, accompany
with parent. On my side, let it please you to believe me that I am de-
sireous to oblige you in whatever thought or ways that you lik. If you
cannot stop up this way, but rather to be in Santicross [Santa Cruz], I
am very willing to do so. I feel convinced that the merits of your family are not to be estimated by an ordinary standard, and that their most
ardent wish is to promote your comfort and happiness. Believe me I
feel highly honour of being worthy elevated in such a family. In grant-
ing me this most agreeable favour, you will, my dear girl, not only dis-
pel the peevish gloom which I am confident will hang over me if I
should be deprive of your society. My greatest happiness depends
upon your immediate answer. Please speak a word of regard in your

parents ears.—I remain, dear Lesia, yours truly love, _____ _____.
19. 1. '64.

V

Dear love,—I have the liberty of writing these few lines, hopeing that
it may found you well. I writ to hare [hear] from you wether
[whether] you intend to make me a fool. If you intent to, come before
it is too late. If you witch [wish] you can come up, fear [for] I is not
an pewpy show [puppet-show], that if you tink you will find any better than me. My mother said that she not understand how you always
come here and you not tel her any thin [thing] about me. I witch to
send the yam hed [yam-heads for planting], but I do not know wether
I will reap the benefit of it. Love is strong as death. Jelous is as cruel
as the grave. The rose in June is not so sweet. Like to meet and kiss
you. please to send me answer as quick as passable.

VI

Dear Eliza,—I take the liberty of myself to inform you this few lines
hoping you may not offend as often is. I had often seen you in my
hearts. Their are myriads of loveliness in my hearts toward you. My
loving intentions were realy unto another female, but now the love
between I and she are very out now entirely. And now his the expected time I find to explain to my lovely appearance [presumably
"apparent love"], but whether if their be any love in your hearts or
mind towards me it is hard for I to know, but his I take the liberty to
inform you this kind, loving, and affectionate letter. I hope when it
received into your hand you receive with peace and all good will,
pleasure, and comforts, and hoping that you might answer me from
this letter with a loving appearance, that in due time Boath of us
might be able to join together in the holy state of matremony. I hoping
that the answer which you are to send to me it may unto good intention To me from you that when I always goine to write you again I
may be able to write, saying, my dear lovely Eliza.—Your affectionate
lover, affraied [afraid] J.S. Dear Eliza, wether if you are willing or not,
Please to sent me an ansure back. Do, my dear.

The last we shall give is a genuine negro valentine:

VII

Mrs. Agostiss R_____,—I hope you know Valintine is now is seson. I will take the pleasure to write you this, my hearth is yours and your are mine; but you do not know it. I love you as the bee love the flower. The flower may fade, but true love shall never. My love for you is a love that cannot be fade. You shall be my love here an' in heaven for ever. The Rose in June is not so sweet as when two lovers kisses meet. Kiss me quick and go my honey. I still remain true lover.

NAMES

MATTHEW GREGORY LEWIS, *Journal of a West India Proprietor* (London, 1834), 349.

February 19. [1818]
Neptune came this morning to request that the name of his son, Oscar, might be changed for that of Julius, which (it seems) had been that of his own father. The child, he said, had always been weakly, and he was persuaded, that its ill-health proceeded from his deceased grand-father's being displeased, because it had not been called after him. The other day, too, a woman, who had a child sick in the hospital, begged me to change its name for any other which might please me best: she cared not what; but she was sure that it would never do well, so long as it should be called Lucia. Perhaps this prejudice respecting the power of names produces in some measure their unwillingness to be christened. They find no change produced in them, except the alteration of their name, and hence they conclude that this name contains in it some secret power; while, on the other hand, they conceive that the ghosts of their ancestors cannot fail to be offended at their abandoning an appellation, either hereditary in the family, or given by themselves.

GREVILLE JOHN CHESTER, *Transatlantic Sketches in the West Indies, South America, Canada, and the United States* (London, 1869), 78–79.

It is a marked peculiarity of the negroes that except in the mechanical movements of music and dancing they have not the slightest idea of time and scarcely any of number. Constantly they have not the faint-

est idea of their own age, or of that of their children. Their only ep-
ochs are "Freedom," Cholera" and "Dust." Thus a man told me he
"was eight years old at Dust, but didn't know how old he was now."
By Dust he meant the extraordinary fall of volcanic particles and
ashes, which lasted during an entire day of darkness at the time of the
frightful eruption of the Souffriere in St. Vincent, May 1, 1812.

The negroes share with the "Bims" in their love of fine language
and "talk-talk." They have also an extravagant fondness for fine
names, such as Adriana, Elvira, Moletta, Sativa. I knew a man who
insisted on having his child christened "Monumon," and another who
grumbled because his clergyman demurred at naming his infant
"Ether." Many titles such as Queen, Prince, King, Captain, &c., are
also used as proper names. The ancient African names still linger,
such as Auco, Quacco, Mingo, Quow, Ambo, Wambo, Quamin, Qua-
mina, Quasheba, Jubba, Bimba, Coubah, Crobah, Miah, Phibba, and
Mimba.* Very quaint combinations are found in the parochial register
books, as *e.g.*, "Gift and Miniky," "Quamin and Kitty," "Wonder Wall-
cott and Leah Bispham," "York and Madam," "Quow and Mercy."
One young lady's name I found given as "Sucky Venus," but I afterwards discovered that this was a Cambridge M. A.'s manner of spelling the more ordinary "Sukey."

REV. H. V. P. BRONKHURST, *The Colony of British Guyana and its
Labouring Population* (London, 1883), 377.

The late Rev. Henry Bleby, in his *Missionary Father's Tales,* Third
Series, gives the name of a fugitive or runaway slave as "Shadrach-

---

*P. H. Gosse, in a work on the natural history of Jamaica, states that these "names in-
dicate the day of the week on which the individual was born":

	Male	Female
Sunday	Quashe, *(Cooashe)*	Quasheba, *(Cooa-sheba)*
Monday	Cudjo, *(Coojo)*	Juba, *(Coo-jo-ba)*
Tuesday	Cubena, *(Coobena)*	Benaba, *(Coo-bena-ba)*
Wednesday	Quacco, *(Cooa-co)*	Cooba, *(Cooa-co-ba)*
Thursday	Quao, *(Cooa-o)*	Abba, *(Coo-a-ba)*
Friday	Cuffee *(Coofee)*	Feeba, *(Coo-fee-ba)*
Saturday	Qyanubm *(Cooamin)*	Mimba, *(Coo-mim-ba)*

" 'Ba,' being a mark of the feminine gender, 'Coo,' or 'Qua,' less exclusively of
the masculine."

The knowledge of this has died out in Barbados, and the names are applied indiscriminately. As the word "mimba" means "palm wine" on the Gaboon River in
Western Africa, it is possible that the slaves in the first instance gave that name to Saturday, as on that evening a week of toil was concluded, and they had more time for
refreshment.

Meshach-Abednego-Hannibal"; and Rev. M. C. Osborn, who paid a
visit to British Guyana in the fall of 1878, in a speech he made at the
Exeter Hall Annual Missionary Meeting in 1879, said, speaking of his
work in Jamaica, "I several times administered the sacrament of Holy
Baptism, and I am credibly informed that a good number of little male
darkies, *in esse* and *in posse,* will at a future time be known by the
name of Marmaduke Osborn; and I should not be surprised if some
are called 'General Secretary,' and others go down to posterity as so
many 'Deputations.' " I do not know what has been done in Jamaica,
and the other West Indian Islands the Reverend gentleman visited. So
far as the Colony of British Guyana is concerned, I have not heard of
any one as yet being baptized, or named, "Marmaduke Osborn," or
"General Secretary," or "Deputation."

REV. J. SCOLES, *Sketches of African and Indian Life and Indian Life
in British Guiana* (Demerara, 1885), 38–39.

If our friend fails somewhat in his speech and uses his British liberty
to the disadvantage of many a long latinized word, so too he seems
free and unfettered in his letter-writing, indulging at times in a delicious simplicity. For instance, a few months ago a poor black man
writing to the Catholic Bishop of these parts upon matters no doubt of
grave importance signed himself thus: "Your affectionate brother the
grave-digger!" Poor fellow, seeing so much "dust to dust" made him
take *la liberté* of thinking of *fraternité* just then and *egalité* later on to
be.

X. BEKE, *West Indian Yarns* (Demerara and London, 1890), 4–7.

The predilection which Negroes have for grand names, alluded to by
Marryat in one of his novels, is well known. In some of the West India
Islands every darkie has a play-name, or name for common every day
use, which is as a rule, short and so to speak, handy. Their baptismal
names, on the contrary, are lengthy and romantic, being borrowed
from the pages of "Standard novels," or from the heroes and heroines
of "penny dreadfuls." In the olden days, Shakespeare was greatly resorted to as a sponsor; and sable Hamlets, Othellos, Romeos, and
Macbeths abound among the older Negroes. Often in the desire for a
polysyllable name its uncomplimentary or inappropriate character is
overlooked, and hence some more or less worthy people are found
whose names bear the prefixes of Mendacious, Abnormal, Abdominal,

Ananias, &c. One man I know, christened Hobbledehoy, tries to conceal the unfortunate name by a strong accent on the second syllable. I have even known a Camomile Brown.

"Massa," said a respectable dark gentleman to a Registrar of Births, &c., "Massa, me make you for know dat for me wife confine Tuesday gone, and she gie me twin, both of dem boys, and me ax you be so kind as gie me name for dem."

"Well," said the Registrar, "let us see, I think you had better call one 'Waverley' and the other 'Guy Mannering.' "

"Tank you, me massa, dem name fustrate, but me beg you write dem on a 'crip of paper, else me no member dem." The Registrar did so and Mr. Pompey went away rejoicing. Some weeks after, the following conversation was overheard between Pompey and a friend:—

"Well, buddie (brother) and how does dem two picknie get on?"

"Fustrate! hearty," replied Pompey.

"Dey is christened yet?"

"Oh! yes, dey baptize last Sunday at chapel."

"And what name you gie dem?"

"Well, me friend, for tell de troot me scarce able for get my tongue round de words, but de name well handsome. Ah! dey call um 'Waberley' and 'Guy Maddering,' someting so."

"Eh! me fadder!" said Pompey's friend, "where ebber you get dem name?"

"Registrar gie um, and write um down for no make mistake."

"And parson take um?"

"Yes, me friend. Fust he say he nebber hear 'Guy Maddering' before, but he know 'Waberly' been one pusson as write plenty good book, so he speck praps dey been brudders, and so he receive de name for me picknies and dem." The "parson" no doubt was one of the locus preacher tribe whose reading did not extend to Scott.

Two black girls, labourers on a friend's estate in the island of St. Maria, returning from work, met on the road. They had but a scanty amount of clothes, but each had a baby in her arms. There was some quarrel between them, and a wordy combat ensued. At its close one damsel, turning away, said, "Well, I don't want no more discoorse wid you, 'Miss Teraza.' "

"Me make you for know, marm," retorted the other girl, "that for me name no Teraza, but Tereesa."

"Well, me dear," was the reply, "Teraza else Tereesa, both de same, for me name a better name that for your own, for me name Diana de Goddess of Chaste;" and Diana strutted off with a swing of her tattered skirt and toss of the head that would have become a duchess.

A Negro often takes as his "bragging" or "play" name that of his master, and in their social gatherings these names alone are used, while the gait and manner, or any other peculiarities of their employers, are also imitated.

Servants and labourers are addicted to bestowing on their offspring the names of their masters and mistresses, and often when, as is the custom in some of the colonies, a son takes as his surname the christian name of his father, the result is embarrassing. For instance, if Mr. Brown Robinson's groom, Jack Caesar, calls his son "Robinson Caesar," the latter, when he has a boy, will probably christen him as . . . "Brown Robinson," so that proper-minded persons are apt, on finding the aristocratic name to be borne by a small coloured boy, to shake their heads and make edifying reflections on the morality of the original Robinson.

This mark of respect or of admiration for the name, and sometimes the rank of a superior was curiously exemplified some years ago in, as I think, Jamaica, where the wife of a black military labourer marched up to the font with her infant, and in the presence of a scandalized congregation gave its intended name as "George Frederick Augustus Snodgrass Adjutant."

PROVERBS

BRYAN EDWARDS, *The History, Civil and Commercial, of the British Colonies in the West Indies* (Dublin, 1793), vol. II, 78–79.

One instance recurs to my memory, of so significant a turn of expression in a common labouring Negro, who could have had no opportunity of improvement from the conversation of White people, as is alone, I think, sufficient to demonstrate that Negroes have minds very capable of observation. It was a servant who had brought me a letter, and, while I was preparing an answer, has, through weariness and fatigue, fallen asleep on the floor: as soon as the papers were ready, I directed him to be awakened; but this was no easy matter. When the Negro who attempted to awake him, exclaimed in the usual jargon, *You no hear Massa call you?* that is, Don't you hear your Master call you? *Sleep,* replied the poor fellow, looking up, and returning composedly to his slumbers, *Sleep hab no Massa!* (Sleep has no master.)

JAMES STEWART, *A View of the Past and Present State of the Island of Jamaica* (Edinburgh, 1823), 257, 264.

Their ideas cannot be expected to extend to abstract and metaphysical subjects. Of the existence and attributes of a Deity, of a future state, and of duration and space, they have but very imperfect notions. They cannot dilate and subdivide their conceptions into minuter distinctions and more abstract combinations; yet they will often express, in their own way, a wonderfully acute conception of things. These conceptions they sometimes compress into short and pithy sentences, something like the sententious proverbs of the Europeans, to which many of them bear an analogy. Their sayings often convey much force and meaning, and would, if clothed in a more courtly dress, make no despicable figure even among those concepts of wisdom which are ascribed to wiser nations. When they wish to imply, that a peaceable man is often wise and provident in his conduct, they say, *"Softly water run deep";* when they would express the oblivion and disregard which follows them after death, they say, *"When man dead grass grow at him door";* and when they would express the humility which is the usual accompaniment of poverty, they say, *"Poor man never vex."*

. . .

Although the proverbial sayings of the negroes have often much point and meaning, they, however, no sooner begin to expatiate and enter more minutely into particulars, than they become tedious, verbose, and circumlocutory, beginning their speeches with a tiresome exordium, mingling with them much extraneous matter, and frequently traversing over and over the same ground, and cautioning the hearer to be attentive, as if fearful that some of the particulars and points on which their meaning and argument hinged should escape his attention. So that by the time they arrive at the peroration of their harangue, the listener is heartily fatigued with it, and perceives that the whole which has been said, though it may have taken up half an hour, could have been comprised in half-a-dozen words.

TRELAWNY WENTWORTH, *The West India Sketch Book* (London, 1834), vol. I, 14, 16.

". . . me work for me massa—me now old no can work." "Well, well . . . but you're very happy, you have a house, and children, and a pig, and cow; and"—

"Hey! Me, Massa—him no 'blong me—es *Kraub tan naw he hole ee nebber fat,* him 'blong Quasheba." ("If a crab does not leave its hole it never gets fat." This is one of numerous proverbs of the negroes, implying that if we do not move about to promote our interest we cannot get rich.)

. . .

Cheep good haut, . . . da kow no hab no tail, Gor-a-mity brush fly—(p. 17—Keep a good heart; if cow has no tail, God Almighty brushes the flies . . . *i.e.,* a reliance on the deity, if a manifestation of his goodness and protection in their necessities. . . . *"Gor-a-mighty never shet he yie"* . . . *"Gor-a-mighty no lub angry."*

ROBERT BAIRD, *Impressions and Experiences of the West Indies and North America in 1849* (London, 1850), 81.

Popular sayings in common use among these descendants of the sons of Africa are ofttimes very amusing. "When cattle* lose tail, who for brush fly?" is the common negro form for pointing out how essential one person is to another: "Night no hab eye," is the apology for a negro woman's evening dishabille: and "When cockroach gib dance, him no ask fowl," was the explanation given by a negro to a friend and myself, when charged by us with a breach of contract in not getting us an invitation to a "Dignity ball."

L. D. POWLES, *Land of the Pink Pearl* (London, 1888), 165–67.

The darkies are also great at proverbs. I subjoin a small collection.

> "Come see me is notin, come lib wid me something!"
> "Follow fashion break monkey neck."
> "Goat say him hab wool; sheep say him hab har!"
> "Greedy choke puppy!"
> "Hab money hab friend!"
> "Hog run for him life; dog run for him character!"
> "Hungry fowl wake son."

This proverb is particularly appropriate to Nassau.

> "If you see a fippence you know how dollar made!"
> "John Crow nebber make house till rain come!"
> "Lizard no plant corn but him hab plenty."
> "Man can't whistle and smoke one time."

---

*Throughout the West Indies you seldom hear of a bull, an ox, a cow, &c.; the word "cattle," is used in the singular as well as in the plural.

This is a favorite proverb, but I deny its truth.

> "Misfortune nebber trow cloud."
> "No eberyting you yerry (hear) good fe talk!"
> "No trow away dirty water before you hab clean!"
> "Ole firestick no hard fo catch."
> "One tief no like see oder tief carry long bag."

This proverb reminds me of a story of a negro Methodist who has stolen some goods which were after stolen from him. Next time he went to class-meeting he ejaculated, "Oh, Lord, de tief am bad, but when tief tief from tief, oh, Lord, him too much proboking!"

> "Parson christen him own pickanninny first."
> "Rain nebber fall at one man door."
> "Stone at sea bottom no know sun hot."
> "Seven year no 'nough for washy speckly off guinea hen back."
> "Shoe know if stocking hab hole."
> "Sleep hab no massa."
> "Spider and fly no make bargain."
> "When man no done climb hill he should no trow away him stick."
> "John Crow tink him pickanninny white."
> "When man say him no mind, den he mind."
> "When hand full him hab plenty company."
> "You shake man hand, you no shake him heart."
> "Trouble nebber blow shell."

This is an allusion to the custom of using shells as horns to blow through.

> "Time longer dan rope."
> "When fowl drinky water him lift up him head and say, 'Tank God,' but man drinky water and no say noting."
> "When eye no see, mout no talk."
> "When man no done grow him nebber should cuss long man."
> "Stranger no know whar de deep water."
> "Cuss cuss (calling names) no bore hole in skin."
> "Cunning better dan strong."
> "De rope you pulling, no de rope I cutting."
> "Ebbery day fishing day, but no ebbery day catchy fish."
> "Hot needle burn thread."
> "Big blanket make man sleep late."
> "When cockroach gib dance him no ax fowl."
> "Cockroach nebber so drunk he no crossy fowl-yard."
> "Dead hog ne fear biling water."

3

Anancy Tales

"Anancy stories" or "Nancy stories" (often ambiguously pronounced as "nasty story" or "nonsense story") is the general name for folktales in much of the English-speaking Caribbean. They derive the name from the spider-hero who appears in many of them. The spider is a common figure in many West African folktale traditions (see, for example, the Twi *ananse* [spider] tales), one who functions in ways quite familiar to those of us who know the Brer Rabbit cycle of Joel Chandler Harris. Anancy, like Brer Rabbit, is a trickster, surviving through guile and wit, and is a small figure in a world of larger ones. Much debate has surrounded the role and sources of the rabbit in the United States but no one has questioned Anancy. (A curious aside: Anancy and Brer Rabbit both speak a "lower" form of black English dialect in their respective traditions—"lower," for example, than those of their tellers.) The survival qualities of Anancy continue to appeal to many, and it is common to see West Indian political writers use the folktale form in Jamaica, but also in Canada and Britain.

Contemporary reports of these tales suggest that they were not fully reported upon in these earlier renditions. Anancy's doings, it seems, were simply too scandalous to be printed—for he is a voracious eater, indeed a cannibal, a carrion eater, and so on. Likewise, his sexual appetite finds no bounds.

MATTHEW GREGORY LEWIS, *Journal of a West India Proprietor* (London, 1834), 253–59, 290–96, 301–07.

May 7 [1816]

A negro song.—"Me take my cutacoo, (i.e. a basket made of matting,) and follow him to Lucea, and all for love of my bonny man-O—

My bonny man come home! Doctor no do you good. When neger fall into neger hands, buckra doctor no do him good more. Come home, my gold ring, come home!" This is the song of a wife, whose husband had been Obeahed by another woman, in consequence of his rejecting her advances. A negro riddle: "Pretty Miss Nancy was going to market, and she tore her fine yellow gown, and there was not a taylor in all the town who could mend it again." This is a ripe plantain with a broken skin. The negroes are also very fond of what they call Nancy stories, part of which is related, and part sung. The heroine of one of them is an old woman named Mammy Luna, who having left a pot boiling in her hut, found it robbed on her return. Her suspicions were divided between two children whom she found at play near her door, and some negroes who had passed that way to market. The children denied the theft positively. It was necessary for the negroes, in order to reach their own estate, to wade through a river at that time almost dry; and on their return, Mammy Luna (who it should seem, was not without some skill in witchcraft), warned them to take care in venturing across the stream, for that the water would infallibly rise and carry away the person who had stolen the contents of her pot; but if the thief would but confess the offence, she engaged that no harm should happen, as she only wanted to exculpate the innocent, and not to punish the guilty. One and all denied the charge, and several crossed the river without fear or danger; but upon the approach of a *belly-woman* to the bank, she was observed to hesitate. "My neger, my neger," said Mammy Luna, "why you stop? me tink, you savee well, who thief me?" This accusation spirited up the woman, who instantly marched into the river, singing as she went (and the woman's part is always changed in chorus, which the negroes call, "taking up the sing").

> "If da me eat Mammy Luna's pease-O,
> Drowny me water, drowny, drowny!"

"My neger, my neger," cried the old woman, "Me sure now you the thief! me see the water wet you feet. Come back, my neger, come back." Still on went the woman, and still continued her song of

> "If da me eat Mammy Luna's pease, etc.

"My neger, my neger," repeated Mammy Luna, "me no want punish you; my pot smell good, and you belly-woman. Come back, my neger, come back; me see now water above your knee.'" But the woman was obstinate; she continued to sing and to advance, till she reached the middle of the river's bed, when down came a tremendous flood, swept her away, and she never was heard of more; while Mammy Luna warned the other negroes never to take the property of another; always to tell the truth; and, at least, if they should be betrayed into telling a lie, not to persist in it, otherwise they must expect to perish like their companion. Observe, that a moral is always an indispensable part of a Nancy story. Another is as follows:—"Two sisters had always lived together on best terms; but, on the death of one of them, the other treated very harshly a little niece, who had been left to her care, and made her a common drudge to herself and her daughter. One day the child having broken a water-jug, was turned out of the house, and ordered not to return till she could bring back as good a one. As she was going along, weeping, she came to a large cotton-tree, under which was sitting an old woman without a head. I supposed this unexpected sight made her gaze rather too earnestly, for the old woman immediately enquired—'Well, my piccaniny, what you see?' 'Oh, mammy,' answered the girl, 'me no see nothing.' 'Good child!' said again the old woman; 'and good will come to you.' Not far distant was a cocoa-tree; and here was another old woman, without any more head than the former one. The same question was asked her, and she failed not to give the same answer which had already met with so good a reception. Still she travelled forwards, and began to feel faint through want of food, when, under a mahogany tree, she not only saw a third old woman, but one who, to her great satisfaction, had got a head between her shoulders. She stopped, and made her best curtsey—'How day, grannie!' 'How day, my piccaniny; what matter, you no look well?' 'Grannie, me lilly hungry.' 'My piccaniny, you see that hut, there's rice in the pot, take it, and yam-yamme; but if you see one black puss, mind you give him share.' The child hastened to profit by the permission; the 'one black puss' failed not to make its appearance, and was served first to its portion of rice, after which it departed; and the child had but just finished her meal, when the mistress of the hut entered, and told her that she might help herself to three eggs out of the fowl-house, but that she must not take any of the *talking* ones: perhaps, too, she might find the black puss there, also; but if she did, she was to take no notice of her. Unluckily all the eggs seemed to be as fond of talking as if they had been so many old maids; and the moment that the child entered the fowlhouse, there was a cry of 'Take *me!* Take *me!*' from all quarters. However she was punctual in her obedience; and although the conversable eggs were remarkably fine and large, she searched about till at length she had collected three little dirty-looking eggs, that had not a word to say for themselves. The old woman now dismissed her guest, bidding her to return home without fear; but not to forget to break one of the eggs under each of the three trees near which she had seen an old woman that morning. The first egg produced a water-jug exactly similar to that which she had broken; out of the second came a whole large sugar estate; and out of the third a splendid equipage, in which she returned to her aunt, delivered up the jug, related that an old woman in a red docker (i.e. petticoat) had made her a great lady, and then departed in triumph to her sugar estate. Stung by envy, the aunt lost no time in sending her own daughter to search for the same good fortune which had befallen her cousin. She found the cotton-tree and the headless old woman, and had the same question addressed to her; but instead of returning the same answer—'What me see?' she said; 'me see one old woman without him head!' Now this reply was doubly offensive; it was rude, because it reminded the old lady of what might certainly be considered as a personal defect; and it was dangerous, as, if such a circumstance were to come to the ears of the buckras, it might bring her into trouble, women being seldom known to walk and talk without their heads, indeed, if ever, except by the assistance of Obeah. 'Bad child!' cried the old woman; 'bad child! and bad will come to you!' Matters were not better managed near the cocoa-tree; and even when she reached the mahogany, although she saw that the old woman had not only got her head on, but had a red docker besides, she could not prevail on herself to say more than a short 'How day?' without calling her 'grannie.' [Among negroes it is almost tantamount to an affront to address by the name, without affixing some term of relationship, such as 'grannie,' or 'uncle,' or 'cousin.' My Cornwall boy, George, told me one day, that 'Uncle Sully wanted to speak to massa.' 'Why is Sully your uncle, George?' 'No, massa, me only call him so for honour.'] However, she received the permission to eat rice at the cottage, coupled with the injunction of giving a share to the black puss; an injunction, however, which she totally disregarded, although she scrupled not to assure her hostess that she had suffered puss to eat till she could eat no more. The old lady in the red petticoat seemed to swallow the lie very glibly, and despatched the girl to the fowl-house for three eggs, as she had before done her cousin; but having been cautioned against taking the talking eggs, she conceived that these must needs be the most valuable; and, therefore, made a point of selecting those three which seemed to be the greatest gossips of the whole poultry yard. Then, lest their chattering should betray her disobedience, she thought it best not to return into the hut, and, accordingly, set forward on her return home; but she had not yet reached the mahogany tree, when curiosity induced her to break one of the eggs. To her infinite disappointment it proved to be empty; and she soon found cause to wish that the second had been empty too; for, on her dashing it against the ground, out came an enormous yellow snake, which flew at her with dreadful hissings. Away ran the girl; a fallen bamboo lay in her path; she stumbled over it, and fell. In her fall the third egg was broken; and the old woman without the head immediately popping out of it, told her, that if she had treated her as civilly, and had adhered as closely to the truth as her cousin had done, she would have obtained the same good fortune; but that as she had shown her nothing but rudeness, and told her nothing but lies, she must be contented to carry nothing home but the empty eggshells. The old woman then jumped upon the yellow snake, galloped away with incredible speed, and never showed her red docker in that part of the island any more."

■   ■   ■

April 19. (Sunday) [1816]

I have not been able to ascertain exactly the negro notions concerning the *Duppy;* indeed, I believe that his character and qualities vary in different parts of the country. At first, I thought that the term Duppy meant neither more nor less than a ghost; but sometimes he is spoken of as "the Duppy," as if there were but one, and then he seems to answer to the devil. Sometimes he is a kind of malicious spirit, who haunts burying-grounds (like the Arabian ghouls), and delights in playing tricks to those who may pass that way. On other occasions, he seems to be a supernatural attendant on the practitioners of Obeah, in the shape of some animal, as familiar imps are supposed to belong to our English witches; and this latter is the part assigned to him in the following "Nancy-story":

"Sarah Winyan was scarcely ten years old, when her mother died, and bequeathed to her considerable property. Her father was already dead; and the guardianship of the child devolved upon his sister, who had always resided in the same house, and who was her only surviving relation. Her mother, indeed, had left two sons by a former husband, but they lived at some distance in the wood, and seldom came to see their mother; chiefly from a rooted aversion to this aunt; who, although from interested motives she stooped to flatter her sister-in-law, was haughty, ill-natured, and even suspected of Obeahism, from the occasional visits of an enormous black dog, whom she called

Tiger, and whom she never failed to feed and caress with marked distinction. In case of Sarah's death, the aunt, in right of her brother, was the heiress of his property. She was determined to remove this obstacle to her wishes; and after treating her for some time with harshness and even cruelty, she one night took occasion to quarrel with her for some trifling fault, and fairly turned her out of doors. The poor girl seated herself on a stone near the house, and endeavoured to beguile the time by singing—

> 'Ho-day, poor me, O!
> Poor me, Sarah Winyan, O!
> They call me neger, neger!
> They call me Sarah Winyan, O!'

But her song was soon interrupted by a loud rushing among the bushes; and the growling which accompanied it announced the approach of the dreaded Tiger. She endeavoured to secure herself against his attacks by climbing a tree: but it seems that Tiger had not been suspected of Obeahism without reason; for he immediately growled out an assurance to the girl, that come down she must and should! Her aunt, he said, had made her over to him by contract, and had turned her out of doors that night for the express purpose of giving him an opportunity of carrying her away. If she would descend from the tree, and follow him willingly to his own den to wait upon him, he engaged to do her no harm; but if she refused to do this, he threatened to gnaw down the tree without loss of time, and tear her into a thousand pieces. His long sharp teeth, which he gnashed occasionally during the above speech, appeared perfectly adequate to the execution of his menaces, and Sarah judged it most prudent to obey his commands. But as she followed Tiger into the woods, she took care to resume her song of

> 'Ho-day, poor me, O!'

in hopes that some one passing near them might hear her name, and come to her rescue. Tiger, however, was aware of this, and positively forbad her singing. However, she contrived every now and then to loiter behind; and when she thought him out of hearing, her

> 'Ho-day, poor me, O!'

began again; although she was compelled to sing in so low a voice, through fear of her four-footed master, that she had but faint hopes of its reaching any ear but her own. Such was, indeed, the event, and Tiger conveyed her to his den without molestation. In the meanwhile, her two half-brothers had heard of their mother's death, and soon arrived at the house to enquire what was become of Sarah. The aunt received them with every appearance of welcome; told them that grief for the loss of her only surviving parent had already carried her niece to the grave, which she showed them in her garden; and acted her part so well, that the youths departed perfectly satisfied of the decease of their sister. But while passing through the wood on their return, they heard some one singing, but in so low a tone that it was impossible to distinguish the words. As this part of the wood was the most unfrequented, they were surprised to find any one concealed there. Curiosity induced them to draw nearer, and they soon could make out the

'Ho-day! poor me, O!
Poor me, Sarah Winyan, O!'

There needed no more to induce them to hasten onwards; and upon advancing deeper into the thicket, they found themselves at the mouth of a large cavern in a rock. A fire was burning within it; and by its light they perceived their sister seated on a heap of stones, and weeping, while she chanted her melancholy ditty in a low voice, and supported on her lap the head of the formidable Tiger. This was a precaution which he always took when inclined to sleep, lest she should escape; and she had taken advantage of his slumbers to resume her song in as low a tone as her fears of waking him would allow. She saw her brothers at the mouth of the cave: the youngest fortunately had a gun with him, and he made signs that Sarah should disengage herself from Tiger if possible. It was long before she could summon up courage enough to make the attempt; but at length, with fear and trembling, and moving with the utmost caution, she managed to slip a log of wood between her knees and the frightful head, and at length drew herself away without waking him. She then crept softly out of the cavern, while the youngest brother crept as softly into it: the monster's head still reposed upon the block of wood; in a moment it was blown into a thousand pieces; and the brothers, afterwards cutting the body into four parts, laid one in each quarter of the wood."

From that time only were dogs brought into subjection to men; and the inhabitants of Jamaica would never have been able to subdue those ferocious animals, if Tiger had not been killed and quartered by Sarah Winyan's brothers. As to the aunt, she received the punishment which she merited, but I cannot remember what it was exactly. Probably, the brothers killed and quartered *her* as well as her four-footed ally: or, perhaps, she was turned into a wild beast, and supplied the vacancy left by Tiger, as was the case with the celebrated Zingha, queen of Angola; who, although she embraced Christianity on her death-bed, and died according to the most orthodox forms of the Romish religion, still had conducted herself in such a manner while alive, that shortly after her decease, the kingdom being ravaged by a hyena, her subjects could not be persuaded but that the soul of this most Christian queen had transmigrated into the body of the hyena. Yet this was surely doing the hyena great injustice; for she, at least, had never been in the habit of composing ointments by pounding little children in a mortar with her own hands; an amusement which Zingha had introduced at the court of Angola. It took surprisingly; shortly, no woman thought her toilette completed, unless she had used some of this ointment. Pounding children became all the rage; and ladies who aspired to be the leaders of fashion, pounded their own.

■　　■　　■

April 29. [1816]

An African Nancy-story—"The headman (i.e. the king) of a large district in Africa, in one of his tours, visited a young nobleman, to whom he lost a considerable sum at play. On his departure he loaded his host with caresses, and insisted on his coming in person to receive payment at court; but his pretended kindness had not deceived the nurse of the young man. She told him, that the headman was certainly incensed against him for having conquered him at play, and meant to do him some injury; that having been so positively ordered to come to court, he could not avoid obeying; but she advised him to take the river-road, where, at a particular hour, he would find the king's youngest and favourite daughter bathing; and she instructed him how to behave. The youth reached the river, and concealed himself, till he saw the princess enter the stream alone; but when she thought fit to regain the bank, she found herself extremely embarrassed.—'Ho-day! what is become of my clothes? ho-day! if any one will bring me back my clothes, I promise that no harm shall happen to him this day— O!'—This was the cue for which the youth had been instructed to wait. 'Here are your clothes, missy!' said he, stepping from his concealment: 'a rogue had stolen them, while you were bathing; but I took them from him, and have brought them back.'—'Well, young man, I will keep my promise to you. You are going to court, I know; and I know also, that the headman will chop off your head, unless at first sight you can tell him which of his three daughters is the youngest. Now I am she; and in order that you may not mistake, I will take care to make a sign; and then do not you fail to pitch upon me.' The young man assured her, that, having once seen her, he never could possibly mistake her for any other, and then set forwards with a lightened heart. The headman received him very graciously, feasted him with magnificence, and told him that he would present him to his three daughters, only that there was a slight rule respecting them to which he must conform. Whoever could not point out which was the youngest, must immediately lose his head. The young man kissed the ground in obedience, the door opened, and in walked three little black dogs. Now, then, the necessity of the precaution taken by the princess was evident; the youth looked at the dogs earnestly; something induced the headman to turn away his eyes for a moment, and in that moment one of the dogs lifted up its fore paw. 'This,' cried the youth—'this is your youngest daughter';—and instantly the dogs vanished, and three young women appeared in their stead. The headman was equally surprised and incensed; but concealing his rage, he professed the more pleasure at that discovery; because, in consequence, the law of that country obliged him to give his youngest daughter in marriage to the person who should recognize her; and he charged his future son-in-law to return in a week, when he should receive his bride. But his feigned caresses could no longer deceive the young man: as it was evident that the headman practised Obeah, he did not dare to disobey him; and knew that to escape by flight would be unavailing. It was, therefore, with melancholy forebodings that he set out for court on the appointed day; and (according to the advice of his old nurse) he failed not to take the road which led by the river. The princess came again to bathe; her clothes again vanished; she had again recourse to her 'Ho-day! what is become of my clothes?' and on hearing the same promise of protection, the youth again made his appearance. 'Here are your clothes, missy.' said he; 'the wind had blown them away to a great distance; I found them hanging upon the bushes, and have brought them back to you.' Probably the princess thought it rather singular, that whenever her petticoats were missing, the same person should always happen to be in the way to find them: however, as she was remarkably handsome, she kept her thoughts to herself, swallowed the story like so much butter, and assured him of her protection. 'My father,' said she, 'will again ask you which is the youngest daughter; and as he suspects me of having assisted you before, he threatens to chop off *my* head instead of yours, should I disobey

him a second time. He will, therefore, watch me too closely to allow
of my making any sign to you; but still I will contrive something to
distinguish me from my sisters; and do you examine us narrowly till
you find it.' As she had foretold, the headman no sooner saw his destined son-in-law enter, than he told him that he should immediately
receive his bride; but that if he did not immediately point her out, the
laws of the kingdom sentenced him to lose his head. Upon which the
door opened, and in walked three large black cats, so exactly similar
in every respect, that it was utterly impossible to distinguish one from
the other. The youth was at length on the point of giving up the attempt in despair, when it struck him, that each of the cats had a slight
thread passed round its neck; and that while the threads of two were
scarlet, that of the third was blue. '*This* is your youngest daughter';
cried he, snatching up the cat with the blue thread. The headman was
utterly at a loss to conceive by what means he had made the discovery; but could not deny the fact, for there stood the princesses in their
own shape. He therefore affected to be greatly pleased, gave him his
bride, and made a great feast, which was followed by a ball; but in
the midst of it the princess whispered her lover to follow her silently
into the garden. Here she told him, that an old Obeah woman, who
had been her father's nurse, had warned him, that if his youngest
daughter should live to see the day after her wedding, he would lose
his power and his life together; that she, therefore, was sure of his intending to destroy both herself and her bridegroom that night in their
sleep; but that, being aware of all these circumstances, she had
watched him so narrowly as to get possession of some of his magical
secrets, which might possibly enable her to counteract his cruel designs. She then gathered a rose, picked up a pebble, filled a small
phial with water from a rivulet; and thus provided, she and her lover
betook themselves to flight upon a couple of the swiftest steeds in her
father's stables. It was midnight before the headman missed them: his
rage was excessive; and immediately mounting his great horse,
Dandy, he set forwards in pursuit of the lovers. Now Dandy galloped
at the rate of ten miles a minute. The princess was soon aware of her
pursuer: without loss of time she pulled the rose to pieces, scattered
the leaves behind her, and had the satisfaction of seeing them instantly grow up into a wood of briars, so strong and so thickly planted,
that Dandy vainly attempted to force his way through them. But, alas!
this fence was but of a very perishable nature. In the time that it
would have taken to wither its parent rose-leaves, the briars withered
away; and Dandy was soon able to trample them down, while he con-

tinued his pursuit. Now, then, the pebble was thrown in his passage; it burst into forty pieces, and every piece in a minute became a rock as lofty as the Andes. But the Andes themselves would have offered no insurmountable obstacles to Dandy, who bounded from precipice to precipice; and the lovers and the headman could once more clearly distinguish each other by the first beams of the rising sun. The headman roared, and threatened, and brandished a monstrous sabre; Dandy tore up the ground as he ran, neighed louder than thunder, and gained upon the fugitives every moment. Despair left the princess no choice, and she violently dashed her phial upon the ground. Instantly the water which it contained swelled itself into a tremendous torrent, which carried away every thing before it,—rocks, trees, and houses; and 'the horse and his rider' were carried away among the rest—*'Hic finis Priami fatorum!'* There was an end of the headman and Dandy! The princess then returned to court, where she raised a strong party for herself; seized her two sisters, who were no better than their father, and had assisted him in his witchcraft; and having put them and all their partisans to death by a summary mode of proceeding, she established herself and her husband on the throne as headman and headwoman. It was from this time that *all* the kings of Africa have been uniformly mild and benevolent sovereigns. Till then they were all tyrants, and tyrants they would all still have continued, if this virtuous princess had not changed the face of things by drowning her father, strangling her two sisters, and chopping off the heads of two or three dozen of her nearest and dearest relations.

MRS. LANIGAN, *Antigua and the Antiguans* (London, 1844), vol. 2, 115.

After dancing, I think the next favourite pastime of the negroes, particularly among the younger ones, is to collect together upon a fine moonlight night, and talk "Nancy stories," (which, as before remarked, generally consist of tales of *diablerie*), and the far-famed "Scheherezade" of the "Arabian Nights" could scarcely invent more marvellous ones. Some tell of a wondrous bird, (equalling in magnitude Sinbad's roc), which in other days appeared, and completely covered Antigua for some time, obliging the good people to "light candle all de day, so dat dey neber no when night come self"; others tell of men turning into monkeys (no uncommon thing nowadays); some of demons, and their deeds; and others, again, of golden houses, and streets of silver, flying dragons, and talking birds. These "Nancy stories" are generally given in a species of recitative; but the conclusion to them all is the same—"I was dere, an see it well done, and I get a glass of wine for me pains!" The relater of the tales is held in great repute, and to obtain instruction in the art, many a little negro will give their dinners, and go hungry to-bed.

MRS. HENRY LYNCH, *The Wonders of the West Indies* (London, 1856), 170–73.

Amongst insects, the Anansi spider holds a prominent place as the spirit of evil. We heard an African slave drawl out the following Anansi tale in a melancholy tone, making it strangely impressive by suddenly lowering her voice to a whisper, and then all at once swelling out into wild earnestness. She sat on the ground as she related it, giving a kind of emphasis to the metre with her foot, regularly striking the earth with it at every pause.

> "Oh, mother, sweet mother, my pickney child,
> That a living star on my path has smiled,
> Lies scorched in the fever's burning embrace,
> With pain's dark touch on her soft sweet face;
> My spirit is troubled, the life-blood chill
> Sends shivering through me the sense of ill.

> The dark Anansi,
> Oh, it came to me
> At the crimson fall of day;
> With a stealthy creep,
> As my babe did sleep,
> On her guileless breast it lay!

> Go thou forth, my daughter, go forth when night
> Wears its crystal dew gems all fresh and bright,
> When the all-spice tree, with its shining bark,
> Sends silvery light through the foliage dark;
> When the fire-fly flits o'er the wavy cane,
> And when insects burr on the dusky plain;
> Then go forth, my flower, and it may be
> Thou shalt learn thy doom from the Anansi.

> The young Quadroon wrapped the crocus plaid
> Round the babe which soft on her breast was laid,
> When the evening breeze in a love-lorn sigh
> Woo'd the graceful palm trees in passing by;
> She wound her way through the deep arcade

By the gleaming myrtles and citrons made,
With a failing step, and with trembling frame,
To the crystal banks of the stream she came!

> Anansi, Anansi,
> Alone, alone with thee,
> And night, and dews undefiled,
> Shall the kindled torch
> Of this fever scorch
> To the death my hapless child!

> In the reedy grass
> Where the shadows pass,
> Silently over the ground,
> In the silvery coil
> Of its spidery toil
> Lay the dark Anansi bound!

And a whispering sound, such as elfish sprite,
Breathes of coming doom to the silent night,
Passed her, whizzing low with a rustling sigh,
She knew the Anansi in truth was nigh.
Speak, oh speak, she cried, I am strong to bear,
And break the chain of this grim despair!

> Three times the sun
> His course shall run,
> Three times the weeping flowers
> Shall bow to the rain
> And awake again
> All gemmed by pearly showers.

Then shall fall on thy way the Anansi's curse,
Foaming waters shall be the plumed hearse,
And rocking billows thy babe shall nurse;
> And Death shall smile,
To see how, when fever had failed to bring
Thy babe to the shade of his dusky wing,
The poor little helpless unconscious thing
> Was his the while.

> Woe is me! woe is me!
> Anansi, Anansi,
> And the mother tore her hair;
> I'm off and away,
> Ere the third sad day,
> From the vile Anansi's lair."

CHARLES RAMPINI, *Letters from Jamaica, "The Land of Streams and Woods"* (Edinburgh, 1873), 115–28.

Reference has frequently been made in the preceding pages to the popular tales—the Annancy stories—of the negroes in Jamaica. Corresponding to the fairy tales of more northerly regions, they have been the delight and the amusement of many a generation of young Creoles, white, black, brown, and yellow. Nor, indeed, have they wanted admirers amongst children of a larger growth. No pleasanter picture of peasant comfort and enjoyment is to be seen in Jamaica than that of a circle of negroes seated around some village storyteller as he recounts the cunning exploits of Annancy.

The chief repositories of this traditional literature are children and old women. It is essentially the literature of a race, not of a nation. Essentially a child of the soil, its subjects are almost exclusively drawn from the common daily incidents of a country life. "It scarcely ever rises above Gungo peas and Afoo yams. It reflects the inward feeling and outward circumstances of a very simple and a very unpolished peasantry."[*]

The principal hero of this autochthonic literature is the large black Annancy spider. He is the personification of cunning and success—two qualities which have an especial charm for the negro mind.[†] "He is the Jove, the Thor, the Bramah of negro mythology. His great strength is in his cunning, and in his metamorphic versatility; he out-Proteuses Proteus. His parentage is utterly unknown—nor indeed does it seem referred to in any of the Annancy stories."[‡] The other personages who figure in the tales are Annancy's wife Crookie, and Tacooma his reputed son. "Tacooma is a person quite by himself. He

---

[*]From an admirable Paper on Negro Literature in the Transactions of the Jamaica Royal Society of Arts and Agriculture. New Series, vol. i, no. 4, p. 64.

[†]The philosophy of these stories is well explained by Dr. Dasent in his Norse Tales: "They are called 'Ananzi Stories,' because so many of them turn on the feats of Ananzi, whose character is a mixture of 'the Master-thief,' and of 'Boots'; but the most curious thing about him, is that he illustrates the Beast Epic in a remarkable way. In all the West Indian Islands, 'Ananzi' is the name of spiders in general, and of a very beautiful spider with yellow stripes in particular. The Negroes think that this spider is the 'Ananzi' of their stories, but that his superior cunning enables him to take any shape he pleases. In fact, he is the example which the African tribes, from which these stories came, have chosen to take as pointing out the superiority of wit over brute strength. In this way they have matched the cleverness and dexterity of the Spider against the bone and muscle of the Lion, invariably to the disadvantage of the latter."—*Introduction to Appendix*, p. 485.

[‡]"Negro Literature"—*Trans. Jamaica Royal Soc.*, vol. i, p. 65, new series.

seems without parallel in any other mythology. He helps his father or not, as he thinks fit. He is stronger than his father, but has less cunning; and when he, the strong, and the father, the cunning, do unite, woe to the victim they attack! As regards Annancy and his wife, they engage in squabble, which, had the pair been human, might have led them to the Divorce Court, but which, for matrimonial objurgation, are fit to rank with those splendid 'passages' between Jupiter and Juno."[§]

Many of the Annancy stories exist only as pointless, disjointed, mutilated fragments. Others of them break off abruptly just when the interest has reached its highest point.

The specimens which follow have been taken down from the lips of the narrators. Much of their dramatic effect must, of necessity, be lost in their transcription. The action, the imitation of Annancy's drawl, the alternation of tones by which the various personages are distinguished, the little fragments of song introduced, it was of course impossible to reproduce. To have given them too, in all the baldness of the negro dialect, would have rendered them unintelligible to the English reader. Still we trust that we have deprived them of no part of their essential character.

Without further preface, therefore, here follows the legend of

Annancy and the Tiger

Once upon one time, long before Queen Victoria come to reign over we, Annancy and Tiger were both courting de same young lady. Dey was both bery jalous of each other. So when Annancy one day go to dis lady's yard, him say to her dat Tiger was noting better dan his father's old riding-horse. Little time after Tiger come to call 'pon him sweetheart. But de young lady say to him, "Go 'long, sa! How can you come courting me when you know you is noting but Missa Annancy's father's old riding-horse?"

"Warra!" cried Tiger, "who tell you dis one great big lie?"

"Hi!" said de lady, "is dis a way to speak to me? Go 'long wid you, you old good-for-noting jackass riding-horse!"

"My fader!" said Tiger, "what is dis? It favour like you have a suspich 'pon me, ma'am. (It looks as if you were suspicious of me.) But I tell you, ma'am, what I will do. I will go straight 'long to Breda (Brother) Annancy, an' make him to tell me what time I eber turn his fader's old jack-ass riding-horse."

§"Negro Literature," *ut supra*, p. 65.

So de lady say to him, "Well, go 'long, sa!"

Then Tiger take up him stick, and him stick him junky pipe in his cheek, and go straight to Annancy's yard. When him get there, he found Annancy lying in his bed down with fever. So him lift de latch, and call out, "Breda Annancy! Breda Annancy!"

Annancy hear him bery well; but him jus' say, so soft, "Dear Tiger, you call me?"

Tiger reply, "Yes, I call you. I come to you. I want to hear good from you today, because lady tell me you say I noting but your fader's old Jackass riding-horse, and I come to make you prove it."

"Hi!" said Annancy, "don't you see I hab fever? My stomach pain me bad, an' I hab jus' taken doctor's medicine!"

"Cho!" replied Tiger.

"After I hab jus' eaten two pills, Breda Tiger, how you think I can go to de lady yard to prove that rude word to-night?"

"I don't want to hab any conconsa (argument) wid you, Breda," replied Tiger, "but you mus' jus' show the lady dis night when I turn you fader old jackass riding-horse."

"O king!" cried Annancy, " 'an' dis cataplasm upon my breast, it burn me so! Howsomever, I will try to go wid you to de lady."

Then Tiger say, "Well, Breda, since you so kind, don't mind; I will carry you on my back."

"Wait a minute, den, Breda, an' I will try to rise out of my bed."

But him fall back. Den him cry out, "Dear! I can't get up at all. Do, I beg you, Breda, come raise me up." Tiger raised him up.

So when Annancy rise up, him go to the rafter, and take down him saddle.

"Hi!" said Tiger, "what you going to do wid dat?"

"Jus' to put it upon your back, Breda, for me to sit down soft becausing you see I am well sick."

"Neber mind, den," said Tiger, "put it on."

Then Annancy got his bridle and reins.

"Hi' " said Tiger, "an' what are you going to do wid dat?"

"Jus' to put 'pon your mouth, Breda, to pull you up when you walk too fast."

"All right," said Tiger, "put dem on."

Then Annancy took out his horse-whip.

"Hi!" said Tiger, "an' what are you going to do wid dat?"

"When fly come 'pon your ear, Breda, I will take dis whip and lick it off."

Tiger say, "Well, take it."

Then Annancy put on his spurs.

"Hi!" said Tiger, "what are you going to do wid dat?"

"When fly come 'pon your side, Breda, I will touch dem wid my spur, an' make them fly off."

"Nebber mind, den," said Tiger, "put them on."

Then Annancy called out, "Now, den, Breda Tiger, stoop down," an' Annancy mounted 'pon him back. Tiger den began to walk off.

But as him walk too fast, Annancy pull him up wid de bridle.

"Stop, Breda! take time; my head hurt me so!"

Tiger went on till he go a mile. In a little, Annancy take him horse-whip and fetch Tiger a lick on the ear.

"Hi!" said Tiger, "what dat fo, sa?"

"Cho!" replied Annancy, "what a 'tupid fly! Shoo, you fly!"

"All right, Breda," said Tiger, "but nex'time don't lick so hot."

Tiger go on again for anoder mile. Then Annancy stick his spur into his side.

Tiger gabe one big jump, and cry out, "Warra! what dat?"

"Dem bodersome flies, Breda; dey bite your side so."

Then Tiger go on for another half-mile, till he come to the lady's yard.

Now de lady's house had two doors, a front one and a back one. Just as he came to de entrance of de yard, Annancy rise up in him saddle, like how jockey run race on Kingston racecourse, and him take out him whip and him lash Tiger well.

"Hi!" cried Tiger, "you lick too hot!" But Annancy lash him up the more, till Tiger gallop. Then Annancy took his spurs and stuck dem into Tiger's side, till he drove him right up to de lady's door-mouth.

Then Annancy took off his hat, an' waved it above his head, and say to the lady, who was standing at the door, "Hi! Missis, me no tell you true dat dis Tiger noting but my fader's old riding-horse?" So him leap off Tiger, and go into de lady's house. But Tiger gallop off, and never was heard of no more.

Many of the Annancy stories serve to illustrate natural facts. In the following, for instance, the baldness of head of the Carrion Crow or Turkey Buzzard is amusingly illustrated. These vultures, the scavengers of tropical cities, cannot fail to attract the attention of the traveller, almost upon his first arrival in Jamaica. So useful are they deemed to be by the Creoles that a local Act inflicts a fine upon any person who kills one. Their sense of smell is exquisite; and it is stated as a curious fact, that during the so-called Rebellion of 1865, the island was deserted by the John Crows, except in the parishes of St. Thomas and Portland, where the frightful scenes of carnage and of slaughter were being enacted.

Why the John Crows have Bald Pates

In a time before time there libed a man who hated de John Crows and wanted to destroy dem. But howsomdever him neber get de opportunity, an' de John Crows still libed to vex him.

But John Crow tink himself dandy man, an' it griebe him heart to tink that after all him had neber been christened. So him call a meeting of all him frien' an' relation, an' dey resolve to go ask man to christen him an' gib him a name.

When man hear this he rejoice greatly, an' him say to himself, "Cunny (cunning) better dan 'trong (strength). Now I will hab my vengeance 'pon my enemies."

So him appoint a day, an' him tell John Crow to mek a feast, an' to kill a big hog, an' to buy a little rum an' a little port-wine, an' plenty of salt fish an' yam an' oder vittles.

On de day him name all de John Crows of dat country gadered demselves togeder. And one brought beef, an' anoder brought ham, an' anoder a sucking pig, an' anoder fowls; an' dere was yams and cocoas, an' sweet potatoes, an' ebryting, an' plenty of liquor.

An' when de man com to de place where de eating match was to be, him bring wid him a big barrel full of American flour, which him said was him contribution to de feast. Den all de John Crows clapped deir wings wid joy, an' said: "Hi! de good buckra!" But de man only smile to himself an' say, " 'To-day fe me, to-morrow fe you'; 'When fowl merry, hawk catch him chicken;' 'Hide fe me, to-morrow fe you;' 'You shake my han', but you no shake my heart!' "‖ Then him turn to de John Crows and say, "When you hab plenty you boil pot," an' he bid dem light a fire, for he said he would need to boil de flour an' water togeder to make a grand cake for de christening.

When de barrel of flour was empty an' de flour an' de water was boiling, bubblin' up 'pon de fire, he call all de John Crows roun' him an' say, "You see dis barrel ya (here)?"

‖Negro proverbs.

Dey all say, "Yes, we see it."

"Bery well," he say, "come roun' an' put all you heads into it, an' you musn' lif' up your head or look roun' till I tell you, fo I hab someting secret to mek ready fe de christening." So dey all put deir head into de barrel, an' de barrel was chockful of deir head.

Den de man took de cauldron of boilin' water an' him step up behind dem softly, softly, an' den he lift up de pot an' pour all de boiling stuff 'pon deir heads, an' him laugh an' him say, "Dead fe true! Dis is de way I christen you, John Crow!"

But after all dey was not dead. Only when dey got better dey found all deir head peel (Bald) where de boilin' water fell 'pon dem.

An' dis is why John Crows hab bald pates to dis day.

Of the same kind is the story entitled

Why Hawks eat Fowls

Long time ago Fowl was Hawk's mother. One day Hawk was going to him work when he see little Ground Dove playing on a flute, and singing so sweet,

"Fee, fee, fee tender!"#

"Marning, Ground Dove," said Hawk.

"Marning, sa," him reply, "how you is to-day?"

"So-so, I tank you. Hi! what a pretty ting dat is you play 'pon you flute!"

"Tink so, sa?" said Ground Dove; an' him put up him flute to him mouth an' play again,

"Fee, fee, fee tender!"

"Do, I beg you, len' me you' flute, cousin Ground Dove. It soun' so sweet."

But Ground Dove say, "No cousin, me couldn' do it."

"Hi!" say Hawk, "you so quarry-quarry** you no let I mek my old moder Fowl hear you flute?"

"No, cousin," answer Ground Dove. "You no know what de old-time people say, " 'Pider (Spider) an' fly no mek good bargains! I could n' do it, sa, I could n' do it."

Den Hawk spring 'pon Ground Dove, an' tear up him feathers,

#An imitation of the note of the ground dove.
**Quarrelsome.

an' mash him up wid him beak, an' lef (leave) him fe dead 'pon de dirt.[††] An' him take away him flute, an' so carry away go home.

An' when Hawk come to him house he go into him hall to de ches' of drawers dat stan' da, an' him open de one drawer, de two drawer, de tree drawer, de four drawer, de five drawer, de six drawer, till him come to de twelve drawer; an' him put de flute into de twelve drawer, an' come back sit down.

Den he turn to him moder Fowl an' say, "Grandie, if any come to you, ask you fer give him de flute me put in de twelve drawer, you is not to give it him. Yerry?" (do you hear?) An' him moder say, "Yes, sa! me hear." Den Hawk say, "An', Grandie, you mus' hab my breakfas' ready an' keep him hot till me come back from de field. Yerry?"

An' him moder say, "Yes, sa! me yerry."

Den Hawk take up him hoe an' him machette an' go to him ground.

But all dis time little Ground Dove had followed Hawk, an' when him tell him moder where him put de flute, him listen behin' de door, an' hear what him did say.

So when Hawk gone, Ground Dove come out from behin' de door, an' go into Hawk's house. By dis time Grandie fowl done cook Hawk breakfas', an' was sitting aside de kitchen fire smokin' her pipe.

"Good-day, godmother," said Ground Dove.

"Good-day, my dear."

"Godmother," said Ground Dove, "Cousin Hawk sent me to tell you to gib me him breakfas' to carry to him in de field, and de flute which him put in de twelve-drawer to make him play an' sing."

But Fowl say, "Go long wid you, pickny! You tell me one big story—me no go give you one ting."

Ground Dove begin to cry. Den him say, "Godmother, you tink a little ting like me would tell you such a lie? no, ma'am! me wouldn' do it; me wouldn' do it."

But Fowl still sit by de fire an' smoke him pipe.

Ground Dove cry more.

Den Fowl get angry and say, "Hi! Cho! you too foolish. Don't winka-winka at me (neigh like a horse). Go long wid you, Cho!"

But Ground Dove cry on still.

"Cho!" said Fowl, "it 'tan too 'tupid" (The matter is too absurd).

But Ground Dove go on cry so bad dat at las' Fowl get terrify. Den she rise up from her seat, take de flute from de drawer, and gib

††Earth-ground.

it, wid de breakfas', to Ground Dove, fe go carry it to Hawk in him
field. Ground Dove dry him eyes, put him flute to him mout' an' play
so sweet,

> "Fee, fee, fee tender,"

and so go leave de house.

As him went along him eat Hawk's breakfas', but him take de
flute an' hide him under him wing till him come to a *lignum vitae*
bush close by where Hawk was at work in him field. Then him took
out him flute, and begin to play

> "Fee, fee, fee tender,"

again.

Hawk heard him. Hi! but him well warify (in a great passion)
when him yerry dis. Him throw down him hoe, an' him throw down
him machette, an' him curse him moder for a "cra-cra" (careless),
"Bogro-bogro" (coarse), "takro-takro" (ugly), "chaka-chaka" (disorderly), "buffro-buffro" (clumsy), "wenya-wenya" (meagre), "nana"
(old woman); an' him stalk away out of him ground to his moder
house.

When him come to de yard him call out, "Moder!" But him
moder no answer him. She was afraid. Den him walk into de house,
an' him go up to de ches' ob drawers, an' him open de one drawer,
an' de two drawer, de tree drawer, de four drawer, de five drawer, de
six drawer, till him come to de twelve drawer. But him no find him
flute. Den him cross de yard, an' step up to him moder, an' say, "Hi!
ma'am, you gib my flute to Groun' Dove, do you? Where my
breakfas'?"

But him moder no answer him. She was afraid.

So Hawk say, "Yerry, ma'am? where my breakfas', ma'am?"

Den him moder fall down a' him feet an' say, "Sa! You no' sen'
little Ground Dove ya (here), make I gib him you breakfas' fe go carry
to you in de field, and you flute fe mak you play an' sing?"

"You tief!" said Hawk, "me neber sen' any one ya!"

"Wi! O me moder me dead!"‡‡ cry out poor Fowl.

But Hawk reply, "You tief, you witch! you shall be my breakfas'!"

Den him pounce 'pon Fowl, an' shake her, an' tear her till her
dead: an' den him eat her for him breakfas'!

An' dis is why eber since Hawks eat Fowls.

---

‡‡An exclamation implying great fear and personal danger.

HENRY G. MURRAY, *Manners and Customs of the Country a
Generation Ago, Tom Kittle's Wake* (Kingston, Jamaica, 1877), 24–29.

But let us listen to Tom's Nancy Story.

"Once upon a time in a Chookoo dere was hard time dere. Nobody couldn't get nuttin to eat. Bud dem fly all bout da look for someting to eat, but dem couldn't get nuttin; so tay one day, de word come
say, one gentleman corn piece far y-o-n-d-e-r—hab plenty corn; and
de corn well an ripe. As de news come so pigeon dem all da fly fe go
dere. Mudfish in a water; from him wake da morning, so tay in a
breakfast time, him yery bud wing da go ya—pa, pa, pa; pa, pa, pa;
him say, 'poor me boy! da warra disha ya to-day?' Him swim go da
shore side, den when pigeon dem top da riverside fe drink water, him
hax dem say, 'Bra, whi side unoo da go?' Dem say, 'Ha Bra! buckra
corn piece ripe, sa! We da go dere!' Mudfish say, 'Bra unoo carry me
go wid unoo, no?' Pigeon dem say, 'Cho, mudfish! tan where you day,
man. What you da go do da cornpiece!' Mudfish wouldn't satisfy; him
tan dere da shoreside, so pigeon dem come da waterside come drink
water, him beg dem, 'Bra, unoo carry me go, no!' Dem say, 'Mudfish,
tan where you day, man.' Mudfish top dere, neber move, tay bambye* good-belly pigeon come dere come drink water. Mudfish say to
him, 'Bra pigeon carry me go wid you, no!' Him say, 'Bra, what you
da go do a cornpiece?' Mudfish say, 'Me too love corn, Bra.' Him say,
'how you fe go!' Him say, 'Bra, you no make me lie down da you
back.' Him say, 'Bra, suppose you fall down?' Him say 'Bra, me will
hold on.' Him say, 'Bra Mudfish, me no want car you.' Him say, 'Bra
car me!' Good-belly pigeon take him so carry him. When dem catch
da cornpiece, dem put Mudfish da ground; den so de pigeon dem da
eat corn a top, Mudfish da da bottom da pick up wha drop, da eat.
When dem all busy da eat, yery word come say 'Watchman da come;'
pigeon dem begin da fly da go way—ya, pa, pa, pa, Mudfish say,
'Good-belly pigeon take me up no?' Him say, 'Bra, we cant wait fe
you. Bra me ben tell you say you must'nt come ya; da you hard ears
you take so come ya.'—Mudfish say, 'poor me boy, me done for to-
day.' So dem order pigeon da fly da go, him beg dem fe take him up.
Dem say, 'Cho man, who do go boder with you? Dat man bring you
ya, make him take you no!' Dem all lef Mudfish go way. When Watchman come, him see Mudfish, him say, 'wha you da do ya? How you
lef water so come ya?' Him say, 'Bra, da pigeon bring me come ya.'

*Good natured.

Watchman take him up an put him da him kutakoo, say, 'I wi carry you to buckra make you tell him wha you da do ya.' So Watchman da walk da go 'long, so, him da sing. Mudfish talk to himself say 'Dis Watchman ya love sing.' Watchman say, 'I love sing, yes.' Mudfish say, 'Ah! Bra Watchman, ef you want fe hear man sing, da me.' Watchman say, 'a so?' Mudfish say 'yes, but I cant sing widout water; put me in a one packy o' water and I wi sing fe you.' Watchman do so. Mudfish shake himself, den begin fe sing—

> 'Yerry groomer corn pempeny,
> Groomer yerry;
> Pigeon bring me da groomer yerry.'

Watchman dance. Him say, 'Mudfish you sing well, sa.'—Mudfish say, 'put me in a tub o' water an I wi sing better, Bra.' Watchman put him in a big washing tub o' water. Mudfish sing again; Watchman dance so, till de sweat drop off da him face. Him say, 'Mudfish, you sing too sweet.' Mudfish say, 'Dis put me riber side make I smell riber water.' Him say, 'No Mudfish! bambye you make me fool!' Mudfish say, 'No Bra, no cajon put my body, dis put my tail, make it touch de water, and I will sing fe you make you dance like you mad.' Watchman say, 'I will do it, but take care you make me fool.' Him say, 'No, Bra Watchman, put me down.' Mudfish begin sing; Watchman begin dance. So Mudfish da sing, so him da wriggle him tail. How de sing sweet Watchman him neber look 'pon Mudfish. Mudfish wriggle and sing—Mudfish wriggle and sing, till him get into de water; as him get in dere so, him raise up him head an him say, 'Bra Watchman, me gone, yerry!'—Watchman jump after him, but bufo you coulda say 'Jack,' Mudfish gone! A dat make you hear dem say 'neber make Mudfish tail touch water.' "

This story was duly applauded, and wound up with the usual "Jack Mandora."

I have said that Bartibo was a proverb of *good appetite*. He was none of your dainty epicures, that looked to the *piquant* quality of his dish beyond anything else. Joe's delight was in *quantity* rather than *quality*. To use his own expressions he liked a "*proper belly full.*" It will afford no surprise, therefore, to hear, that he feasted heartily upon Tom's slaughtered pig. As he feasted, he waxed eloquent—"Dis by chance, sir, I hear dat de old man dead, sir. Dis by chance!" said he, with a mouthful of pork in his mouth. "Umphoo!" said Maria, "ef him no been taste dis pork meat ya, it would a mek ebery body sick, de bex him been da go bex." Old Joe did not hear her.

"Well sir, I jis come from Sandy Bay. I was down dere, because I did hear say Misser Telford down dere hab a Taffy, an him say dat him wi gie de Taffy to any man dat wi eat him liber wid a grain o' salt. Sis I, my massa, da me da you man, sir. Well, sir, him gie me Taffy, an I kill him, sir, and I mash up one o' de biggest grain o' coarse salt I could a find, an me an me boy Peter clean off de liber bufo you could a say Jack. Well, sir, I tek me drink o' grog, an I smoke my pipe, and go to my bed. As I drop asleep, so I hearee in a my sleep:

> 'Tarra tell lie pon tarra
> Tarra tell lie pon tarra.'

I wake Peter. Me say, 'Peter, you hear dat?' Him say, 'Daddy, da de people da eat dem new nyams.' Me say, 'Peter, my boy, ef "tarra tell lie pon tarra," dis not a good place; we wi get in a trouble.' Well, I go sleep till bufo day, nummo come yerry dem Eboe fellow—

> 'Broke Whanica Penny comb
> Kill de debil moder,
> Kill de debil moder.'

Me say—whoy! Poor me boy, dis is a turrable place! I must go 'way. I wake Peter. My good sir, Peter mek up one face! nuff fe cruddle any milk! Me ax him say—'Boy, you hab pain o' tomach?' Him say, 'Daddy, what you da boder me for! You cant mek people sleep?' Me say 'Boy, you yery dat?' Him say, 'Daddy me no tell you da de new nyams!' Me say, 'No boy, tek up de meat mek we go. Ef dem kill de debil moder ya, we better go boy, else we wi get in a trouble. Debil no man fe mek fun wid, my son!' So said, sir, I lick myself in a my canoe name John Francis, and paddle up to Great Riber. As I come dere, sir, dat greedy little fellow, Missa Jacky bawl out say, 'Ah, mammy, daddy bring meat fe we eat wid de pear and de nyams.' I say, 'Go long way, sir, you greedy little chap. I neber see a chap lub meat so.—Dem tell me say Tom Kittle ded, an him wake fe keep up to-night.' Says I to my wife, 'my dear, you know I lub old Tom, so I gwine to him wake; eat one leg o' de mutton you and dem pickney, and corn de rest till I come. Ef de leg done before I come back, take care you touch any more!—Too much meat don't good fe children.' I paddle my canoe, sir, an you see me ya."

Maria looked at him with a quiet smile of contempt as she witnessed his power of deglutition, and the rapidity with which choice pieces of meat slipped away through his teeth.—After a while, lifting her head from her jaw, on which it had been resting for some time, she called to him:

"Ole Massa!"
"Yes, gal!"
"Bud mus a ben carry de news down da Great Riber say old Tom lef hog fe kill, no sir?" "Gal, what you mean!" "Me no mean nuttin, old massa. Nummo me ben tink say after you ben lub old Tom so you might a ben bring half a de goat meat fe gie people da him wake." "Gal mind you self," said old Joe, who knew well enough *what* she meant.

"Come boys," said William Hinds, "gib us a song." Now William had a man called Blackam, who was his *umbra*, Blackam, knew what sort of song William wanted, and at once he struck up a Stevedore's song, to which Thomas kept chorus *(Sing.):—*

> "Bony was a good boy,
> Sing hal le ho!
> Bony was a good boy,
> Sing hal le ho!

> "O! poor Bony, boy.
> Sing hal le ho!
> O! poor Bony, boy.
> Sing hal le ho!

> "Bony mek de Dubs fly,
> Sing hal le ho,
> Bony mek de Guineas fly,
> Sing hal le ho, &c."

"Ah," said William, at the close of this song, "Bony was a good boy, but him could'nt no match fe de Duke, sa, I tell you. Bony was a noble feller fe fight sir, but him was nuttin to de Duke. One day, sir, Bony little son come to him fader, and him say, 'Pupa! I was lookin pon Englan trough my 'py glass, an it's a bery small place—what mek you don't take it my fader?' 'Ah, my son,' said Bony, 'Englan is a small garden but she hab some bery bitter weeds.'"

Then follows William's celebrated story of "Bony and the Duke," which cannot be written. It may be summed up in this, that according to our veracious chronicler, the battle of Waterloo lasted for "five days and five nights"—that at length "Bony" saw that the tide had turned quite against him, and so giving "the boy who had been holding his horse a macarony," he said, "boy, go buy sumting fe drink

I is off." It was at this moment that the Duke espied him, and gave chase. "De Duke was mounted, pon dat his celebrated, 'Rabian grey chestnut colt, an he call out to his officers and his mans dem, 'right rank in the rear! Mek we go after dat feller.'" Then occurred the terrible chase. "Uphill and down dale," through "mud-mud, an san; an putto-putto," till overtaking Bony, the Duke "hit him wid dat him silber mounted 'py glass 'pon de back, an say 'top you villain you, top.'" This brought Bony to a halt, and thus he came to grief.

REV. CHARLES DANIEL DANCE, *Chapters from a Guianese Log-Book* (Demerara, 1881), 85–90.

The Coast and River Creoles of British Guiana, with indeed all creoles of the West Indies, are famous for their "Death Wakes."

The night following the death of a villager is spent by the deceased's relatives and friends, and friends' friends, in the house or yard in which the body is laid; and the visitors employ themselves according to their pleasure. Those who are musically and religiously inclined *keep inside* the house, or if it be too small for the accommodation of all, some seat themselves on benches near the door, and sing hymns, sometimes with fiddle or clarionette accompaniment, diversifying the music with extempore prayers, recitative and durge-like. Outside, and farther away in the yard, groups of persons congregate—some playing at forfeits, the proceeds of which are devoted to the purchase of candles, peppermint and beer. Others are putting riddles to be solved, or narrating "Anansie Stories."

"Anansie" is a spider from which man is thought to have been developed. The "Anansie" of the stories is the half-developed man from the spider, who in his transitional state combines the agility and craftiness of the insect with the intelligence of the man, and is always represented as speaking in a snuffling indistinct manner.

In these "stories" (the African Aesop's Tales) the animals are made to talk and act as men; and each story has its moral, sometimes rather far-fetched. There are scores of these fables of ridiculous humour, but they are hardly admissible on account of their Aristophanic simplicity; and to attempt to dress them up would be only to spoil them. I shall select a few of the most decorous.

I. *Anansie—Yawarri—and Asoonu* (supposed to be an Elephant).

Anansie, who is recovering slowly from illness and consequent starvation, is seen, every morning at daybreak, bringing home a small bit of fresh meat. Yawarri, who is both inquisitive and envious, often teases Anansie to tell him whence he procured his supplies every morning; but Anansie puts him off the scent by giving him false accounts.

Yawarri is despairing to discover the secret, so much so, that he falls ill. His friend the monkey is grieved at his illness; and learning the cause of it, he advises Yawarri to keep a watch near Anansie's house at night, and to follow him as he goes out for the fresh meat. This advice Yawarri takes. He watches by Anansie's house, and steadily follows his footsteps. Anansie—unaware of Yawarri's presence—scales the wall of the King's park, when Yawarri calls out to him and tells him that if he does not promise to take him as a partner he shall cry out an alarm of "Thief!"

So Anansie promised; and taking Yawarri with him, he explained how that every night, while the king's elephants slept in the park, he entered into the bowels of one of them, cut off a moderate piece of meat, and made his retreat, taking care not to trouble the same elephant a second time.

When these companions had proceeded a little way, they came up to two elephants into which they entered,—each into the one of his choice,—Yawarri first losing some time in ascertaining, by sight, which of the two elephants was the more fat and fleshy.

Anansie very soon came out of his elephant, after cutting his usual moderate bit of meat. After waiting a long time and becoming impatient, he said,—"Bru Yawarri! Bru Yawarri! (brother Yawarri), come out—the day will soon be dawning!" But Yawarri, putting his head out, and in the greatest excitement, answered—"O Bru! What fine meat! what fat meat! I cannot come; go if you like, but I must cut all day: to-night do send my wife and children to assist me in taking home what I cut. Good-bye!"

So saying, Yawarri popped in his head and continued his work of slashing and cutting the entrails of the elephant, so that by the dawn of day it was dead.

The king had a *post-mortem* examination at once, for the keepers of the elephants had told him that, although the elephant was certainly dead, a strange noise was continually heard within it. Judge their surprise and indignation when, on laying open a part of the body of the Asoonu, they saw Yawarri, who, so busy at his own work, did not at first perceive the work of the doctors. He was taken prisoner, had a fair trial and was killed.

That night the keepers of the Asoonu were vigilant.

As for Anansie, he sent Yawarri's family as he was directed; but, fearing some mishap, did not venture himself any nearer than the top of the wall, whence he saw Yawarri's wife and children shot by the keepers.

Moral. Be moderate in all things.

II. *The Sign of a Tiger's Death.*

Once Tiger had a happy thought. He called his wife, and bade her blow a shell through the forest, to notify to all his friends that he was ill, and at the point of death.

The next morning he bade his wife to bandage his jaws slightly, and spread him out on his bed, and lay a cloth over his body. This done, he sent her round the neighbourhood to proclaim his death, and with sound of shell to invite all his friends to the burying.

That afternoon Tiger—with one eye slyly open—saw a goodly number of prime animals all fat and sleek making a hubbub of grief. (Here a long list of the animals present is mentioned, and each one's manner of crying is ludicrously assimilated to loud weeping.)

Just then Anansie came to the door, and with a great show of authority ordered everyone to go outside, as he wanted to confer privately with Mrs. Tiger.

Having put the animals all out of the house, he spoke thus to Mrs. Tiger: "Madam, it is one's duty to condole with the losses of his friend; but it is a happier office to dissipate her sorrows and restore her happiness. Are you sure that my best of friends is dead?"

"Sure, Mr. Anansie?" said the sorrowing widow, all in tears—"who can know better than I who attended him in his last moments, and laid him out?"

"Poor, poor Bru Tiger, how my heart is ready to burst! How long, Madam, has he been dead?"

"Since daybreak."

"And has he *sneezed* since his death?" asked Anansie, his eyes red with tears, and his countenance evincing the deepest sympathy.

"*Sneezed*, Mr. Anansie? Are you come to mock the sorrows of a widow's broken heart? Who ever heard of the dead sneezing?"

"Ah, Mrs. Tiger," answered Anansie, "you have no experience: neither you nor our dear friend there ever saw a tiger dying. Now I have, in my travels, witnessed the death of several tigers: and believe me that a tiger is never truly dead until he has sneezed many times after the breath has left him. Take comfort, your husband will recover."

At this point of the conversation, Tiger—fearing that the report getting out to the company that he was not dead would sadly interfere with his projects of a wholesale slaughter—gave a series of very emphatic sneezes, which sent Anansie to the roof of the house laughing, and caused all the other animals to scamper into the forest.

Moral. See that your plans are perfect before you work them.

III. *Anansie Refuses to Marry a King's Daughter.*

Anansie goes every night to steal from the king's garden, and is always escaping the trap laid for him by the gardener. At last he is caught. The gardener cuts out the form of a man in wood, plants it in the ground firmly, and then covers it with a very adhesive substance. Anansie (who is ever a coward, although cunning and clever to get out of scrapes) pretends to be one of the under-gardeners, and accosts the supposed man, requiring to know from him why he has ventured to rob another man's field. Receiving no reply, he is assured that it is not a gardener but a thief that he sees, and waxing bold by the silence of the supposed thief, he threatens to beat him if he will not answer.

He puts his threat into execution by inflicting a blow, and the result is that he is held firmly by the adhesive matter on the image. "Let me go," says Anansie, "or I shall strike you with my left hand, which never fails to kill." He strikes with the left hand, which is also held as in a vice. Anansie implores to be let loose, and then threatens terrible evils. He then butts with his forehead, by which his head is fastened to the wooden man. Now he kicks with one foot and with the other, both of which likewise get fastened. Rendered desperate, he strikes with his belly, his elbows, and his knees, and behold Anansie so fastened that he can neither turn nor wriggle.

The day is breaking, and Anansie is offering fabulous wealth for his release, but in vain, not a word in answer does he get.

By-and-by the sound of horns and of the baying of dogs is heard, and he knows that the king with his gardener and his assistants and the huntsmen are approaching.

Terrified nearly to death already, another terror has now seized poor Anansie; for he sees Tiger (whose ire he has incurred by innumerable tricks played on him) approaching.

As Tiger approaches, he hears Anansie, as unconscious of Tiger's presence, and as in a great rage, saying—"I shall rather die than suffer my affections to be forced in such a manner!"

"What is it that you say, Bru Anansie?" questions Tiger, who is greatly perplexed between his desire to avail himself of the tempting opportunity to eat up Anansie, and his curiosity to know the meaning of Anansie's strange imprisonment and words. Anansie then tells him that because he refused the offer of the king to take his daughter the princess in marriage, with a marriage gift of a hundred oxen, he was placed there to compel his consent. "Hark!" said he, "do you hear them coming? But I shall rather remain here fastened all day, and exposed to the sun's heat, than marry contrary to my inclinations."

"Would the king accept me for a son-in-law?" asked Tiger.

"Accept! yes," said Anansie, "he will accept anybody, so anxious is he to get off his daughter."

Tiger quickly released Anansie, and would then have eaten him up; but finding that the pitch alone could not keep him to the block, and knowing that Anansie was an old hand at rope-tying, he spared him. "A hundred oxen did you say? Why that will feed me and my family for a year. Tie me tightly, Bru Anansie—I will marry the princess."

Anansie had time just to tie Tiger so firmly that he could by no means escape, and then nimbly clamber up a tree, when the king and his followers came up.

Tiger not quite liking the situation, and fearing the dogs, cried out quickly—"Release me, king: I am ready to marry your daughter."

"Marry my daughter! you impudent knave," said the king. "Do you pretend to be mad after robbing my garden?"

And amidst the unavailing roars of Tiger that he was ready to marry the princess and take the hundred oxen, the king set his dogs at him, who worried him until, by his constant wriggling, he displanted the block, and got away with it into the bush, vowing vengeance against Anansie, who all the while was in the tree heartily enjoying the scene.

Moral. Mind your own business; go straight on your own road; don't believe all you hear.

4

Religion and Magic: Beliefs and Practices

European observers of Afro-American life were supremely aware of magical and religious practices. Mention of *obeah* and *myal*, for example, is made by nearly every observer of West Indian life at one time or another. Included in this section are extended discussions, often case studies taken from court records or similar reportage. Some of this almost obsessive concern is of course rooted in points of contrast and conflict between European and African practices, but there are also points of overlap, points where European folk magic coincided with that of the Africans. (Oral evidence continues to insist that slave obeah specialists often served the slaveholders themselves.) But the social consequences of these beliefs were also matters for practical concern. Obeah practitioners often became figures of leadership on plantations and joined an uncomfortable configuration of slaveowner, overseers, and slave preachers. There was also general fear of the possibility of obeah workers inciting and leading slave rebellions, and indeed this was the case in many instances, certainly in more than we will ever know for certain. In Jamaica, for example, the "Tacky Rebellion" of 1760 was said to be obeah inspired. And among maroons, obeah workers provided enduring leadership—Jack Mansong ("Three-Finger Jack"), as an instance. (Although historians downplay the fact, slave rebellions in the United States were also often led or aided by obeah workers or other religious leaders.)

Unfortunately, these writings on religion and magic are spotty, confused, and inconsistent. The amount of detail on the paraphernalia of practices is staggering, but surprisingly, few of these observers tried to discover the system of correspondences lying behind the objects and their uses. Obeah, for example, was (and remains today) the catchall term for all forms of magic and sorcery. Under this heading fall dream interpreters, grave-dirt collectors, makers of love potions, specialists in herbal medicine, and poisoners. Or it is used simply to refer to belief in spirits—*duppies, shadows*, and the like—or the supernatural. Throughout the accounts there is additionally a confusion with *myal*, but *myalism* (a still poorly described and understood Jamaican religion derived in part from Ashanti practices and beliefs) is itself opposed to obeah and has always promised defense against obeah practices.

Criticism of these early accounts should be tempered by the fact that with rare exceptions (such as Jane Beck's recent book, *To Windward of the Land: The Occult World of Alexander Charles* [Bloomington: Indiana University Press, 1979]), we still lack adequate descriptions and analyses of these phenomena. On obeah, again, we do know that it is still a general term for a wide variety of individuals and their practices: curing the ill, helping in financial and love matters, identifying criminals to their victims, injuring others in the name of their clients, and protecting their clients from being injured by others; we know that these practices are assembled from a variety of African, European, and Amerindian traditions (from African supernatural beliefs, Christian symbolism, Amerindian herbal knowledge, in addition to the numerology and dream interpretation publications of the De Laurance Company of Chicago such as *The Sixth and Seventh Books of Moses* [1919]); and we have come to understand that obeah is divided into "science" or "book-magic" on one hand, and "medicine" or "bush-medicine" (the knowledge of herbal and animal remedies for human illnesses) on the other. But, overall, understanding of such practices remains as schematic and distant as in these early accounts.

To make any sense at all of West Indian religious beliefs and practices we have to look at every scrap of writing which relates to the supernatural. The lines drawn among magic, superstition, religion, funeral practices, and obeah belong more to European cosmology than they do to Afro-West Indian. Thus it is under the heading of "superstition" that we can find bits of magic, religious practices, as well as lists of spirits—of the water, the woods, and the graveyard—and lists of what Europeans call "superstitions," formulaic-type proscriptions and prescriptions of all sorts.

In this section we have grouped together materials in the supernatural domain into the three categories of beliefs and superstitions, funerals, and obeah. These are the areas of primary focus in the observations. But they are also in part a response to the areas of cultural focus among slaves, and as such these categories represent something of a presentation of real cultural concerns. Given the continuing paucity of writings on these subjects, they remain critical and provide a basis for a much needed reassessment of Afro-American systems of religious belief and practice. Nowhere does the lack of documentation seem so imposing, for recent studies of black life remind one of the continuing central place of religion and the church and bespeak the continuity of culturally distinctive ways of conceiving of the relationship between man and God, the community and the Holy Spirit or Soul.

RELIGIOUS BELIEFS
AND
SUPERSTITIONS

CHARLES LESLIE, *A New and Exact Account of Jamaica*, 3d ed. (Edinburgh, 1740), 323–24.

Their Notions of Religion are very inconfident, and vary according to the different Countries they come from: But they have a Kind of occasional Conformity, and join without Distinction in their solemn Sacrifices and Gamboles. They generally believe there are Two Gods, a good and a bad One; the First they call *Naskew* in the *Papaw* Language, and the other *Timnew:* The good God, they tell you, lives in the Clouds, is very kind and favours Men; 'twas he that taught their Fathers to till the Ground, and to hunt for their Subsistence. The evil God sends Storms, Earthquakes, and all Kind of Mischief. They love the one dearly, and fear the other as much. Their Notions are extremely dark; they have no Idea of Heaven, further than the Pleasures of returning to their native Country, where they believe every Negro goes after Death: This Thought is so agreeable that it cheers the poor Creatures, and makes the Burden of Life easy, which otherways would be quite intolerable. They look on Death as a Blessing: 'Tis indeed surprising to see with what Courage and Intrepidity some of them will meet their Fate, and be merry in their last Moments; they are quite transported to think their Slavery is near an End, and that they shall revisit their happy Native Shores, and see their old Friends and Acquaintance. When a Negroe is near about to expire, his Fellow-Slaves kiss him, wish him a good Journey, and send their hearty Recommendations to their Relations in *Guiney*. They make no Lamentations, but with a great deal of Joy inter his Body, firmly believing he is gone home and happy.

When any Thing about a Plantation is missing, they have a solemn Kind of Oath which the oldest Negroe always administers, and which by them is accounted so sacred, that except they have the express Command of their Master or Overseer, they never set about it, and then they go very solemnly to Work. They range themselves in that Spot of Ground which is appropriate for the Negroe's Burying place, and one of them opens a Grave. He who acts the Priest takes a little of the Earth, and puts into every one of their Mouths; they tell, that if any has been guilty, their Belly swells and occasions their Death. I never saw an Instance of this but one; and it was certainly Fact that a Boy did swell, and acknowledged the Theft when he was dying: But I am far from thinking there was any Connection betwixt the Cause and the Effect; for a Thousand Accidents might have occasioned it, without having Recourse to that foolish Ceremony.

J. G. STEDMAN, *Narrative of a Five Years' Expedition against the Revolted Negroes of Surinam* (Amherst: University of Massachusetts Press, 1971 [1796]), 364–66.

No people can be more superstitious than the generality of negroes; and their *Locomen,* or pretended prophets, find their interest in encouraging this superstition, by selling them *obias* or amulets, as I have already mentioned, and as some hypocrites sell absolution in Europe, for a comfortable living. These people have also amongst them a kind of *Sibyls,* who deal in oracles; these sage matrons dancing and whirling round in the middle of an assembly, with amazing rapidity, until they foam at the mouth, and drop down as convulsed. Whatever the prophetess orders to be done during this paroxysm, is most sacredly performed by the surrounding multitude; which renders these meetings extremely dangerous, as she frequently enjoins them to murder their masters, or desert to the woods; upon which account this scene of excessive fanaticism is forbidden by law in the colony of Surinam, upon pain of the most rigorous punishment: yet it is often practised in private places, and is very common amongst the Owca and Seramica negroes, where captains Fredericy and Van Geurick told me they had seen it performed. It is here called the *winty-play,* or the dance of the mermaid, and has existed from time immemorial; as even the classic authors make frequent mention of this extraordinary practice. *Virgil,* in his sixth book, makes Eneas visit the Sibyl of Cuma; and *Ovid* also mentions the same subject, lib. 14, where Eneas wishes to visit the ghost of his father.

But what is still more strange, these unaccountable women by their voice know how to charm the *ammodytes*,* or *papaw* serpent, down from the tree. This is an absolute fact; nor is this snake ever killed or hurt by the negroes, who, on the contrary, esteem it as their friend and guardian, and are happy to see it enter their huts. When these sibyls have charmed or conjured down the ammodytes serpent from the tree, it is common to see this reptile twine and writhe about their arms, neck and breast, as if the creature took delight in hearing her voice, while the woman strokes and caresses it with her hand. The sacred writers speak of the charming of adders and serpents in many places, which I mentioned only to prove the antiquity of the practice;† for nothing is more notorious, than that the Eastern Indians will rid the houses of the most venomous snakes by charming them with the sound of a flute, which calls them out of their holes. And it is not many years since an Italian woman brought over three tame snakes, which crawled about her neck and arms: they were four or five feet long, but not venomous.

Another instance of superstition amongst the negroes I must relate; there is a direct prohibition in every family, handed down from father to son, against the eating of some kind of animal food, which they call *treff*; this may be either fowl, fish, or quadruped, but whatever it is, no negro will touch it; though I have seen some good Catholics eat roast-beef in Lent, and a religious Jew devouring a slice from a fat flitch of bacon.

However ridiculous some of the above rites may appear, yet amongst the African blacks they are certainly necessary, to keep the rabble in subjection; and their *gadomen* or priests know this as well as the infallible Pontiff of the Roman church. These illiterate mortals differ, however, in this respect from the modern Europeans, that whatever they believe, they do it firmly, and are never staggered by the doubts of scepticism, nor troubled with the qualms of conscience; but whether they are, upon this account, better or worse, I will not pretend to determine.—I however think that they are a happy people, and possess so much friendship for one another, that they need not be

---

*This creature is from three to five feet long, and perfectly harmless; it has not the least apprehension of being hurt *even* by man, while the unparalleled brilliancy of its colours may be another inducement for the adoration of the negroes.

†See the 58th Psalm, ver. 4, and 5: "They are like the deaf adder, that stoppeth her ear; which will not hearken to the voice of charmers, charming never so wisely."—Jerem. chap. viii. ver. 17,—and the Book of Ecclesiastes, chap. x. ver. 11, &c.

told to "love their neighbour as themselves"; since the poorest negro, having only an egg, scorns to eat it alone; but were a dozen present, and every one a stranger, would cut or break it into just as many shares; or were there one single dram of rum, he would divide it among the same number: this is not done, however, until a few drops are first sprinkled on the ground, as an oblation to the gods.—Approach then here, thou canting hypocrite, and take an example from thy illiterate sable brother!—From what I sometimes throw out, however, let it not be understood that I am an enemy to religious worship—God forbid!

MATTHEW GREGORY LEWIS, *Journal of a West India Proprietor* (London, 1834), 98–100.

Last Saturday a negro was brought into the hospital, having fallen into epileptic fits, with which till then he had never been troubled. As the faintings had seized him at the slaughter-house, and the fellow was an African, it was at first supposed by his companions, that the sight and smell of the meat had affected him; for many of the Africans cannot endure animal food of any kind, and most of the Ebres in particular are made ill by eating turtle, even although they can use any other food without injury. However, upon enquiry among his shipmates, it appeared that he had frequently eaten beef without the slightest inconvenience. For my own part, the symptoms of his complaint were such as to make me suspect him of having tasted something poisonous, especially as, just before his first fit, he had been observed in the small grove of mangoes near the house; but I was assured by the negroes, one and all, that nothing could possibly have induced him to eat an herb or fruit from that grove, as it had been used as a burying-ground for "the white people." But although my idea of the poison was scouted, still the mention of the burying-ground suggested another cause for his illness to the negroes, and they had no sort of doubt, that in passing through the burying-ground he had been struck down by the duppy of a white person not long deceased, whom he had formerly offended, and that these repeated fainting-fits were the consequence of that ghostly blow. The negroes have in various publications been accused of a total want of religion, but this appears to me quite incompatible with the ideas of spirits existing after dissolution of the body, which necessarily implies a belief in a future state; and although (as far as I can make out) they have no outward forms of religion, the most devout Christian cannot have "God bless you" oftener on his lips than the negro; nor, on the other hand, appear to feel the wish for their enemy's damnation more sincerely when he utters it.

RICHARD WATSON, *A Defense of the Wesleyan Methodist Missions in the West Indies* (London, 1817), 17.

The whole of their theology, if I may so call it, consists in a confused notion of *"somebody at top."* But their notions of him have not the least tendency to restrain their vicious propensities. The following conversations which I had with some of them will inform you respecting their superstitions. The first occurred in Barbadoes, in 1804. Early one morning I was going through the heathen (unbaptized) burying ground, my attention was arrested by an old female slave, sitting upon a grave, eating out of a calabash. I approached her and said, *What are you doing? Massa, me feed dead. Who is buried here? Me sissa,* (sister, a name used in common for all females.) *Can the dead eat? Yes, Sir. But are you not eating, not the dead? Yes, Massa, but dead eat too.*

The negroes may be ·divided into two classes, such as are employed as house servants, and such as are engaged in the work of the estates: the former had a little knowledge, from their intercourse with white people. The state of the field negroes was deplorable indeed. I will not say that they had no idea of the being of a God, or of the immortality of the soul, but the traces of these doctrines were so faint, as to have little or no effect upon their moral conduct. They believed in the existence of spirits, which they called *Jumbees,* and sometimes spread victuals on the graves of those who were recently dead, that their spirits might return and eat. I have often seen the graves made up with lime and stone in the form of a coffin, and a small earthen cup placed on the breast, for the purpose of containing meat or drink. They were so exceedingly degraded, debased, and vicious, that many doubted whether they had immortal souls; and I myself have thought, that some of them differed very little from the cattle of the field, except in the possibility of being raised from the ruins of their fall.

H. T. DE LA BECHE, *Notes on the Present Conditions of the Negroes in Jamaica* (London, 1825), 30–31.

Some negroes entertain ideas of the transmigration of the soul; an old woman on my estate, whom the Wesleyan Missionary (the Rev. I.

Crofts), was instructing previous to baptism, stated her belief that people when they died turned into dust like brick-dust; that those who
had behaved ill during their lives became mules, horses, flies, &c.;
but that those who had led a good life were born again, and occupied
similar situations to those they had previously filled; that blacks
would be blacks again, and whites whites.

A belief in ghosts is rather common among the people: a fatal
instance of the power of this impression occurred upon my estate
while I was there. A negro woman, named Julina Brown, who was
slightly affected with a liver complaint, surprised us much, by refus-
ing almost all food for about six weeks: we at first thought she la-
boured under the influence of Obeah; it however turned out that she
fancied her mother's ghost had appeared to her, and warned her of
her death, and that whenever she attempted to take any nourishment,
the spirit washed its hands in the broth, gruel, or whatever else it
might be;—her expression was, that her mother had "put her hand
upon her." To prevent the ghost from doing her any bodily mischief,
she had tied her caul round her neck in a piece of blue stuff; this the
negroes fancy has that effect. She died of exhaustion: her death would
not, I am inclined to think, have taken place, had we sooner known
the cause of her refusal to eat; for it was only after repeated questions
from the Missionary, that she informed us of it; she appeared at last to
be convinced of her error, though not in sufficient time to prevent the
effects of her abstinence.

B. J. VERNON, *Early Recollections of Jamaica* . . . (London, 1848),
14–16.

Returning home one night at a late hour, on foot, through the high
woods, accompanied by a young slave, we had great difficulty in
keeping the track; and often losing it for several minutes, it became a
question whether we had not better select a spot to rest in, and patiently wait the return of day. The unpleasant nature of the accommodation, rife with snakes, lizards, scorpions and centipedes, (not to
mention enormous rats) induced me to persevere and as often as we
regained the lost path, hope revived and we pressed forward. At last
a glimmering light appeared every now and then through the bushes.
On asking my companion what he thought it could be, he replied it
must be a runaway's fire, and advised me strongly not to approach it
any nearer. Being determined to discover what it was, and having a
good sharp cutlass in my hand, I cautiously advanced, holding the boy

firmly by his smock frock, lest fear should lead him to desert. He trembled from head to foot, and it was difficult to prevail on him to move: by dint of whispered threats, however, he was made to proceed. When we had arrived within a few yards of the object, nothing could induce the Negro to advance another step. His teeth chattered, and his whole frame shook. I was therefore obliged to make a closer inspection alone. It was manifest that no danger was to be apprehended, although I could not understand the nature of the strange appearance.

It seemed to be a mass of phosphorescent light, about two feet high, the same in breadth, and eight feet long; emitting such a glare as to illuminate objects around for many yards. I approached closer, and stuck the point of my cutlass into it with considerable force. It trembled and sent forth a hollow sound. The frightened boy declared it must be a "Duppy," (Evil Spirit) nor could I persuade him until I had broken off a large piece, that it was nothing more than a rotten fragment of a decayed tree. The piece I had broken off served admirably for a torch to guide our way. On reaching home I frightened some relatives who were in bed, by rushing with the seeming fire brand, close up to the gauze mosquito curtains.

MRS. HENRY LYNCH, *The Wonders of the West Indies* (London, 1856), 168–70.

Duppies are ghosts, whose appearance augers always some approaching evil. These shadowy personages, according to the belief of the negro, have taken possession of some of the old Spanish houses in Jamaica. A favourite resort of their's, is Salt Ponds near Spanish Town. We were there for some weeks, and could not prevail on a single servant to remain with us. In the time of the Buccanneers, the Banditti Chiefs held their revels there; concealed their stores of gold, indulged in their lawless entertainments, where cruelty and brutality formed a part of enjoyment; imprisoned their innocent captives in the dungeons below, and stained the dark places of the old dwelling with blood. The rats now hold carnivals there; and rushing noisily about on their predatorial excursions, convince the credulous blackies, that the ghosts of those who were slaughtered, are restlessly hurrying to and fro in search of revenge. The sad influence of slavery, whilst it extinguished many a noble feeling, could not crush the fanciful part of the negro's nature, and in his belief of omens, tokens, and warnings, he perhaps exceeds the poor of our own land.

If an owl flap its wings heavily, evil of a serious nature is approaching. If the wind have a wail in its tone which, strange to say, is not often the case in those tropical regions, it is considered the herald of evil tidings. If bats cross each other diagonally in the crimson stream of sunset, some powerful friend will shortly be at variance with you; and if you set a duppy at defiance, going towards it in the endeavour to prove that the supernatural appearance is caused by some undulation of light, or by the shadow flickering on the curtain-fold; illness of a dangerous or, perhaps, fatal nature, is likely to be the sure consequence.

Two large white screech-owls had built their nests in some guinea-trees, not far from this haunted place, and although these birds of evil omen generally contrived to remain invisible during the day, they became very apparent in the silvery moonlight. It seemed, truly, they were lords of the woods at that time; their piercing shrieks were melancholy and startling, and the flapping of their wings, unusually loud and distinct, was heard in the stillness of the night.

> "In the hollow tree, or the old grey tower,
>   The spectral owl doth dwell;
> Dull, hated, despised in the sunshine hour,
>   But at dusk he's abroad and well!
> Not a bird of the forest e'er mates with him;
>   All mock him outright by day:
> But at night, when the woods grow still and dim,
>   The boldest will shrink away!
> Mourn not for the owl, nor his gloomy plight,
>   The owl hath its share of good;
> If a prisoner he is in the broad day light,
>   He is the lord of the dark green wood.
> Nor lonely the bird, nor his ghastly mate.
>   They are each unto each a pride;
> Thrice fonder, perhaps, since a strange dark fate
>   Hath rent them from all beside."

REV. CHARLES DANCE, *Chapters from a Guianese Log-Book* (Demerara, 1881), 78–84.

Obeahism has already obtained so vile a notoriety that it is unnecessary to explain it here.

The belief in the "Water Mama," or "Mermaid," a being of supernatural power, is common to all people of a certain stage of mental development who live in the neighbourhood of the sea, lakes, or large rivers. But the formation of a society founded on a belief of its existence and superhuman intelligence, and for the purpose of its glorification by an obscene worship, is peculiar, as far as I know, to Africans and their descendants. On the coast of British Guiana the offspring of the old African slaves still continue in its worship, although it must be admitted that it is fast disappearing under the potent influence of Christian civilization; and yet it must be confessed, at the expense of some degree of shame, that several of the present members of the Water Mamma Society have a tolerable knowledge of the Holy Scriptures, and can read and write.

Endeavours have been made to trace the Water Spirit to the manatee (seacow, cuimure or quemoa); and although it very probably is the origin of the existence of the mythic creature in these waters, yet every one of the Indians and creoles, with whom I have spoken on the subject, denies that the two are identical. Whether it be a very degraded corruption, indeed, of "the wise old man of the sea," the Ægean Nereus who had the power of prophesying the future and of appearing to mortals in different shapes; or of one of the nymphs of the sea and of the fresh water, may not be an unreasonable conjecture.

The attachment of the Water Spirit to human beings is mostly sexual, and if there be not more than one of these mysterious creatures, it must be of an hermaphrodital nature. But there is abundant willing testimony to the fact that they are many—if not numerous—and of both sexes.

In the lower part of the rivers and on the coasts the Water Spirit attaches itself mostly to men, and strange to say, evinces a peculiar *penchant* for married men.

A young married man is absent for a week or more from his young wife, whom he persuades to believe that he has received a mysterious mandate to go somewhere, which, on pain of death to him, her, and their child or children, he may not neglect: when the husband returns after his absence, he talks to his wife of heaps of money, for the Water Spirit is liberal with silver; but the wife sees none of it. The man's absence then becomes long and frequent. The young wife must bear her wrongs and her grief in silence, lest evil come on her and her husband and their little ones. She is henceforth a wife in nothing but in name.

A portion of the mystery of the Minje Mamma, Water Spirit, or Mermaid is cleared when we get to the knowledge of the society organized by its votaries. Men and women are admitted as members; and at their gatherings sensual dances excite the imagination until the dancers fall on the ground in ecstatic convulsions; and profligacy of the most atrocious kind seems to be their bond of union.

Of the minor superstitions of the coast there are—

1. *Rolling Calves.*—These are the furious spirits of bad men who died unpardoned. They appear in form of calves dragging long chains at night through the streets and in the yards of houses, making hideous noises, and with eyes of fire. They are supernatural police to restrain people within doors during the unseasonable hours, and in this light they discourage housebreaking, robbery, and midnight debauchery.

"Why not call them roaring calves?" I said to a person who was speaking of them; "calves roar rather than roll."

"There is nothing to prevent a calf from rolling on the ground," was his reply; "and these calves are said to roll over and over while they utter dreadful noises."

2. *Long Bubbies* are the ghosts of certain dead women. These appear with the right breast elongated or lengthened at pleasure, with which they threaten certain night walkers and flog others. They are scavengers of the night, terrifying or chastising according to the requirement of the case.

3. *The Cabresses.*—These are the spirits of courtesans, who visit dancing houses and other places of public resort,—seem to enjoy the amusements, join in them, attach themselves to some reckless lovers of pleasure, and luring them to some desolate spot, break their necks or press them to death in the moments of dalliance.

4. *Then the Warning Spirits of Dead Relatives.*—These sometimes intimate the death of those to whom they appear, or warn them against evil committed or permitted by them.

An instance is told of a young man who, after the death of his mother, forsaking the advantages of his early careful Christian training, had fallen into dissolute habits. One night, on going homewards, partly drunk, he made an assignation on the street with a woman who accompanying him to the door of his dwelling, appeared suddenly transformed to the likeness of his dead mother. She then reproved his vicious habits, and warned him that it would be ill with him if he did not amend at once. The apparition had some deterring effect for a time; but assuming that it was only a trick of his imagination fired with intoxicating drink, he shortly resumed his evil ways. Another night while tipsy he followed a woman, who, when he asked her where she lived, answered that she would show him her home. They walked on and talked until they arrived at the gates of the burial

ground which contained the remains of the young man's mother. Here
the woman changed from the appearance of the young vivacious cour-
tesan of the streets, and his mother stood before him in her grave-
clothing. She mourned over him, and then said, "You asked to go
home with me: thus far I have brought you; but you will very soon,
too soon, alas! be carried through these gates to the home you are
recklessly seeking." So saying she flew over the gates of the burial
ground, and was lost to sight. It was with deep remorse and a determination to amend the habits which his follies had made injurious to
him in every way, that the young man went home that night. He not
only sorrowed for the grief he was causing his mother in her grave,
but was seriously anxious respecting his impaired health, and the
threat held out by his mother's spirit to his persistence in evil. But
who does not know that habit is second nature, and that an evil once
allowed is stamped, as it were, on plastic clay, every additional indulgence hardening the stamped impression to the consistency of
iron; and "if one hear not Moses and the Prophets, neither will he be
persuaded though one rose from the dead" to warn him? The young
man's pent-up passions broke through the feeble attempt at restraint,
and he was once more, but with the aggravation of desperation, a confirmed drunken street-walker. At last, one night, at the steps of his
own door, an apparition so frightful presented itself to him, that his
emaciated frame of body and mind could not bear it: he burst open
his door and fell down in a fit. The next evening sorrowing friends
followed his dead body, borne through the gates over which he had
seen his mother's ghost pass.

5. *Witches.*—The coast people are also not without their firm
faith in Witches, or Old Hags, whose greatest claim to the appellation
is their old age. These old women, by the recitation of some absurd
lines, are said to be empowered to take off their skin, which they fold
up and hide in a convenient place. They then anoint their skinless
bodies, and assume superhuman powers. They fly through the air;
they enter closed rooms, and suck the life-blood of infants. During the
time that they remain without their skin, a lurid halo surrounds them.
If the wrapped-up and hidden skin can be found and pickled while
the owner of it is skimming the air high overhead, or, like a vampire
bat, gorging and disgorging infant blood, it ceases to be of use when
the hag attempts to replace it, for it burns the skinless body; and the
charm being only for one aerial trip each night, the old wretch is
bound to be discovered in the morning. Another mode of detecting an

old hag is to throw down before her skin an odd number of grains of Indian corn, which she is bound to pick up and reckon before she can put on her skin; but as she can pick them up only in pairs, two grains at a time, the last odd one troubles her, and so she has to throw them down again and reckon each time to make them an even number, and thus she must continue until daylight discovers her to the enraged community.

It is inconvenient to the old women of a village when a child becomes suddenly ill; for the mother, in such case, unhesitatingly attributes its illness to the influence of witchcraft, and the oldest neighbour is *prima facie* adjudged to be the offender. She must then be flogged with calabash switches (for none other can she feel) until she restores the child's health, or is rescued from her merciless tormentors. I once saw an old woman in this trouble. In vain did she deny her guilt. The child was thrust into her arms, and she was told to "cure it—or take the consequences." Sagaciously attributing the child's illness to neglect and starvation, she, by careful nursing and feeding it with rice, restored it to health and strength.

The staunch defender of the old women of a certain village was the missionary residing there. The dames who, on the report of a child made ill by blood-sucking, were fortunate enough to hobble to his house were safe, for the time, from the approaching *witch hunt;* for the whole sisterhood came in, at such times, for a share of the abuse and mud pelting.

The reverend gentleman was eccentric in some matters, but he was a faithful minister of the Gospel—dreaded by the evil-doers of the village, and respected and beloved by those who were trying to be good. But he would sometimes digress during the sermon, which was frequently embellished with personalities, to answer the retort of an offended party. Sometimes a deacon was remiss in his duties, and he would get his share of reproof before the whole congregation. Once while the minister was engaged in the Sunday morning's service, a man—who was then making his first appearance in chapel a few days after a penal servitude for the theft of sugar from an estate—dressed in the most extravagant style of village fashion, his woolly hair parted in the middle, brass chains with seals crossing and recrossing his waistcoat, and his stiff fingers expanding a pair of white cotton gloves—came noisily stepping up on the. wooden floor, and diverting the attention of the congregation. The missionary, angry at this interruption, directed the attention of the people to the priggish thief—

"Who wishes to see the latest Massaruni fashion-dandyism from the Penal Settlement blooming in the midst of us plain village people? Look round and see our friend Tommy Coll!"

On another occasion the minister saw a man in chapel who was paying off his "head-tax" by reporting to the commissary the villagers who had neglected to register their names. He was not forgotten. After the service the man accosted the preacher to know if the remarks were intended for him. "Does the cap fit? Wear it. Does the shoe pinch? Get rid of it," was his only reply.

He practiced homeopathy, and took delight in the study and application of herbal medicines, so much so, and with such success, that the doctor appointed to visit the village had little practice. His attention to the sick, whether of his own flock, of the Church of England, or of no church whatever, was unremitting. Often when the village—from bad drainage—was flooded, he was seen with naked feet wading knee deep in mud and water, visiting the sick. He was the only medical attendant in the time of the cholera.

I was present with him at a deathbed scene. As *doctor* Henderson he had attended aunty 'Vina; and as *parson* Henderson had directed her faith, (she was a good churchwoman; and as there was no resident clergyman there at the time, the rector of the parish had tacitly acknowledged Mr. Henderson as curate). And now that the spirit of the aged woman was about to take its flight,—he, as friend, brother, father Henderson, poured out pathetic prayers in heart-stirring accents for her safe entrance into bliss, and for the good conduct of her several children. And when the old woman called up her children and grandchildren, and gave them her last advice and blessing, the hard features of the Scotchman softened, and his eyes sympathised in teardrops with the sorrows of aunty 'Vina's children. I heard afterwards that the "aunty," who had been an excellent nurse, had frequently been a co-village labourer with the missionary at the bedside of the sick.

6. The *Adopi*.—The superstition of the *adopi* is, that they are a kind of little men with extraordinary physical strength, and are superhuman, or at least not altogether human. They are the black men of the woods, and seem to take, in the tropics, the place of the "green men" or fairies of the north. They do not possess the advantage of thumbs; and to propitiate them when met in the bush, one must not expose his thumbs to their view, or their first object of assault will be to break them off.

We must conclude with another feature of the superstitions of the creole population of the coast, viz., that known as—

7. *Kenna.*—This is the belief that certain meats are, more or less, unwholesome; that the human blood is affected by the kinds of meats consumed; that the blood of each family differs from that of another, and that each family has a predisposition to certain diseases which may be developed or suppressed by the use of or abstinence from such meats; and that the meats good for one family may be blood poison to another. The observers therefore of *kenna* scrupulously abstain from that which they have heard to be the kenna of their family,—the forbidden meats unused by their ancestors. To some families fowl is forbidden, or tortoise, or certain kinds of fish; to others fresh pork, venison, or goat mutton and goat milk. Scrofulous and leprous cases are frequently attributed to a breach of the rule of kenna. This law, originating in Africa, is of a piece with the Mosaic and Mohammedan prohibitions, and is founded on the unsuitableness of much meat in tropical countries.

REV. H. V. P. BRONKHURST, *The Colony of British Guyana and its Labouring Population* (London, 1883), 380–86.

9. Speaking of superstitions, I may say that the following handed down by tradition, are fervently believed in many parts of America, and in the Colony of British Guyana.

> White specks on the nails are luck.
> Whoever reads epitaphs loses his memory.
> To rock the cradle when empty is injurious to the child.
> To eat while a bell is tolling for a funeral causes a toothache.
> The crowing of a hen indicates some approaching disaster.
> When a mouse gnaws a hole some misfortune may be apprehended.
> He who has his teeth wide asunder must seek his fortune in a distant land.
> Whoever finds a four-leaf trefoil shamrock should wear it for good luck.
> Beggar's bread should be given to children who are slow learning to speak.
> If a child less than twelve months old be brought into a cellar, he becomes fretful.
> When children play soldiers on the roadside, it forebodes the approach of war.

A child grows proud if suffered to look into the mirror when twelve months old.

He who proposes moving into a new house must first send in bread and a new broom.

Whoever sneezes at an early hour either hears some news or receives some present the same day.

The first tooth cast by a child should be be swallowed by the mother to insure a new growth of teeth.

Buttoning the coat awry, or drawing on a stocking inside out, causes matters to go wrong during the day.

By bending the head to the hollow of the arm the initial letter of one's future spouse is represented.

Women who sow flax seed should, during the process, tell some confounded lies, otherwise the yarn will never bleach white.

When women are stuffing beds, the men should not remain in the house, otherwise the feathers will come through the tick.

When a person enters a room, he should be obliged to sit down, if only for a moment, as he otherwise takes away the children's sleep with him.

Among the Creoles I observe that until the ceremony of baptism is performed on an infant, a Bible is always placed under its pillow. A horse shoe is nailed on the door to secure the inmates from the attack of hogs or witches. On the death of a relation the children are crossed over the coffin before it is taken from the house to the burial; should any one sneeze at the time of this performance, it indicates the death of another near relation. Among the Coolies the cat passing across the road is a bad omen, the business begun is obstructed. The chirping of a lizard from the south of any person is a favourable omen. The flight of a heron, from right to left, across the path of a person first setting out on a journey, is inauspicious. If at the time of a person getting married the dog growls or barks, or a cat rushes in, it is a sure sign of the marriage being an unhappy one.

REV. J. SCOLES, *Sketches of African and Indian Life in British Guiana* (Demerara, 1885), 59–65.

Some of the foolish customs out here must have come originally from England or perhaps it may be *vice versa*. For instance, you will in your walks out here as frequently come across the ugly rusty horse shoe, tightly nailed against the door or out-buildings of the poorer sort of people as in England, Wales, or Scotland, where the iron shoe is supposed to bring good luck; while out here it is accounted a sover-

eign remedy against the attack of hogs, and moreover has the power
of keeping off the evil machination of witchcraft or witches.

The poor African people, like the poor uneducated class of other
nations, are full of vain fears and foolish fancies; and in proportion to
their ignorance, so are they naturally superstitiously inclined.

They have a great dread of graveyards during the night, and fear
much after dusk being near old tombs, or ancient tombstones, scattered as these are on all sides, in the house garden or in the adjoining
paddock, on the roadside or in the plantation; for in days gone by,
men buried their dead friends just where they bury their dead horses
now—that is, just where they liked—whether among their roses or
among the thorns, at the foot of a mango tree or the head of a walk, or
in the midst of the tall para grass hard by.

Again, African people, big and little, are as frightened about
ghosts, spirits, hobgoblins, and all that very interesting class of invisible beings, as country servant girls or foolish nursery maids at home.
And now that we have got so far, it is high time to introduce our readers to the renowned or far-famed ghost of our colony, and hand up his
card with JUMBI written on it.

Now Jumbi be it known is a great power out here, and we may
almost add, a sort of public pet, for so many things have been given
or dedicated to him, and on so many things such as trees, flowers,
seeds, berries and birds his name like a trade mark or sign appears.

Although out here our thin card-board houses, with their
wooden walls not much thicker than our writing desks or dining tables! devoid too of all dark corners, chimney breasts, double-doors,
ancient hangings, and the like, and furthermore mostly of modern
build, would seem to be proof against all ghostly intrusion, still in
spite of all these jumbi disadvantages, we have some romance left on
our rich mud shores, for certain houses in Town and lonesome mansions in the Country are pointed *out,* and pointed *at,* as veritable
haunted houses; for:—

> "O'er all there hangs the shadow of a fear,
> A sense of mystery the spirit daunted,
> And said as plain as whisper in the ear,
> The place is *haunted.*"

Few, it may be, but *genuine* haunted houses we have! enjoying
all the special privileges, rights, titles, and immunities of haunted
dwellings! where mysterious sights are seen, blue lights, lurid and

ghastly forms, where strange sounds and unearthly noises are heard, where mosquito-curtains shake, and thin doors bang, and where the weaker sex grow pale and speechless for a time, and then, all nervous, beg of their fretful husbands in spite of his many rat-traps to quit at once the place and seek nocturnal peace and quietness somewhere else.

But Jumbi has other privileges besides the possession of houses. He is a favourite as said above, and has his garden dinners, and his wedding feasts in these tropical parts. And first a word about his dinner-parties. The poor ignorant people fearing at times that Jumbi is not well pleased with them for something done, or is annoyed at something neglected to be done, try to appease his ghostship by spreading out, now and again, upon the grassy ground, a repast of boiled rice and cooked fowl, most scrupulously avoiding the admixture of the slightest particle of salt,—children and children alone, are allowed to be guests at this sumptuous garden spread, and are told by their deluded parents that Jumbi-ghost is all the while in their very midst, silently and invisibly partaking of the savoury fowl and unsalted rice. . . .

Our Jumbi-ghost, besides his silent dinner-parties, has as mentioned above his wedding feasts, and these are of a noisy nature. There is a fine quick-growing tree in these parts known by the learned as the *Hura crepitans* and called by the unlearned the sandbox tree.* Now when its impatient seed vessels, being of the size and general form of a Spanish onion, but flattened and deeply furrowed— or perhaps better described, as more like to a large well-formed tomato—though of a hard and horny texture;—now when these seedvessels burst with a loud sharp explosive sound, sending their many seeds of waistcoat-button shape all rattling among the branches and rolling on the ground, then young Africa, or older Africa, if passing by that way and hearing the noisy sound, cries out, "Ah, ah, Jumbi wedding-day—Jumbi go married;" and Jumbi and his mysterious family have, be it remarked, many weddings during the season; and should your easy-chair, or hammock, be in close proximity to some prolific sand-box tree, and you are suddenly disturbed in your day dreams or

*Possibly, and we throw it as a mere suggestion, the sand-boxes of the *Hura crepitans* were used in former times to contain sand for blotting up purposes before the invention or introduction of blotting paper. Sand to this day is used in many places and in public offices on the continent for such purposes. The seed vessels of the sand-box tree, which do not burst asunder if picked and cured in time, are just the size, and shape, and construction for the suggested use.

nightly slumbers, you are not quite in the humour or at all inclined to impart a nuptial blessing on Jumbi ghost or his marriage feast.[†]

The sand-box tree has another curious name of its own; it is also called *Monkey dinner bell tree;* whether the noisy habit alluded to, arouses and calls the monkey to his dinner, in the shape of the many button-like seeds scattered on the ground, or whether the noise is only a general summons to Master Monkey to attend to his corporal wants is a question for the learned to decide. The flat nutty seeds however be it remarked, are a dangerous cathartic and have at times destroyed young children, who indulged in the too free eating thereof; moreover we are told these seeds are used by the wicked obeah-man in making up his deadly compounds to destroy the victims of his wickedness.

Leaving the sand-box Jumbi tree, we pass on to consider the eccentric habits of the silk-cotton tree *(Eriodendron anfractuosus)* and the strange African traditions and superstitions connected with it. This tree is of a stately growth and gigantic height, with far extending roots and flying buttress-like supports at base. It is said by some to bloom but once every three years, and pretty and elegant are its silken blossoms, whether triennial or not.

The tree however has strange untree-like habits or propensities of its own, for in spite of its immense size and outstretching roots and quasi buttress supports, at dead of night "when mortals in slumber are bound" it walks about, crosses and recrosses wide and deep rivers, but is always active and sharp enough to find its way back to its place, before the break of day, and moreover manages to escape detection in its nightly walks or nocturnal wanderings!—so say the common African people together with many of their somewhat fairer descendants. This tree also is sometimes known as Jumbi tree; often it is called the devil's tree. One thing is clear and that is, you must not "trouble that tree"; and another thing is more certain still, and that is the difficulty there exists in finding men who will dare cut down that tree or otherwise destroy it, be the labourers required for the work, black men, or men of a more coffee colour; for they all say, the executioner will not long survive the cutting of the tree.[‡] Hence while trees around have yielded to the axe, and become furniture wood or fire fuel, the

---

[†]By some, these explosive feasts are called Lizard Weddings.

[‡]The same superstition about this tree exists in some of the West Indian islands, Jamaica and St. Vincent among others. Had the silk cotton tree been a profitable wood, useful and fit for furniture, probably Europeans would have done away with the superstition long ago!

silk-cotton tree has been left proudly standing, a monument, it is true, to African fear and local superstition. It is at the foot of this strange tree that the obeah-man often makes up his detestable obeah-bags.

But 'tis time to finish with Jumbi and his trees,—to make no reflection on his cap! which by-the-bye is the lowly toad-stool of Cryptogamian class and fungus form, raised to a high dignity, and called *jumbi cap;* nor must we forget to look serious when we think or speak of Jumbi bird all neatly dressed in black, and blest with one white spot of perfect contrast.

The visits of this black bird are alarming and of course unwelcome, for when he flutters around inhabitable dwellings, it is sad omen that one among the living will quickly be numbered among the dead. Ravens elsewhere, and some say owls, are supposed to be birds of the same bad, or evil omen.

We may laugh or smile at African superstition here, and in other matters too, but if we do stoop down to pick up stones to cast at the poor Africans for their childish folly or superstitions, let us not be the first to throw them or fling them hard; for, are there not stout hearts among us at home or even here who possibly with a prayer book in the pocket, have a mortal dread of sitting down to dinner thirteen at a time,—who are miserably unhappy till some one of the thirteen sacrifices his meal, *pro bono publico,* and begs to retire, (ill of course!) or till the unlucky number has been changed to fourteen, by insisting upon the butler or some poor boy sitting down to do justice to the good things prepared?

EDEN PHILLPOTTS, *In Sugar-Cane Land* (London, 1894), 166–67.

Then arose a distant weird sound of wailing and ululation. It was, we learned, the screaming of mourners. They would sit round the dead woman's cottage all night and sing a dirge to keep away Jumbies.

A Jumby is an extremely sinister evil spirit with ghoulish tendencies. A deathbed is his particular weakness but as might be expected, he has no music in his wicked soul, and a negro chorus persisted in, arrests the progress of the most eager Jumby.

Superstition is deeply rooted in the black man's nature. The distant songsters will all go to church tomorrow and conduct themselves with entire propriety but Jumbies and Obi are still as much a part of Quashie's beliefs—as sacred and as real—as anything missionaries have taught him. Those well-meaning mourners afforded a happy example of the new order blending with the old. They were discouraging and harrassing the Jumbies with "Hymns Ancient and Modern."

Another Ethiopian monster, akin to the vampire or were-wolf, is the loup-garou. These have similar vile tendencies as the Jumbies. Loups-garou, however, are addicted to habits which render them assailable. They always take off their skins when at work, to be cooler no doubt, and they invariably hide these coverings at the root of a silk-cotton tree. If anybody finds a skin, he can put the loup-garou who owns it in an extremely awkward position because, if not returned, the owner catches a chill and grows faint and poorly from exposure, and ultimately fades away altogether.

BESSIE PULLEN-BURRY, *Jamaica As It Is, 1903* (London, 1903), 137–38.

There is no doubt that superstition, which always goes hand-in-hand with ignorance, is born and bred in the descendants of Ham. Nowhere, I learn, is this more the case than amongst the Jamaican negroes inhabiting the mountainous parts of the island. In the Blue Mountains, where wooded heights and musical murmuring streams suggest supernatural agencies, one finds weird ideas among their folklore. If you can persuade some native to talk about the "duppy," you may learn that that which is most feared is a rolling calf; you will be told how the sight of it foretells great misfortune, and those who have witnessed the awful phantom describe it as a huge animal with fire issuing from its nostrils, and clanking chains as it rolls down the mountain-side, burning everything in its path. Other apparitions of a cat as large as a goat, with eyes burning like vast lamps, are said to have been seen by the mountain dwellers at nightfall in the woods. Some of these story-tellers will eat a raw rat before relating the ghost stories, to give them, as they express it, a "sweet mout."

BESSIE PULLEN-BURRY, *Ethiopia in Exile: Jamaica Revisited* (London, 1905), 147, 150–53.

. . . . Were it not for such uplifting influences, for the continuous zeal of the teachers of religion, we should hear of a recrudescence of the spells of Obeah, with its senseless, demoralizing insignia—grave-dirt, cocks' feathers, wood shaped like a coffin, birds' feathers, snakes' teeth. To terrify the timid, to detect crime, but generally to obtain re-

venge, resort is even now occasionally had to Obeah. Myalism, apparently, is a name given to counter-witchcraft. Native supserstitions and
fears revolve round the deathbed, or ghost of the departed, which latter is locally known as the "duppy."

The principle of grieving for the departed as night advances is
soon lost sight of: at midnight, orgies of the lowest character, tinged
with the spirit of religious revivalism, are a perfect nuisance to the
community. The second ceremony, which is held nine days after the
first, is a repetition of the wake, rendering night hideous to the respectable community—drinking and immorality marking the proceedings.

It is, however, interesting from the standpoint of folklore, for it
embodies a vestige of pagan superstition to the effect that the ghost
roams over the earth until the ninth day, when it may be conciliated
before taking its departure for spiritual spheres. Some say weird and
terrible formulas are gone through and the "duppy" implored to go in
peace and not haunt the house and relatives. Formerly, so it is said,
the watchers tremblingly lifted the sheet from the dead face and
asked the phantom if it were still there, when they begged it to have
mercy and not appear to them.

Another custom used to be observed. When a death took place
in a family, every drop of water in the house at the time was thrown
away, for Death cools his dart in the water as he departs, and it would
be highly injurious to drink it. In the house of more enlightened folk,
mirrors and looking-glasses have been known to be turned to the wall
lest the spirit of the departed should be reflected in them. In some
families, immediately after the removal of a corpse a jar of water was
placed in the room, and a light kept burning for nine days—the idea
being that during this time the deceased would return to his room,
needing a light to guide his footsteps and water to quench his thirst.
From a Jamaican source I quote the following:—

"One of the superstitions of a more serious nature is the belief
that the devil sometimes comes for the soul of the departed who has
spent his life in this world as the wicked often do. I am not aware that
his Satanic Majesty is ever seen, but as he comes at night and is supposed to be black his invisibility may be accounted for. However, the
rattling of the chains which he brings for the souls of the deceased is
distinctly heard, and not by one or two persons, but by a whole neighbourhood; and the traces of his cloven feet along the sand of the street
in which the deceased resided are next morning clearly seen. I could
name a case in which it is believed by a great many persons, many of

them leaders in church, that these circumstances occurred; that the rattling of the chains was heard; that just previous to the departure of life a seeming internal struggle was observed to take place in the body of the deceased; that a whole neighbourhood was disturbed by the clanking noise of the chains, and that crowds of persons went, the succeeding morning, to view the marks of the devil's feet."

■   ■   ■

From another source I find that the negro connects the moon with agriculture, certain of her phases being favourable to the planting of crops.

All Fools' Day is thought best for sowing corn. The 15th of April is the favourable day for sowing peas. If a man points at a young pumpkin with his finger the negro declares it will drop off and be no good; in the same way it is most unlucky to inspect the soil when tobacco has been sown, before it has appeared above the surface. Nothing gives us a better insight into the characteristics of a people than a study of their folk-lore, and in Jamaica a number of letters bearing on native superstitions were collected a short time since for a competition.

Some are worth noting. West African students very probably could produce analogous ideas in comparing them with the tribal folk-lore of their former habitat, which would tend to explain their origin. The following superstitions are still believed by some in Jamaica.

If any one kills an annancy (spider) it makes him, or her, liable to break plates.

A person about to proffer a request putting the right foot first will meet with success, but if he put the left he will be disappointed.

If a man is at enmity against another and wishes to injure him, he catches his enemy's shadow in a bottle and corks it tightly. So long as the bottle is corked, so long has the possessor absolute mastery over the destiny of the person who is thus rendered incapable of hurting him. If the shadow should escape through the uncorking of the bottle, the only way to bring it back is to boil rice and put it at the bottom of the bottle. The effect of bottling a man's shadow is to make him stupid and imbecile. The Jamaica black bird—the John Crow—is regarded with great superstition.

A writer narrates that one day while passing through the market he saw a black bird fly across. Instantly a large number of ragged boys were pushed forward by their elders, who cried out: "Pickney oo' no see bad luck bird," a shrill chorus, "Kirry out! kirry out!" was repeated with "Pepper an' salt fe your mammy." This treatment satisfying all parties, they quickly retired. No one dares to throw a stone at this bird, as it is believed fever would result from such an action.

In no part of Jamaica will gravediggers commence digging a grave without imbibing freely of rum. Often some of the liquid is thrown round the spot to give it to an unseen being to whom they talk as they dig the grave. This custom prevails still when cutting down a cotton-tree, which, as the home of "duppies," they hold sacred, or when building a tank, or when washing a "dead."

The bitter-bush shrub has been repeatedly mistaken for a terrible phantom; the backs of the leaves are white, and if looked at from a distance in moonlight are spectrelike when, the wind suddenly blowing them, they gleam momentarily forth from the surrounding foliage. The belief in unseen spirits pervades the African-Jamaican mind. According to blacks, it is disastrous to refer to duppies. If, unconscious of this strange remnant of African superstition, you innocently point to a peculiar object which strikes you, the negro in an excited undertone mutters, "No talk, no talk!"

It is recorded of bygone days that when an infant was to be bathed, a tub of water would be placed in the sun in order that the chill should be taken off—this was done at midnight. At twelve o'clock in daytime, as well as at night, "duppies" are abroad. To prevent them from playing with the water, the mother would place two sticks across the tub, thereby making the sign of the cross to scare away unseen spirits.

The story which won the prize at the competition I have mentioned is worthy of quotation, and describes the handing over and receiving again of a surviving twin-baby across the coffin of the other, which is lying inside, lest the dead child should return for the survivor, the idea in so doing being that the living babe is supposed to be given to the departed and taken back. In the Dark Continent it is well known that many widespread beliefs are connected with the birth of twins. Sometimes the mother was put to death, and I learnt that years ago, in Jamaica, a woman who gave birth to twins was persecuted and reviled by her black neighbours, who regarded the event as execrable and to the last degree unlucky. The love of the negro for music is so well known that it is hardly worth comment. Before me, however, is an amusing incident of how a negro preacher, probably a fisherman, illustrating his texts by alluding to the familiar objects of his calling, describes the patience of Job:—

"Me will tell you. Fisherman go out all night; his fish-fish-fish ta daybroke and no' mo' ketch so tru prat (three sprats I imagine to be the correct translation). Him came home—him put him tree prat pon top-a-house fer dry. John Crow come, tek one, berry well—John Crow come tek nadda—him come tird time, tek tarra. De prat all gone, but fisherman no say—John Crow!! Dat da Job-pashance!"

FUNERALS

SIR HANS SLOANE, *A Voyage to the Islands of Madera, Barbados, Nieves, St. Christophers, and Jamaica,* . . . (London, 1707), vol. I, xl.

The Negroes from some countries think they return to their own country when they die in *Jamaica,* and therefore regard death but little, imagining they shall change their condition, by that means from servile to free, and so for this reason often cut their own Throats. Whether they die thus, or naturally, their Country people make great lamentations, mournings, and howlings about their expiring, and at their Funeral throw in Rum and Victuals into their graves, to serve them in the other world. Sometimes they bury it in gourds, at other times spill it on the Graves.

CHARLES LESLIE, *A New and Exact Account of Jamaica* (Edinburgh, 1739), 325, 326.

I have discoursed them anent the Immortality of the Soul, and some other important Points; but I observed their Notions of these Matters were extremely obscure, yet from the Customs they use at their Burials, I can gather some faint Remains of their Knowledge in that Article. When one is carried out to his Grave, he is attended with a vast Multitude, who conduct his Corps in something of a ludicrous Manner: They sing all the Way, and they who bear it on their Shoulders, make a Feint of stopping at every Door they pass, and pretend, that if the deceast Person had received any Injury, the Corps moves toward that House, and that they can't avoid letting it fall to the Ground when before the Door. When they come to the Grave, which is generally made in some Savannah or Plain, they lay down the Coffin, or whatever the Body happens to be wrapt up in; and if he be one whose Circumstances could allow it (or if he be generally liked, the Negroes contribute among themselves) they sacrifice a Hog. The Way they do it is this; the nearest Relation kills it, the Intrails are buried, the four Quarters are divided, and a kind of Soup made, which is brought in a

Calabash or Gourd, and, after waving it three Times, it is set down, then the Body is put in the Ground; all the while they are covering it with Earth, the Attendants scream out in a terrible Manner, which is not the Effect of Grief but of Joy; they beat on their wooden Drums, and the Women with their Rattles make a hideous Noise: After the Grave is filled up, they place the Soup which they had prepared at the Head, and a Bottle of Rum at the Feet. In the mean Time cool Drink (which is made of the *Lignum Vitae* Bark) or whatever else they can afford, is distributed amongst these who are present; the one Half of the Hog is burnt while they are drinking, and the other is left to any Person who pleases to take it; they return to Town or the Plantation singing after their Manner, and so the Ceremony ends.

J. G. STEDMAN, *Narrative of a Five Years' Expedition against the Revolted Negroes of Surinam* (Amherst: University of Massachusetts Press, 1971 [1796]), 375.

. . . . and when he is no more, his companions or relations carry him to some grove of orange-trees, where he is not interred without expense, being generally put in a coffin of the very best wood and workmanship, while the cries and lamentations of his surviving friends, who sing a dirge, pierce the sky. The grave being filled up, and a green turf neatly spread over it, a couple of large gourds are put by the side, the one with water, the other with boiled fowls, pork, cassava, &c. as a libation, not from a superstitious notion, as some believe, that he will eat or drink it, but as a testimony of that regard which they have for his memory and ashes; while some even add the little furniture that he left behind, breaking it in pieces over the grave. This done, every one takes his last farewell, speaking to him as if alive, and testifying their sorrow at his departure; adding, that they hope to see him, not in *Guinea*, as some have written, but in that better place, where he now enjoys the pleasant company of his parents, friends, and ancestors; when another dismal yell ends the ceremony and all return home. Next a fat hog being killed, with fowls, ducks, &c. a general feast is given by his friends to all the other negroes, which concludes not till the following day. The nearest connections and relations of the deceased, both male and female, now cut their hair* and shave their heads, round which having tied a dark blue handkerchief, they wear this mourning for a whole year; after which,

*We are told Job did the same.

once more visiting the grave, they offer a last libation, and taking their
final farewell, another hog and fowls being killed, the funeral rites are
quite ended by a second feast, which finishes with a joyful dance, and
songs in memory and praise of their dear departed friend or relation.

JOHN LUFFMAN, *A Brief Account of the Island of Antigua* (London,
1789), 109–13.

LETTER XXV
To _____

St. John's, Antigua,
Dec. 8, 1787.

Dear Sir,

Slaves are not permitted to marry consequently take one anoth-
ers words, and change their husbands and wives (as they term them)
when, and as often as they please. Baptism is allowed by some owners, but the slave must pay the priest for executing his office and the
price is a dollar. Negroes and colored people are not buried in the
same church-yard as the whites, even if free; the distinction, and
the superiority which the European race claim over the African, are
extended as far as they can possibly go: to the grave! but there they
must cease, and the hereafter, when the reign of human pride is over,
will be directed according to the fear we have had of God, and the
love we have borne one another during our earthy state of trial.

Negroe funerals, particularly such as are of old Creole families,
or in esteem among their fellows, are numerously attended; I have
seen from one or two hundred men, women, and children, follow a
corpse, decently dressed in white, which dress has been recom-
mended to them by the Methodist and Moravian preachers, whose
meetings are crowded by these people, and to whose discourses they
listen with seeming attention. If the party deceased has been christened, and their friends can afford to pay for the ringing of the church
bell, they may have that ceremony performed, as also the burial service, the first of these is sometimes done, the latter very seldom. The
body is mostly inclosed in a wooden shell or coffin, which, during the
procession to the grave, is covered with a sheet, by way of pall, and
such as have it in their power, bring liquor, fruit, &c. to the house of
their deceased uncle or aunt, brother or sister, (the common appella-
tions, whether related in consanguinity or not) which are consumed
by the company while things are getting into readiness. Before I leave

the subject of negroe burials, I cannot avoid remarking to you, one among many other singularities, possessed by these people, as it will serve to shew in what manner they feel, and express their feelings: when one of their brotherhood dies, as they suppose by ill-usage; as soon as the body is brought out of the place where it was deposited, taken upon the shoulders of the bearers, and has remained in that situation a few seconds, they (the bearers) begin to reel and stagger about surprisingly, going in zig-zags, and hurrying from one side of the street to the other, as if forced by some supernatural impulse, when after carrying on this joke for sometime, and probably tired themselves with their retrograde motions, one or two of the mourners walk up to the head of the coffin, and talk in a low voice to their departed brother or sister, the purport of which is to request the deceased to go in an orderly manner to the place of interment; to see them thus agitated gives great trouble to their friends, who are very sorry for what has happened, and that Gorramitee, (the negroe manner of expressing God Almighty) will punish those who have done them ill. This exordium always appeases the defunct, who then goes *quietly* to interment.

I remain, &c. &c.

WILLIAM BECKFORD, *A Descriptive Account of the Island of Jamaica* (London, 1790), vol. II, 388–90.

Their principal festivals are at their burials, upon which occasions they call forth all their magnificence, and display all their taste; and the expence with which the funerals of the better sort of negroes upon a plantation are attended, very often exceed the bounds of credibility; and of this position many instances might be given. Their bodies lie in state; an assemblage of slaves from the neighbourhood appears: the body is ornamented with linen and other apparel, which has been previously purchased, as is often the custom, this solemn occasion; and all the trinkets of the defunct are exposed in the coffin, and buried in the grave with the remains. The bier is lined with cambric and with lace; and when closed, it is covered with a quantity of expensive cloth, upon which are sometimes deposited wines and other liquors for the recreation of the guests, while a hog, poultry, and other viands, are offered up as an expiatory sacrifice. When the body is carried to the grave, they accompany the procession with a song; and when the earth is scattered over it, they send forth a shrill and noisy howl, which is no sooner re-echoed, in some cases, than forgotten.

After this ceremony, which in civilized countries is considered as a melancholy one, but of which few traces can be found in the sepulture of a negro, the affected tear is soon dried, the pretended sight is soon suppressed, and the face of sorrow becomes at once the emblem of joy. The instruments resound, the dancers are prepared; the day sets in cheerfulness, and the night resounds with the chorus of contentment; and the day only rises to awaken in their minds the regret of a necessary departure, and to summon them to their expected work.

GEORGE PINCKARD, *Notes on the West Indies* (London, 1806), vol. I, 270–73.

Seeing a crowd in one of the streets, and observing a kind of procession, we followed the multitude, and soon found ourselves in the train of a negro funeral. Wishing to witness the ceremony of interment we proceeded to the burial ground, with the throng. The corpse was conveyed in a neat small hearse, drawn by one horse. Six boys, twelve men, and forty-eight women walked behind, in pairs, as followers, but I cannot say as deeply afflicted mourners. The females were neatly clad, for the occasion, and mostly in white. Grief and lamentations were not among them: nor was even the semblance thereof assumed. No solemn dirge was heard—no deep-sounding bell was tolled—no fearful silence held. It seemed a period of mirth and joy. Instead of weeping and bewailing, the followers jumped and sported, as they passed along, and talked and laughed, with each other, in high festivity. The procession was closed by five robust negro fishermen, who followed behind playing antic gambols, and dancing all the way to the grave.

At the gate of the burying ground the corpse was taken from the hearse, and borne by eight negroes, not upon their shoulders, but upon four clean white napkins placed under the coffin. The body was committed to the grave, immediately, on reaching it, without either prayer or ceremony; and the coffin, directly, covered with earth. In doing this, much decent attention was observed. The mould was not shovelled in roughly with the spade, almost disturbing the dead, with the rattling of stones and bones upon the coffin, but was first put into a basket, and then carefully emptied into the grave; an observance which might be adopted in England very much to the comfort of the afflicted friends of the deceased.

During this process an old negro woman chanted an African air, and the multitude joined her in the chorus. It was not in the strain of a hymn, or solemn requiem, but was loud and lively, in unison with the other gaieties of the occasion.

Many were laughing and sporting the whole time with the fishermen, who danced and gambolled, during the ceremony, upon the neighbouring graves. From the moment the coffin was committed to the earth, nothing of order was maintained by the party. The attendants dispersed in various directions, retiring, or remaining, during the filling up of the grave, as inclination seemed to lead.

When the whole of the earth was replaced several of the women, who had staid to chant, in merry song, over poor Jenny's clay, took up a handful of the mould, and threw it down again upon the grave of their departed friend, as the finishing of the ceremony, crying aloud "God bless you, Jenny! good-by! remember me to all friends t' other side of the sea, Jenny! Tell 'em me come soon! Good-by, Jenny, good-by! Send for me good——to-night, Jenny! Good-by, good night, Jenny, good-by!" All this was uttered in mirth and laughter, and accompanied with attitudes and gesticulations expressive of any thing but sorrow or sadness.

MICHAEL SCOTT, *Tom Cringle's Log* (London: J. M. Dent, 1969 [1829–1833]), 142–44.

The following night there was to be a grand play or wake in the negro houses, over the head cooper, who had died in the morning, and I determined to be present at it, although the overseer tried to dissuade me, saying that no white person ever broke in on these orgies, that the negroes were very averse to their doing so, and that neither he, nor any of the white people on the estate, had ever been present on such an occasion. This very interdict excited my curiosity even more; so I rose about midnight, and let myself gently down through the window, and shaped my course in the direction of the negro houses, guided by a loud drumming, which, as I came nearer, every now and then sunk into a low murmuring roll, when a strong bass voice would burst forth into a wild recitative; to which succeeded a loud piercing chorus of female voices, during which the drums were beaten with great vehemence; this was succeeded by another solo, and so on. There was no moon, and I had to thread my way along one of the winding footpaths by starlight. When I arrived within a stone-cast of the hut before which the play was being held, I left the beaten track, and crept onwards until I gained the shelter of the stem of a wild cotton-tree, behind which I skulked unseen.

The scene was wild enough. Before the door a circle was formed by about twenty women, all in their best clothes, sitting on the ground, and swaying their bodies to and fro, while they sung in chorus the wild dirge already mentioned, the words of which I could not make out; in the centre of the circle sat four men playing on *gumbies,* or the long drum formerly described, while a fifth stood behind them, with a conch-shell, which he kept sounding at intervals. Other three negroes kept circling round the outer verge of the circle of women, naked all to their waist cloths, spinning about and about with their hands above their heads, like so many dancing dervishes. It was one of these three that from time to time took up the recitative, the female chorus breaking in after each line. Close to the drummers lay the body in an open coffin, supported on two low stools or trestles; a piece of flaming resinous wood was stuck in the ground at the head, and another at the feet; and a lump of kneaded clay, in which another torchlike splinter was fixed, rested on the breast. An old man, naked like the solo singer, was digging a grave close to where the body lay. The following was the chant:—

> "I say, broder, you can't go yet."
>   THEN THE CHORUS OF FEMALE VOICES.
> "When de morning star rise, den we put you in a hole."
>   CHORUS AGAIN.
> "Den you go in a Africa, you see Fetish dere."
>   CHORUS.
> "You shall nyam goat dere, wid all your family."
>   CHORUS.
> "Buccra can't come dere; say, dam rascal, why you no work?"
>   CHORUS.
> "Buccra can't catch Duppy,* no, no."
>   CHORUS.

Three calabashes, or gourds, with pork, yams, and rum, were placed on a small bench that stood close to the head of the bier, and at right angles to it.

In a little while, the women, singing-men, and drummers, suddenly gave a loud shout, or rather yell, clapped their hands three times; and then rushed to the surrounding cottages, leaving the old grave-digger alone with the body.

*Duppy, *Ghost.*

He had completed the grave, and had squatted himself on his hams beside the coffin, swinging his body as the women had done, and uttering a low moaning sound, frequently ending in a loud *pech*, like that of a paviour when he brings down his rammer.

I noticed he kept looking towards the east, watching, as I conjectured, the first appearance of the morning star; but it was as yet too early.

He lifted the gourd with the pork, and took a large mouthful.

"How is dis? I can't put dis meat in Quacco's coffin, dere is salt in de pork; Duppy can't bear salt," another large mouthful—"Duppy hate salt too much,"—here he ate it all up, and placed the empty gourd in the coffin. He then took up the one with boiled yam in it, and tasted it also.

"Salt here too—who de debil do such a ting?—must no let Duppy taste dat." He discussed this also, placing the empty vessel in the coffin as he had done with the other. He then came to the calabash with the rum. There is no salt there, thought I.

"Rum! ah, Duppy love rum—if it be well strong, let me see— Massa Niger, who put water in a dis rum, eh? Duppy will never touch dat"—a long pull—"no, no, never touch dat." Here he finished the whole, and placed the empty vessel beside the others; then gradually sank back on his hams with his mouth open, and his eyes starting from the sockets, as he peered up into the tree, apparently at some terrible object. I looked up also, and saw a large yellow snake, nearly ten feet long, let itself gradually down directly over the coffin, between me and the bright glare (the outline of its glossy mottled skin glancing in the strong light, which gave its dark opaque body the appearance of being edged with flame, and its glittering tongue that of a red-hot wire), with its tail round the limb of a cotton tree, until its head reached within an inch of the dead man's face, which it licked with its long forked tongue, uttering a loud hissing noise.

I was fascinated with terror, and could not move a muscle; at length the creature slowly swung itself up again, and disappeared amongst the branches.

Quashie gained courage, as the rum began to operate, and the snake to disappear. "Come to catch Quacco's Duppy, before him get to Africa, sure as can be. De metody parson say de debil old sarpant— dat must be old sarpant, for I never see so big one, so it must be de debil."

He caught a glimpse of my face at this moment; and it seemed that I had no powers of fascination like the snake, for he roared out,

"Murder, murder, de debil, de debil, first like a sarpant, den like himself; see him white face behind de tree; see him white face behind de
tree;" and then, in the extremity of his fear, he popt, head foremost,
into the grave, leaving his quivering legs and feet sticking upwards,
as if he had been planted by the head, like a forked parsnip reversed.

MATTHEW GREGORY LEWIS, *Journal of a West India Proprietor*
(London, 1834), 97–98.

The negroes are always buried in their own gardens, and many
strange and fantastical ceremonies are observed on the occasion. If
the corpse be that of a grown person, they consult it as to which way
it pleases to be carried; and they make attempts upon various roads
with success, before they can hit upon the right one. Till that is accomplished, they stagger under the weight of the coffin, struggle
against its force, which draws them in a different direction from that
in which they had settled to go; and sometimes in the contest the
corpse and the coffin jump off the shoulders of the bearers. But if, as
is frequently the case, any person is suspected of having hastened the
catastrophe, the corpse will then refuse to go any road but the one
which passes by the habitation of the suspected person, and as soon
as it approaches his house, no human power is equal to persuading it
to pass. As the negroes are extremely superstitious, and very much
afraid of ghosts (whom they call the *duppy*), I rather wonder at their
choosing to have their dead buried in their gardens; but I understand
their argument to be, that they need only fear the duppies of their
enemies, but have nothing to apprehend from those after death, who
loved them in their lifetime; but the duppies of their adversaries are
very alarming beings, equally powerful by day as by night, and who
not only are spiritually terrific, but who can give very hard substantial
knocks on the pate, whenever they see fit occasion, and can find a
good opportunity.

JAMES STEWART, *A View of the Past and Present State of the Island
of Jamaica* (Edinburgh, 1823), 274–76.

At their funerals, the African negroes use various ceremonies, among
which is the practice of pouring libations, and sacrificing a fowl on the
grave of the deceased—a tribute of respect they afterwards occasionally repeat. During the whole of the ceremony, many fantastic motions and wild gesticulations are practised, accompanied with a suit-

able beat of their drums and other rude instruments, while a melancholy dirge is sung by a female, the chorus of which is performed by the whole of the other females, with admirable precision, and full-toned and not unmelodious voices. When the deceased is interred, the plaintive notes of sympathy are no longer heard, the drums resound with a livelier beat, the song grows more animated, dancing and apparent merriment commence, and the remainder of the night is usually spent in feasting and riotous debauchery.

Previous to the interment of the corpse it is sometimes pretended that it is endowed with the gift of speech; and the friends and relatives alternately place their ears to the lid of the coffin, to hear what the deceased has to say. This generally consists of complaints and upbraidings for various injuries,—treachery, ingratitude, injustice, slander, and, in particular, the non-payment of debts due to the deceased. This last complaint is sometimes shewn by the deceased in a more *cogent* way than by mere words; for, on coming opposite the door of the negro debtor, the coffin makes a full stop, and no persuasion nor strength can induce the deceased to go forward peaceably to his grave till the money is paid; so that the unhappy debtor has no alternative but to comply with this demand, or have his creditor palmed upon him, as a lodger, for some time. Sometimes, however, the deceased is a little unconscionable, by claiming a fictitious debt. In short, this superstitious practice is often made subservient to fraudulent extortion. A negro, who was to be interred in one of the towns, had, it was pretended by some of his friends, a claim on another negro for a sum of money. The latter denied any such claim; and accordingly, at the funeral of the deceased, the accustomed ceremonies took place opposite the door of his supposed debtor; and this mummery was continued for hours, till the magistrates thought proper to interfere, and compelled the defunct to forego his claim, and proceed quietly on to his place of rest.

ALEXANDER BARCLAY, *A Practical View of the Present State of Slavery in the West Indies* . . . (London, 1826), 131–33, 158–62.

. . . . even if christening the negroes had done nothing else but put an end to night funerals among them, humanity could not have considered it altogether in vain; as this truly pernicious custom, which their native superstition regarded as a solemn rite on no account to be dispensed with, was, perhaps, of all others that ever existed, the most fruitful in disorder and suffering. The whole night, or the greater part of it, was spent in drumming on the gumbay, singing, dancing, and drinking:—before committing the corpse to the earth the whole party issued forth in a state of intoxication, two of them bearing the coffin on their heads, and proceeded in a body, dancing and singing, to every house in the plantation village, into which the deceased was carried to take leave. This, however, was not always done on friendly terms; sometimes the corpse was made to charge the owner of the house with having done him an injury, or with owing him money; and in this case the persons carrying him pretended that he would not go away, and that they were not able to take him away, till satisfaction was given. When I had been but a few weeks in Jamaica, I was one night suddenly awakened out of sleep by a strange and unearthly sound of music, unlike any thing I had ever before heard. I started out of bed, and throwing up the window, directly under it beheld a large body of negroes, two of them with a coffin on their heads, with which they were wheeling round and dancing; the others carrying torches, and all dancing and singing, or rather yelling unlike any thing human. I shall never forget the impression of horror which this spectacle made on my mind, and which was long after kept alive by the death-beat of the gumbay heard almost every night on some one or other of the plantations in the neighbourhood.*

The extinction of this most barbarous custom is a very happy and important change. The very sight of it was horrible to an European; and to the negroes it was the occasion, not of casual but of continual excesses, producing a degree of over-excitement by drinking and carousing, which, just as surely as the next morning dawned, incapacitated some of those thoughtless creatures from attending their duty,

*The following air is one I have heard sung by them on these occasions, and probably African; to me it appears strikingly wild and melancholy, associated as it is in my mind with such recollections, and heard for the first time sung by savages interring their dead at the midnight hour.

and consequently subjected them to punishment. To avoid this for the moment, but greatly to aggravate it in the end, the conscious offender deserted his duty, and suffered the consequences. Negro funerals now take place in the day-time: if none of themselves are qualified, a white person always attends to read the burial service; I have often done so myself; and there is invariably the utmost solemnity observed.

■ ■ ■

When Mr. Stephen descends from general accusations to specific charges, there is no difficulty in meeting him. Thus, after describing in this chapter how much attention was paid by the Athenians, the Romans, and in more modern times by the French, to the funerals of their slaves, he goes on to say—

> "But we should search in vain in the laws or practices of any of the British colonies, speaking generally as to the practice, for equal humanity. There when no longer animated with that soul which groaned under oppression, and no longer fit for the master's purposes, is abandoned with unfeeling disregard, to the care of kindred wretches, to be interred at their discretion in the nearest vacant soil. The funereal rites commonly paid to ordinary plantation slaves are supplied, not by the care of the master, but by their relatives on the same estate; and are in the forms of African superstition, not of christian worship" (p. 275).

Never was there a more palpable misrepresentation. As formerly mentioned, the slaves about 20 years ago were, with few exceptions, buried at night; and the funereal rites were in the forms of African superstition. But as religion advanced, this barbarous custom gradually disappeared; and a positive law in 1816 put an end to night funerals, that source of crime and misery. Christianity would have effected this before now, if no such law had been enacted. But had this change (beneficial as I have shewn it to be) been attempted by law twenty years sooner, with the superstitious veneration the negroes then attached to night funerals, they would have felt it as a deprivation of a solemn rite which they owed to the dead; and, I need scarcely add, they would have resisted its abolition accordingly. Can enthusiasm, which vainly thinks to mould the human mind as a potter does his clay, not read in such facts as useful lesson, to let education and religion take their course in eradicating superstition and conveying light into the darkness of paganism, without attempting to accomplish in a day what can only be the work of years? What the utmost stretch of power could scarcely have effected then, has now been, without a murmur, almost imperceptibly accomplished.

The funerals of slaves in Jamaica for years past have in no respect differed from those of white people. When a negro's death is occasioned by an acute disorder, it happens in the hospital, where he has been under the care of the medical attendant;[†] when it occurs from a decay of life, he is not removed from the comforts which his own house affords; but in either case he has the kind offices of those most nearly related to him by the ties of blood and affection. When he expires, notice is brought to the master or overseer, and generally communicated in the short but emphatic expression, such as one "is gone." Immediate directions are given to the carpenters on the plantation to make a coffin; and some little things are always given for the funeral, such as rum and sugar, and a little flour and butter to make cakes or rusks; often on such occasions, I have known masters, and even managers of estates, give from their own private stock half a dozen bottles of Madeira wine, and a dozen of brown stout, to shew their respect for a valuable and faithful servant.

The shroud and furniture for the coffin are provided by the family of the deceased; white if a single, and black if a married person, with corresponding mounting or plates; in short, in every respect the same as in the case of white persons. During the night, and it is never more than one, that the corpse is in the house, a few religious friends attend, psalms are sung, and prayers given by some of their own (negro) preachers. The following day the funeral takes place, and is always numerously attended by the relations of the deceased, by all the old and invalided of the plantation village, and by the women, exempted from labour on account of pregnancy or attention to their families; nor, indeed, is permission to attend ever refused to a slave on a neighbouring plantation, if the deceased has been his intimate friend, relation, or countryman. At the hour appointed, a white person attends, accompanied frequently by others, to read the service appointed by the church of England, in committing dust to dust; and this most solemn and impressive ceremony is listened to by white and black, with an attention and humility evincing a sense, that "our brother here departed," has gone where we must all follow, and where human distinctions are at an end. While the grave is closing, bread and wine are handed round, which, from seeing it done at the funerals of white persons, the negroes perhaps consider a part of the ceremony; of course, it is little more than a matter of form, and a cou-

---

†Every plantation has an hospital, and these buildings are so respectable in size and appearance, that they are often mistaken by strangers for the mansion-houses.

ple of bottles of Madeira is the usual quantity procured for the occasion by the ordinary class of slaves.

From a latent taint of African superstition, the negroes universally attach great importance to having what they call "a good burial." Hence those who are in only indifferent circumstances, are often careful to reserve means for the purpose; others, indifferent to the morrow, are still more so as to what shall follow, when the wants of life are at an end; yet a thoughtless improvident creature of this description, *"not sorry for himself,"* as the negroes express it, is respected in death by his friends, who would consider it as an indelible disgrace to themselves, if he was not buried *"as a Christian ought."*

Near towns, and on some plantations, a piece of ground is enclosed as a burial-place for the negroes; but the more common practice upon plantations with both whites and blacks, is to inter the dead in a small corner of their respective gardens set aside for the purpose; and as the negroes attach an importance to the burial of the dead, they extend the same feeling to the graves, over which they erect tombs built commonly of brick, and neatly white-washed. The white-washing is carefully repeated every Christmas morning, and formerly it was on these occasions customary to kill a white cock, and sprinkle his blood over the graves of the family; but this last part of the ceremony seems now to be little attended to, and is likely to be soon extinct. In public negro burial grounds on plantations they build into the tombs, at one end, a piece of hard and almost imperishable wood, placed upright and having the top cut into rough outlines of the human figure, which gives the spot a very striking and not unimposing effect.

Such are negro funerals, as I have seen them, and such, however much at variance with Mr. Stephen's account of the matter, I avouch to be the general practice.

R. R. MADDEN, *A Twelve Month's Residence in the West Indies, . . .* (London, 1835), vol. I, 183–84, 187–88.

A negro burial used formerly to be as joyous a solemnity as an Irish wake. There was dancing, singing, drinking, feasting, and a little fighting, not unfrequently, to enliven the mourners. There was a striking resemblance in the rites of both. There was a Willyforce nigger gone kickeraboo, instead of "a beautiful corpse" of a Paddy—plenty of new rum, in place of whisky—a gong and a bongau, in lieu of the bagpipes—howling negro wenches, instead of keeners—stories of duppies, in place of banchees—vows to a Fetish, instead of St. Patrick—songs about Bushas and Buckras, in place of Sassenachs—nyaming of goat and wegitabs, instead of rashers of bacon and prateesn and may-be there wasn't a wedding or two knocked up at the wake, and a stranger or two knocked down, for recreation at the berne! But these happy times are gone: the negroes are no longer permitted to bury their dead by torchlight; to dance over their departed friends, and to frighten the isle from its propriety with barbarous music. Many, however, of the more peaceable practices are still observed; but so carefully are the white people excluded from the exhibition of them, that it is more difficult, I am persuaded, to get a sight at a negro wake than the preparation for a Turkish funeral.

. . .

I was requested some days ago by a family in my neighborhood to attend a negro funeral. . . .

On proceed to the negro grounds, I heard the lugubrious concert of many African and Creole voices strike up, as I approached the hut of the deceased negro. The sounds were "not musical, but most melancholy." I stopped at a little distance to endeavour to catch the words, but I was not sufficiently acquainted with nigger tongue to make out more than a few words here and there of the chaunt they were giving, somewhat in the fashion of a recitative. There were no Af allusions to Fetish divinities, but an abundance of scriptural paraphrases, strangely applied to their ideas of happiness of a future state, and the deserts of the dead woman. The expressions were a mixture of genuine piety and fanaticism—at least if the colloquial familiarity of their mode of addressing God deserved the latter name:—

> "Gar Amighty see this very wicked world—
> Him say, 'Sister, come away,
> What for you no come to me?'
> Sister say, 'O Gar Amighty,
> Too much glad to come away!
> When one die, him sickness over;
> Him leave all trouble in dis sinful world;
> Him no nyam, no clothes, no sleep,
> Him much too glad to come away.' "

The last line was a chorus that was frequently repeated. I do not say these were the exact words, but they are very near the sense, and only a very small part of the chaunt in which they were repeated. The singing was stopped when I came up to the door; there were a number of negroes assembled in the room. In the centre a handsome mahogany coffin was placed on trestles. At the end of the room a table was spread out with cakes, wine-glasses, and a decanter of Madeira, which had not been touched, and I suppose was intended for the white man's entertainment. The negroes stood up when I entered; and the daughter of the deceased, a decent-looking woman dressed in black, offered me refreshment. I told them when they were quite ready I would attend the funeral. . . .

REV. CHARLES DANIEL DANCE, *Chapters from a Guianese Log-Book* (Demerara, 1881), 90–91.

. . . the previous attention to the dying or dead still warrants a little excusable display of kindly interested authority in the arrangements made for conducting the funeral,—the ordering or retarding of the start of the procession, even if thereby a little additional confusion is promoted,—the running alongside of the procession to occasionally arrange a silk cloak or a hatband of one of "the followers,"—with a sufficiently audible sigh while turning round to the spectators to show (and who of them is not passionately fond of display?) there her officiousness at the funeral of the deceased arises from the right of sympathetic affinity.

I once had the opportunity of observing unobserved the preparations for a funeral procession about to leave the house. Before the dead was lifted out, the little daughter of the deceased man was hoisted over the coffin from one side to the other. This was thought to be a charm for the protection against the interference of evil spirits in general, and the spirit of the dead parent in particular. They then proceeded with the corpse into the street towards the hearse, singing very mournfully.

It was a pity that the wife of the deceased was not, as well as the little daughter, hoisted over the coffin, or had not herself stridden across it; for, according to her own statement, she was very much troubled at night by the presence of her dead and buried husband.

The remedy, as practised here, for such ghostly persecution is to go to the grave of the troublesome dead, and *"curse"* him. She went to curse, but at the grave the remembrance of their former love did not permit her to curse, she merely remonstrated. But the remonstrance did not quiet the dead, for he appeared to her that very night, and stroking her face with his cold hand told her that "she had too much tongue"; then, kissing her, he left her kicking up her heels and thumping about in a fit of hysterics.

It should be stated that the disconsolate widow, used to her
dram-drinking, had been solacing herself too freely during the first
few days of her widowhood.

Bessie Pullen-Burry, *Jamaica As It Is, 1903* (London, 1903),
140–41.

Not long since an aged labourer on a neighboring plantation was attacked with disease. The proprietor ordered special food to be cooked
for him, and a servant was told off to look after him. The latter never
went near the old black, so the result was that the master, who was a
good-hearted man, took personal charge of him, whilst his wife
brought food to him, even cooking it herself. The old negro, however,
died, and then the friends, who had not been near him for days,
crowded to the little hut, and not only had the corpse laid out in a fine
new suit of white duck, but held a wake for three nights, when they
disposed of enough rum and tea, in celebrating his decease, to have
kept the old fellow going months during his life-time.

Bessie Pullen-Burry, *Ethiopia in Exile: Jamaica Revisited*
(London, 1905), 147.

The funeral wakes and "ninth-day" feasts are occasions of great excitement among the blacks. Those who live close by a negro settlement are familiar with the awful din proceeding from a dead man's
house as soon as darkness has settled over the earth. The body, cof-
fined or otherwise, lies in the inner apartment; friends and relatives
collect in the outer room, sing hymns, lament the dead, and solace
their grief with plentiful potations of rum. The only difference between an Irish wake and a negro one is that the former is more hu-
morous in its character, the corpse being in the centre of the lament-
ing friends and kinsfolk.

OBEAH

Bryan Edwards, *The History, Civil and Commercial, of the British
Colonies in the West Indies* (Dublin, 1793), vol. II, 82–92.

. . . With them, equally with the Whites, nature shrinks back at approaching dissolution; and when, at any time, sudden or untimely
death overtakes any of their companions, instead of rejoicing at such

an event, they never fail to impute it to the malicious contrivances
and diabolical arts of some practitioner in *Obeah,* a term of African
origin, signifying sorcery or witchcraft, the prevalence of which,
among many of their countrymen, all the Negroes most firmly and implicitly believe. We may conclude, therefore, that their funeral songs
and ceremonies are commonly nothing more than the dissonance of
savage barbarity and riot; as remote from the fond superstition to
which they are ascribed, as from the sober dictates of a rational
sorrow.

Having mentioned the practice of *Obeah,* the influence of which
has so powerful an effect on the Negroes, as to bias, in a considerable
degree, their general conduct, dispositions, and manners, I shall conclude the present chapter by presenting to my readers the following
very curious account of this extraordinary superstition, and its effects:
it was transmitted by the Agent of Jamaica to the Lords of the Com-
mittee of Privy Council, and by them subjoined to their report on the
slave trade; and, if I mistake not, the publick are chiefly indebted for
it to the diligent researches, and accurate pen, of Mr. Long.

The term *Obeah, Obiah,* or *Obia* (for it is variously written) we
conceive to be the adjective, and *Obe* or *Obi* the noun substantive;
and that by the words *Obia*-men or -women, are meant those who
practice *Obi.* The origin of the term we should consider as of no
importance in our answer to the questions proposed, if in search
of it, we were not led to disquisitions that are highly gratifying to curiosity. . . .

As far as we are able to decide from our own experience and information when we lived in the island, and from the current testimony
of all the Negroes we have ever conversed with on the subject, the
professors of *Obi* are, and always were, natives of Africa, and none
other; and they have brought the science with them from thence to
Jamaica, where it is so universally practiced, that we believe there are
few of the large estates possessing native Africans, which have not
one or more of them. The oldest and most crafty are those who usually
attract the greatest devotion and confidence; those whose hoary
heads, and somewhat peculiarly harsh and forbidding in their aspect,
together with some skill in plants of the medicinal and poisonous species, have qualified them for successful imposition upon the weak and
credulous. The Negroes in general, whether Africans or Creoles, revere, consult, and fear them; to these oracles they resort, and with the
most implicit faith, upon all occasions, whether for the cure of disorders, the obtaining revenge for injuries or insults, the conciliating of

favour, the discovery and punishment of the thief or the adulterer, and the prediction of future events. The trade which these impostors carry on is extremely lucrative; they manufacture and sell their *Obies* adapted to different cases and at different prices. A veil of mystery is studiously thrown over their incantations, to which the midnight hours are allotted, and every precaution is taken to conceal them from the knowledge and discovery of the White people. The deluded Negroes, who thoroughly believe in their supernatural power, become the willing accomplices in this concealment, and the stoutest among them tremble at the very sight of the ragged bundle, the bottle or the egg-shells, which are stuck in the thatch or hung over the door of a hut, or upon the branch of a plantain tree, to deter marauders. In cases of poison, the natural effects of it are by the ignorant Negroes, ascribed entirely to the potent workings of *Obi*. The wiser Negroes hesitate to reveal their suspicions, through a dread of incurring the terrible vengeance which is fulminated by the *Obeah-men* against any who should betray them; it is very difficult therefore for the White proprietor to distinguish the *Obeah professor* from any other Negro upon his plantation; and so infatuated are the Blacks in general, that but few instances occur of their having assumed courage enough to impeach these miscreants. With minds so firmly prepossessed, they no sooner find *Obi set for them* near the door of their house, or in the path which leads to it, than they give themselves up for lost. When a Negro is robbed of a fowl or a hog, he applies directly to the *Obeah* man or woman; it is then made known among his fellow Blacks, that *Obi is set* for the thief; and as soon as the latter hears the dreadful news, his terrified imagination begins to work, no resource is left but in the superior skill of some more eminent *Obeah-man* of the neighborhood, who may counteract the magical operations of the other; but if no one can be found of higher rank and ability, or if, after gaining such an ally, he should still fancy himself affected, he presently falls into a decline, under the incessant horror of impending calamities. The slightest painful sensation in the head, the bowels, or any other part, any casual loss or hurt, confirms his apprehensions, and he believes himself the devoted victim of an invisible and irresistible agency. Sleep, appetite, and cheerfulness forsake him, his strength decays, his disturbed imagination is haunted without respite, his features wear the settled gloom of despondency; dirt, or any other unwholesome substance, become his only food, he contracts a morbid habit of body, and gradually sinks into the grave. A Negro, who is taken ill, enquires of the *Obeah-man* the cause of his sickness, whether it will prove mortal or not, and within what time he shall die or recover? The oracle generally ascribes the distemper to the malice of some particular person by name, and advises to set *Obi* for that person; but if no hopes are given of recovery, immediate despair takes place, which no medicine can remove, and death is the certain consequence. Those anomalous symptoms which originate from causes deeply rooted in the mind such as the terrors of *Obi*, or from poisons, whose operation is slow and intricate, will baffle the skill of the ablest physician.

Considering the multitude of occasions which may provoke the Negroes to exercise the powers of *Obi* against each other, and the astonishing influence of this superstition upon their minds, we cannot but attribute a very considerable portion of the annual mortality among the Negroes of Jamaica to this fascinating mischief.

The *Obi* is usually composed of a farrago of materials, most of which are enumerated in the Jamaica law, viz. "Blood, feather, parrots beaks, dogs teeth, alligators teeth, broken bottles, grave-dirt, rum, and egg-shells."

With a view to illustrate the description we have given of this practice, and its common effects, we have subjoined a few examples out of a very great number which have occurred in Jamaica; not that they are peculiar to the island only, for we believe similar examples may be found in other West India colonies. *Pere Labat,* in his history of Martinico, has mentioned some of which are very remarkable.

▪   ▪   ▪

It may seem extraordinary, that a practice alleged to be so frequent in Jamaica should not have received an earlier check from the legislature. The truth is, that the skill of some Negroes in the art of poisoning has been noticed ever since the colonists became much acquainted with them. Sloane and Barham, who practiced physics in Jamaica in the last century, have mentioned particular instances of it. The secret and insidious manner in which this crime is generally perpetrated, makes the legal proof of it extremely difficult. Suspicions therefore have been frequent, but detections rare: these murderers have *sometimes* been brought to justice, but it is reasonable to believe that a far greater number have escaped with impunity. In regard to the older and more common tricks of *Obi,* such as hanging up feathers, bottles, eggshells, etc. etc. in order to intimidate Negroes of a thievish disposition from plundering huts, hog-styes, or provision-grounds, these were laughed at by the White inhabitants as harmless stratagems, contrived by the more sagacious, for deterring the more simple and superstitious Blacks, and serving for much the same purpose as the scare-crows which are in general used among our English farmers and gardeners. But in the year 1760, when a very formidable insurrection of the Koromantyn or Gold Coast Negroes broke out in the parish of St. Mary, and spread through almost every other district of the island, an old Koromantyn Negroe, the chief instigator and oracle of the insurgents in that parish, who had administered the Fetish or solemn oath to the conspirators, and furnished them with a magical preparation which was to render them invulnerable, was fortunately apprehended, convicted, and hung up with all his feathers and trumperies about him; and his execution struck the insurgents with a general panic, from which they never afterwards recovered. The examinations which were taken at that period first opened the eyes of the public to the very dangerous tendency of the *Obeah* practices, and gave birth to the law which was then enacted for their suppression and punishment. But neither the terror of this law, the strict investigation which has ever since been made after the professors of *Obi*, nor the many examples of those who from time to time have been hanged or transported, have hitherto produced the desired effect. We conclude, therefore, that either this sect, like others in the world, has flourished under persecution; or that fresh supplies are annually introduced from the African seminaries.

The following paper referred to in the preceding account.

OBEAH PRACTICE

"We have the following narratives from a planter in Jamaica, a gentleman of the strictest veracity, who is now in London, and ready to attest the truth of them.

"Upon returning to Jamaica in the year 1775, he found that a great many of his Negroes had died during his absence; and that of such as remained alive, at least one half were debilitated, bloated, and in a very deplorable condition. The mortality continued after his arrival, and two or three were frequently buried in one day; others were taken ill, and began to decline under the same symptoms. Every means were tried by medicines, and the most careful nursing, to preserve the lives of the feeblest, but in spite of all his endeavours, this depopulation went on for above a twelve month longer, with more or less intermission, and without his being able to ascertain the real cause, though the *Obeah practice* was strongly suspected, as well by himself as by the doctor and other White persons upon the plantation, as it was known to have been very common in that part of the island, and particularly among the Negroes of the *Papa* or *Popo* country. Still he was unable to verify his suspicions, because the patients constantly denied their having any thing to do with persons of that order, or any knowledge of them. At length a Negress, who had been ill for some time, came one day and informed him, that feeling was impossible for her to live much longer, she thought herself bound in duty, before she died, to impart a very great secret, and acquaint him with the true cause of her disorder, in hopes that the disclosure might prove the means of stopping the mischief, which had already swept away such a number of her fellow-slaves. She proceeded to say, that her step-mother (a woman of the *Popo* country, above eighty years old, but still hale and active) had put *Obi upon her,* as she had also done upon those who had lately died; and that the old woman had practised *Obi* for as many years past as she could remember.

"The other Negroes of the plantation no sooner heard of this impeachment, than they ran in a body to their master, and confirmed the truth of it, adding, that she had carried on the business ever since her arrival from Africa, and was the terror of the whole neighborhood.— Upon this he repaired directly, with six White servants, to the old woman's house, and forcing open the door, observed the whole inside of the roof (which was of thatch) and every crevice of the walls, stuck with the implements of her trade, consisting of rags, feathers, bones of cats, and a thousand other articles. Examining further, a large earthen pot or jar, close covered, was found concealed under her bed.—It contained a prodigious quantity of round balls of earth or clay of various dimensions, large and small, whitened on the outside, and variously compounded, some with hair and rags or feathers of all sorts, and strongly bound with twine; others blended with the upper section of the skulls of cats, or stuck around with cat's teeth and claws, or with human or dog's teeth, and some glass beads of different colours; there were also a great many eggshells filled with a viscous or gummy substance, the qualities of which he neglected to examine, and many little bags stuffed with a variety of articles, the particulars of which cannot at this distance of time be recollected. The house was instantly pulled down, and with the whole of its contents committed to the flames, amidst the general acclamation of all his other Negroes. In regard to the old woman, he declined bringing her to trial under the law of the island, which would have punished her with death; but, from a principle of humanity, delivered her into the hands of a party of Spaniards, who (as she was thought not incapable of doing some trifling kind of work) were very glad to accept and carry her with them to Cuba. From the moment of her departure his Negroes seemed all to be animated with new spirits, and the malady spread no farther among them. The total of his losses in the course of about fifteen years preceding the discovery, and imputable solely to the *Obeah practice,* he estimates, at least, at one hundred Negroes."

OBEAH TRIALS

"Having received some further information upon this subject from another Jamaica gentleman, who sat upon *two* trials, we beg leave to deliver the same in his own words, as a supplement to what we have already had the honour of submitting.

"In the year 1760, the influence of the professors of the *Obeah art* was such, as to induce a great many of the Negroe slaves in Jamaica to engage in the rebellion which happened in that year, and which gave rise to the law which was then made against the practice of *Obi.*

"Assurance was given to these deluded people, that they were to become invulnerable; and in order to render them so, the *Obeah-men* furnished them with a powder, with which they were to rub themselves.

"In the first engagement with the rebels, nine of them were killed and many prisoners taken; amongst the latter was one very intelligent fellow, who offered to disclose many important matters, on condition that his life should be spared; which was promised. He then related the active part which the Negroes, known among them by the name of *Obeah-men,* had taken in propagating the insurrection; one of whom was thereupon apprehended, tried (for rebellious conspiracy), convicted, and sentenced to death.

N. B. This was the Koromantyn Obeah-man alluded to in our first paper.

"At the place of execution, he bid defiance to the executioner, telling him, that 'It was not in the power of the White people to kill him.'—And the Negroes (spectators). were greatly perplexed when they saw him expire. Upon other *Obeah-men,* who were apprehended at that time, various experiments were made with electrical machines and magic lanterns, but with very little effect, except on one, who, after receiving some very severe shocks, acknowledged that 'This master's *Obi* exceeded his own.'

"The gentleman from whom we have this account, remembers having sat twice on trials of *Obeah-men,* who were both convicted of selling their Obeah preparations, which had occasioned the death of the parties to whom they had been administered; notwithstanding which, the lenity of their judges prevailed so far, that they were only punished with transportation. To prove the fact, two witnesses were deemed necessary, with corroborating circumstances."

MATTHEW GREGORY LEWIS, *Journal of a West India Proprietor* (London, 1834), 94–95, 133–38.

January 12 [1816]

The belief in Obeah is now greatly weakened, but still exists in some degree. Not above ten months ago, my agent was informed that a negro of very suspicious manners and appearance was harboured by some of my people on the mountain lands. He found means to have him surprised, and on examination there was found upon him a bag containing a great variety of strange materials for incantations; such as thunder-stones, cat's ears, the feet of various animals, human hair, fish bones, the teeth of alligators, etc.: he was conveyed to Montego Bay; and no sooner was it understood that this old African was in prison, than depositions were poured in from all quarters from negroes who deposed to having seen him exercise his magical arts, and, in particular, to his having sold such and such slaves medicines and charms to deliver them from their enemies; being, in plain English, nothing else than rank poisons. He was convicted of Obeah upon the most indubitable evidence. The good old practice of burning has fallen into disrepute; so he was sentenced to be transported, and was shipped off the island, to the great satisfaction of persons of all colours—white, black, and yellow.

•   •   •

January 24 [1816]

But now came the most puzzling business of the day. About four years ago, two Eboes, called Pickle and Edward, were rivals, after being intimate friends: Pickle (who is an excellent faithful negro, but not very wise) was the successful candidate; and, of course, the friendship was interrupted, till Edward married the sister of the disputed fair one. From this time the brothers-in-law lived in perfect harmony together; but, during the first festival given on my arrival, Pickle's house was broken open, and robbed of all his clothes, &c. The thief was sought for, but in vain. On Monday last I found Pickle in the hospital, complaining of a pain in his side; and the blood, which had been taken from him, gave reason to apprehend a pleurisy arising from cold; but, as the disorder had been taken in its earliest stage, nothing dangerous was expected. The fever abated; the medicines performed their offices properly; still the man's spirits and strength appeared to decline, and he persisted in saying that he was not better, and should never do well. At length, to-day, he got out of his sick bed, came to the house, attended by the whole body of drivers, and accused his brother-in-law of having been the stealer of his goods. I asked, "Had Edward been seen near his house? Had any of his effects been seen in Edward's possession? Did Edward refuse to suffer his hut to be searched?" No. Edward, who was present, pressed for the most strict scrutiny, and asserted his perfect ignorance; nor could the accuser advance any grounds for the charge, except his belief of Edward's guilt. "Why did he think so?" After much beating about the bush, at length out came the real *causa doloris*—"Edward had *Obeahed* him!" He had accused Edward of breaking open his house, and had begged him to help him to his goods again; and "Edward had gone at midnight into the bush" (i.e. the wood), and "had gathered the plant whangra, which he had boiled in an iron pot, by a fire of leaves, over which he went puff, puffie!" and said the sautee-sautee; and then had cut the whangra root into four pieces, three to bury at the plantation gates, and one to burn; and to each of these three pieces he gave the name of a Christian, one of which was Daniel; and Edward had said, that this would help him to find his goods; but instead of that, he had immediately felt this pain in his side, and therefore he was sure that, instead of using Obeah to find his goods, Edward had used it to kill himself. "And were these all his reasons?" I enquired. "No; when he married, Edward was very angry at the loss of his mistress, and had said that they never would live well and happily together; and they never *had* lived happily and well together."

This last argument quite got the better of my gravity. By parity of reasoning, I thought that almost every married couple in Great Britain must be under the influence of Obeah! I endeavoured to convince the fellow of his folly and injustice, especially as the person accused was the identical man who had detected the Obeah priest harboured in one of my negro huts last year, had seized him with his own hands, and delivered him up to my agent, who had prosecuted and transported him. It was, therefore, improbable in the highest degree, that he should be an Obeah man himself; and all the bystanders, black and white, joined me in ridiculing Pickle for complaints so improbable and childish. But anger, argument, and irony were all ineffectual. I offered to christen him, and expel black Obeah by white, but in vain; the fellow persisted in saying, that "he had a pain in his side, and, *therefore*, Edward must have given it to him"; and he went back to his hospital, shaking his head all the way, sullen and unconvinced. He is a young strong negro, perfectly well disposed, and doing his due portion of work willingly; and it will be truly provoking to lose him by the influence of this foolish prejudice.

January 25 [1816]

I sent for Edward, had him alone with me for above two hours, and pressed him most earnestly to confide in me. I gave him a dollar to convince him of my good-will towards him; assured him that what- ever he might tell me should remain a secret between us; said, that I was certain of his not having used any poison, or done any thing really mischievous; but as I suspected him of having played some monkey- tricks or other, which, however harmless in themselves, had evidently operated dangerously upon Pickle's imagination, I begged him to tell me precisely what had passed, in order that I might counteract its baleful effects. In reply, Edward swore to me most solemnly, "by the great God Almighty, who lives above the clouds," that he never had gone into the wood to gather whangra; and that he had considered Pickle, from the moment of his own marriage, as his brother, and had always, till then, loved him as such. His eyes filled with tears while he protested that he should be as sorry for Pickle's death as if it were himself; and he complained bitterly of having the ill name of an Obeah man given to him, which made him feared and shunned by his companions, and entirely without cause. But he said that he was cer- tain that Pickle would never have suspected him of such a crime, if a third person had not put it into his head. There is a negro on my es- tate called Adam, who has been long and strongly suspected of having connections with Obeah men. When Edward was quite young, he was under this fellow's superintendence, and he now assured me, that Adam had not only endeavoured to draw him into similar practices, but had even pressed him very earnestly to lay a magical egg under the door of a book-keeper whose conduct had been obnoxious. Ed- ward had positively refused: from that moment his superintendent, from being his protector, had become his enemy, had shown him spite upon every occasion; and he it was, he had no doubt, who, for the purpose of injuring him, had put this foolish notion into Pickle's head.

Upon enquiry it appeared, that on the very morning succeeding Pickle's entering the hospital, this suspected man had gone there also, on pretence of sickness, and had remained there to watch the invalid; although it was so evident that nothing was the matter with him, that the doctor had frequently ordered him to the field, but the man had always found means for evading the order. The first thing that we now did was to turn him out of the sickhouse, neck and heels; I then took Edward with me to Pickle's bedside, where the former told his brother-in-law, that if he had ever done any thing to offend him, he heartily begged his pardon; that he swore by the Almighty God that he had never been in the bush to hurt him, nor any where else; on the contrary, that he had always loved him, and wished him well; and that he now begged him to be friends with him again, to forget and forgive all former quarrels, and to accept the hand which he offered him in all sincerity. The sick man also confessed, that he had always loved Edward as his brother, had "eaten and drunk with him for many years with perfect good-will," and that it was his ingratitude for such affection which vexed him more than any thing. On this I told him, that I insisted upon their being good friends for the future, and that I should never hear the word Obeah, or any such nonsense, mentioned on my estate, on pain of my extreme displeasure. I promised that, as soon as Pickle should be quite recovered, I would buy for him exactly a set of such things as had been stolen from him; that Edward should bring them to his house, to show that he had rather give him things than take them away; and I then desired to see them shake hands. They did so, with much apparent cordiality; Edward then went back to his work; and this evening, when I sent him a dish from my table, Pickle desired the servant to tell me, that he had hardly any fever, and felt "quite so so," which, in the negro dialect, means "a great deal better." I begin, therefore, to hope that we shall save the foolish fellow's life at last, which, at one time, appeared to be in great jeopardy.

JAMES STEWART, *A View of the Past and Present State of the Island of Jamaica* (Edinburgh, 1823), 276–79.

The most dangerous practice, arising from a superstitious credulity, prevailing among the negroes is, what is called *obeah*,* a pretended

---

*This practice is less common at present than it used to be.

sort of witchcraft. One negro who desires to be revenged on another, and is afraid to make an open and manly attack on his adversary, has usually recourse to *obeah*. This is considered as a potent and irresistible spell, withering and palsying, by undescribable terrors and unwonted sensations, the unhappy victim. Like the witches' caldron in Macbeth, it is a combination of many strange and ominous things— earth gathered from a grave, human blood, a piece of wood fashioned in the shape of a coffin, the feathers of the carrion-crow, a snake's or alligator's tooth, pieces of egg-shell, and other nameless ingredients, compose the fatal mixture. The whole of these articles may not be considered as absolutely necessary to complete the charm, but two or three are at least indispensable. It will of course be conceived, that the practice of *obeah* can have little effect, unless a negro is conscious that it is practised upon him, or thinks so; for as the whole evil consists in the terrors of a superstitious imagination, it is of little consequence whether it be really practised or not, if he only imagines that it is. But if the *charm* fails to take hold of the mind of the proscribed person, another and more certain expedient is resorted to—the secretly administering of poison to him. This saves the reputation of the sorcerer, and effects the purpose he had in view.[†] An *obeah* man or woman (for it is practised by both sexes) is a very wicked and dangerous person on a plantation; and the practice of it is made felony by the law, punishable with death where poison has been administered, and with transportation where only the charm is used. But numbers may be swept off by its infatuation before the crime is detected; for, strange as it may appear, so much do the negroes stand in awe of those *obeah* professors, so much do they dread their malice and their power, that, though knowing the havock they have made, and are still making, they are afraid to discover them to the whites; and others, perhaps, are in league with them for sinister purposes of mischief and revenge. A negro under this infatuation can only be cured of his terrors by being made a Christian: refuse him this boon, and he sinks a martyr to imagined evils. The author knew an instance of a negro, who, being reduced by the fatal influence of *obeah* to the lowest state of dejection and debility, from which there were little hopes of his recovery, was surprisingly and rapidly restored to health and cheerfulness by being baptized a Christian. A negro, in short, considers him-

---

†The negroes practising *obeah* are acquainted with some very powerful vegetable poisons, which they use on these occasions.

self as no longer under the influence of this sorcery when he becomes a Christian.

But, though so liable to be perverted into a deadly instrument of malice and revenge, *obeah*—at least a species of it—may be said to have its uses. When placed in the gardens and grounds of the negroes, it becomes an excellent guard or watch, scaring away the predatory runaway and midnight plunderer with more effective terror than gins and spring-guns. It loses its power, however, when put to protect the gardens and plantain-walks of the *Buckras*. When an oath is taken by a negro, according to a certain *obeah* process, it binds by ties the most sacred. This ceremony is usually performed over a grave. The creoles, however, think it equally binding to swear on *Buckra book*—the Bible.

The negroes believe in apparitions, and stand in great dread of them, conceiving that they forebode death or some other great evil to those whom they visit; in short, that the spirits of the dead come upon earth to be revenged on those who did them evil when in life.

H. T. DE LA BECHE, *Notes on the Present Conditions of the Negroes in Jamaica* (London, 1825), 29–31.

Christianity is the more easily introduced among the negroes, as its progress is not obstructed, as it is in India and many other places, by the influence of prejudices in favour of any existing system of religion among them. Obeahism can scarcely be called a religion, being little more than the superstitious dread of power of certain men, who are supposed capable of injuring others by certain preparations.* The be-

*I once received information that a strange negro was in the habit of frequenting my negro houses for the purpose of practising Obeah; after a few weeks spent in vain endeavours to secure him, I was one day fortunate enough to do so; upon searching him we found a handkerchief in his hat, containing small pieces of chalk, broken bits of various woods of a certain length, roots of grass, pieces of eel skin, two wings of a bat, two or three pieces of old leather, &c.: he endeavoured to throw this bundle away among the brushwood and trees where I came up with him. At the bottom of his breeches pocket, the search of which he violently resisted, we discovered an *Oznaburgh bag*, containing a round piece of leather, painted different colours, to the rim of which were attached small bags of various sizes, an English sixpence, a gilt button, the gilt handle of a small drawer, with a small string of beads, the little bags contained several singular mixtures, some of which were most probably poisons (for where the Obeah man cannot produce an effect on the mind, he generally has recourse to poison); in one bag was a human tooth, enveloped in a mixture, that seemed principally composed of brown soap. Such is the dread the negroes entertain of these people, that I could prevail on none of

lief in the power of Obeah men has very considerably declined of late; but some spells or preparations are still by many considered effective.[†]

CYNRIC WILLIAMS, *A Tour Through the Island of Jamaica,* . . . (London, 1826), 25–27.

We overtook a tall, strapping negro, so like in figure to one of my friend's slaves, that he saluted him with "how d' ye, Cudjoe? Which way are you going?" But before he could get an answer, looking in the man's face, he perceived his mistake, and asked again, "What's your name? Whom do you belong to? Where are you going? This is no pass."—The man replied, "Me belong to massa; me watchman; me going to mountain." My friend inquired again sharply, "What massa? What mountain?" "You massa; for you mountain, me no your neegar Cuffie?" "Well," says my friend, "this is a curious piece of effrontery; I think I ought to know all my own negroes. You must be a runaway, my man, and about no good here; so turn about, and walk with me to the works." The negro found himself in a scrape, and looked about to see how he could escape; but we headed him, and manoeuvred with our horses to keep him in the road till he came to the negro houses, where he jumped over a penguin fence that protected the gardens from the road, hoping, no doubt, to hide himself among them before we could get round by the gate. But my friend was too active for him,

them to appear and charge him with practising Obeah, though it was notorious that he had done so. He was (when I left Jamaica) to be tried for having "materials in his possession notoriously used in the practice of Obeah," which is punishable under the 53rd clause of the consolidated Slave Act, by transportation from the island, "or such other punishment, not extending to life, as the court shall think proper to direct."

[†]The negroes continue to place watchmen (as they call them), in their provision grounds, though the practice is by no means so general as formerly, these are commonly composed of pieces of the wood-ant's nest, the roots of a particular grass, grave dirt, bunches of feathers, &c., either singly or together. Some people even make small boxes, resembling the coffins of infants, line them with black or white cloth, and then fill them up with earth, and very often grave-dirt. These various "watchmen" have ceased to be much attended to by the habitual plunderers of provision grounds: two of my people were overheard one day addressing one of the coffin boxes, and telling it, that it might, if it could, inform its owner of the depredations they had committed in his provision grounds; they laughed heartily, and seemed to enjoy the joke.

Many negroes suppose that grave-dirt trod upon by a thief, if placed in his way for that purpose, will seriously injure or kill him; for example, I once heard a Halse Hall woman, passing my house early in the morning on her way to work, exclaim in a great passion, "Dem somebody tief my corn, I go lay grave-dirt in a pass (the road or path), and kill dem; me no care, Henry (meaning me) hab no nager (negroes).

and, giving his horse rein and spur, cleared the fence like an old hunter. It was negro dinner-time, and the driver and his gang were at home. Of course Cuffie was instantly secured, and led to the overseer's house, where an examination immediately took place. Partly by his own confession, and partly by the recollection of a white man present, we discovered that he belonged to a neighbouring estate, and my friend was going to send him there in custody, with a note to his overseer, according to the usual practice in such cases among neighbours, when a sharp lad, a book-keeper, said to my friend, "I wish, sir, you would let me search his (cutacoo); I have a strange fancy he has something there he ought not to have." It is impossible to convey to the reader, by description, an idea of the look which the culprit gave the young man, when he observed, in answer to his suggestion, "Warra debbil cun poor negar hab in him cutacoo, but lilly bit nyam-nyam?" However, permission was given to search. The young man, in an instant, leaped down off the steps, grappled with Cuffie, who made stout resistance, and at last succeeded in wresting the cutacoo from his grasp. The contents were immediately displayed on the steps of the overseer's house. There was an old snuff-box, several phials, some filled with liquids and some with powders, one with pounded glass; some dried herbs, teeth, beads, hair, and other trash; in short, the whole farrago of an Obeah man. The old Scotch carpenter's attention was attracted by the snuff-box, and he had taken out of it a pinch of the contents, which he was conveying to his nose, when the young lad jumped up in great agitation, with, "What are you doing? don't you know it's poison?" and with a smart rap on the knuckles kindly baulked the carpenter's gratification. We were all easily convinced of the uses to which these articles were intended to be applied, and the confusion of the man himself, at this discovery, confirmed our opinion of his guilt. My friend, on further inquiry, found that this fellow had been for some time frequenting his negro houses, and therefore in some degree accounted for sundry abortions among his women, and some other fatal occurrences among his negroes, which had previously much distressed him. He could not, however, by any direct proof, bring home to this man any interference in the calamities which he deplored, and therefore pursued his former resolution of sending him to the estate to which he said he belonged. The messenger and the culprit soon returned with a note from the overseer, stating that it was true Cuffie had formerly belonged to that estate, but having been convicted of Obeah, he had been sentenced to transportation.

R. R. MADDEN, *A Twelve Month's Residence in the West Indies, . . .*
(London, 1835), vol. II, 93–109.

To Dr. Webster.

Kingston, Sept. 8, 1834.

My dear Sir,

An obeah man was lately committed to the Spanish Town prison
for practising on the life of a negro child. It appeared in evidence that
he went to a negro hut, and asked for some fire to light his pipe; that
he was seen to put some *bush* (herb) into the pipe, and then placing
himself to windward of the child, commenced smoking, so that the
fumes were directed by the wind towards the child. Immediately after
he went away, the child was taken alarmingly ill; the father pursued
the man suspected of obeahing, and brought him back. He was accused of being an obeah man, of having injured the child; and being
threatened with violence if he did not take off the obeah, he con-
sented to do so, and accordingly performed certain ceremonies for
that purpose: the child improved and he was suffered to depart. The
improvement however was only temporary: he was again sent for, and
with a similar result.

I have copied the account of his examination by the attorney-
general, from the original document. He confessed that he was a prac-
tiser of obeah; that he did it not for gain or vengeance, but solely because the devil put it into his head to do bad. He had learned the use
of the bush from an old negro man on _____ estate, where master had
been poisoned by the old man. It was a small plant which grew in the
mountains, but did not know the name of it: (he gave some of the
dried leaves to the attorney, who showed them to me for examination;
but they were so broken that nothing was to be made of them). He
said it did him no hurt to smoke this plant; but whoever breathed the
smoke was injured by it: he had no spite against the father or mother
of the child, no wish to injure them. He saw the child, and he could
not resist the instigation of the devil to obeah it; but he hoped he
would never do it any more: he would pray to God to put it out of his
head to do it. Such was the singular statement made to the attorney-
general by the prisoner; and the attorney informed me, made with an
appearance of frankness and truth which gave a favourable impression
of its veracity.

My opinion of this case was, that notwithstanding the confession
of the man, and the evidence against him, the plant was innoxious in
the way it was administered. I did not conceive it possible to smoke

a poisonous substance with impunity, which was yet capable, when the fumes of it were only partially inhaled by another, to produce fatal effects. The man's own confession however was subjected to my opinion. The confession appeared to me to be of less importance than the evidence against him. There was hardly an unfortunate witch hanged in England or Scotland for many a year, that was not convicted chiefly on her own confession; and it need not be stated how such confessions were obtained. On further inquiry into this case, I discovered that the threat of the torture of thumb-screwing had been had recourse to by the father of the child and other negroes before the confession was made. But why should an innocent man persist in a confession of guilt extorted from him in a moment of terror, when he is no longer subjected to its tyranny? To this I answer—The impression of great terror is not so easily effaced, even by the removal of the cause that inspired it; the importance of the means in self-defence adopted for its dissipation becomes an exaggerated sentiment, which dupes the enfeebled mind, and actually converts a deceit into a delusion. It was said by *Warren Hastings,* when he listened to his impeachment in the House of Commons, that such was the overwhelming effect of the language in which the atrocities ascribed to him were couched by his accuser, that he actually believed himself at the time the guilty wretch he was represented to be. If such an effect could be produced for a moment on the mind of an enlightened man, by an accusation that involved not life or limb, a graver accusation that placed both in jeopardy might well have a permanent influence on the uncultivated intellect. The man was not prosecuted.

A negro was brought before me and Dr. Maglashan, one of the local magistrates, previous to August, charged with obeahing the only child of a negro woman, after having caused the death of three others of her children. The mother gave her evidence in a state of great excitement; several of her female neighbours confirmed it, and it amounted to this—that the prisoner's wife had no children, and was jealous of the complainant on this account; that she had persuaded her husband to obeah her children one after another, till they had all died, and had now put obeah on herself, in order to prevent her having any more.

Dr. Maglashan took the utmost pains to soothe her excitement, and persuade her of the error she was labouring under.

Here there was no charge of poisoning, but of killing by the supernatural agency of obeah: I also endeavoured to convince her of the delusion; but it was only when I called on the man to declare, that even if he had the power to put obeah on her, which was impossible, he would never do it, that she appeared at all satisfied, or the friends who accompanied her. In this instance the man bore an excellent character, and there was no earthly ground for the charge: nevertheless, in former years he might have been hanged on such a charge, for an obeah man. The excellent old gentleman, whose name I had occasion to mention in this case, has since died: happy would it be for Jamaica, if the local magistracy consisted solely of persons like this venerable man; for one more humane, more intelligent, and in every respect more efficient than this gentleman, who, I believe, was one of the oldest inhabitants of St. Andrews, I have not met with. There are two descriptions of obeah; one that is practised by means of incantations; and the other, by the administration of medicated potions—in former times, it is said of poisons, and these practitioners were called *myal men.*

A negro was tried some years ago at *Spanish Town,* for practising obeah, under the following circumstances: Dr. _____ being about to get married, a person of colour, who up to this period had been his housekeeper, had recourse to an obeah man, to break the Doctor's attachment to his betrothed lady: suspicion of what was going on brought the Doctor to the house; and on his entrance, he found the customary obeah dance going on, both repeating incantations,—the necessary part of the ceremony, ablutions, and the administering of a potion having taken place. In this dance the principal part of the initiated person's vesture is dispensed with: there was an iron pot in the centre of the room, round which the dancing was going on, and in it was a cock's head, serpents' eggs, blood, and grave dirt. The principal facts were deposed to on the trial, by the Doctor: the man was condemned for life to the workhouse, and he died in jail about 1827. Many instances of this kind, and under similar circumstances, have occurred.

In the criminal record-book of the parish of St. Andrews, I find the following obeah cases:—

1773. Sarah, tried "for having in her possession cats' teeth, cats' claws, cats' jaws, hair, beads, knotted cords, and other materials, relative to the practice of obeah, to delude and impose on the minds of the negroes."—Sentenced to be transported.

1776. Solomon, "for having materials in his possession for the practice of obeah."—To be transported.

1777. Tony, "for practising obeah, or witchcraft, on a slave named Fortune, by means of which, said slave became dangerously ill."—Not Guilty.

1782. Neptune, "for making use of rum, hair, chalk, stones, and other materials, relative to the practice of obeah, or witchcraft."—To be transported. . . .

The description of the ingredients in the above indictments, made use of in these African incantations, reminds one forcibly of the ingredients for the charmed cauldron of the Weird sisters—

One of the necessary ingredients for the obeah ceremony, is either the head, feathers, or claws of a fowl; but there is nothing held in so much estimation for obeah rites, as a perfectly white cock; and if it happens to crow while the ceremony is going on, it is reckoned a good omen, and the fetish who presides over the ceremony is supposed to be propitiated. There are two obeah ordeals in use here, which I do not remember to have seen mentioned in any work:

The Book Ordeal

To find out the person who has committed a theft, all parties present are called upon to open a Bible, 10th chapter of Kings: they then place a key between the leaves, and tie it in the closed book with a slender thread; the key is held between the tips of the two second fingers; the book is then struck after a portion of the 50th psalm has been read, and if the person is present who committed the theft, the key will remain in the hands of the holder, and the book will fall to the ground. This is a singular instance of an African superstition engrafted on Christianity.

The Broom Ordeal

The broom ordeal is practised by cementing two layers of light broom, with ashes mixed with water: the suspected person is then placed on a stool, and calls on God to show who is the guilty person. The slight broom wicker is then pressed round his throat: if it happens to give way, it is a proof that he is innocent; but if the pressure should cause him to fall from the stool, that circumstance is an evidence of his guilt. . . .

. . . . Edwards' observations on the derivation of this word deserve attention:—"The general term," he says, "in Jamaica, denotes those Africans who in that island practise witchcraft or sorcery; comprehending, also, the class of what are called myal men, or those who, by means of a narcotic potion, made with the juice of a herb said to be branched callalu,—a species of solanum, which occasions a trance, or profound sleep of a certain duration,—endeavour to convince the deluded spectators of their power to re-animate dead bodies." The influence of the terror of obeah over the Negroes some twenty or thirty years ago, was almost incredible: even at the present time it is greatly dreaded by the least instructed of the Negroes. In this, as in many other matters, the exertions of the missionaries have been evidently beneficial to the negroes: obeah no longer has the power of producing mischief to the extent it formerly did. The dread of it is greatest amongst the Africans. Some of the Creole negroes affect to laugh at it; but when I have seen their courage put to the test when they have been menaced with obeah, or they think it has been set for them, the old superstition takes possession of their fears. When I lived in St. Andrews, in one of my morning rambles between my house and Mr. Hall's, I found a piece of dirty rag tied up like a bag, about the size of a walnut. It contained some dried brown leaves broken into small bits, shreds of red wood rolled up, mixed with hair and some dirt. This was obeah that in all probability had been set for some person. I took it home and had it placed over the door of an old Mulatto woman,—a very troublesome old lady, who carried water for us, and who had a mortal aversion for Johnny Crows whenever she was indisposed. Her antipathy to this black angel of death, Captain Mason and myself were often in the habit of rallying her about: one day she lost patience, and told me it was only for buckra the Johnny Crows were flapping their big wings.

The Johnny Crows made me feel the less repugnance to give the old woman a fright in order to give the other negroes a lesson: the dirty bag of evil augury was placed over her door so conspicuously that it was sure to be discovered. It was discovered. A volley of moans and groans, and devotional ejaculations, gave us intimation of her having found it: "Her enemies had found her out: they had set obi for her; it could be placed there for nobody else." The other negroes were nearly as much frightened, with the exception of a servant-boy who was in on the secret. I soon relieved the old lady's apprehensions after some time, on the score of being obeahed; but if it were not for the boy's testimony, I think she would hardly have believed me: as it was, it was very difficult to convince her of the folly of her fears.

The fetish is the African divinity, invoked by the negroes in the practice of obeah. When they take an oath, they say they "take the fetish"; and when they worship, they "make fetish." I believe the word is peculiar to the dialect of Guinea, and signifies "a charm or incantation," as well as a divinity.

They have a singular idea that, if they swear falsely on the fetish, their stomachs will burst, their faces will be scratched, and their fingers will drop off, and, what is still more, a great many of them have the same apprehension, coupled with their ideas of the obligation of an oath in the Christian scriptures. A Mrs. Panther, a whited-brown lady, brought a negro girl before me, to give evidence against one of her apprentices. I inquired of her if the girl, who was about seventeen or eighteen, knew the nature of an oath? She seemed a little hurt at a question which, she thought, implied a doubt of the girl's being duly instructed. I repeated the question, however; and, to the great discomfiture of Mrs. Panther, and the no small surprise of a crowded court, the poor girl replied, "Massa, if me swear false, my stomach (I will not vouch for this word) would burst, my face would be scratched, and my fingers drop off." I could not avoid complimenting her mistress on the result of the pains that had been taken with the poor girl's improvement, and the case was dismissed for want of better testimony.

I have heard the same idea expressed respecting the obligation of an oath on two other occasions. The negro Sharp, who was one of the chief planners of the late rebellion, reluctantly confessed the part he had taken in the conspiracy, and the form of oath administered to the negroes, when they came to be sworn in, at a house on Retrievo estate, some weeks before Christmas. A bible was brought, and put on the table. The person to be sworn got up and said, "If ever I witness any thing against my brother and sister concerning this matter, may hell be my portion!"

Edwards mentions a mode of administering an oath, which, I heard, in the late rebellion was practised by the negroes, either by the immediate descendants of Africans, or those not attached to the religious societies of any Christian sect.

"Human blood, and earth taken from the grave of some near relative, are mixed with water, and given to the party to be sworn; who is compelled to drink the mixture, with an imprecation that it may cause the belly to burst, and the bones to rot, if the truth be not spoken. This test is frequently administered to their wives, on the suspicion of infidelity; and the resemblance which it bears to the trial of jealousy, by the bitter water, described in the book of Numbers, is a curious and striking circumstance."

Formerly, the influence of obeah practitioners was very great over the negroes. Hundreds have died of the mere terror of being under the ban of obeah. A little bag, with a few trumpery and harmless ingredients, hung up over a door, was sufficient to break down the health and spirits of the stoutest-hearted African. The Koromantyn rebel who was capable of facing death in its most appalling form without a murmur, has been often driven into rebellion by the terror of an obeah bag, and an intimation that he had not taken the fetish, or the oath of fidelity to a new conspiracy. In 1760, an obeah instigator to rebellion was put to death. During the twenty years subsequent to this period, a great many negroes were hanged for obeah crimes. Those charged with them were generally old, misshapen, or deformed negroes, of African origin. In the slave law, passed 1831, the capital crime of obeah is defined to be, the administering of any poisonous or deleterious ingredient, such as pounded glass, although death may not ensue therefrom.

But the ingredients that are now in use for obeah purposes are harmless substances: cats' claws, parrots' beaks, grave dirt, &c. strung up in little bags, over people's doors; and the charmers are generally old women, whose wrinkles are their chief titles to the character of wise women. So long as these poor bodies were hanged and flagellated for the exercise of their African sorcery, obeah flourished—like some other things, which, the more they are prosecuted, the more they prosper; but when humanity came to the aid of legislative wisdom, and softened down some of the most prominent barbarities of former enactments—that especially respecting obeah, the practice was deprived of the principal source of the reverence it exacted, when the exposure of its absurdities was divested of the cruelties which made a merit, in former times, of persisting in them. But though judicial barbarities were practised in Jamaica within the last forty years, which have been unknown to Europe for upwards of a century, and executions for witchcraft or obeah, and torturing practices (though not by course of law, by means of thumb-screws), been had recourse to,—even much later, instances have occurred in Great Britain, within the last thirty years, in which the mob have endeavoured to revive the savagery of the law, and have taken into their own hands the punishment of the crime of witchcraft. . . .

Hundreds of poor negroes, I am convinced, have been executed in Jamaica for witchcraft equally weak in intellect. The Africans, like all other people who profess the Mahometan faith, have an opinion that insanity and supernatural inspiration are frequently combined, and, consequently, knaves and lunatics (partially insane) are commonly the persons who play the parts of santons and sorcerers. The Africans carried most of their superstitions to our colonies, and, amongst others, their reverence for those, either whose physical or mental peculiarities distinguished them from the multitude,—and such were the persons who, in advanced age, usually took on themselves the obeah character. It is evident to any medical man who

reads these trials, that in the great majority of cases the trumpery ingredients used in the practice of obeah were incapable of producing
mischief except on the imagination of the person intended to be
obeahed.

ANONYMOUS, *Missionary Work and Adventure* (London, 1838),
136–39.

One Sabbath evening, in a meeting of session, B_____ of *Success* estate was charged with having gone to a reputed Obea man to help him
out of a scrape. M_____, the Obea man, was one I had often exhorted,
without knowing his character, but always in vain. He pretended
sometimes to be stupid, unable to understand what was said to him;
and at other times excused himself from coming to church by his
watchman's duties in the provision grounds. Of late a great change
had appeared in him, and his testimony on this occasion surprised me,
by the intelligence and change of views it evidenced. He said that
B_____ had come to his hut with the usual fees, money and rum,
begging for help, for he was in trouble, and no man could get him out
of it like M_____. Instead of complying, he reproved B_____, saying
that he had given up all these bad ways, and begun to hear the gospel;
and why should B_____, who had long time heard the good word,
want to go back to them again. He advised B_____ to follow the light
as he was trying to do, and to confess his sin if he had done anything
bad, and repent, and pray God to help him, for he only could. Old
M_____ spoke with a clearness and animation quite refreshing, and
his evidence confounded poor B_____, who, self-condemned, had
nothing to say.

  "*May* 11, 1838.—G_____ T_____ came to-day to explain his
wife's case, which, he assured me, had been misreported. She has
been long in bad health, and nothing the white doctor could do was
of any use. A Christian sister, however, who was staying with them
lately, had made his wife drink of herbs, which, in the middle of the
night, caused her to sneeze violently, and cast out of her nostrils two
pieces of bottle glass. These he showed me, and he believed they had
caused her sickness. How they got into her head he could not tell; but
sure he was they came out of it in the way he described, and now he
expected she would get better."

  This strange story, which he told with the utmost gravity, and
expected me to believe, was in every particular destitute of truth. The
fact was, that he and his wife had gone to a Myal woman, of great re-

pute on Iron Shore estate, for a cure. That woman's mode of practice being *(secundum artem nigram),* or of a genuine African kind, was one we discouraged, as both unlawful and deceptive. Her system was to extract from the diseased body the vitiating substances, which some unknown enemy had, by magic arts, imbedded there. By sucking, or sneezing, or retching, she caused the pins, glass, or nails to be extracted from the sufferer's flesh. This came out at our next examination.

"*May* 20—G_____ T_____ and his wife appeared before the session. She admitted having gone to the Myal woman, by her husband's desire, for the cure of her sickness, and showed a piece of bottle glass that had been sucked out of her shoulder, and said that since then she had felt better. In vain were all attempts of the session to convince them of their error. The example of Ahaziah, who died in the sickness for which he had sought a cure from a strange god, was no warning to them. She knew when she was sick and when she was well, and that was enough for her. They were both suspended from membership, till they should show more both of faith and sense."

It may be well to state here what we knew at that time of the *Myal* system, which came a few years afterwards to be so fully revealed. It must not be confounded with *Obea,* to which indeed it was wholly opposed. It affected to cure the sicknesses, and remove other evils, which the Obea produced. The Myal practitioners counted themselves angels of light, and called those of the opposite craft angels of darkness.

It was part of the art and power of a Myal man also to *catch the shadow* of a deceased person, and retain it for purposes of necromancy. It must be caught at the grave, at or soon after interment; therefore in the dusk of the evening, when burials usually took place, or by moonlight, a fitting time for such mysterious proceedings. In the midst of the people encircling the grave, the Myal man saw, what was unseen by others, the shadow or spirit of the departed hovering over its last tenement; and he tried by many violent gestures, leaping and grasping, to seize it, or by strange voices to charm it, as it flitted about and evaded him. When he succeeded, he secured it in a tiny coffin ready for the purpose, to be buried in the same grave, or deposited in the house, and under the bed, of the practitioner for future use. Sometimes it could not be easily caught, and escaped to the pastures or bush, whither the by-standers followed the Myal man in pursuit, over hedges and ditches, stone dykes and all difficulties, following may be a fire-fly, or night bird, anything or nothing, till the leader had gained his object and secured the ghost.

This kind of work was long kept a secret. It had begun to be disused, checked by severe legislative repression and increasing Christian light. The Guinea negroes never spoke to "Buckra" of their "country fashions"; and not till we had Christian young men growing up around us could certain information be obtained on those subjects. Even they spoke about them with such reserve and dread as the idea of "a familiar spirit," a "medium" of communication with the invisible world, was fitted to create.

The delusion went the length of supposing that the shadow could be lost even before death; that someone could steal away another's soul. I knew a girl about sixteen years of age, who was greatly afflicted with the idea that she had lost her shadow. Someone had stolen it, she said; and she went seeking it by the bushy banks of streams, or round the gigantic cotton tree, or in other haunted spots, by moonlight, among all the shadows of such places at such a time. She was not lunatic, I was assured by her friends, who brought her to me for a cure; and though they did not believe in such things, they affirmed that many others did. My prayers and good words were unable to relieve her mind and dry her tears; my faith perhaps being too weak to cast out devils.

These strange superstitions came from Africa. We found them afterwards at Calabar. Some persons were believed to be able to call up departed souls, and question them on important business. Others believed not only that the soul or shadow could live apart from the body, but that the body could live apart from it, as is the case with the inferior animals, destitute of a soul like man. The chief of Old Town had a sacred grove, near a spring of water, where his soul was kept safely; and he complained that the labourers belonging to the mission house there, who were clearing the ground all about, went too near the sacred spot, and troubled his soul. "You always tell us," said he to the missionary, "that every man must mind his soul. Why do your men go trouble my soul at that place?" The Calabar word for soul is that used for shadow. In his last sickness he believed that someone had possessed himself of his soul, and bottled it up to prevent its returning to him. He even complained to the kings of Duke Town and Creek Town that some one had stolen his soul; and these rulers had proclamation made that the audacious thief, whoever he might be, should let the shadow escape, or whenever detected, die the most terrible death. Nothing availed, however, to cure his delusion or restore his lost spirit. The chief of another town having been long ill, got persuaded that certain persons had stolen his soul or shadow, and buried

it, and so held him bound in sickness. He charged them with it, and
desired they should clear themselves by the poison ordeal. The accused did not say that the charge was absurd, or unheard of, but simply that they were not guilty of the crime imputed to them, and wisely
refused the dangerous trial.

ANONYMOUS, *Letters From the Virgin Islands* (London, 1843), 148.

. . . And superstition is on the wane among our negroes; they seem to
confess that whatever appetis (spells) their magicians could once effect, these have long since failed before superior Christian cantations.
The Obeah man with his cutacoo—whose nuptic contents usually
comprise an old snuff box, human hair, dried grass and other trash—
cannot protect himself when discovered, nor gather a poor pittance
from his old devotees. The more harmless pageant of Jonkanoo also,
with its little emblem of Noah's Ark, have fallen into disuse together
with Obeah.

MRS. HENRY LYNCH, *The Wonders of the West Indies* (London,
1856), 160–77.

The great superstition amongst the negroes in the West Indies is that
of Obeahism. The witch of Endor is called in the Hebrew language
Obi; the word therefore has reached Africa through the Arabic of the
Mohammedans. In Hayti, the term Obeah is not known. The charms
are spoken of as *Arranga,* and the enchanter as *Macandai.* Amongst
the Egyptians, a serpent is called Obion; and Moses in the name God,
forbad the Israelites ever to enquire of the demon Obi, translated in
the Bible, Wizard.

At first sight this Obeahism appears but a harmless delusion; and
it is only when we look closely into it, that the dark mischief it works
becomes apparent. The Obeah Chief is on all occasions looked up to
as an oracle. He is considered potent to heal diseases; to discover
crime, and for the bribe of gold, he will through risk and danger find
means to satisfy the applicant's wildest thirst for revenge. The more
terrible the appearance of the Obeah man, the more power can he exert over his victims. If his face be deeply furrowed with the harshest
lines of age; if his beard be matted and grizzled; his gait loitering, and
his figure deformed; so much the better for his purpose. Knowing well
the peculiar nature of the people on whom he seeks to impose; he effects a husky and croaking voice, and thus more effectually imposes

on the negro. The shrivelled old man is viewed as the unerring prophet; and the implicit belief in his pretended communion with demons is apparent in the horror-stricken countenances of those around him. And this pandering with the deepest emotions of the human heart, was by no means an unprofitable employment. Obeahism assumed a power over health and illness, life and death. The shadows of night gave a mysterious influence to the midnight incantation, and the self-deceived enquirer at this evil shrine was soon led to imagine, that a supernatural power was at work on his enemy.

A fair young girl from England became perhaps unsuspectingly the bride of some creole planter. She thought that her husband had been free to seek her affections; and little dreamed she had, by her marriage, displaced from the situation of housekeeper one of Africa's dusky daughters; who with a burning jealousy at her heart, was plotting with the Obeah man a scheme for her rival's destruction. So baneful was the nature of this Obeah practice, that the negro woman, who would have stood aghast at the very thought of murder, fancied herself quite justified in "turning the eyes," as the expression is, of her young mistress; and to accomplish this would not hesitate to set Obi for her, or in other words to receive from the Obeah man a slow poison which she dexterously inserted in the food of her unsuspecting victim, a mission which she is generally most careful to fulfill, having received from the old man the prophetic assurance, that by thus acting, she will regain the lost affections of her master. The bodily disease, the natural consequence of poison, is immediately attributed by the infatuated slave to the power of the Obeah chief; and if the agent of this sin-stained man feel any latent compunction, any sharp pang of conscience, when she looks on the success of her scheme in the drooping form and sunken cheeks of her mistress, on the very system of papal indulgences, for a little more money given to the Obeah man, she is assured that all is right, and she watches calmly her helpless rival sink into the grave.

With the advance of civilization attendant on freedom, this obeahism has almost passed away from the British West Indies. The present race of English negroes, though still listless and idle, and almost entirely devoid of enterprise, are comparatively an enlightened set, as the ignorance which was justly considered an indispensable requisite for slavery is unnecessary for free labour; the blacks are no longer shut out from the means of improvement; schools are established throughout the West Indies, and the rising generation in many instances, excels in knowledge the village poor of England.

We are now speaking of obeahism, as it was more than fifty years ago. With the grand-daughter of a lady who lost her life from the practice of Obeah, we were intimately acquainted. This lady noticed a mysterious community of interest among some of the negroes on the estate. In the hut of one of the slaves was found a collection of feathers, bottles, rags, alligator's teeth, fish bones, and egg shells; and whilst her husband passed them by with a laugh, as symbols of a harmless superstition, she felt convinced that some deep and terrible mischief lay hidden under these fantastic emblems. As if consumption had marked her for its own, the lady passed away from life, withering as a summer flower sometimes does, with sunshine gleaming around it; and many long years afterwards when she was but imperfectly recollected as a dream of the morning, a dying negro woman revealed the terrible fact to her startled master, that she had long, long ago poisoned his fair English bride. Knowing her mistress' practice of taking every morning a fresh egg for breakfast, she had contrived to insinuate poison through the shell, and thus to work out the Obeah which had been put on her mistress. The woman died a few hours after this confession.

When a negro is put under Obeah; strange as it may seem, poison is not necessary to deprive him of life. The effect of this superstition on his mind is most astonishing. If a garden or poultry yard has been robbed, the proprietor, himself a negro, applies to the man of witchcraft, to set Obi for the thief. It is talked of among the neighbours, and as soon as the culprit discovers that he is under Obi, his imagination conjures up a thousand horrors, which playing riot in his heart, work a real ruin on the physical part of his nature. A settled despondency overshadows him, and the terror in his soul saps the very springs of life. The negro is peculiarly susceptible and credulous, and the anticipation of indefinite evil hurries the emaciated victim to his grave.

If a negro is taken ill, he enquires of the Obeah man, whether the sickness be unto death. Should this dire prophet give a chance of recovery, all is well. But if on the contrary when the infatuated inquirer has laid open the anxieties of his soul, he receive an indefinite or doubtful answer, terror and fear become the able ministers of disease, and the poor man finds himself in a very short time standing on the very confines of life.

Many years ago, the proprietor of a fine lowland estate in Jamaica observed that there was a great mortality amongst his negroes. There was no fever prevalent; neither was there any epidemic at that time in the island. Sometimes two or three persons were buried in one day, and the doctor began to suspect, that Obeah was practised on the place. At length in the extremity of her fear, a young woman told her master that all the negroes who had died, had previously been put under Obi, and this led to further investigation. The house of the accused was searched; a variety of articles belonging to the practice of the superstition were found in her house, and her master feeling persuaded that she was an Obeah enchantress, sent her off to one of the other West India islands. This punishment had the desired effect. She never again followed those evil courses, and the negroes on the estate from which she was banished were soon restored to their usual health and tranquillity.

Myalism is said to be the disenchanter of Obeahism. Their impositions are very nearly related to each other. The Myalmen by means of a narcotic potion made from a species of calalue, pretend to be able to reanimate dead bodies, and assert, that they can at any time keep the stern messenger death from themselves.

Although these superstitions are, with the dark ignorance fostered by slavery, passing gradually away in the West Indies, some three or four years ago, Dr. T_____ travelled through Jamaica successfully practising Myalism, and actually pressing out of the credulity of the negro not less than fifteen or twenty pounds a day.

There was an estate in the country, on which, after a season of drought, the river which was a large one became dry. Under the influence of some inconceivable infatuation, the proprietor, an educated Englishman, drove Dr. T_____ in his own carriage to the river side. There was a well near its banks into which the doctor was let down; when he appeared again, he brought an alabaster doll from his bosom, and told the negroes who crowded round him, for he had not quite hardihood enough to look at the proprietor, that he had brought up in his arms the mermaid who kept the waters from flowing. He received a handsome fee for thus capturing the spirit of the drought, and though some time passed away before the stream again bore its burden of waters to the ocean; yet when the drought ceased it was attributed with solemn gravity to the influence of Dr. T_____ over the mermaid, and He who sends the early and the latter rain was unthought of. At length the doctor was sentenced to imprisonment for raising money under false pretences, and though he contrived to impress his fellow convicts with an idea of his control over the last enemy, they were soon made sensible of the folly of their credulity by the circumstance of his sudden death from a large stone which fell on him.

PLATO

During the last century there was another man who rose to some celebrity as an Obeah chief. A runaway slave named Plato, established
himself in the heart of the Jamaica mountains, and soon had a lawless
and wild banditti at his command. Robbery and murder lengthened
the catalogue of their crimes. But Plato's detection was no easy matter; for any negro who ventured to hint at the place of his retreat, gave
way from that very moment to a melancholy foreboding of evil, he became tortured with dreams, and in every shadow on his way fancied
he discovered the dark presence of the evil one; he never doubted
that this Obeah chief, learning by intuition the revelation he had
made, set Obi for him. Plato threatened that whoever put a hand on
him should not only suffer physically, but should endure spiritual tor-
ments, and that these would be the fearful precursors of insanity. He
was a handsome athletic man, and collected at his home many of the
young negro women who were discontented with their masters. The
furniture of this mud-walled house is said to have been uncommonly
good; and to supply his many wives with sumptuous apparel, he
robbed the Creole ladies of their finery, as they were on their way to
the sessions in Spanish Town; and if the waiting-maid were in any
way attractive, he ran off with her as well as with the band-box.

Unfortunately for Plato, he persuaded himself that he could not
live without drinking ardent spirits; and this was not the caprice of
the moment, rum had become almost necessary to his existence. At
one time, having established himself in the neighborhood of Montego
Bay, he started at twilight into the town to purchase his favourite potion. He was recognised by a negro, who immediately gave the alarm
that Plato was in sight. Echo wafted the dreaded name from tree to
tree, but alas, no one was within hearing. The angry Obeahman
rushed on the frightened slave, and raising the axe with which he was
armed, aimed a heavy blow at his enemy, who escaped it by flying
precipitately before his pursuer. Plato however, was very swift of foot,
and gained every moment on the negro, who suddenly ascended into
a bread-fruit tree which presented itself at the road side. Plato could
not follow, for he was no climber, but he began to hew down the tree
with his axe, and would soon have succeeded in so doing if his enemy
had not contrived to pelt him on the head with pieces of the tree,
which he brake from the boughs around him. This so delayed Plato in

his work, that the shrieks of the slave were heard before it was completed, and the Obeah man was obliged in his turn to seek safety by flight.

Having one day purchased some spirits, he could not resist putting the tempting draught to his lips on his way home; and to drink with moderation, being at all times a difficulty with Plato, he quaffed the whole of the dangerous potion, and very soon lay senseless at the road side. In this condition he was easily made prisoner, and shortly after he was tried at the quarterly sessions at Montego Bay. He was convicted of more than one murder and speedily condemned to die. Plato heard his sentence with extraordinary calmness, and with an odd wild smile, which indifference the negroes attributed to the power of Obeahism. He told the magistrates, and it is affirmed that his skin grew supernaturally black as he spoke, that God would avenge his death by a terrible storm, which that very year should shake the island to its foundations, and cause the waters that surrounded it to rush in as a destroying flood upon the land; and those who know anything of the records of the West Indies will be aware, that in that very year, 1780, a fearful hurricane devastated Jamaica, and that the sea passing its usual boundaries, rolled in and deluged the land.

There were trembling hearts in that Court of Justice, and Plato told his executioner that he had set Obi for him, and that he being the minister of his public ignominy should meet his retribution by death before the expiration of the year. The unfortunate young man became care-worn and emaciated, and medical skill could do nothing for the fear which was gnawing at his heart. He was sent to America in the hope that change of air might revive him: no expense was spared, but all was in vain.

Religion was not much in vogue at that time in the West Indies. It was considered dangerous to instruct a slave in the precepts of Christianity; and no one spoke to the poor man of the Balm in Gilead. Mental suffering undermined his constitution, and in the midst of sympathising friends and experienced doctors, without any tangible disease, he pined away, and, before the year was over, died.

These accidental circumstances were looked upon as miraculous by the negroes. Plato's name was mentioned reverently, and in a mysterious whisper. Obeahism was more implicitly believed in than ever; and, for years after Plato's death, the stoutest-hearted negro trembled and turned pale if he had to walk at night in the vicinity of this Obeah chief's old habitation; for it was confidently asserted that his duppy roamed about in the starlight, and had more than once been seen, axe in hand, under the very bread-fruit-tree which had witnessed his discomfiture.

Choice Notes from "Notes and Queries"—Folklore (London, 1859), 229.

OBEISM

In the early part of this century, Obeism was very common among the slave-population in the West Indies, especially on the remoter estates—of course of African origin—not as either a "religion" or a "rite," but rather as a superstition; a power claimed by its professors, and assented to by the *patients,* of causing good or evil to, or averting it from them; which was of course always for a "consideration" of some sort, to the profit, whether honorary, pecuniary, or other, of the dispenser. It is by the pretended influence of certain spells, charms, ceremonies, amulets worn, or other such incantations, as practised with more or less diversity by the adepts, the magicians and conjurers, the "false prophets" of all ages and countries.

On this matter, a curious phenomenon to investigate would be, the process by which the untonsured neophyte is converted into the bonneted doctor; the progress and stages of his mind in the different phases of the practice; how he begins by deceiving himself to end in deceiving others; the first uninquiring ignorance; the gradual admission of ideas, what he is taught or left to imagine; the faith, or what is fancied to be so, the mechanical belief; then the confusion of thought from the intrusion of doubt and uncertainty; the adoption of some undefined notions; and, finally, actual unbelief; followed by designed and systematic injustice in the practice of what first was taken up in sincerity, though even this now perhaps is not unmixed with some fancy of its reality. For this must be the gradation more or less gone through in all such things, whether Obeism, Fetichism, the Evil Eye, or any sort of sorcery or witchcraft, in whatever variousness of form practised; cheats on the one hand, and dupes on the other: the *primum mobile* in every case being some shape or other of *gain* to the practitioner.

It seems, however, hardly likely that the Obeism should now be "rapidly" gaining ground again there, from the greater spread of Christianity and diffusion of enlightenment and information in general since the slave-emancipation; as also from the absence of its feeding that formerly accompanied every fresh importation from the coast: as, like mists before the mounting sun, all such impostures must fade away before common sense, truth, and facts, whenever these are allowed their free influence.

The conclusion, then, would rather be, that Obeism is on the decline; only more apparent, when now seen, than formerly, from its attracting greater notice.

M.

I was for a short time on the island of Jamaica, and from what I could learn there of Obeahism, the power seemed to be obtained by the Obeah-man or woman, by working upon the fears of their fellow-negroes, who are notoriously superstitious. The principal charm seemed to be, a collection of feathers, coffin furniture, and one or two other things which I've forgotten. A small bundle of this, hung over the victim's door, or placed in his path, is supposed to have the power of bringing ill luck to the unfortunate individual. And if any accident, or loss, or sickness should happen to him about the time, it is immediately imputed to the dreaded influence of Obeah! But I have heard of cases where the unfortunate victim has gradually wasted away, and died under this powerful spell, which, I have been informed by old residents in the island, is to be attributed to a more natural cause, namely, the influence of poison. The Obeah-man causes a quantity of *ground glass* to be mixed with the food of the person who has incurred his displeasure; and the result is said to be a slow but sure and wasting death! Perhaps some of your medical readers can say whether an infusion of powdered glass would have this effect. I merely relate what I have been told by others.

D. P. W.

CHARLES RAMPINI, *Letters from Jamaica* (Edinburgh, 1873), 131–42.

Of all the motive powers which influence the negro character, by far the most potent, as it is also the most dangerous, is that of Obeah.

"Obeah in Jamaica," says Mr. Beckford Davis, in his evidence before the Royal Commission,* "is a twofold art. It is the art of poisoning, combined with the art of imposing upon the credulity of ignorant people by a pretence of witchcraft." The obeah man or woman is one of the great guild or fraternity of crime. Hardly a criminal trial

---

*Jamaica Royal Commission, 28th day, p. 521.

occurs in the colony in which he is not implicated in one way or another. His influence over the country people is unbounded. He is the prophet, priest, and king of his district. Does a maiden want a charm to make her lover "good" to her? does a woman desire a safe delivery in child-birth? does a man wish to be avenged of his enemy, or to know the secrets of futurity?—the obeah-man is at hand to supply the means and to proffer his advice. Under the style and title of a "bush doctor," he wanders from place to place, exacting "coshery" from his dupes on all hands: supplied with food by one, with shelter by another, with money by a third, denied nought, from the mysterious terror with which he is regarded, and refused nothing from fear of the terrible retribution which might be the consequences of such a rash act. His pretensions are high: but he has means at hand to enforce them. He can cure all diseases; he can protect a man from the consequences of his crime; he can even reanimate the dead. His knowledge of simples is immense. Every bush and every tree furnishes weapons for his armoury. Unfortunately, in too many instances more potent agents are not wanting to his hand. His stock-in trade consists of lizards' bones, old eggshells, tufts of hair, cats' claws, ducks' skulls, an old pack of cards, rusty nails, and things of that description. "Gravedirt," that is, earth taken from where a corpse has been buried, is also largely used. "It is supposed that if an obeah-man throws it at a person he will die."[†] But ground glass, arsenic, and other poisons, are not unfrequently found among the contents of the obeah-man's "pussskin" wallet; and it is not difficult to conjecture for what purposes these are employed.

As an outward and visible sign of his power, the obeah-man sometimes carries about with him a long staff or wand, with twisted serpents, or the rude likeness of a human head carved round the handle. He has his cabalistic book, too, full of strange characters, which he pretends to consult in the exercise of his calling. One of these is now in my possession. It is an old child's copy-book, well thumbed and very dirty. Each page is covered with rude delineations of the human figure, and roughly-traced diagrams and devices. Between each line there runs a rugged scrawl, intended to imitate writing. The moral precepts engraved at the head of each page seem strangely out of place with the meaningless signs and symbols which occupy the remainder of its space.

†Mr. Davis's Evidence, Royal Commission, p. 522.

There is something indescribably sinister about the appearance of an obeah-man, which is readily observed by persons who have mixed much with the negroes. With a dirty handkerchief bound tightly round his forehead, and his small, bright, cunning eyes peering out from underneath it, he sometimes visits the courts of petty sessions throughout the island, if some unfortunate client of his who has got into trouble requires his aid to defend him. On one occasion a notorious thief was brought up before one of these local tribunals, charged with stealing a few shillings' worth of ground provisions. Instead of employing a lawyer he committed his defence to an obeah-man, who promised him, in consideration of a fee of £3, 3s., that on the day of trial he would attend in court, and by "fixing the eye" of the presiding magistrate, obtain the prisoner's acquittal. But, all the same, the man was convicted and sentenced to three months' imprisonment, with hard labour.

Serpent or devil worship is by no means rare in the country districts; and of its heathen rites the obeah-man is invariably the priest. Many of them keep a stuffed snake in their huts as a domestic god—a practice still common in Africa, from which of course the custom has been derived.[‡] One of the commonest deceptions which the obeah-man practices upon his dupes, is by persuading them that they have lost their shadows.[§] "I was present," says Mr. Barclay, "some years ago, at the trial of a notorious obeah-man, driver on an estate in the parish of St. David, who, by the overwhelming influence he had acquired over the minds of his deluded victims, and the more potent means he had at command to accomplish his ends, had done great injury among the slaves on the property before it was discovered. One of the witnesses, a negro belonging to the same estate, was asked— 'Do you know the prisoner to be an obeah-man?' *'Ees, massa; shadow-catcher true.'* 'What do you mean by shadow-catcher?' *'Him heb coffin* [a little coffin produced] *him set fo catch dem shadow.'* 'What shadow do you mean?' *'When him set obeah for summary* (somebody) *him catch dem shadow and dem go dead.'* And too surely they were soon

---

[‡]Among the annual festivals is the pilgrimage of the nation of Fida to the great serpent. The people, collected before the house of the serpent, lying upon their faces, worship his supposed divinity, without daring to look upon him."—Prichard, *Natural History of Man*, p. 533. The Fida, besides the great serpent which is adored by the whole nation, have each their particular smaller serpents, which are worshipped as household gods, but are not esteemed so powerful by far as the great one to whom the smaller serpents are subjected.—Prichard, p. 527.

[§]See case given in Waddell's *West Indies and Central Africa*, p. 138. London, 1863.

dead, when he pretended to have caught their shadows, by whatever means it was effected."‖ The same superstition was found by Mr. Waddell in full force in Calabar; and it may assist in enabling us to understand its meaning, when we keep in view that in the language of that country the word for "shadow" is the same as that for "soul."#

I have before me the records of the slave courts held for the parish of Portland between the years 1805 and 1816. They are full of cases of Obeah. One woman attempts to murder her master by putting arsenic into his noyeau; another by mixing pounded glass with his coffee; a third is charged with practicing upon the credulity of his fellow-slaves by pretending to cure another of a sore in his leg, and "taking from thence sundry trifles,—a hawk's toe, a bit of wire, and a piece of flesh."

On 22d February 1831 William Jones was tried and sentenced to death "for conspiring and contriving to destroy William Ogilvie, overseer of Fairy Hill estate in the parish of Portland." The notes of the evidence taken at the trial state:—"This prosecution arises out of the confession of Thomas Lindsay, who was shot to death pursuant to the sentence of a court-martial, on the 31st day of January 1832. The part of the confession which inculpates William Jones is as follows:— 'About three weeks before Christmas me and David Anderson, and William Rainey, and Alexander Simpson being together, the devil took hold of us, tell us we must destroy the overseer; and he agreed to go to a man named William Jones, belonging to Providence Mountain, an obeah-man, to give us something to kill the busha, so that his horse may throw him down and break his neck in a hole. Jones said as this was a great thing he could not do it for less than a doubloon, and we had only five shillings to give him. But we agreed to carry him a barrow (a hog) with five dollars, and a three-gallon jug of rum, and three dollars in cash. He then gave us something and told us to give it to the waiting-boy to throw it in the water and that would kill him. The waiting-boy, James Oliver, did throw it into the water, but it did the busha no harm, and the waiting-boy said the obeah-man was only laughing at us. We then went to the obeah-man, and he said the waiting-boy could not have put the things into the water. And then he came himself one day, took the bag of an ant's house, etc. etc. etc.' " "Here," says the report, "follows an account of obeah tricks practiced." It then goes on:—"*David Anderson,* sworn. He [witness] was

‖Barclay, *A Practical View of the Present State of Slavery in the West Indies,* London, 1826, 185–86.
#Waddell, p. 139.

run away three months before Christmas in consequence of the over-seer flogging him for stealing some rum from his brother Henry Simpson and putting water in the place of it. He and four others went to William Jones. William Rainey explained the cause of their coming—that he carried one macaroni, and four bitts, and a jug of rum, and that Alexander Simpson carried a pig. The obeah-man (the prisoner) asked a doubloon. He gave them something in a nancy bag pounded up, which James Oliver put into the busha's drink, but it did not do him. That they then fetched the obeah-man down to the estate, where he gave them something to put in the step of the door—all to kill the busha. The prisoner had a cutacoo. They gave him a two-dollar piece, besides the money they had before given.

"*Benny Simpson*, Fairy Hill, sworn—Says the prisoner came into the house of her father, Adam Fisher, where he stayed two weeks, and that he was employed making obeah to kill the busha. She was afraid of the man. Thomas Lindsay, Davy Anderson, and Sammy Taylor brought him there. She was not allowed to go into the house, as he was making obeah to kill the busha. William Rainey showed the guilty parties the pass to find out prisoner. When her daddy, Adam Fisher, heard that James Purrier was taken up, he went away, saying he would destroy himself. He has not been heard of since."

On the 13th April of the same year William Fisher was tried and convicted for pretending to supernatural power. Edward Francis, slave to Fairfield, being "sworn and admonished," said:—"On Wednesday, about the first week in May of last year, I was at my father-in-law's house. This was shortly after Mr. Speed came as over-seer to the estate. Tom, *alias* Richard Mein, Richard Passley, the driver of Fairfield, prisoner, and others, came in. Fisher called for a fowl's egg, which he put into a basin. Tom Crowder sat beside him. Fisher threw rum over the egg, and set it on fire, and when the egg was boiled in the rum he broke it, gave it to Tom to suck, who declined. Fisher, after sucking the egg, rubbed part of the shell in his hand until it was mashed. He then put it with some stuff which he said was cinnamon into a phial. It was a thing which he said would turn anybody's mind. He then gave it to me, and said it was to be given to driver Richard, who would give it to the horse-stable boy, to put under the horse's tail, when the horse would throw the busha, Mr. Speed, down and break his neck. I was obliged to go back to Fairfield to fetch the money before he gave me the phial. He would not trust me without I got the money from Justina. Fisher likewise gave me some of the eggshell, and [told me] to rub it up and strew it about the yard—that if the stuff in the phial did not make the horse throw the busha, this would. Robert Mein [slave] to Cold Harbour, had a bad leg. Fisher pricked the place, and black blood came. Fisher then sucked the part and spit out two beads. At another time, when I ran away, I met Fisher in the pass, and he took me up to his mountain and gave me a bush to chew, and said if I went home without it I should get fum fum, as the busha was swearing after me very much. I gave him four bits for it. When I went home busha did fum me, and I then went back to Fisher to get the money from him. He said, 'No, there is a different way to manage the busha,' which was to kill him. On the Wednesday night before mentioned, Fisher gave Solomon Passley a little bit of stick, which he told him to chew and spit it all about the pass, and this would kill busha. The whole estate said they would go to somebody to kill the busha. They all agreed to look out for a man for that purpose.

"*By Court.*—What money did you give Fisher for the stuff in the phial?"

"Half-a-dollar, which Justina gave me."

"Did you not go to fetch Fisher?"

"No; driver Richard sent me to get the stuff. He said in the mill-house that every one must throw up money to kill the busha."

"Did Justina complain to you of your having kept the money and not given it to Fisher?"

"She said I had eaten the money, I had not given it to Fisher, as no good had come. Fisher had not killed the busha, and the money was given for so-so."

"What did you do with the phial?"

"I carried it and broke it against the horse-stable, and covered it with dirt."

"Was it the intention of the whole estate's people to kill Mr. Speed?"

"Yes, we all employed Fisher."

"*Alexander Hartley to Fairfield,* sworn—saith that he knows Fisher. He is a Mungola man. He is a bush man—an obeah man. Heard when runaway, and living in a cave, that money had been thrown up for the purpose of killing Mr. Speed."

The practice of Obeah amongst the humbler classes is still, unfortunately, as prevalent at the present day, despite the severely penal laws against it, as it was in the beginning of the century.

A local paper, *The Gleaner* of 26th January 1869, quoting from *The Falmouth Post*, relates the following story:—

"During the past week the town of Lucea was kept in a state of considerable excitement, in consequence of a report which was circulated and believed, not only by the lower but middling classes, that a Spanish jar, containing a large quantity of gold coins, had been discovered in the yard adjoining the premises of a black man, named Johnson, near the Weir Park settlement, about a mile from the town of Lucea. The report of the discovery was strengthened by the assertion of several persons, male and female, that preparations on an extensive scale, and commensurate with the stated value, were being made for the purpose of taking up the jar and its contents. We instituted an inquiry, and ascertained that many of the friends of the man Johnson were assisting in doing all he suggested,—that obeah-men were employed by the parties immediately concerned,—that the obeah-men were supplied with an abundance of food and liquor,— and that nights were passed in the performance of superstitious rites which disturbed the Christian-minded villagers in the neighbourhood. A white cock was killed on one occasion, for the purpose of carrying out one of the objects that was declared necessary, and there were sacrifices of goats and pigs, the spilling of blood in all directions, and the commission of other abominations, which we have neither time nor inclination to mention.

"On Sunday, 17th instant, the excitement was greater than on preceding days. One of the crowd remarked, that all attempts made to take the jar from the earth would be unavailing, until human blood was sprinkled on the land,—'that human blood must be used, for nothing else would answer.' On hearing this remark, and seeing that hundreds of persons were on their way to the spot, and that the constabulary were proceeding thither for the maintenance of order, we determined upon accompanying them. On arriving in front of Johnson's house, where upwards of 400 men, women and children, were assembled, an inspection was made of the piece of land where the treasure was said to be, and one of the constables, having been engaged a few minutes in turning up the earth, while Johnson and his family were giving utterance to angry expressions, aided by a young man named Langshaw (a clerk in one of the stores in Lucea), who talked about the rights of property, etc., found a clayed cooking utensil, called a yabba, and a common water jar, both of which had been evidently placed in the newly-excavated earth by Johnson and his associates. At the discovery of the imposture, a shout of indignation was raised by some of the assembled people, and between them and Johnson's family there was a violent altercation. Upon a gentleman remarking that the whole affair was a compound of Obeahism, Myalism, and Revivalism, some of the bystanders observed, that if the white people had not interfered the jar and money would have been found. One of the black lookers-on said, 'The jar began to sink down as soon as the white people began to trouble it.' The house of Johnson was afterwards searched by the constabulary, who took from it blocks and ropes that Langshaw had supplied for lifting up the treasure; and on inquiry being made, the fact was ascertained that Obeahism had been at work for several days and nights. We are informed that three Obeah-men, who were not apprehended at the time we left Lucea, had received £10 for their services, and that for some months past they have had other and well-paying customers in Lucea, some of whom are among the most earnest in professions of Christianity."

The Obeah-man must not be confounded with the Myalman, who is to the former what the antidote is to the poison. He professes to undo what the other has injured; but it must be confessed that both in its operation and its results, the cure is often worse than the disease. In truth, the boundary line between the two classes of professors is oftentimes but a shadowy one.

Obeah, apparently, is not destined to die an inglorious death,— *quia caret vate sacro*. In 1817, there was published in London a book, entitled, "Poems, chiefly on the Superstition of Obeah,"—a curious work, on a curious and far from uninteresting subject.

H. V. P. BRONKHURST, *The Colony of British Guyana and its Labouring Population* (London, 1883), 382–86.

One great superstitious abomination practiced and believed in by the black Creoles of the Colony, and other West Indian Islands, as Trinidad, Jamaica, Hayti, &c., is Obeahism, which seems to defy all the efforts of the Legislature to stamp it out. The law does not trifle with offenders when they are brought under it and their offence is brought home to them, but it is very seldom that an Obeahman is publicly catted for practising his abominable and diabolical calling, and yet it is patent to every one who takes any notice of the habits and customs of the labouring Creole population, that their belief in and their fear of the Obeahman are strong and deeply grounded. It is the people's childish fear of the impostor that constitutes his main safety. Imbued with the superstitious feelings of their ancestors, they firmly believe in the Obeahman's power to work evil for them, and, weak-minded and timid as they are, they hesitate to place themselves in antagonism to what they consider to be supernatural powers that are able to deprive them not only of health but of life itself. The Obeahman or Piaiman (from the Caribi word *"Puiai,"* which signifies a sorcerer, and equivalent to the Tamil word *Pey-Karan* or *Pey-Pidittavan,* literally devil-man, one possessed of the devil) is consulted in cases of sickness and adversity. If the patient is strong enough to endure the disease, the excitement, the noise, and the fumes of tobacco in which he is at times enveloped, and the sorcerer observes signs of recovery, he will pretend to extract the cause of the complaint by sucking the part affected. After many ceremonies he will produce from his mouth some strange substance, such as a thorn or a gravel-stone, a fish bone or bird's claw, a snake's tooth or a piece of wire, which some malicious Yauhahu is supposed to have inserted in the affected part. As soon as the patient fancies himself rid of this cause of his illness his recovery is generally rapid, and the fame of the sorcerer greatly increased. The Obeahman, generally speaking, is deformed, ugly, with a lot of wrinkles on his face, and altogether a frightful object. Some folks go even so far as to believe that the Obeahman can transport himself from place to place at his pleasure, like an unseen spirit; and hence they dread him. Nor is the dread of Obeah confined to the uneducated classes; it exists in the minds of men and women who have received a liberal education, but who, instead of labouring to defeat the impostor's power by ridiculing it or exposing its contemptible nature, pay it homage, and in some cases call in its aid to help out their special purposes. The following account, taken from the *Royal Gazette* of Georgetown, Demerara, will give my reader some idea of what Obeahism really is:—

> "It is useless to look to the lowest class in the country to rebel and throw off the Obeah yoke as long as their superiors in position and general advantages are content to remain in bondage, and Ministers and others who are bent on eradicating the evil should direct their crusade, in the first place, not against the lowest grade of society, but against a higher class which provides the Churches of the Colony with the great bulk of their members. When this class has been brought to see Obeah in its true light, then it will be easier to prevail on those at the bottom of the ladder to laugh at the threats of the Obeahman; but until then the Ministers' efforts will be almost in vain.
>
> "In the meantime the profession goes on flourishing, and provides a large and regular income to a number of blackguards who are either located in some district populous enough to support them, or who perambulate the country on the hunt for work, which is seldom hard to get.

It is seldom their prosperity is interrupted, but occasionally a man is found sensible enough to lay a trap for the scamps, and then the Magistrate's Court becomes the means of giving the general public some idea of the ceremonies performed during the working of the magic, and the articles that are necessary to render it effective. Such a case has just occurred in Berbice. A policeman received notice from a man that an Obeahman was going to practice at his house that night. The policeman concealed himself where he could see and hear everything that was going on; and after the magic was performed, he arrested the magician himself. The evidence given in the Court, one would think, would suffice to break the power of Obeah without one word being added against it. As is usual in these cases, the Obeahman pretended he had been hired to kill the man in whose house he then was, for which deed he was to receive six dollars; it being understood, of course, that if the Obeahman was to receive six dollars for killing, he ought to be paid at least double that for disappointing his customer, and letting the intended victim live. To make the bargain binding, the Obeahman then called for a tumbler, into which he poured some of the contents of a bottle; he then called for another tumbler and poured some of the bottle's contents into it also, he then called for a third tumbler, but he did not pour anything into it. He called for a looking-glass and six bits, a pair of scissors, a reel of black thread, a razor, five pins and two needles, and arranged these articles on a table before him. He then called the man whom he was engaged to kill, and putting his hand on the victim's stomach muttered something which nobody could understand. Whether the spell was complete at that stage we cannot say, but the policeman stepped in and arrested both the magic and the magician, and seized the whole of the household articles which were being made such a mysterious use of. The ludicrous ceremony thus disclosed in Court is, no doubt, a fair specimen of the performance by the generality of Obeahmen in presence of their believers; and it shows how deep-rooted and firm the superstition must be in the minds of the people, when such childish, silly, and contemptible forms can awe them. In this case the victim had sense enough to know that the Obeahman was a law-breaking rascal, and that the jail was the best place for him; but he is a great exception to the ordinary run of his class, who would not dare to betray the presence of the Obeahman, for fear of the awful consequences that, in their opinion, would be sure to follow. The light way the Obeahman talked of being engaged to do murder is, in a manner, very amusing. He was engaged at six dollars to murder the man in whose house he was; but this was a cheap job; for in the course of conversation he stated that he was engaged to go to Lochaber that night to throw a man into the boiling tache, for which he was to get forty dollars. The policeman, in arresting him, thus spoilt a good night's business, and interfered with the magician's income; it is to be hoped the law will see its way clear to indemnify the Obeahman for this loss by providing him with free board and lodging for some time, and with such other attention as the ordinance regarding the practice of Obeah recommends. It is humiliating to think that a superstition of pins and needles should, after fifty years of freedom, flourish as bravely as it did in the days of slavery."

The following I extract from a recent number of the *Berbice Asylum Journal*:—

"That a firm belief in Obeahism is widely diffused amongst the people of this Colony any one who is brought into intimate contact with them is not long in discovering. This belief is not true in Obeahism only as a mode of secret poisoning, a materialistic and gross view of the craft, but in it as a form of enchantment, after the style of that of which we read in the *Arabian Nights*. By its means it is believed that the fortunes of men can be made or marred. When any one wishes to wreak his vengeance on his enemies without danger to himself, it is to the Obeah doctor he applies. An incident which took place a few years ago at the Asylum so strongly illustrates both the belief in Obeah and its mode of working as to be worth relating. One morning the senior attendant, a fair-skinned, almost white, man, and one of fair intelligence, made a complaint that an attempt had been made to Obeah him. He said that early that morning an Obeah bottle had been found upon the doorstep of his cottage, and as he was the first person likely to pass it, it must have been intended for him: although he made the complaint, he was loud as usual in his expression of unbelief in Obeah. He could he, a Christian, believe in such a thing? At the same time he showed great reluctance to bring the bottle, and only did so after a good deal of pressure had been put upon him. He treated it much after the same manner as one can suppose an infernal machine is handled when its character is known. It was afterwards found out that he had, before leaving his cottage that morning, looked out the window, and saw the thing of horror upon his doorstep. At once a hue and cry was raised to bring assistance from outside, as no one dared pass it. A woman living near came and undertook to exorcise the demon of the bottle, which she did by performing the usual rites of invocation, and a liberal application of salt and water. When examined, this terrible thing was found to be an ordinary eau-de-cologne bottle filled with a heterogeneous collection, after the approved style of necromancy. Here were—

> 'Eye of newt and toe of frog,
> Wool of bat and tongue of dog,
> Adder's fork and blind worm sting,
> Lizard's leg, owlet's wing,'

or their local equivalents. Conspicuously standing above the cork was a hair, certainly much like one from the head of the attendant who complained, and its presence was said to act as a guide to direct the mischief towards him. The bottle was afterwards used as a test of the belief in Obeahism amongst the attendants, and its effects were very marked. The application of the test was made in this manner. First came the question—'Have you had anything to do with this Obeah business? Do you believe in it?' 'O, Sir! how could I believe in such a thing?' 'It is a good thing you don't believe in it, for then you will be able to tell me what you think of this.' On which the bottle suddenly appears. The abrupt start, the tremor, and change of complexion, in one instance a bolt made for the door, showed that the heart did not confirm the denial made by the tongue. The bottle is still in existence, but its contents have dried up, so it is feared that its virtue may have departed from it."

X. BEKE, *West Indian Yarns* (Demerara and London, 1890), 44–49.

When Mrs. _____ came to stay with us she brought her maid, a black girl some twenty-two years of age. One day on my return home, I was informed that "Blossom," the girl in question, was in deep distress, because Wellington (my groom) had "obeahed" her.

Now, obeah, pure and simple, and unaccompanied with the administration of poison, only does harm by affecting the imagination; but the negro who believes that obeah has been worked against him, often pines away from sheer fright.

Sometimes he has recourse to some obeah practitioner who undertakes to counteract the evil, and when the patient believes this has been done, he recovers. The mere punishment of a detected obeahman by a magistrate does the victim of the fraud no good; the law cannot undo the mischief.

I interviewed "Blossom" who was in a terrible state of agitation, trembling like a leaf. Wellington had got some of her hair and wore it around his waist and was working obeah for her. "He want for marry me, but me no want him."

I rode off to the stables where I found Mr. Wellington. I made him stoop on some pretext, when his jersy rose up, and round his waist I saw a string with "bobs" of wool,—Blossom's hair, tied at intervals. I collared the fellow and sent for Blossom; told her to bring me a white handled razor, and made her cut off the string, because I informed her only an unmarried person must do that. She followed my directions, but her hand trembled and Wellington wriggled so that he narrowly escaped a slash. We then formed a small procession to the house, the girl carrying the string with outstretched arm. A coal pot was brought and the magic cord and hair duly burned. Wellington, however, still protesting his innocence, a bottle of ether was brought by Blossom and was dubbed, after the Chinese method, "lie water." Wellington agreed with much hesitation to the ordeal, and Blossom poured what was intended to be a few drops, but what her trembling hand caused to be near a spoonful on Wellington's extended tongue;—a yell, as he dashed from my side, followed, and the last I saw of Wellington for many months was my gentleman bounding like a deer through the guinea grass. He spread my fame as a head obeahman, and Blossom recovered her spirits and health. It afterwards occurred to me that I had been practising "an occult art" and had rendered myself liable to fine or imprisonment.

These obeahmen are often called upon by those who should know better, to assist in recovering stolen property, and persons too, whose education should have taught them better, often stand in dread of these practitioners. A clergyman once applied for a warrant against one Archie Sam, who, to a legitimate business as cooper, no doubt added that of obeah doctor.

I asked what was the offence—and the circumstances.

It turned out that the reverend gentleman had gone down the coast the previous Sunday to officiate at a church usually served by his curate. On his arrival, he ran against Mr. Archie Sam who lived in a different part of the island. Just before ascending the pulpit, the rector took a glass of water from a "goglet" in the vestry room, and shortly after commencing his sermon was attacked by a feeling of dizziness, which, however, soon passed off.

I explained that I did not see how anything could be charged against Archie, but Mr. _____ got very angry, and said there were the facts of the appearance of the obeahman in the village far from his home—and the unusual effect of the glass of water; for his part he thought the case was clear.

I differed, and declined to issue a warrant. The rector complained to the governor, who reported the circumstances to the bishop, from whom the parson received an admonition, *vulgò*, a wigging.

The materials used are of various kinds—bone, needles tied crosswise with black thread and rubbed with tallow, nails, wire, coals, salt, a looking-glass, cards, and earth from a grave. There is nothing which may not be employed. In the incantations, a white cock, and, of course, rum, are indispensable. I knew an old fool who was cheated out of all his earnings, and ultimately out of his house and home, by a rascal who assured him there was much hidden treasure in his garden, and, who drew heavily on him for the materials necessary for its discovery.

The practice of obeah was kept up in many places by men of the W. I. regiments who were recruited in Africa, and, who, on being pensioned, added to their means by setting up as obeahmen.

I remember several years ago, a rascal being brought before me charged with practising obeah. The police corporal, however, who was somewhat hasty and premature, had arrested the man before he had actually done any act which constituted that offence.

The prisoner was an important character, as he was firmly believed in by the country people, and I felt that his acquittal would be considered as a striking instance of his powers rather than as the result of the corporal's precipitancy.

I could not convict him, but I determined he should not go scot free. Pointing to a small bag he wore suspended from his neck by a dirty cord, I asked him what was in it?

"No harm, me washup, it only one ting I does wear fo' keep away pain."

I insisted on its being taken off his neck and placed on the table, and ordered the fellow to open it. This he refused to do.

A group of the townspeople had edged up to my table, every one of whom had been repudiating all belief in obeah, and in undertones expressing wonder how anybody could be so foolish "as believe in such a thing." To one of these gentry who was a churchwarden, and in some respects a well educated man, I handed one of the prisoner's razors with a request that he would cut open the little packet. A very decided "no" was the result, and so with each of the non-believers who shrank back from the mysterious oddments spread before me. In the end I cut it open myself, and, as I expected, found it filled with earth probably taken from a grave.

"What is this stuff?" I asked the obeahman.

"Dat no harm, Sah, he no poison."

"Then," said I, "you will eat it."

"Eat it my washup?"

"Yes, eat it up—you say it is no harm."

"Me eat it?"

"Yes, eat it up."

I shall never forget the man's face as I fixed my eyes on his and uttered these words. I subsequently found that he had been told I was a chief obeahman and whether he fancied my powers were real and greater than his I do not know, but gazing steadily at me, he began to tremble, and, eventually stretching out his hand, grasped the bag, which he then raised very slowly from the table.

"Eat it up," I repeated.

By degrees he raised it to his lips, and placing the contents between his lips, he swallowed them.

As he finished I said "Now be off; if ever you return to this district you shall be severely punished."

I waved my hand to him, and, darting through the door, he made his exit. I have since heard that he still lives, and that the above occurrence has been handed down to present times, when small boys delight in dubbing the obeahman, "Eat it up."

5

Festivals, Carnival, Holidays, and JonKanoo

The travel literature in any "exotic" region abounds with descriptions of strange foods, manners, dress, and surprising behaviors. Nothing fascinates or threatens the observer more than having these different practices and values dramatized in festival format. By their very nature, festivities invoke license, releasing selected members of the community from the rules and boundaries imposed in everyday life. That this should be all the more a time of anxiety in plantation America should come as little surprise, for it was during Christmas and New Year's (in the United States and the Eastern Caribbean) or Carnival (on the U.S. Gulf Coast and in the originally French and Spanish islands) that the slaves were permitted not only to dance, sing, and beg or even coerce openly, but they were allowed a great deal more social and physical freedom. Little wonder then that during these times the plantocracy most feared open rebellion, and as our earliest account, from the *Journal of a Lady of Quality,* points out: "It is necessary to keep a look out during this season of unbounded freedom; and every man on the island [Antigua] is in arms." This point is repeated throughout the travel and journal literature, with the additional recognition that to eliminate the practices would backfire and almost certainly lead directly to rebellion.

Yet we do have considerable evidence that many rebellions which occurred did begin during one or another season of license. Robert Dirks, for example, has reckoned that at least 35 percent of the rebellions in the British Caribbean were planned or executed in late December.[1]

Still it would be difficult to accept the reasoning behind the

1. Robert Dirks, "Slaves' Holiday," *Natural History,* 84, no. 10 (Dec. 1975), 82–84, 87–88, 90.

planters' fears as sufficient to the defensive posture which they assumed, and to the attempts documented here, to eliminate the most
licentious practices on some islands. Again, as our Lady of Quality
points out, the fully dressed militia contributed greatly to the festive
atmosphere, as did the ritual firing of guns traditionally carried out in
some places on New Year's Eve!

We have assembled here observations on a variety of public festivities: those of their main holidays, Trinidadian Carnival, mumming,
set girls, the Rose and the Marguerites, and JonKanoo. The general
nature of public festivities is discussed in the introduction along with
tea meetings but some of these events require a few more words of
explanation.

Several islands of the Caribbean originally had festivals of the
Roses and Marguerites, but St. Lucia has had them continuously for at
least 175 years. On the Feast of St. Rose of Lima (August 30) the Societies of the Flowers hold fetes that involve an elaborate panoply of
kings, queens, soldiers, pages, nurses, et al. in parades, dances, grand
marches, and dinners. St. Lucia was virtually divided into moities by
these groups, and all levels of the island's society have participated in
them. Special dances and songs have been developed for these
groups, and they hold practice meetings throughout the year. Their
institutions also had the power to levy fines on socially and ritually
errant behavior by means of which they gained money for sponsoring
fetes. There is a long history attached to these groups which remains
to be documented;[2] Breen's account reprinted here remains the central document.

"Set Girls," on Jamaica, like the Flower Societies on St. Lucia,
expressed themselves in performance: in this case, by means of set
dances of European origin—Lancers, polkas, waltzes, the schottische,
and so forth. (This is nicely complicated by the fact that these dances
began as peasant dances in Europe and spread to the upper classes,
only to be changed; then they were carried to the West Indies by European planters whose slaves took them up and again changed them!)
Behind the development of the sets, as in many Afro-West Indian performances, there is an element of imitation and reaction to European
discrimination. Those excluded from white performances stage their
own parallel performances within their own social and cultural frame-

2. See Daniel J. Crowley, "Festivals of the Calendar in St. Lucia," *Caribbean Quarterly*, 4 (1955), 99–121; "La Rose and Marguerite Societies in St. Lucia," *Journal of
American Folklore*, 71 (1958), 541–52; and Harold F. C. Simmons, "The Flower Festivals of St. Lucia," *The Voice of St. Lucia*, Aug. 27, 1953.

work. Yet the symbolic and social elaboration (and from the European's perspective, *over*-ornamentation) of these events suggests a much more complex history and set of social factors behind them. In the introduction we attempt to show how this works in the creolized nature of such activities as parades, tea meetings, and *plays* (tales) but there is much more to be investigated.

The story of JonKanoo has been told many times but seems far from having been fully analyzed for all its significance. Here we have included all the historically relevant descriptions. That this practice is, in the main, a mumming like that still practiced throughout the Eastern Caribbean is clear. But the practice has achieved a symbolic place in Jamaican national life, a fact which takes it far beyond a simple seasonal festival. Although there have been so many reportings of JonKanoo, including a number of recent ones, beyond Silvia Wynter's suggestive remarks on the subject and Judith Bettelheim's recent survey, nothing of a synthetic and overarching sort has been attempted.

JANET SCHAW, *Journal of a Lady of Quality* . . . (New Haven, 1927), 107–09.

December, 1724

Last Saturday was Christmas. . . . We met the Negroes in joyful troops on the way to town with their Merchandize. It was one of the most beautiful sights I ever saw. They were universally clad in white Muslin; the men in loose drawers and waistcoats, the women in jacket and petticoats; the men wore black caps, the women had handkerchiefs of gauze or silk, which they wore in the fashion of turbans. Both men and women carried neat white wicker baskets on their heads, which they balanced as our milk maids do the pails. These contained the various articles for Market, in one a little kid raised its head from amongst flowers of every hue, which were thrown over to guard it from the heat; here a lamb, there a Turkey or pig, all covered in the same elegant manner. While others had the baskets filled with fruit, pine-apples reared over each other; Grapes dangling over the loaded basket: oranges, Shaddacks, water lemons, pomegranates, grandillas, with twenty others, whose names I forget. They marched in a regular order, and gave the agreeable idea of a set of devotees going to sacrifice to the Indian Gods, while the sacrifice offered just now to the Christian God is, at this Season of all others the most proper, and I may say boldly, the most agreeable, for it is a mercy to the creatures of the God of mercy. At this Season the crack of the inhuman whip must not be heard, therefore some days, it is an universal Jubilee;

nothing but joy and pleasantry to be seen or heard, while every Negro in fact can tell you, that he owes this happiness to the good Buccara God, that he can be no hard Master, but loves a good black man as well as a Buccara man, and that Master will die a bad death, if he hurt poor Negro on his good day. It is necessary however to keep a look out during this season of unbounded freedom; and every man on the island is in arms and patrols go all round the different plantations as well as keep guard in the town. They are an excellent disciplined Militia and make a very military appearance.

EDWARD LONG, *The History of Jamaica* (London, 1774), vol. II, 424–25.

In all the towns, during Christmas holidays, they have several tall robust fellows dressed up in grotesque habits, and a pair of ox-horns on their head, sprouting from the top of a horrid sort of vizor or mask, which about the mouth is rendered very terrific with big boar-tusks. The masquerader, carrying a wooden sword in his hand, is followed with a numerous crowd of drunken women, who refresh him frequently with a cup of aniseed-water, whilst he dances at every door, bellowing out John Connú! with great vehemence; so that, what with the liquor and the exercise, most of them are thrown into dangerous fevers; and some examples have happened of their dying. This dance is probably an honourable memorial of John Conny, a celebrated cabocero of *Tres Puntas*, in Axim on the Guiney coast; who flourished about the year 1720. He bore great authority among the Negroes of that district. When the Prussians deserted Fort Brandenburgh, they left it to his charge; and he gallantly held it for a long time against the Dutch, to whom it was afterwards ceded by the Prussian monarch. He is mentioned with encomium by several of our voyage-writers.

In 1769, several new masks appeared; the Ebos, the Papaws, &c. having their respective Connús, male and female, who were dressed in a very laughable style.

PETER MARSDEN, *An Account of the Island of Jamaica* (Newcastle, 1788), 33–34.

At Christmas the slaves are allowed three days holiday during which time they are quite at liberty, and have herrings, flour, and rum. The prime negroes and mulattoes pay a visit to the white people during the festivity, and are treated with punch; one of them attends with a fiddle, and the men dress in the English mode, with cocked hats, cloth coats, silk stockings, white waistcoats, Holland shirts, and pumps. They dance minuets with the mulattoes and other brown women, imitating the motion and steps of the English but with a degree of affectation that renders the whole truly laughable and ridiculous. When the holidays are over, without the least appearance of fatigue from their extraordinary exertions night and day, they cheerfully return to their work. Every Saturday night many divert themselves with dancing and singing, which they style plays; and notwithstanding their week's labour, continue this violent exercise all night. But their own way of dancing is droll indeed; they put themselves into strange postures and shake their hips and great breasts to such a degree, that it is impossible to refrain from laughing, though they go through the whole performance with profound gravity, their feet beating time remarkably quick; two of them generally dance together, and sometimes do not move six inches from the same place. After the interment of corpses they always dance and sing dolefully; but there is no way of knowing what they say on these occasions. They used formerly to have other instruments than a bow with two or three wires, which they struck with a stick, making a noise strangely dissonant and uncouth.

I have been entertained very much during the last week by the negroes paying their highly absurd compliments of the season to every person from whom they think a trifle can be drawn, and their common wish, upon those occasions, is—"Long life and crosperity"— not prosperity, (observe, I mention this, lest you should suppose it to be an error of my pen). The holidays consist of three days, including Christmas-day, and so careful are they to prevent any encroachment on this privilege, that were their owners to give them double the time in lieu thereof, at any other season of the year, they would not accept it. A gentleman some years ago was murdered here by his slaves, purely because he obliged them to work on the days appointed for holidays.

WILLIAM BECKFORD, *A Descriptive Account of the Island of Jamaica* (London, 1790), vol I, 386–92.

The doors of the manor-house were by prescription opened: the smiles of welcome met the stranger at the threshold, and conducted him to his feat; for modesty was then a sufficient introduction to the honest and open heart, which not only received its own happiness in that of others, but was grateful to the source from whence the envied ability of doing good, so largely flowed.

"A merry Christmas" was in former times a pleasing, as a proverbial salutation: but now the manners of the world are changed, and
luxury has trampled upon simplicity, and hospitality resigned its
place to pride and ceremony. The country mansion is closed at this
season of the year; and the remembrance of former mirth and conviv-
iality lies buried in those vaulted domes which were used to smoak
with abundance, and resound with music.

As small communities are too apt to affect the manners of the
great, the customs that prevail in capitals will consequently find their
way into the provinces, and from thence into the more distant de-
pendencies; and hence it is, that in Jamaica this festival is hardly
kept; or if it be remembered, it occurs with a sameness and frigidity
by no means correspondent to that warmth of hospitality which is observed at other times to flow with so much fervour.

You observe, indeed, the white people riding from one plantation to another, and returning perhaps overcharged with liquor at
night, when it is doubly incumbent upon them, at such a season of
riot and inebriety, to keep themselves sober, and to preserve a proper
authority upon the plantation.

The negroes at this season of the year are in continual hurry and
confusion; nor do they ever seem to form any regular plans for the
conduct or amusement of those days which they anticipate with so
much pleasure, and which they generally consume with as little
thought.

Their occupations and diversions seem to arise from the impulse
of the moment; and many pass their time in dull and sedentary inac-
tion, who were previously determined to give themselves up to song
and dance.

The first day of this recurring holiday they generally spend
among the mountains, in collecting provisions for their own use, or in
raising money to expend again in dress and trifles at the neighbouring
town: the more wealthy sell poultry, or kill a hog, (by which they
make a considerable profit), or give an entertainment to their friends,
or make a public assembly, at which every person pays a stipulated
sum at his admittance.

The mulattoes likewise at this season have their public balls,
and vie with each other in the splendour of their appearance; and it
will hardly be credited how very expensive their dress and ornaments
are, and what pains they take to disfigure themselves with powder
and with other unbecoming imitations of the European dress. Their
common apparel, at other times, and mode of attiring, are picturesque
and elegant; and as the forms of the young women are turned with

equal grace and symmetry, and as their motions in the dance are well calculated to show off their make to the greatest advantage, the most pleasing attitudes, as well as the most various inflections of body and of limbs, may be taken from them when thus engaged in their most favourite amusement.

At Christmas the negroes upon neighbouring estates are divided, like other communities, into different parties: some call themselves the blue girls, and some the red: and their clothes are generally characteristic of their attachment.

The plantation negroes always make a point to visit their masters at Christmas, when they array themselves in all their finery: they divide themselves upon the different estates; and those belonging to one property go down in procession together; and those of another, though belonging to the same master, detach themselves in like manner, and proceed with music and singing to the place of their destination; at which, when arrived, and after having made their salutations, they begin the song and dance, for it is almost impossible to do one without the other; and the very children so soon as they are able to walk, at the first sound of the cotter (which I shall hereafter explain) put their little elbows in motion—their feet shortly follow, and in a little time the whole body seems to be in action.

I have often been surprised to observe how infinitely more the negro appears to be affected by music and by dancing, than the white children in Jamaica; and for this fact I know not how in any manner to account. The same customs are daily before the eyes of both; nay, the Creole infants are suffered to associate too much with those of the negroes: they converse and play together, and are too apt, as they grow up, to copy their manners, and to imitate their vices: nor do I think that the parents in general are sufficiently studious to prevent their forming connexions with those whose bad example may, and frequently has, conducted to ruin.

When the negroes are assembled at Christmas in all their finery, and select a spreading tree, under the shadow of which they assemble, they certainly form many very picturesque and pleasing groups; and though a general resemblance of colour and features may be thought at a little distance to prevail,—yet the most common observer will, upon a near inspection, perceive a very striking discrimination of both.

Some negroes will sing and dance, and some will be in a constant state of intoxication, during the whole period that their festival at Christmas shall continue; and what is more extraordinary, several of them will go ten or twelve miles to what is called a play, will sit up and drink all night, and yet return in time to the plantation for their work the ensuing morning: many, indeed, are consequently laid up in the hospitals; and too many, I fear, fall victims to continued watchfulness, fatigue, and inebriety.

ANONYMOUS, "Characteristic Traits of the Creolian and African Negroes in Jamaica, &c. &c," *Colombian Magazine*, April–October 1797 (Reprinted in 1976, Barry Higman, ed. [Mona, Jamaica: Caldwell Press, 1976], pp. 21–22, 22–23).

It is a remarkable circumstance that the vulgar of several nations have some general object of ridicule or merriment. Mr. Addison in his 47th Spectator mentions those of Holland, France, Italy, and Great-Britain.

The Negroes have their droll, which, however it may be dressed, is always called a John Canoe; a whimsical character, variously habited according to the ability and capacity of the negroes. Sometimes they wear two faces, different from each other; as usually they have but one, which is often rendered hideous by beards and boar's tusks; a great variety of ornaments is used on the embellishment of those figures, some of which cost many pounds and considerable ingenuity to compleat. Formerly their conceptions and execution were comparatively rude to what has been exhibited for the few last years: their aim was then a savage but is now often a polite appearance. They were content with an insignificant or ugly mask—a close waistcoat and trowsers, chequered like a Harlequin's coat, or hung with shreds of various coloured cloth dangling like a loose shag: but many of their present figures claim attention for the fantastic modern cut of their cloaths, often of silk and sometimes enriched with lace; a quantity of hair on the head as preposterously dressed as some European beaux: and over that a representation of an edifice, sometimes very prettily devised and executed in the stile of a baby house, shewing different fronts with open doors, glazed windows, stair cases, piazas & balconies, in which diminutive figures are placed. They now and then salute with the discharge of little guns placed in some of the buildings. Small looking glasses are also used to embellish the person. Before this principal figure, several fellows occasionally march with painted sticks or wands, strutting with much formality and grimace.

This character in its former unpolished state was attended thro' the town by a great number of negroes, beating old canisters, or pieces of metal, singing "ay, ay, John Canoe," in the time expressed by three quavers and two semiquavers, but with little inflexion of the voice: the words "ay, ay," being frequently repeated like a chorus.

They carry a stick in their hands which they flourish somewhat in the manner of a cudgel-player, and when two of those accidently meet in their walks, they exchange several grimaces before they pursue their respective ways.

Different trades-men distinguish themselves by the impliments of their several employments, and in this manner go through the town stopping at such houses as they expect to receive a gratuity from.

The figure exhibited by the Butchers, is clad in the hide of an ox with horns, which is held up with a rope and frequently lashed with a cart-whip.

■   ■   ■

Sets

The approach of the Christmas holydays is carefully noted by the negroes, most of whom make some provision for their being better dressed.—It is upon this occasion that the women form themselves into parties which they call sets; distinguishing them by various names, as the Golden Set, the Velvet Set, the Garnet Ladies, &c. They endeavour and often succeed in procuring dresses like each other of the same set. These consist of particular patterns of cloth for the bed gowns, handkerchiefs, ornamented hats, &c. These preceded by a negro fiddler, go through the town singing and marching in a fantastic manner in the streets, or entering into dwelling houses where they have acquaintance or hope to get a present.

It is no easy matter to account for several of them getting such finery, as few have more than a weekly allowance of two shillings and sixpence currency, and many of them not so much, unless we suppose they make theft and prostitution subservient to their fine appearance.

The negroes from different districts in Guinea associate in parties and wander about the town, diverting themselves with their own peculiar singing, instruments, and dances, the last of which they stop to perform.

The negroes ideas of pleasure are rude and indistinct: They seem chiefly to consist in throwing off restraint and spending two or three days in rambling and drinking. Aniseed is generally used on this occasion with which the women often debauch.

The confusion occasioned by the rattling of chains and slings from the wharves, the mock-driving of hoops by the coopers, winding the postmens horns, beating militia and negroe drums, the sound of the pipe and tabor, negroe flutes, gombas and jaw-bones, scraping on the violin, and singing of men women and children, with other incidental noises, make Kingston at this time a very disagreeable residence.

MARIA NUGENT, *Lady Nugent's Journal,* ed. Frank Cundall (London, 1907 [1839]), 65–66.

[*December*] *25th* [*1801*].—Christmas Day! All night heard the music of Tom-Toms, &c. Rise early, and the whole town and house bore the appearance of a masquerade. After Church, amuse myself very much with the strange processions, and figures called Johnny Canoes. All dance, leap and play a thousand anticks. Then there are groups of dancing men and women. They had a sort of leader or superior at their head, who sang a sort of recitative, and seemed to regulate all their procedings; the rest joining at intervals in the air and the chorus. The instrument to accompany the song was a rude sort of drum, made of bark leaves, on this they beat time with their feet. Then there was a party of actors.—Then a little child was introduced, supposed to be a king, who stabbed all the rest. They told me that some of the children who appeared were to represent Tippoo Saib's children, and the man was Henry the 4th of France.—What a *mélange*! All were dressed very finely, and many of the blacks had really gold and silver fringe on their robes. After the tragedy, they all began dancing with the greatest glee.—We dined in the Council Chamber, but went to bed early, but not to rest, for the noise of singing and dancing was incessant during the night. . . .

26th.—The same wild scenes acting over and over again.

27th.—The town very quiet. . . .

28th.—The Christmas sports recommenced, and we don't like to drive out, or employ our servants in any way, for fear of interfering with their amusements. Poor things, we would not deprive them of one atom of their short-lived and baby-like pleasure.—The whole day, nothing but singing, dancing, and noise. . . .

MICHAEL SCOTT, *Tom Cringle's Log* (London: J. M. Dent, 1969 [1829–33]), 241–45.

[ca. 1806–22]

This was the first day of the Negro Carnival or Christmas Holydays, and at the distance of two miles from Kingston the sound of the negro drums and horns, the barbarous music and yelling of the different African tribes, and the more mellow singing of the Set Girls, came upon the breeze loud and strong.

When we got nearer, the wharfs and different streets, as we successively opened them, were crowded with blackamoors, men, women, and children, dancing, and singing and shouting and all rigged out in their best. When we landed on the agents' wharf we were immediately surrounded by a group of these merrymakers, which happened to be the Butchers' John Canoe party, and a curious exhibition it unquestionably was. The prominent character was, as usual, the John Canoe or Jack Pudding. He was a light, active, clean-made young Creole negro, without shoes or stockings; he wore a pair of light jean small-clothes, all too wide, but confined at the knees, below and above, by bands of red tape, after the manner that Malvolio would have called cross-gartering. He wore a splendid blue velvet waistcoat, with old-fashioned flaps coming down over his hips, and covered with tarnished embroidery. His shirt was absent on leave, I suppose, but at the wrists of his coat he had tin or white iron frills, with loose pieces attached, which tinkled as he moved, and set off the dingy paws that were stuck through these strange manacles, like black wax tapers in silver candlesticks. His coat was an old blue artillery uniform one, with a small bell hung to the extreme points of the swallow-tailed skirts, and three tarnished epaulets; one on each shoulder, and O ye immortal gods! O Mars armipotent! the biggest of the three stuck at his rump, the *point d' appui* for a sheep's tail. He had an enormous cocked hat on, to which was appended in front a white false-face or mask, of a most methodistical expression, while Janus-like, there was another face behind, of the most quizzical description, a sort of living Antithesis, both being garnished and over-topped with one coarse wig, made of the hair of bullocks' tails, on which the chapeau was strapped down with a broad band of gold lace.

He skipped up to us with a white wand in one hand and a dirty handkerchief in the other, and with sundry moppings and mowings, first wiping my shoes with his mouchoir, then my face, (murder, what a flavour of salt fish and onions it had!) he made a smart enough pirouette, and then sprung on the back of a nondescript animal, that now advanced capering and jumping about after the most grotesque fashion that can be imagined. This was the signal for the music to begin. The performers were two gigantic men, dressed in calf-skins entire, head, four legs, and tail. The skin of the head was made to fit like a hood, the two fore-feet hung dangling down in front, one over each

shoulder while the other two legs, or hind feet, and the tail, trailed
behind on the ground; deuce another article had they on in the shape
of clothing except a handkerchief, of some flaming pattern, tied round
the waist. There were also two flute players in sheep skins, looking
still more outlandish from the horns on the animals' heads being pre-
served; and three stout fellows, who were dressed in the common
white frock and trousers, who kept sounding on bullocks' horns.
These formed the band as it were, and might be considered John's immediate tail or following; but he was also accompanied by about fifty
of the butcher negroes, all neatly dressed—blue jackets, white shirts,
and Osnaburgh trousers, with their steels and knife-cases by their
sides, as bright as Turkish yataghans, and they all wore clean blue
and white striped aprons. I could see and tell what *they* were; but the
Thing John Canoe had perched himself upon I could make nothing of.
At length I began to comprehend the device.

The *Magnus Apollo* of the party, the poet and chief musician, the
nondescript already mentioned, was no less than the boatswain of the
butcher gang, answering to the driver in an agricultural one. He was
clothed in an entire bullock's hide, horns, tail, and the other particulars, the whole of the skull being retained, and the effect of the voice
growling through the jaws of the beast was most startling. His legs
were enveloped in the skin of the hind-legs, while the arms were
cased in that of the fore, the hands protruding a little above the hoofs,
and, as he walked reared up on his hind-legs, he used, in order to support the load of the John Canoe who had perched on his shoulders,
like a monkey on a dancing bear, a strong stick, or sprit, with a crutch
top to it, which he leant his breast on every now and then.

After the creature, which I will call the *Device* for shortness, had
capered with its extra load, as if it had been a feather, for a minute or
two, it came to a stand-still, and, sticking the end of the sprit into the
ground, and tucking the crutch of it under its chin, it motioned to one
of the attendants who thereupon handed, of all things in the world, a
fiddle to the ox. He then shook off the John Canoe, who began to caper
about as before, while the *Device* set up a deuced good pipe, and
sung and played, barbarously enough, I will admit, to the tune of
Guinea Corn, the following ditty:—

> "Massa Buccra lob for see
> Bullock caper like monkee—
> Dance, and shump, and poke him toe,
> Like one humane person—just so."—

And hereupon the tail of the beast, some fifty strong, music men, John Canoe and all, began to rampage about, as if they had been possessed by a devil whose name was legion:—

> "But Massa Buccra have white love,
> Soft and silken like one dove.
> To brown girl—him barely shivel—
> To black girl—oh, Lord, de Devil!"

Then tremendous gallopading, in the which Tailtackle was nearly capsized over the wharf. He looked quietly over the edge of it.

"Boat-keeper, hand me up that switch of a stretcher," (Friend, if thou be'st not nautical, thou knowest what a *rackpin*, something of the stoutest, is.)

The boy did so, and Tailtackle, after moistening well his dexter claw with tabacco juice, seized the stick with his left by the middle, and balancing it for a second or two, he began to fasten the end of it into his right fist, as if he had been screwing a bolt into a socket. Having satisfied himself that his grip was secure, he let go the hold with his left hand, and crossed his arms on his breast, with the weapon projecting over his left shoulder, like the drone of a bagpipe.

The *Device* continued his chant, giving the seaman a wide birth, however:—

> "But when him once two tree year here,
> Him tink white lady wery great boder;
> De coloured peoples, never fear,
> Ah, him lob him de morest nor any oder."

Then another tumblification of the whole party.

> "But top—one time bad fever catch him,
> Colour'd peoples kindly watch him—
> In sick room, nurse voice like music—
> From him hand taste sweet de physic."

Another trampoline.

> "So alway come—in two tree year,
> And so wid you, massa—never fear
> Brown girl for cook—for wife—for nurse;
> Buccra lady—poo—no wort a curse."

"Get away, you scandalous scoundrel," cried I; "away with you, sir!"

Here the morrice dancers began to circle round old Tailtackle, keeping him on the move, spinning round like a weathercock in a whirlwind, while they shouted, "Oh, massa, one *maccaroni** if you please." To get quit of the importunity, Captain Transom gave them one. "Ah, good massa, tank you, sweet massa!" And away danced John Canoe and his tail, careering up the street.

In the same way all the other crafts and trades had their Gumbimen, Horn-blowers, John Canoes, and Nondescript. The Gardeners came nearest of anything I had seen before to the Mayday boys in London, with this advantage, that their Jack-in-the-Green was incomparably more beautiful, from the superior bloom of the larger flowers used in composing it.

The very workhouse people, whose province it is to guard the Negro culprits who may be committed to it, and to inflict punishment on them, when required, had their John Canoe and *Device;* and their prime jest seemed to be every now and then to throw the fellow down who enacted the latter at the corner of the street, and to administer a sound flogging to him. The John Canoe, who was the workhouse driver, was dressed up in a lawyer's cast-off gown and bands, black silk breeches, no stockings or shoes, but with sandals of bullock's hide strapped on his great splay feet, a small cocked hat on his head, to which were appended a large cauliflower wig, and the usual white, false-face, bearing a very laughable resemblance to Chief-Justice S _____, with whom I happened to be personally acquainted.

The whole party which accompanied these two worthies, musicians and tail, were dressed out so as to give a tolerable resemblance of the Bar broke loose, and they were all pretty considerably drunk. As we passed along, the *Device* was once more laid down, and we could notice a shield of tough hide strapped over the fellow's stern frame, so as to save the lashes of the cat, which John Canoe was administering with all his force, while the *Device* walloped about and yelled, as if he had been receiving punishment on his naked flesh. Presently, as he rolled over and over in the sand, bellowing to the life, I noticed the leather shield slip upwards to the small of his back, leaving the lower story uncovered in reality; but the driver and his tail were too drunk to observe this, and the former continued to lay on and laugh, while one of his people stood by in all the gravity of drunkenness, counting, as a first lieutenant does, when a poor fellow is polishing at the gangway,—"Twenty—twenty-one—twenty-two"—and so on, while the patient roared you, an' it were anything but a nightin-

*A quarter dollar.

gale. At length he broke away from the men who held him, after receiving a most sufficient flogging, to revenge which he immediately fastened on the John Canoe, wrenched his cat from him, and employed it so scientifically on him and his followers, giving them passing taps on the shins now and then with the handle, by way of spice to the dose, that the whole crew pulled foot as if Old Nick had held them in chase.

The very children, urchins of five and six years old, had their Lilliputian John Canoes and *Devices*. But the beautiful part of the exhibition was the Set Girls. They danced along the streets, in bands of from fifteen to thirty. There were brown sets, and black sets, and sets of all the intermediate gradations of colour. Each set was dressed pin for pin alike, and carried umbrellas or parasols of the same colour and size, held over their nice showy, well put on *toques*, or Madras handkerchiefs, all of the same pattern, tied round their heads, fresh out of the fold.—They sang, as they swam along the streets, in the most luxurious attitudes. I had never seen more beautiful creatures than there were amongst the brown sets—clear olive complexions, and fine faces, elegant carriages, splendid figures,—full, plump, and magnificent.

Most of the Sets were as much of a size as Lord _____'s eighteen daughters, sailing down Regent Street, like a Charity School of a Sunday, led by a rum-looking old beadle—others again had large Roman matron-looking women in the leading files, the *figurantes* in their tails becoming slighter and smaller, as they tapered away, until they ended in *leetle picaniny, no bigger as my tumb*, but always preserving the uniformity of dress, and colour of the umbrells or parasol. Sometimes the breeze, on opening a corner, would strike the sternmost of a set composed in this manner of small fry, and stagger the little things, getting beneath their tiny umbrellas, and fairly blowing them out of the line, and ruffling their ribbons and finery, as if they had been tulips bending and shaking their leaves before it. But the *colours* were never blended in the same set—no blackie ever interloped with the browns, nor did the browns in any case mix with the sables— always keeping in mind—black *woman*—brown *lady*.

MATTHEW GREGORY LEWIS, *Journal of A West India Proprietor* (London, 1834), 50–59; 73–76.

1816—January 1
At length the ship has squeezed herself into this champagne bottle of a bay! Perhaps, the satisfaction attendant upon our having overcome the difficulty, added something to the illusion of its effect; but

the beauty of the atmosphere, the dark purple mountains, the shores covered with mangroves of the liveliest green down to the very edge of the water, and the light-coloured houses with their lattices and piazzas completely embowered in trees, altogether made the scenery of the Bay wear a very picturesque appearance. And, to complete the charm, the sudden sounds of the drum and banjee, called our attention to a procession of the *John-Canoe,* which was proceeding to celebrate the opening of the new year at the town of Black River. The John-Canoe is a Merry-Andrew dressed in a striped doublet, and bearing upon his head a kind of pasteboard house-boat, filled with puppets, representing, some sailors, others soldiers, others again slaves at work on a plantation, etc. The negroes are allowed three days for holidays at Christmas, and also New-years' day, which being the last is always reckoned by them as the festival of the greatest importance. It is for this day that they reserve their finest dresses, and lay their schemes for displaying their show and expense to the greatest advantage; and it is then that the John-Canoe is considered not merely as a person of material consequence, but one whose presence is absolutely indispensable. Nothing could look more gay than the procession which we now saw with its train of attendants, all dressed in white, and marching two by two (except when the file was broken here and there by a single horseman), and its band of negro music, and its scarlet flags fluttering about in the breeze, now disappearing behind a projecting clump of mangrove trees, and then again emerging into an open part of the road, as it wound along the shore towards the town of Black River.

> _____ "Mano telluris amore
> Egressi optatâ Tröes potiuntur arenâ."

I had determined not to go on shore, till I should land for good and all at Savannah la Mar. But although I could resist the "telluris amor," there was no resisting John-Canoe; so, in defiance of a broiling afternoon's sun, about four o'clock we left the vessel for the town.

It was, as I understand, formerly one of some magnitude; but it now consists only of a few houses, owing to a spark from a tobacco-pipe or a candle having lodged upon a mosquito-net during dry weather; and although the conflagration took place at mid-day, the whole town was reduced to ashes. The few streets—(I believe there were not above two, but those were wide and regular, and the houses looked very neat)—were now crowded with people, and it seemed to be allowed, upon all hands, that New-year's day had never been celebrated there with more expense and festivity.

It seems that, many years ago, an Admiral of the Red was superseded on the Jamaica station by an Admiral of the Blue; and both of them gave balls at Kingston to the "Brown Girls"; for the fair sex elsewhere are called the "Brown Girls" in Jamaica. In consequence of these balls, all Kingston was divided into parties: from thence the division spread into other districts: and ever since, the whole island, at Christmas, is separated into the rival factions of the Blues and the Reds (the Red representing also the English, the Blue the Scotch), who contend for setting forth their processions with the greatest taste and magnificence. This year, several gentlemen in the neighbourhood of Black River had subscribed very largely towards the expenses of the show; and certainly it produced the gayest and most amusing scene that I ever witnessed, to which the mutual jealousy and pique of the two parties against each other contributed in no slight degree. The champions of the rival Roses,—the Guelphs and the Ghibellines,—none of them could exceed the scornful animosity and spirit of depreciation with which the Blues and the Reds of Black River examined the efforts at display of each other. The Blues had the advantage beyond a doubt; this a Red girl told us that she could not deny; but still, "though the Reds were beaten, she would not be a Blue girl for the whole universe!" On the other hand, Miss Edwards (the mistress of the hotel from whose window we saw the show), was rank Blue to the very tips of her fingers, and had, indeed, contributed one of her female slaves to sustain a very important character in the show; for when the Blue procession was ready to set forward, there was evidently a hitch, something was wanting; and there seemed to be no possibility of getting on without it—when suddenly we saw a tall woman dressed in mourning (being Miss Edwards herself) rush out of our hotel, dragging along by the hand a strange uncouth kind of a glittering tawdry figure, all feathers, and pitchfork, and painted pasteboard, who moved most reluctantly, and turned out to be no less a personage than Britannia herself, with a pasteboard shield covered with the arms of Great Britain, a trident in her hand, and a helmet made of pale blue silk and silver. The poor girl, it seems, was bashful at appearing in this conspicuous manner before so many spectators, and hung back when it came to the point. But her mistress had seized hold of her, and placed her by main force in her destined position. The music struck up, Miss Edwards gave the Goddess a great push forwards; the drumsticks and the elbows of the fiddlers attacked her from the rear; and on went Britannia willy-nilly!

The Blue girls called themselves "the Blue girls of Waterloo." Their motto was the more patriotic; that of the Red was the more gallant:—"Britannia rules the day!' streamed upon the Blue flag; "Red girls for ever!" floated upon the Red. But, in point of taste and invention, the former carried it hollow. First marched Britannia; then came a band of music; then the flag; then the Blue King and Queen—the Queen splendidly dressed in white and silver (in scorn of the opposite party, her train was borne by a little girl in red); his Majesty wore a full British Admiral's uniform, with a white satin sash, and a huge cocked hat with a gilt paper crown upon the top of it. These were immediately followed by "Nelson's car," being a kind of canoe decorated with blue and silver drapery, and with "Trafalgar" written on the front of it; and the procession was closed by a long train of Blue grandees (the women dressed in uniforms of white, with robes of blue muslin), all Princes and Princesses, Dukes and Duchesses, every mother's child of them.

The Red girls were also dressed very gaily and prettily, but they had nothing in point of invention that could vie with Nelson's Car and Britannia; and when the Red throne made its appearance, language cannot express the contempt with which our landlady eyed it. "It was neither one thing nor t'other," Miss Edwards was of opinion. "Merely a few yards of calico stretched over some planks—and look, look, only look at it behind! you may see the bare boards! By way of a throne, indeed! Well, to be sure, Miss Edwards never saw a poorer thing in her life, that she must say!" And then she told me, that somebody had just snatched at a medal which Britannia wore round her neck, and had endeavoured to force it away. I asked her who had done so? "Oh, one of the Red party, of course!" The Red party was evidently Miss Edwards's Mrs. Grundy. John-Canoe made no part of the procession; but he and his rival, John-Crayfish (a personage of whom I heard, but could not obtain a sight), seemed to act upon quite an independent interest, and go about from house to house, tumbling and playing antics to pick up money for themselves.

A play was now proposed to us, and, of course, accepted. Three men and a girl accordingly made their appearance; the men dressed like the tumblers at Astley's, the lady very tastefully in white and silver, and all with their faces concealed by masks of thin blue silk; and they proceeded to perform the quarrel between Douglas and Glenalvon, and the fourth act of "The Fair Penitent." They were all quite perfect, and had no need of a prompter. As to Lothario, he was by far the most comical dog that I ever saw in my life, and his dying scene exceeded all description; Mr. Coates himself might have taken hints from him! As soon as Lothario was fairly dead, and Calista had made her exit in distraction, they all began dancing reels like so many mad people, till they were obliged to make way for the Waterloo procession, who came to collect money for the next year's festival; one of them singing, another dancing to the tune, while she presented her money-box to the spectators, and the rest of the Blue girls filling up the chorus. I cannot say much in praise of the black Catalani; but nothing could be more light, and playful, and graceful, than the extempore movements of the dancing girl. Indeed, through the whole day, I had been struck with the precision of their march, the ease and grace of their action, the elasticity of their step, and the lofty air with which they carried their heads—all, indeed, except poor Britannia, who hung down hers in the most ungoddess-like manner imaginable. The first song was the old Scotch air of "Logie of Buchan," of which the girl sang one single stanza forty times over. But the second was in praise of the Hero of Heroes; so I gave the songstress a dollar to teach it to me, and drink the Duke's health. It was not easy to make out what she said, but as well as I could understand them, the words ran as follows:—

> "Come, rise up, our gentry,
> And hear about Waterloo;
> Ladies, take your spy-glass,
> And attend to what we do;
> For one and one makes two,
> And one alone must be.
> Then singee, singee Waterloo,
> None so brave as he!"

—and then there came something about green and white flowers, and a Duchess, and a lily-white Pig, and going on board of a dashing man of war; but what they all had to do with the Duke, or with each other, I could not make even a guess. I was going to ask for an explanation, but suddenly half of them gave a shout loud enough "to fright the realms of Chaos and old Night," and away they flew, singers, dancers, and all. The cause of this was the sudden illumination of the town with quantities of large chandeliers and bushes, the branches of which were stuck all over with great blazing torches: the effect was really beautiful, and the excessive rapture of the black multitude at the spectacle was as well worth the witnessing as the sight itself.

I never saw so many people who appeared to be so unaffectedly happy. In England, at fairs and races, half the visiters at least seem to have been only brought there for the sake of traffic, and to be too busy to be amused; but here nothing was thought of but real pleasure; and that pleasure seemed to consist in singing, dancing, and laughing, in seeing and being seen, in showing their own fine clothes, or in admiring those of others. There were no people selling or buying; no servants and landladies bustling and passing about; and at eight o'clock, as we passed through the market-place, where was the greatest illumination, and which, of course, was most thronged, I did not see a single person drunk, nor had I observed a single quarrel through the course of the day; except, indeed, when some thoughtless fellow crossed the line of the procession, and received by the way a good box of the ear from the Queen or one of her attendant Duchesses. Every body made the same remark to me; "Well, sir, what do you think Mr. Wilberforce would think of the state of the negroes, if he could see this scene?" and certainly, to judge by this one specimen, of all beings that I have yet seen, these were the happiest. As we were passing to our boat, through the market-place, suddenly we saw Miss Edwards dart out of the crowd, and seize the Captain's arm—"Captain! Captain!" cried she, "for the love of Heaven, only look at the *Red* lights! Old iron hoops, nothing but old iron hoops, I declare! Well! for my part!" and then, with a contemptuous toss of her head, away frisked Miss Edwards triumphantly.

January 6

This was the day given to my negroes as a festival on my arrival. A couple of heifers were slaughtered for them: they were allowed as much rum, and sugar, and noise, and dancing as they chose; and as to the two latter, certainly they profited by the permission. About two o'clock they began to assemble round the house, all drest in their holiday clothes, which, both for men and women, were chiefly white; only that the women were decked out with a profusion of beads and corals, and gold ornaments of all descriptions; and that while the blacks wore jackets, the mulattoes generally wore cloth coats; and inasmuch as they were all plainly clean instead of being shabbily fashionable, and affected to be nothing except that which they really were, they looked twenty times more like gentlemen than nine tenths of the bankers' clerks who swagger up and down Bond Street. It is a custom as to the mulatto children, that the males born on an estate should never be employed as field negroes, but as tradesmen; the females are brought up as domestics about the house. I had particularly invited "*Mr.* John-Canoe" (which I found to be the polite manner in which the negroes spoke of him), and there arrived a couple of very gay and gaudy ones. I enquired whether one of them was "John-Crayfish"; but I was told that John-Crayfish was John-Canoe's rival and enemy, and might belong to the factions of "the Blues and the Reds"; but on Cornwall they were all friends, and therefore there were only the father and the son—Mr. John-Canoe, senior, and Mr. John-Canoe, junior.

The person who gave me this information was a young mulatto carpenter, called Nicholas, whom I had noticed in the crowd, on my first arrival, for his clean appearance and intelligent countenance; and he now begged me to notice the smaller of the two John-Canoe machines. "To be sure," he said, "it was not so large nor showy as the other, but then it was much better *proportioned* (his own word), and altogether much prettier"; and he said so much in praise of it, that I asked him whether he knew the maker? and then out came the motive: "Oh, yes! it was made by John Fuller, who lived in the next house to him, and worked in the same shop, and indeed they were just like brothers." So I desired to see his *fidus Achates*, and he brought me as smart and intelligent a little fellow as eye ever beheld, who came grinning from ear to ear to tell me that he had made every bit of the canoe with his own hands, and had set to work upon it the moment that he knew of massa's coming to Jamaica. And indeed it was as fine as paint, pasteboard, gilt paper, and looking-glass could make it! Unluckily, the breeze being very strong blew off a fine glittering umbrella, surmounted with a plume of John Crow feathers, which crowned the top; and a little wag of a negro boy whipped it up, clapped it upon his head, and performed the part of an impromptu Mr. John-Canoe with so much fun and grotesqueness, that he fairly beat the original performers out of the pit, and carried off all the applause of the spectators, and a couple of my dollars. The John-Canoes are fitted out at the expense of the rich negroes, who afterwards share the money collected from the spectators during their performance, allotting one share to the representator himself; and it is usual for the master of the estate to give them a couple of guineas apiece.

RICHARD WATSON, *A Defense of the Wesleyan Methodist Missions in the West Indies* (London, 1817), 121–22.

Amongst the many unspeakable advantages which have resulted from the missions, in the West Indies, a very evident one appears at the season of Christmas. At this period, the negroes in general have some time allowed them for holidays. They have also a certain portion of provision allotted. It is well known that thirty years ago, they used to spend their time at this festival, in gluttony, drunkenness, quarrelling, fighting, dancing, and carousing; and, in general, very much mischief was done by them. The island of Nevis, for instance, may serve as a

specimen. This is the native place of Mrs. Dace, and she can well remember, that if the managers did not deal out the Christmas allowance to please the slaves; they, out of resentment, would do any mischief to the estates, which lay in their way. Sometimes they would go
and set fire to a whole piece, or track, of sugar canes; so that the
greater part would be destroyed before the flames could be quenched.
Sometimes the poor cattle would suffer, either by being maimed or
killed. The gentlemen of the island were under the necessity, therefore, at this season, of forming themselves into an armed body; their
place of rendezvous was the Church, and while a part stood on guard
there, the rest formed into parties, and travelled in different circuits,
through, and round their respective estates. This was done in the
night, to prevent mischief, overawe the negroes, and preserve their
own lives and property. My wife's father used to make one of these
parties, and I have heard the inhabitants relate the same things. At
Tortola, also, I have heard some of our old leaders and members, and
several of the white inhabitants say, that it certainly was a happy day,
when the Methodist missionaries arrived there; for before, many, both
of the coloured and white inhabitants, used to dread the approach of
Christmas, among the slaves; there was then so much rioting, obeah
(a kind of witchcraft,) cruelty, and wickedness. All old grudges were
sure to be remembered and repaid then; and very often murder was
committed. They have told me, it has been thought well, if one murder only, was committed at that season. Thefts and robberies were
innumerable.

Now these are plain and undeniable facts, visible to all ranks
and colours, to friends and enemies. But how very different is the case
now? No guard is kept in Nevis at all, at the Christmas festival; nor
has been kept for a great many years. The ungodly spend this season,
it is true, in a loose and thoughtless manner; but even *they* do not
"run to the same excess of riot." A very great and manifest alteration
has taken place in general; but there are hundreds and thousands of
the religious slaves, who observe Christmas, not only with order and
sobriety, but in the most religious manner.

JAMES STEWART, *A View of the Past and the Present State of the
Island of Jamaica* (Edinburgh, 1823), 273–74.

On new-year's-day, it is customary for the creole negro girls of the
towns, who conceive themselves superior to those on the plantations,
to exhibit themselves in all the pride of gaudy finery, under the de-

nomination of *Blues and Reds*—parties in rivalship and opposition to each other. They are generally dressed with much taste, sometimes at the expense of their white and brown mistresses, who take a pride in showing them off to the greatest advantage. Their gowns are of the finest muslin, with blue or pink satin spencers, trimmed with gold or silver, according to their party; and gold necklaces, ear-rings, and other expensive trinkets, shine to advantage on their jet black skins. The most comely young negresses are selected, and such as have a fine and tutored voice; they parade through the streets, two and two, in the most exact order, with appropriate flags and instrumental music, accompanied by their voices, the songs being for the most part such as they have caught from the whites, and which they previously practise for the occasion. Each party has its *queen*, who eclipses all the rest in the splendour of her dress. Their appearance, upon the whole, is tasteful and elegant, and would somewhat astonish a stranger who had associated with the idea of slavery other images than those of gayety and costly display.

These exhibitions are not so frequent as they used to be. The mistresses of the slaves, who were the patronesses of them, and at whose expense much of the requisite finery was provided, find that they cost more money and trouble than they can well spare. The negresses must, however, have their annual display of fine clothes and suitable ornaments, if they should go in filth and raggedness all the rest of the year.

H. T. DE LA BECHE, *Notes on the Present Conditions of the Negroes in Jamaica* (London, 1825), 41–42.

At Christmas the negroes are altogether without restraint, and go over the country feasting, dancing, and drinking. Many of the girls form themselves into what they call sets, in which the dresses are nearly alike; these sets travel, preceded by flags, drums, and other music, from estate to estate, dancing at the houses of the white people, and in the negro villages, where they are given money, and very often entertained. Their dresses on these occasions are often very expensive, hats that cost a doubloon (sixteen dollars), and blue or white kid shoes at fifteen shillings per pair are by no means uncommon; those that wish to be particularly smart carry parasols.

The negroes have the amusements of the May-pole and Jack in the Green. A spike of the yellow flowers of the American aloe is employed for the former purpose, and when, as sometimes happens, it

rises from twenty to twenty-five feet high; and is handsomely ornamented with other flowers and gilding, it forms a very beautiful
object.

Some of the negroes go about at Christmas and Easter attended
by drums, &c., and perform much in the same manner as our Mummers. I was much amused on Easter Monday by a party which came
to my house from a neighbouring property, consisting of musicians,
and a couple of personages fantastically dressed to represent kings or
warriors; one of them wore a white mask on his face, and part of the
representation had evidently some reference to the play of Richard
the Third; for the man in the white mask exclaimed, "A horse, a horse,
my kingdom for a horse!" The piece however terminated by a sword
dance with him.

The various African amusements, in which the negroes formerly
took so much delight, are not now kept up with spirit, and Joncanoe
himself is getting out of fashion.

CYNRIC R. WILLIAMS, A Tour through the Island of Jamaica, . . .
(London, 1826), 21–27, 62–64.

I was grumbling in imagination at the incessant clamour of the cocks
on the morning of Christmas-day, when my ears were assailed with
another sort of music, not much more melodious. This was a chorus of
negroes singing "good morning to your night-cap, and health to master and mistress." They came into the house and began dancing. I
slipped on my dressing-gown and mingled in their orgies, much to the
diversion of the black damsels, as well as of the inmates of the house,
who came into the piazza to witness the ceremonies. We gave the fiddler a dollar, and their provisions for two or three days, and we saw
no more of them till the evening, when they again assembled on the
lawn before the house with their gombays, bonjaws, and an ebo drum,
made of a hollow tree, with a piece of sheepskin stretched over it.
Some the women carried small calabashes with pebbles in them,
stuck on short sticks, which they rattled in time to the songs, or rather
howls of the musicians. They divided themselves into parties to
dance, some before the gombays, in a ring, to perform a bolero or a
sort of love-dance, as it is called, where the gentlemen occasionally
wiped the perspiration off the shining faces of their black beauties,
who, in turn, performed the same service to the minstrel. Others performed a sort of pyrrhic before the ebo drummer, beginning gently
and gradually quickening their motions, until they seemed agitated by

the furies. They were all dressed in their best; some of the men in long-tailed coats, one of the gombayers in old regimentals; the women in muslins and cambrics, with coloured handkerchiefs tastefully disposed round their heads, and ear-rings, necklaces, and bracelets of all sorts, in profusion. The entertainment was kept up till nine or ten o'clock in the evening, and during the time they were regaled with punch and santa in abundance; they came occasionally and asked for porter and wine. Indeed a perfect equality seemed to reign among all parties; many came and shook hands with their master and mistress, nor did the young ladies refuse this salutation any more than the gentlemen. The merriment became rather boisterous as the punch operated, and the slaves sang satirical philippics against their master, communicating a little free advice now and then; but they never lost sight of decorum, and at last retired, apparently quite satisfied with their saturnalia, to dance the rest of the night at their own habitations.

I must not omit one circumstance that diverted us all exceedingly during the festivity, and seemed to justify the title of saturnalia, which I have given to it. An old grey-headed man, who had formerly been appointed a watchman to guard the negro-grounds, had occasionally abused his trust, and robbed the grounds he was bound to protect: considering his age and venerable appearance, Mr. Graham had always endeavoured to pacify those who had been robbed, by compelling the thief to make restitution from his own grounds, rather than flogging him: however, the old rogue, having been detected in the very act of some outrageous robbery, had thought it prudent to retire, and had absented himself from the estate for two years previous to this festival, in the midst of which he made his unexpected appearance, and came up to his master laughing with perfect nonchalance. He shook hands with him as the others had done, and said "he was sorry he had been a bad boy, but he never would do so any more." So he received a free pardon.

The next morning, a little after breakfast time, the slaves reappeared, dressed in fresh costume, that of yesterday being, perhaps, a little deranged with their romping. A new ceremony was to be exhibited. First came eight or ten young girls marching before a man dressed up in a mask with a grey beard and long flowing hair, who carried the model of a house on his head. This house is called the Jonkanoo, and the bearer of it is generally chosen for his superior activity in dancing. He first saluted his master and mistress, and then capered about with astonishing agility and violence. The girls also danced without changing their position, moving their elbows and knees, and keeping tune with the calabashes filled with small stones. One of the damsels betraying, as it seemed, a little too much friskiness in her gestures, was reproved by her companions for her *imperance;* they called her Miss Brazen, and told her she ought to be ashamed. All this time an incessant hammering was kept up on the gombay, and the cotta (a Windsor chair taken from the piazza to serve as a secondary drum) and the Jonkanoo's attendant went about collecting money from the dancers and from the white people. Two or three strange negroes were invited to join, as a compliment of respect; they also contributed to the Jonkanoo man, who, I am told, collects sometimes from ten to fifteen pounds on the occasion. All this ceremony is certainly a commemoration of the deluge. The custom is African and religious, although the purpose is forgotten. Some writer, whose name I forget, says that the house is an emblem of Noah's ark, and that Jonkanoo means the sacred boat or the sacred dove—*caken* meaning sacred, and *iona* a dove, in Hebrew or Samaritan: but as I have no pretension to etymology, I leave this subject to the literati.

The negroes have a custom of performing libations when they drink, a kind of first-fruit offering. When the old runaway thief of a watchman reconciled himself to his master, he received a glass of grog in token of forgiveness on the one side, and of repentance on the other; first, that he should not be flogged, and secondly, that he should not run away any more. On receiving the glass of grog, he poured a few drops on the ground, and drank off the rest to the health of his master and mistress.

On all these occasions of festivity the mulattoes kept aloof, as if they disdained to mingle with the negroes; and some of the pious, the regenerated slaves, also objected to participate in the heathen practices of their ancestors. Yet they seemed to cast many a wistful look at the dancers, more especially after they had taken their allowance of grog, which it was no part of their new faith to renounce.

. . .

Being the first day of the new year, another holiday is allowed to the negroes. They turned out a little after day-light to show themselves to the overseer, and were again dismissed to prepare for the festivities of the day, which belong to a contest kept up by the two parties of the women. I very much suspect this is a remnant of the Adonia mentioned by Plutarch. Each party wears an appropriate colour, one red, the other blue, of the most expensive materials they can afford. They select two queens, the prettiest and the best-shaped girls they can find, who are obliged to personate the royal characters, and support them to the best of their power and ideas. These are deco-rated with the ornaments, necklaces, earrings, bracelets, &c. of their mistresses, so that they often carry much wealth on their persons for the time. Each party has a procession (but not so as to encounter each other) with silk flags and streamers, in which the queen is drawn in a phaeton, if such a carriage can be procured, or any four-wheeled ve-hicle which can pass for a triumphal car, that her person may be seen to the best advantage. Thus they parade the towns, priding them-selves on the number of their followers, until the evening, when each party gives a splendid entertainment, at which every luxury and deli-cacy that money can procure are lavished in profusion. The only sub-ject of contest or rivalship is the beauty of the queen and the finery of all the individuals. Mirth and good humour prevail throughout, and the evening is concluded with a ball.

As it was my business to see every thing that could interest me in Jamaica, I accompanied Mr. Mathews to the Bay, where one of these entertainments took place in the house of a free mulatto woman. The music consisted of three fiddles, a pipe and tabor, and a triangle. The dancers, male and female, acquitted themselves famously well, and performed country-dances and quadrilles quite as well, if not bet-ter, than I had ever seen at the country ball in England. Most of the ladies wore pink shoes (as it was the red party whom I attended) and all of them silk stockings, set off by feet that Cinderella's could not have surpassed in elegance. The supper consisted of cold roasted pea-fowls, turkeys, capons, tongues, hams, &c.; fresh and dried fruits, grapes from Kingston, equal to any in the world, and all sorts of wines and liquors, not excepting champaign and noyau.

All these things were laid out in an adjoining room, to which we were particularly invited. The dancing still continued, and small par-ties, as they pleased, retired from the ball-room to partake of the col-lation, and then rejoined the dancers.

There were many free people of colour. The men were very well dressed, and conducted themselves with the greatest propriety.

ANONYMOUS, *Marly; or Life in Jamaica* [a novel] (Glasgow, 1828), 293–94.

... A principal attraction was John Canoe and his wife, each ac-coutred in a manner truly fantastical, according as their fancy, of what was most ridiculous, directed them; but John very prudently carried a small imitation of a canoe, into which he and his wife, with their attendants, expected the donations of onlookers to be deposited. To ensure such more effectually, John and his wife, (who, by the way, was of the male sex, metamorphosed into the appearance of a gigantic female, only by the whimsical dress), danced without intermission, often wheeling violently round, for a great number of times, and all the while singing, or, in more correct language, roaring in an unintelligible jargon, in true stentorian voices. Their performance was truly hideous; and had that fabled personage, Melancholy, been present, even he would have forgot his griefs and his sorrows, and joined the laughing spectators.

John Canoe and his lady, with their favourite gumba, were of true African extraction; and their mode of acting seemed well adapted to please a race who are not over fastidious in their amusements, such as a rude or savage people, who take delight in witnessing the most violent efforts of exertion of body and voice, aided by the means of ludicrous grimace and fantastical unnatural decoration. Accordingly, John appeared to reap some benefit from the exertions of himself and his associate; and owing to their earnest desire of affording amusement, few white people, failed, in passing, to drop something into the canoe, which rendered them not the least happy of all of those who were enjoying Christmas.

ALEXANDER BARCLAY, *A Practical View of the Present State of Slavery in the West Indies* . . . (London, 1826), 10–13.

. . . dances were formerly common, or I should rather say universal, at Christmas; but of late years have much gone out, owing to an idea impressed on the minds of the negroes, principally I believe by the missionaries, that the season ought rather to be devoted to religious exercises. It is now considered more becoming to attend the places of worship, or to have private religious parties among themselves; and in passing through a negro village on a Christmas night, it is more common to hear psalm-singing, than the sound of merriment. The young people, however, still indulge in some amusements on this occasion, one of which may be worth describing. The young girls of a plantation, or occasionally of two neighbouring plantations leagued, form what is called 'a sett.' They dress exactly in uniform, with gowns of some neat pattern of printed cotton, and take the name of Blue Girls, Yellow Girls, &c. according to the dress and ribbon they have chosen. They have always with them in their excursions, a fiddle, a drum, and a tambourine, frequently boys playing fifes, a distinguish-

ing flag which is waved on a pole, and generally some fantastical figure, or toy, such as a castle or tower, surrounded with mirrors. A ma-
tron attends who possesses some degree of authority, and is called
Queen of the Sett, and they have always one or two Joncanoe-men,
smart youths, fantastically dressed, and masked so as not to be known.
Thus equipped, and generally accompanied by some friends, they
proceed to the neighbouring plantation villages, and always visit the
master's or manager's house, into which they enter without ceremony,
and where they are joined by the white people in a dance. Some refreshment is given to them, and the Joncanoe-men, after a display of
their buffoonery, commonly put the white people under requisition for
a little money, to pay the fiddler, &c. A party of forty or fifty young
girls thus attired, with their hair braided over their brows, beads
round their necks, and gold ear-rings, present a very interesting and
amusing sight, as they approach a house dancing, with their music
playing, and Joncanoe-men capering and playing tricks. They have
generally fine voices, and dancing in a room they require no instrumental music.* One of their best singers commences the song, and
unaccompanied sings the first part with words for the occasion, of
course not always very poetical, though frequently not unamusing;
the whole sett joins in the chorus as they mingle in the dance, waving
their handkerchiefs over their heads. All is life and joy, and certainly
is is one of the most pleasing sights that can be imagined.

The last party of this kind which I had the pleasure of seeing
and dancing with, at Christmas 1823, belonged to Reach and Muirton
estates, the property of Mr. William Bryan, and afforded a novelty I
had never before witnessed, in a rude representation of some passages of Richard III which they made sufficiently farcical. The
Joncanoe-men, disrobed of part of their paraphernalia, were the two
heroes, and fought, not for a kingdom but a queen, whom the victor
carried off in triumph. Richard calling out "A horse! a horse!" &c. was
laughable enough. This farce I saw at Dalvey estate, the property of
Sir A. Grant, and it afforded Mr. Bell the manager and his guests no

*The airs they sing and dance to are simple and lively; the following is a specimen:—

small amusement. How the negroes had acquired even the very imperfect knowledge they seemed to have of the play, we could form no idea, and the occasion did not admit of asking questions.[†]

While on the subject of Christmas I may observe, that the whole of the Negroes in Jamaica, have three, and some of them four days allowed for their amusements; and that on this occasion their masters give them an allowance of rum, sugar, and codfish or salt meat; and, generally, the larger estates kill as many cattle as are sufficient to give each family a few pounds of fresh beef. Nor let it be supposed that this is the amount of their enjoyments; the more wealthy slave families kill pigs and poultry, have their Christmas cakes, and in fact abound in good things both to eat and drink.

Memoirs of Charles Campbell (Glasgow, 1828), 16–17.

I reached Montego Bay on the night before new-year's-day, and found my friend, with about half a dozen more young men from Scotland, prepared to celebrate Hogmanay, in honour of the ancient customs of their forefathers. I was made a welcome participator of their festivity, and felt all the agreeable emotions that usually accompany a sudden change from a situation of toil and peril, to one of ease and security. The Negroes enjoy the time from Christmas to new-year's-day as holidays, and the streets were now crowded with splendid processions, or choaked up with crowds of dancers. This is an amusement of which the Negroes are very fond. Their music generally consists of a small drum, or the skull of a horse, which they strike with a stick. The bystanders accompany this uncouth instrument with some favourite tune. In these dances only two perform at once, a male and female. The female generally confines her movements to the modesty of nature; but the male displays what he considers his powers of agility, by performing the most extravagant and hyperbolical saltations, without aiming at any thing like science or art. They take great delight in this exercise, and the most extravagant buffoon is generally the victor in the eyes of the sombre fair ones of Dahomy and Congo. Their processions were really elegant, but, as far as I could learn, they consisted principally of free Negroes. They were well attired in muslins and silks, accompanied with bands of music. They walked arm in arm, males and females. Sometimes a female with a good voice sung a

[†]Since this was written, I have read Mr. De la Beche's pamphlet, who mentions having seen the same thing in a different part of the island.

song, and the whole procession joined in the chorus. They carried at certain intervals, large artificial trees, stuck full of burning tapers. They usually made a halt at the doors of the wealthier inhabitants, and after chanting some stanzas in praise of the occupant, received a gratuity in money.

MRS. A. C. CARMICHAEL, *Domestic Manners and Social Conditions of the White, Coloured and Negro Population of the West Indies* (London, 1833), vol. II, 289–91; vol. I, 293–94.

... I recollect one Christmas morning, I was awoke just as day dawned, by the sound of many merry voices, young and old, wishing massa and misses a good Christmas. We got up, and dressed as quickly as possible to return the compliment, and found upwards of twenty negroes—both Laurel Hill and St. Vincent people. When we came to the door, they all shook hands with us; some made long speeches, full of good wishes; and one female negro expressed what she no doubt considered the best wish of all. She meant that her master should enjoy a good old age; but she expressed it by saying, "Me massa, me hope you live long, very long; me hope you live to bury all your pic-a-ninnies." Songs and dances followed; the songs of their own composition, and full of good wishes for a good crop and good sugar.

The giving out the Christmas allowances is a very merry scene: they flour each other's black faces and curly hair, and call out, "look at he white face! and he white wig!"—with many other jokes of their own. On Christmas Eve, or rather from noon the day preceding Christmas, nothing is done but to bring the grass for the stock—all is bustle and preparation; and this is continued until the evening of Christmas-day, which always terminates in a dance. About eleven in the morning, a party of negroes from Paradise, the adjoining estate, came to wish us a good Christmas. They had two fiddlers, whose hats and fiddles were decorated with many-coloured ribbons. They said they wished to come and play good Christmas to the "young misses." They were very nicely dressed, in clean white shirts, trowsers, and jackets. . . .

. . .

Negroes formerly used to be inclined, I was told, to rioting and fighting upon Christmas day, but now they all go to church; even those who do not go at any other time make a point of attending then. Many still dance upon Christmas night, but the greater proportion would not do so—but dance on the other two holidays I have named. Many of the white population informed me that Christmas holidays used formerly to be looked forward to with dread, but now there was a happy improvement indeed. . . .

TRELAWNY WENTWORTH, *The West India Sketch Book* (London, 1834), 37–38.

Christmas is as much a season of festivity among them as it may be with the veriest holyday rake in Christendom, and if a superproportion of roast beef and plum-pudding, so essential to the enjoyment of their phlegmatic brethren in the parent state, does not gladden their hearts till repletion obscures their understanding, they have other viands provided for them, perhaps better suited to their tastes; and their mirth is not marred by the ill-timed connection *quarter-day* with the anniversary. An ox, or, as the planters usually term that description of animal, "a cattle," is on some estates killed and divided amongst them, or Irish mess port, with an extra allowance of yams, and flour or cornmeal, and a measure of rum, the children receiving a proportionate quantity; and by whatever means they have acquired a knowledge of the privileges which the saturnalia conferred upon the Roman slaves, or whether it be from the deduction of reason that they imagine themselves entitled to them, they do not fail to practice as much impudent vivacity in "paying their respects" to their masters, as marked the conduct of the Roman bondmen in doing honour to the Pagan deity. For 3 days, all business or control over them, and all distinctions of rank cease, so far, at least that they do what they please, within the bounds of justifiable liberty and hilarity. On the Christmas morning, most of them pay their respects at "the Buff," or great house, and deal out their benedictions, and compliments with unrestrained volubility, and the serving of the donation is the exordium of the mirth and merriment which follow. Young and old participate in a reckless spirit of enjoyment, and a marvellous effect is also produced upon the sick, inasmuch as the hospital is generally clearer of patients than at any other time, whatever it may be when the holidays have terminated.

JAMES KELLY, *Voyage to Jamaica* (Belfast, 1838), 20–21.

I must just notice the Christmas holidays before I leave Industry. Mr. Gray had provided a cash of santa (shrub). On the first of these joyous days, we were only visited ceremoniously by the head people, and such of the *ladies* that could exhibit finery enough to please themselves; and I was astonished to see such a display of valuable trinkets—coral and carnelian necklaces, bracelets, &c. The next and following days, however, they took possession of the house *en masse*, with the exception of our bed-rooms. Such a motley assembly!

I had just formed an idea of the revelry of the savages. The Mangolas, the Mandingoes, the Eboes, the Congoes, &c. &c. formed into exclusive groups, and each strove to be loudest in the music and songs, or rather yells, peculiar to their country; and their dance, if dance I must call it, was a display of unseemly gestures. These African groups took up the sides and corners of the hall, whilst the Creoles occupied the centre and piazzas, and evidently considered themselves entitled to the best places, which the Africans cheerfully conceded to them, evincing the greatest deference to the *superior civilization* of the upstarts! The one class, *forced* into slavery, humbled and degraded, and lost everything, and found no solace but the miserable one of retrospection. The other born in slavery, never had freedom to lose; yet did the Creole proudly assume a superiority over the African: and the Creoles danced to fife and drum, with a determination to be the uppermost in noise as well as in place. The discordant assembly continued till late the following day; when fatigue, and the effects of the santa, began to subdue and disperse them.

WILLIAM LLOYD, *Letters from the West Indies, During a Visit in the Autumn of MDCCCXXXVI and the Spring of MDCCCXXXVII* (London, 1839), 56–57.

. . . The Christmas holidays are dear to the Negroes; they have *two* days holiday. They make each other presents, feast together, and then dance the African dance called "Joe and Johnny." The day in George Town was orderly and quiet as any English Sabbath till sun-down, when a few dances were in operation. They are open to anyone; are performed at the back of the houses; the doors are thrown open for all inclined to walk through; a circle is formed, but the space so small I could jump across it, as many as choose recite or sing to a very rude drum (called gombay).

"Which sounds like something, and yet it rings but hollow," played upon by the knuckles; and two or at most four are in the circle at a time performing the evolutions, which are continuous. One party being tired, they hand out others and rest; and so the dance goes on for hours, it may be the whole night. Each one recites what he likes; perhaps the "true Barbadian," who assumes considerable consequence, from its being the oldest British Colony. The amusement is simple and I saw no intoxicating liquors handed about.

I. M. BELISARIO, *Sketches of Character in Illustration of the Habits, Occupations and Costume of the Negro Population in the Island of Jamaica* (Kingston, 1838) (unpaginated).

"Koo-Koo, or Actor-Boy"*

Such is the strange title, by which this Aspirant to Histrionic honors is designated. Ten or twelve years back, several companies of these self-styled Performers, envious of each other's abilities, strolled through the streets, habited in varied costumes, considered by them however, as having been in strict accordance with the *characters* they were called upon to sustain—for be it known, they dared to perpetrate "murder most foul" even on the plays of Shakespeare.

Of late years, this class of John-Canoe† has found but little inducement for the exercise of his talent, wanting that grand stimulant to energy—Competition—candidates for *Dramatic* fame among his brethren, having gradually decreased in numbers, leaving the field open to a few only of these heroes of the *Sock and Buskin* who, from having once figured prominently in the *higher walks of their art,* now descend from their pedestals, and content themselves annually with the public exhibition of their finery, and the performance of certain unmeaning pantomimic actions, which are also repeated at private dwellings,—whereby they contrive to draw largely on the bounty of the parties inviting them.

In order to qualify themselves for the representations above alluded to, a negro who could *read,* and instruct them in committing their parts to memory, was pressed into the service for the purpose— *that portion* of his Pupils' education, having been *unfortunately omit-*

---

*Through the kindness of a friend, we are enabled to furnish the following derivation of the term Koo-Koo. It appears that many years back, this *John-Canoe* performed in pantomimic actions *only,* consisting of supplications for food—as being demanded by his empty stomach. At each request, an attendant chorus repeated "Koo-Koo," this was intended in imitation of the rumbling sound of the bowels, when in a hungry state.

†The term *John-Canoe* has had many derivations applied to it, amongst others, that it has arisen from the circumstance of negroes having formerly carried a house in a boat, or canoe; but it is perhaps more consistent to regard it, as a corruption of *Gens inconnus,* signifying "unknown folks," from their always wearing masks. We are strengthened in this opinion, by the frequent occurrence of foreign appelations, being attached to the various grades of people of colour, fruits, &c. in this Island.

ted—a remunerating sum was paid for him for the four or five weeks so occupied, previous to the Christmas Holidays, at which period, the effect of his labours was manifested to a wondering and admiring audience. "Richard the Third" was a favorite Tragedy with them; but *selections* only were made from it, without paying the slightest regard to the *order* in which the "Bard of Avon" had deemed it proper to arrange his subject: Pizarro was also one of their Stock pieces; but whatever might have been the performance, a Combat and Death invariably ensued, when a ludicrous contrast was produced between the smiling mask, and the actions of the dying man. At this Tragical point, there was always a general call for music—and dancing immediately commenced—this proved too great a provocative usually to be resisted even by the slain, and he accordingly became resuscitated, and joined the merry throng. Scenery was of necessity dispensed with, from the removal of such appendage, proving extremely inconvenient to a Company strolling only from street to street.

If competitors for *Dramatic Excellence* be wanting in the present day, the *vanity of excelling* in costliness of attire at least, has not expired, as may annually be seen, when a struggle for superiority in that respect amongst these "Actor Boys," takes place on the Parade, a large and much frequented thoroughfare in Kingston, near the immediate scene of business, or in front of one of the principal Taverns. Gentlemen who may be passing, are requested to decide which is the smartest dressed.

The majority of voices is considered definitive as by previous arrangement, and the individual thus distinguished, then retires "with all his blushing honors thick upon him": *gratification of feeling alone* forming the prize gained on the occasion, and we may here inquire, what greater reward frequently awaits the achievement of exalted actions in higher life?

The jealousy created by failure in the opposite party, is productive of serious broils when he encounters the more fortunate one—blows are exchanged, and other demonstrations of anger indulged in—of their garments, for which they may have paid five Doubloons, equal to about £15 Sterling. Should these escape uninjured, they are disposed of after the holidays to the negroes in the Country, at a considerable loss, who apply them to the like purpose in the ensuing year. The Band consists of drum and fifes only, to which music the Actor stalks the most majestically, oftentimes stopping to afford the by-standers a fair opportunity of gazing at him. In this position he is represented, with a whip and fan, the former is useful in clearing his path of intruders, and the latter proves serviceable in cooling his face, to effect which the mask is of necessity raised, as will be shown in the succeeding print. A brief description of his extraordinary head-dress may not be altogether considered out of place.—The foundation of it is an old hat, affording the wearer the means of sustaining the super-structure, to which it is firmly attached to a pasteboard form trimmed round the edges with silver lace, surmounted with feathers. The gar-ments are of muslin, silk, satin, and ribbons.

The gayest and most glittering effect of all this finery, is pro-duced at night, when by the light of candles, fixed on a large square frame of wood, supported by men, the hero of the scene being in the centre, parades the town, the enclosure acting as a protection to him against the pressure of the crowd from without. When these Christmas amusements were more in vogue, sums amounting to ten or twelve pounds per day, were collected by the Actors.

French Set Girls

This Set is as much distinguished for the neatness of style in their dress, as their general deportment; differing in these respects greatly from all others, as may be perceived in the subjects of the same class already represented, where every description of finery is employed, without the slightest regard being had to the selection of colours, or the mode in which the garments are worn. The French Sets on the contrary, are invariably observers of taste and decorum, considering it derogatory to dance elsewhere than in dwelling-houses, or within walled premises; on no occasion are they found exhibiting on the light fantastic toe in the streets.

During the eventful year 1794, when devastation was spread over that extensive, and once finely cultivated Island St. Domingo, by the horrors of rebellion, many respectable families took flight from the appalling scenes that were there enacted, to the hospitable shore of Jamaica, followed by their faithful slaves to the number of fifteen hundred or two thousand, amongst whom were Africans, as well as Creoles—who to their credit, have, with few exceptions, strictly abided by the compact then entered into, "viz" that of fidelity to their Owners, and a rigid observance of the Laws of the Land so affording them protection. On becoming fixed residents, they formed them-selves into three Bands or Sets at Christmas, denominated "Royal-ists," "Mabiales," and "Americans." The former was composed wholly of Creoles of St. Domingo, who considered themselves on that account of the highest grade—the 2nd, of Africans from Congo, and the latter‡ of a portion of both. The two first-named have ever been jealous of each other, and to such an extent have they carried their animosity at times, that many valuable domestics have fallen victims to the violence of blows received in their conflicts.

They have their Queen, and allow male companions to join in their dances, during which, two§ drums or "Tamboos" are played, and an instrument shaken, called a "Shaka".‖ The voices of those who are not dancing, chime in, and together form a lively and inspiriting sound. To this music alone will these mirthful souls continue a most animated and graceful movement for two or three hours without cessation, a portion of the Set enjoying the amusement, whilst others rest—the Drummers have no relaxation, and evince an earnestness to preserve an even and regular tone that is truly astonishing, considering the *fingers* are used instead of drumsticks, and the force with which they strike, in most instances producing swollen hands.

The tasteful style in which the French Girls tie their kerchiefs on their heads, has ever been the envy of the *Creole* negroes of Jamaica, who make ineffectual efforts to imitate it. There are frequently twelve in a set, exclusive of males, who are more careful in their attire than the musicians, being admitted (as we have before stated) to the privilege of taking the *Fair Ones* by the hand!! Thirty or forty pounds formerly were collected during the Christmas and New-Year's holidays, and that was expended in a grand repast; but their receipts now fall far short of that amount, still feasting cannot be dispensed with, although on a more limited scale of magnificence!

In closing our account of the Christmas amusements, (as they are indulged in at least in the *present day*) we feel called upon to state for the information of those who have absented themselves from this Island many years, that this description of pastime has *greatly declined*—the change no doubt having been effected by the degree of civilization to which the negroes have attained—the majority considering it disgraceful to join in such vulgar doings!!

In Long's "History of Jamaica" we find an attempt at the deri-

‡The term "Americans" has no doubt been assumed, under the impression they were *variously* composed, as is that Nation.
§They are formed of barrels, having both ends taken out, and a parchment of goat's skin strained over them. A fiddlestring, with several pins, and pieces of quill stuck on it, is affixed across the drum; these produce a buzzing sound, on coming in contact with the parchment, during the vibration of the same.—The player sits on the instrument.
‖A cylindrical tin-box pierced with small holes, and filled with beads, shots, or gravel. This is used by the "Royalists,"—the "Mabiales" content themselves with a dried gourd for the same purpose.

vation of the term "John-Canoe," in these words *"It is probably an honorable memorial of John Conny, a celebrated Cabacera, or head of a Tribe at Tres Puntus in Axim, on the Guinea coast; who flourished about the year 1720. He bore great authority among the negroes of that district."*

H. H. BREEN, *St. Lucia: Historical, Statistical, and Descriptive* (London, 1844), 190–200.

Amongst the lower orders the dance exercises a still greater influence. Not satisfied with aping those above them in finery and dress, the Negroes carry their love of dancing to the most extravagant pitch—much too extravagant perhaps for their means. True, the evil has its bright side in the encouragement of trade and the promotion of a spirit of emulation and industry amongst the labouring classes; but it must greatly impair their physical energies, if it does not ultimately mar their independence. The best that can be said of it is, that it is inherent in, and common to, all colonial populations of French origin; and that it is not to be put down either by preaching or persecution. The spoiled children of artificial enjoyment, French Negroes, like their betters, will have their feasts and festivals, their dressing and dancing. Let us hope that these recreations may long continue to preserve their primaeval character of innocence and simplicity, nor, by contact with fashion and false refinement, become the vehicles of corruption and crime.

In order to gratify their propensity for dancing the Negroes have formed themselves into two divisions, or "societies," under the somewhat fantastic style of "Roses" and "Marguerites."* These "societies" exist by immemorial usage in the French colonies, and are still to be found in more or less activity in St. Lucia, Dominica, and Trinidad. The history of the Antilles is involved in such total obscurity in all that concerns the black population, that it would be impossible at the present time to trace the origin of the Roses and Marguerites. It appears that at one period they were invested with a political character; and their occasional allusions to English and French, Republicans and Bonapartists would seem to confirm this impression. Their connexion with politics must have ceased at the termination of the struggle between England and France, from which period their rivalry has been confined to dancing and other diversions.

*The Marguerites are also sometimes called "Wadeloes."

These *societies*, which had remained almost in abeyance during the latter days of slavery, have been revived within the last five years with unusual *éclat* and solemnity. Although few persons, besides the labouring classes and domestic servants, take any active part in their proceedings, there is scarcely an individual in the island, from the Governor downwards, who is not enrolled amongst the partisans of one coterie or the other. The Roses are patronized by Saint Rose, and the flower of that name is their cherished emblem. The Marguerites are in the holy keeping of Saint Marguerite, and the *Marguerite*, or bachelor's button, is the flower they delight to honour. Each society has three kings and three queens, who are chosen by the suffrages of the members. The first, or senior, king and queen only make their appearance on solemn occasions, such as the anniversary of their coronation or the fete of the patron saint of the society: on all other emergencies they are represented by the kings and queens elect, who exercise a sort of vice-regal authority. The most important personage next to the sovereign is the *chanterelle*, or female singer, upon whom devolves the task of composing their *Belairs*,† and of reciting them at their public dances. Each society has a house hired in Castries, in which it holds its periodical meetings. Here the women, whose attendance is much more regular than that of the men, assemble in the evening to rehearse some favourite "belair" for their next dance, or to receive a *lecture* from the king, who may be seen at one end of the room, pacing up and down with an air of dignity and importance suited to his station. If any member has been guilty of improper conduct since their last meeting, the king takes occasion to advert to it in terms of censure, dwelling with peculiar emphasis upon the superior decorum observed by the rival society. Gross misconduct is punished by expulsion from their ranks.

The "belairs" turn generally on the praises of the respective societies; the comparative value of the Rose and the Marguerite; the good qualities, both physical and mental, of individual members; the follies and foibles of the opposite party, and of persons supposed to be connected with or favourable to them. Nothing can surpass the poetical fecundity of the chanterelles: almost every week produces a fresh effusion and a new belair. Some, indeed, are of a higher order than one would be entitled to look for from untutored Negroes: and it is but natural to suppose that they are assisted in these by their

†The *Belair* is a sort of pastoral in blank verse, adapted to a peculiar tune or air. Many of these airs are of a plaintive and melancholy character, and some are exquisitely melodious.

friends among the educated classes. Of this description are the following stanzas in praise of the Roses, which appeared in print in 1840:—

LES ROSES

Venez aimis; venez, dansons;
De Sainte Rose c'est la fête:
Disons pour elle nos chansons.
Et que chacun de nous repète:
Chantons, amis; rions, dansons.

C'est aujourd'hui jour d'allégresse;
Nargue des soucis, des chagrins;
A nous le plaisir et l'irresse,
A nous les vifs et gais refrains.
　　　Venez, &c.

Des fleurs la Rose est la plus belle:
"Par mon parfum, par mes couleurs,
"Par mon éclat, je suis, dit-elle,
"Oui, je suis la reine des fleurs!"
　　　Venez, &c.

Sur sa tige triste et flétrie
La *Marguerite* nait, périt;
Mais la Rose, toujours fleurie,
Reniait toujours et reverdit.
　　　Venez, &c.

La Rose est la reine du monde,
Elle est aussi celle des amours!
Qu' à nos chansons chacun réponde
Vive la Rose pour toujours!
　　　Venez, &c.

The occasions of festivity and dancing are ushered in with universal demonstrations of gaiety and joyousness. After assisting at a solemn service commemorative of the day, the Messieurs and Dames, decked out in their most costly dresses, proceed in groups to visit their friends amongst the higher classes, distributing cakes and flowers in honour of the fête. The costume of the men differs little from that commonly worn by gentlemen in England or France. The silk or beaver hat, the cloth coat, the swelled cravat, the sleek trowsers, the tassled cane—in short, the whole *tournure* and turn-out of the male exquisites, would do honour to Bond-street or the Palais Royal. But the dress of the women is quite another affair: although in many instances the *Jupe*‡ has given way to the regular English gown; yet, on fête days, the former reasserts its preponderance, as being more in harmony with the general costume. First you have the head-dress set off by the varied and brilliant colours of the Madras handkerchief, erected into a pyramid, a cone, or a castle, according to the fancy of the wearer, and spangled over with costly jewels; next a huge pair of ear-rings of massive gold; then several gold and coral necklaces, taste-fully thrown over the dark shoulders; then the embroidered bodice trimmed with gold and silver tinsel; and lastly, the striped jupe of silk or satin, unfolding its bright tints and broad train to the breeze. Add to these a profusion of bracelets and bouquets, of *foulards* and fa-vours, and you will have a faint impression of this bizarre yet brilliant, grotesque but gorgeous costume. Thus travestied the dancers proceed at sunset to the place appointed for the bamboula.§ A circle is formed in the centre of some square or grass-plot. On one side appear four or five Negroes, quite naked down to the waist, and seated on their *tam-tams*.‖ These, together with two or three timbrels, compose the or-chestra. Flags and banners, richly emblazoned upon a red or blue ground and bearing characteristic legends in gilt letters, are seen flut-tering in the air: and as the groups of dancers advance in all direc-tions, the darkness of the night disappears before the blaze of a thou-sand flambeaux. Now the *chanterelle,* placing herself in front of the orchestra, gives the signal with a flourish of her castanet: she then re-peats a verse of the belair: the dancers take up the refrain; the tam-tams and timbrels strike in unison and the scene is enlivened by a succession of songs and dances, to the delight and amusement of the assembled multitude.

To a superficial observer these exhibitions present somewhat of a profane and even heathenish appearance. In this light they were doubtless regarded by a reverend gentleman, who visited St. Lucia in October 1842, and on witnessing the dance exclaimed with a sapient shake of the head: "Juggernath! Juggernath!" But the truth is, there is

---

‡The *Jupe* is a species of gown worn by the Negresses and some of the coloured women in the French Antilles. Having neither sleeves nor bodice, it presents the exact dimen-sions of a petticoat—hence the name.

§The Negro dances are of two kinds—the ball and the *bamboula*. When conducted within doors it is always called a ball—when "sub dio" a bamboula. The use of them varies according to the state of the weather; but there is a marked predilection for the out-door recreation.

‖The *tamtam* is a small barrel, covered at one end with a strong skin. To this, placed between his legs, the Negro applies the open hand and fingers, beating time to the bel-air with the most astonishing precision.

no Juggernath at all in the matter; and the Christian moralist, who takes the trouble to examine and inquire, will find less to censure in these primeval though fantastic diversions, than in the more civilised seductions of the quadrille, the galopade, and the waltz.

The whole labouring population being divided into Roses and Marguerites, it follows that, upon the good understanding which subsists between them, must mainly depend the peace and prosperity of the Colony. This good understanding, however, is liable to be disturbed by the intrigues of interested partisans, on the one hand, and officious, would-be patrons, on the other: and then their rivalry, habitually characterised by the most friendly relations, will assume all the acerbity of a political feud. Thus in 1840, an attempt was made by an unscrupulous planter to set one society in opposition to the other, by pandering to the worst passions of undisciplined humanity, and exciting their emulation beyond its legitimate sphere. The object was to allure the labourers to his estates and get them to work on his own terms: for this purpose he took one of the societies under his special protection; had himself elected their king; purchased superb dresses for the queens; and got up splendid fêtes for their entertainment. Attracted by these dazzling frivolities hundreds of the labourers hastened to range themselves under the banner of the "white king." For some time all went on well, and the planter had every cause to exult in the success of his scheme; but when the day of reckoning came, and the labourers discovered that all their wages had been frittered away in gilded extravagance, the prestige of the white king's popularity speedily vanished, and his estates were deserted.

Another interruption of the general harmony occurred in September 1841. At the instigation of two or three individuals in the assumed character of Patrons of the Roses, these foolish people procured a blue flag (the colour peculiar to the Marguerites) and paraded it in derision through the streets. In the evening they gave a *bamboula*, and the flag having been again exhibited, a party of the Marguerites rushed into the ring, seized the flag, and were carrying it off in triumph, when the Attorney-General, who happened to be present, ran forward, and by threats of vengeance succeeded in wresting it from the discomfited Marguerites, admist the *vivats* and vociferations of the Roses. The pretext for this proceeding was the prevention of a breach of the peace; but if such had really been the object, a more obvious and efficacious means would have been, to have interdicted in the first instance the insulting display of the rival flag. In fact, the course pursued, instead of allaying the popular excitement, only fanned it into a flame; for when the dance was concluded, and the Roses were returning to their houses, they were assaulted by a numerous body of the Marguerites. A general melee ensued, in which the chief combatants were the women, and their chief weapons the flambeaux which they had brought away from the dance: and these they used with such indiscriminate fury against their opponents, that the respectable inhabitants were compelled to interfere to prevent the town from becoming a prey to the flames.

Mrs. LANIGAN, *Antigua and the Antiguans* (London, 1844), vol. II, 129–30.

Christmas is also the season here, as in England, for roast beef, . . . most of the negroes endeavour to get *one* of these articles, should they not be able to procure them all; but if their pockets are too low to do this, they purchase a few raisins to treat their friends with. "Christmas day" is ushered in with the sound of fiddles and drums; parties of negroes going round the town about four o'clock in the morning, playing upon these instruments for the purpose of breaking people's rest, (for I am sure it cannot amuse;) and then they have the assurance to call at the different houses during the day for payment. At conclusion of this serenade, or *waits,* or whatever else they choose to term it, the musicians generally raise their voices to the highest pitch, and call out, "Good morning to you, massa; good morning to you, misis; good morning to you ladies and gentlemen *all!"* A flourish is then given with fiddle and drum, and they march off to disturb another quiet household.

CHARLES WILLIAM DAY, *Five Years' Residence in the West Indies* (London, 1852), vol. I, 313–16.

. . . The maskers parade the streets in gangs of from ten to twenty, occasionally joining forces in procession. The primitives were negroes, as nearly naked as might be, bedaubed with a black varnish. One of this gang had a long chain and padlock attached to his leg, which chain the others pulled. What this typified, I was unable to learn; but, as the chained one was occasionally thrown down on the ground, and treated with a mock bastinadoing it probably represented slavery. Each mask was armed with a good stout quarter-staff, so that they could overcome one-half more police than themselves, should occasion present itself. Parties of negro ladies danced through the streets, each clique distinguished by bodices of the same colour. Every negro, male and female, wore a white flesh-coloured mask, their wooly hair carefully concealed by handkerchiefs; this, contrasted with the black bosom and arms, was droll in the extreme. Those ladies who aimed at the superior civilization of shoes and stockings, invariably clothed their pedal extremities in pink silk stockings and blue, white, or yellow kid shoes, sandled up their sturdy legs. For the men, the predominating character was Pulinchinello; every second negro, at least, aiming at playing the continental Jack-pudding. Pirates too were very common, dressed in Guernsey frocks, full scarlet trowsers, and red woollen cap, with wooden pistols for arms. From the utter want of spirit, and sneaking deportment of these bold corsairs, I presumed them to have come from the Pacific. Turks also there were, and one Highlander, a most ludicrous caricature of the Gael, being arrayed in a scarlet coat, huge grenadier cap, a kilt of light blue chintz, striped with white, a most indescribable philibeg, black legs of course, and white socks bound with dirty pink ribbon. There were also two grand processions, having triumphal "wans," one of which was to commemorate the recent marriage of a high law-officer; the other, judging from the royal arms in front (worth a guinea of anybody's money, if one for the painting—the lion looking like a recently drowned puppy), and a canopy of red glazed calico, trimmed with silver tinsel, shading a royal pari, who, in conscious majesty, sat within, represented the Sovereign pair of England. This brilliant cortege was marshalled forward by a huge negro, in a celestial dress, made after the conventional fashion of the angel Gabriel; and who stalked along, spear in hand, as if intent on doing dire deeds. The best embodiments were the Indians of South America, daubed with red ochre; personified by the Spanish peons from the Main, themselves half Indian, as testified by their exquisitely small feet and hands. Many of these had real Indian quivers and bows, as well as baskets; and, doubtless, were very fair representatives of the characters they assumed. In this costume children looked very pretty. One personation of Death, having what was understood to be a skeleton painted on a coal-black shape, stalked about with part of a horse's vertebra attached to him, and a horse's thigh bone in his hand; but his most telling movements only elicited shouts of laughter. I noticed that whenever a black mask appeared, it was sure to be a white man. Little girls dressed a la jupe, in the vrai creole negro costume, looked very interesting. All parties with the assistance of bands of execrable music, made a tremendous uproar; and most of us were glad when the priestly saturnalia was over.

MAJOR ALAN CHAMBRE, *Recollections of West End Life in London* . . . (London, 1858), vol. II, 151–53.

Christmas-time is a great season for merry-making amongst the negroes. We were fortunate in witnessing a ceremony or procession, called the "Reds and the Blues." The origin of it is not known correctly; but it most probably arose from some *fete* given by the Admiral of the Blue or the Red on that station becoming, in process of time, a national holiday—sometimes going by the name of "Johnny Canoeing." On the north side of the island it is a splendid affair, but on the south side it is just the reverse. In the latter instance, the negroes dress themselves in bulls' hides, with horns on, into which they are sewn, and go bellowing about the streets, butting all the people they meet. This is the remnant, most probably, of some superstitious African ceremony.

At Montego Bay, Lucea, and Falmouth, the rival factions of Reds and Blues represent all the great personages of the day, and their attendants. The ladies lend their jewels to be worn by the negro women who figure in the procession, and subscriptions are made by the residents to assist in purchasing the paraphernalia and dresses, which are really magnificent. King William IV, Queen Adelaide, The Duke of Wellington, The Archbishop of Canterbury, Earl Grey, the Earl of Derby (then Lord Stanley), Lords Welbourne, Brougham and Nelson, Sir Robert Peel, Messrs. Wilberforce, Daniel O'Connell, and Joseph Hume, besides many of the well-known personages, figured amongst them. Queen Victoria had not then been crowned; her crown was therefore carried before her, on a velvet cushion, by a handsomely dressed negress, who personated the Mistress of the Robes. The Duchess of Kent followed behind her Majesty in the procession. Wearing a blue uniform, I received very gracious bows and curtsies from the party of Blues, who no doubt thought I had put it on in compliment to them. Each set had a champion of their masters' horses, who made a great show, in armour that fitted close to his body, and was composed of gilt livery, or basket buttons, sewn closely together. Both being armed with lances and swords, they became so excited, that the two pugnacious heroes defied each other to single combat on the street; and the affray might have ended fatally to one of the parties, if the police had not interfered.

WILLIAM G. SEWELL, *The Ordeal of Free Labor in the British West Indies* . . . (London, 1862), 216–18.

It was Christmas-eve—a season at which the West Indian negro goes wild with excitement. Old drums, trumpets, kettles, bells, and any thing that can make a noise, are brought out; dancers dance violently, and fiddlers fiddle violently, without any regard to time or tune; and masquerading and psalm-singing are alternately kept up until New-year's day is fairly past. No negro will work for love or money during this carnival time. He is literally demented, and can hardly give a sane answer to the most ordinary question. All night long, and for eight successive nights, an infernal din—a concert of cracked drums, shrill voices, and fire-crackers—is maintained. Those poor devils who can not enjoy this species of amusement suffer the most exquisite torture. I passed the whole season in the country, and saw exhibitions of excitement that made me think the actors fit subjects for a lunatic asylum; but, though I mixed freely among the people, I was always most civilly treated, and never on any of these occasions did I see a negro in a state of intoxication. I do not remember having ever seen a West Indian negro drunk; and the temperate habits of the Jamaica Creoles are the more remarkable, as the spirit manufactured in the island can be obtained for a very trifling cost.

I allude to these Christmas festivities because they afforded me an opportunity to see the people in their holiday time, when, if ever, they would be disposed to be as saucy and insolent as I have heard them characterized. I found them nothing of the kind. The accusation may be true as regards Kingston loafers, who hang about the wharves for chance jobs, and follow strangers with annoying persistency; but it is not true when applied to the peasantry. The people are no longer servile, though they retain, from habit, the servile epithet of "Massa," when addressing the whites; but I have ever seen them most respectful to their superiors, and most anxious to oblige, when they are treated as men, and not as slaves or brute beasts. Individual testimony on this point might be discredited or deemed insufficient, but there is no discrediting the fact that, since their freedom, no people in the world have been more peaceful than the Creoles of Jamaica. They seem to have forgotten all ancient grievances, and never to have entertained a thought of retribution. The contrast in this respect between the reign of freedom and the reign of slavery carries its own lesson and its own warning. Twenty-five years of freedom, and not a murmur of popular discontent! Twenty-five years of slavery—I take any period—and what fears and anxieties and actual outbreaks! It cost the government $800,000 to suppress the single insurrection of 1832, during which private property to the value of $6,000,000 was destroyed. But the outbreak from which the planters then suffered would have been light compared with the one that was ready to burst over the island when liberty appeared in the gap and brought them salvation.

I have also heard the Jamaica people denounced for making Christmas, instead of the anniversary of emancipation, their great gala season of festivity. It is argued that they can care little for the boon of freedom if they do not keep it in remembrance, or regard it as a fit opportunity for national rejoicings.

THURLOW WEED, *Letters from Europe and the West Indies* (Albany, 1866), 345–50 (Reprinted in *Virgin Islands View* [St. Thomas, VI], vol. II, no. 7 [December 1966], 32–38).

The New Year anniversaries which, in joyous succession, have been celebrated at Albany, come back to me here, consecrated by a thousand endearing recollections. I see, in imagination, friends and acquaintances, with elastic step and beaming eyes, exchanging congratulations through every street of our ancient metropolis. I can see, too, the open door, the bountifully loaded board, and the cordial welcome that awaits each visitor in his cheerful rounds. I can imagine also the deep snow and merry bells, or at least the icy streets and piercing winds of a Northern winter. But those of you who have not hailed a New Year in a tropical climate, can form no idea of what is passing here. The hills are clothed in verdue. The trees are loaded with fruit. The rays of a sun as intensely hot as those we encounter in July or August, are shining upon us. We sit with open doors and windows to catch every breath that stirs.

The New Year is celebrated here, too, not by the Planters, but by their slaves, and after their own fashion, which is rude and primitive. The Holidays of the slaves commence with Christmas, and although the law gives them that and the following day, they contrive, in imitation of our Congress, to do very little work between Christmas and New Year. And on these occasions the slave's cup of enjoyment fills to the brim. For several weeks preceding Christmas they are busied with preparations for their festivities. Indeed their toil through the whole year is cheered by their anticipation of holiday happiness. For these festivities, all there is of turban, calico, ribbon, gewgaw and trinket, among them, is reserved to adorn their persons. DANCING is their only festive resource. The slaves on each estate elect their Queen and Princess, with their King and Prince, whose authority is supreme. These have their Maids of Honor, Pages, &c., &c. A Queen retains her rank until by age or otherwise she voluntarily retires as Dowager. The instrument which, on these occasions, "discourses most eloquent music," is a large keg or half barrel, over the head of which a goat skin is drawn, and upon which a negro beats with his hands, as proudly and triumphantly as Ole Bull draws his cat gut. The Dance is opened by the King and Queen. The Prima Donna sings ballads, while the whole gang unite in the chorus, to which the Drums furnish a *very* base, but truly appropriate accompaniment. When the Royal pair are exhausted, they introduce the Prince and Princess, who in turn call up those of inferior rank. The Dance opens with much gravity, but in its progress Dancers and Singers warm into enthusiasm. The voice of the Prima Donna rises; the chorus swells; the drummer turns up the white of his eyes and displays his ivory; the Queen swoons; is supported by maids of honor, who sprinkle "Bay Rum" and ply their fans until she recovers, and joins in the Dance with renewed energy. And thus the revelers consume the day and night. Not more than a dozen of a gang of sixty, seventy or eighty, participate in the Dance, the remainder seeming to find equal enjoyment by straining their lungs and cracking their voices in the Orchestra. Towards the close of the festivities, however, all join in the Dance, all, at the same time, singing most vociferously. Flags, held by the maids of honor, are waving over the heads of the Queens during the Dance.

The first privilege (or duty as they esteem it) of the slaves, on Christmas and New Year's days, is to pay their respects, in a body, to their master, before whom they Dance for an hour or more, paying tribute, in their songs, to his liberality, generosity, &c., after which they are regaled with cakes, cordial, &c., and generally receive presents from their mistress. They then return to their own domicils to pass the day and night in festivities. In the Town the Free Colored People and House Slaves form their parties, elect their Kings, Queens, &c., and Dance in like manner. We went the rounds, among them, and were generally received by some complimentary line thrown, impromptu, into their songs. I do not know whether the minstrelsy of these simple people is worth copying, but I will venture to transcribe a few specimens. The following "Toast," as it was styled, the effort of a "Lady Dowager," was regarded as peculiarly felicitous:

Any one that feel themselves insulted they must call to the girls of the garden—the garden girls—they are the most enchanting girls—they do not fear the lions in the wood—

> Bravo, the ladies of the garden,
> Bravo, the ladies of the garden,
> The garden ladies—they are the most enchanting ladies;
> They have no fear—they will brave any ship of war.

If any are incapable of seeking satisfaction, they must call to the girls of the garden. Hurra! hurra! hurra!—gentlemen we don't fear the lions in the wood.

> Chorus—Bravo! bravo! &c.

Here's a health to all that is around us, not forgetting our most gracious Majesty, King Christian, reigning over us. God bless our most noble King.

> Chorus—Bravo! bravo! &c.

Here's a health to all the Americans, and long may they Reign Independent of all nations, in love and security to themselves.

> Chorus—Bravo! bravo! &c.

Here is a health to Queen Victoria, the Ruler of Great Britain, who liberty proclaimed to the slaves.

> Chorus—Bravo! bravo! &c."

Here are the words of another song, but I cannot render them into either verse or Blank verse:

> "Chain the dogs—let the first rate pass—all the Danish gents, and also the Yankees, for they is just like the Otto of Roses—they is lately from Europe and America—just come for the warm climate, with their nice gaiter boots on and neat cane in their hand, and first rate castors on their head—let them pass for to see the bounding girls, for they are great, like the roses when they are blooming.
>
> Chorus—Chain the dogs—let the white men pass."

The following has reference to a movement making to abolish slavery in the island:

> "All we girls must keep heads together; King Christian have sent to free us all; Governor Sholton had a vote for us; King Christian have sent to grant us all; we all have signed for independence; we all have signed for liberty; our Crown Prince had a vote in it; our Gracious Queen had the highest vote; King Christian have sent to say he will crown us all.
>
> Oh, yes! oh, yes! hurra! hurra!
> All we girls must keep head together."

One of the Queens, in her desire to appear in queenly attire, for the Holidays, was prompted to misapply money belonging to her master, for which she was sent to the fort, and instead of enjoying the highest felicity as a mimic Queen, her fallen majesty is now with a gang of culprits at work upon the streets! This circumstance was lamented in a song by her subjects:

> "Oh yes, oh yes, do buy her for her freedom; do buy Queen Slater, our dear Lady Coahly; we are sorry, we are sorry to tell you Queen Slater in the King's fort; we went to the fort gate to ask our Queen if she sorry for what she done, and said, oh yes, oh yes; we send our Lady Dowager to beg for Queen Slater; our Emperor he will sign much money to buy our Queen Slater freedom.
>> Oh yes, oh yes, do buy her for her freedom."

The following is a much admired effort:

> "Hurra, hurra, hurra, my Rooky Queen—
> Hurra my Sholay Queen—she do not spare no cost.
> We wear the best shaleys—we sport the best de lanes
> We wear the best muslins—we do not spare no cost.
>> Hurra, hurra, hurra, hurra!
> Here is our Queen—she wears the best of linen—
> She sports the best of Cambric and doesn't mind the cost.
>> Hurra, hurra, hurra, hurra!
> Our gents smoke the best segars—they sport the Otto of Roses,
> For they have pockets full of doubloons.
>> Hurra, hurra, hurra, hurra!
> Where is my Lady Dowager? she cannot be seen,
> She is in her easy arm chair writing to her Emperor.
>> Hurra, hurra, hurra, hurra!
> Where is the garden girls? they cannot be seen,
> For they have gone to Bredow's Winder to meet the great heads.
>> Hurra, hurra, hurra, hurra!"

The following was sung with great spirit by a fine looking gang of slaves, owned by our friend Walker, as they came into town from the "Wheel of Fortune" estate, on New Year's morning. It is aimed at an unpopular "Manager" who had been displaced:

> Come along! come along! "Betty's Hope" girls—
> Oh come along "Betty's Hope" girls—
> You could not buy Wheel of Fortune.
> Dunlop sell all de Guinea bird—he sell all de sugar apple,
> But he could not buy "Wheel of Fortune,"
>> Come along! come along!

Wheel of Fortune' niggers don't want no Mulatto mistress,
For now they have their first rate Massa Walker.
    Come along! come along!
Massa Walker give them the best Madrass,
Good brown and bamboo—and care dem well.
    Come along! come along!
Massa Walker, Dunlop mark up "Wheel of Fortune,"
He rake down de rum cellar, he scrape out de curing house,
He pick all de peases; but he could not buy "Wheel of Fortune."
    Come along! come along!
Eliza Clarke, she went to the curing house, where she tried de same;
She tried to bring down de cattle—den she tried de mule pen,
But she could not buy "Wheel of Fortune."
    Come along! come along!
Run and call Massa Walker to kick "Betty's Hope" gang out de great
    house,
And drive the Mulattoes off de "Wheel of Fortune."
    Come along! come along!
Dunlop sell all de potatoes—he sell all de Guinea grass,
But he couldn't raise de cash like Massa Walker,
To buy "Wheel of Fortune."
    Come along! come along!

W. J. GARDNER, *A History of Jamaica* (London, 1873), 183.

In town places domestic slaves had learnt, in process of time, to de-
vise recreations of a more attractive kind. At the Christmas carnival
the younger women adorned themselves with all the finery they could
procure: this was often of a superior kind, for their savings for months
were devoted to the purpose. Nor would their mistresses, whether
white or coloured, refuse to assist them, either with gifts or the loan
of jewellery and other ornaments. Gaily adorned, the damsels paraded
the streets in parties, known as the Reds and Blues, or the Yellows
and Blues, each seeking to outshine the other. A kind of rivalry existed, in which their owners often seemed to feel an equal interest.
Any indication of want of taste, or of imperfection in the arrangements
of the opposite party, was sure to meet with very caustic criticism.

    The effect was striking. These young women, with elastic fig-
ures which many a fair lady of wealth and fashion might have envied,
and adorned with considerable taste, presented a spectacle the be-
holder was never likely to forget. Their frocks were usually of fine
muslin, with satin bodices of the colours named above. In Kingston
and Montego Bay, groups of twenty, thirty or even more, passed

through the streets, singing and dancing as they went. Each party had its queen, dressed far more gorgeously than the rest, and selected for much the same reasons as the May queen of an English village.

Sometimes the "setts," as these companies were termed, were all of the same height. Others varied greatly in this respect, but were carefully arranged, the line tapering down from the portly, majestic women, who led the procession, to quite little children in the rear. But every one in the sett was dressed exactly alike, even in the most minute particulars, not excepting the parasol and the shoes, the latter frequently of white kid, then costing nine or ten shillings sterling a pair. There was another rule from which departure was unknown— blacks and browns never mingled in the same sett. The creole distinction of brown lady, black woman, was in those days of slavery and social distinctions strictly observed; and, except in the smaller towns, different shades of colour did not readily mingle.

While these setts were parading the streets, John Canoe parties also displayed themselves: from an artistic point of view it might be said that these had improved on the original idea. The different trades and occupations formed separate parties, each with its John Canoe man, or some quaint device. In some cases a resemblance might be traced to the English mummers of olden time. Now and then these people were dressed up to represent characters they had seen on the stage. Shakespeare was sadly parodied on such occasions. Richard III, for example, after shouting vociferously for a horse, would kill an opponent, who, however, again revived, and performed a sword dance with the monarch.

A simpler and more picturesque scene was presented at Whitsuntide and Easter, when groups of people often danced around the American aloe, then found in bloom, and which was familiarly known as the Maypole.

L. D. POWLES, *The Land of the Pink Pearl or Recollections of Life in the Bahamas* (London, 1888), 147–49.

. . . The darkies are fond of processions, and never miss an opportunity of getting one up.

About Christmas time they seem to march about day and night with lanterns and bands of music, and they fire off crackers. This is a terrible nuisance, but the custom has the sanction of antiquity, though no doubt it would have been put down long ago if the white young gentlemen had not exhibited a taste for the same amusement.

They are very fond of dancing, and I am afraid no amount of

preaching or singing hymns will ever be able to put down the dance-houses, which are terrible thorns in the side of both magistrate and inspector of police.

A form of open-air dancing has also a great hold upon them. It is called a "fire-dance," and is, no doubt, a relic of savage life. I had heard so much about these fire-dances that I arranged with the Sergeant of police to have one got up for my special benefit. . . . The people formed a circle, and a fire was lighted in their midst. The music consisted of two drums that would not work unless frequently warmed at the fire. The company clapped their hands without ceasing all through the dance, chanting all the while in a sort of dreary monotone, "Oh kindoiah! kindoiah!* Mary come along!" When the dance was about half through, the refrain was suddenly changed to "Come down, come down," repeated over and over again in the same dreary monotone. Every now and then a man or a woman, or a couple together would rush into the centre of the circle and dance wildly about. There appeared to be no stop or idea of figure about the performance, the aim and object of the dancers, as far as one could make it out, being to execute as many extravagant capers in and over, and around, and about the fire as they could without burning themselves. It was, in short, a savage African dance in European dress. Another evening Mr. James C. Smith and myself came suddenly upon one of these "fire dances;" on this occasion, the refrain they sang was, "Go along, Yankee, poor old man."

J. VAN SERTIMA, *Scenes and Sketches of Demarara Life*
(Georgetown, Demerara, 1899), 99, 102.

When the great festal day does not fall on a Sunday, the slumberer is awakened by some music and much noise on the streets at any time between midnight and four o'clock in the morning, and small chance is there for him to dose off again in quietude, for the drum-beaters are nothing if not energetic, and the musicians are nothing if not merry. There is a law here, I believe, for the suppression of the drum, but on such a joyous day as this, custom and inclination rule, and our policemen are forgiving. The street band is accompanied by a motley procession of people whose especial business, it seems is to arouse the whole city, and make grand acclaim touching the advent of the illustrious annual visitor. Sometimes in concert, oft times in confusion,

*An African word.

drum and flute, cornet and clarionet, shac-shac and steel, tom-tom and tambourine proclaim the happy morn, while high above all, in dismal diapason, *vox humana* dins into your ear such proclamation as this:

> Chris'mas ma'nin' come again,
> And' I ent get no cawfee wata.

On such a day as this "cawfee wata," or even dofee, is taboo. The people's "vanity" (to use a Wellerism) is much stronger, and in the plenitude of their patriotism they revel in rum,—rum of colonial manufacture. . . .

These merry-makers go by, and anon other merry makers, equally high-spirited come forward, all stir and sound signifying a season of frolic and festivity and rejoicing. Guitars and other stringed instruments also.

■　■　■

Meanwhile, throughout the day, the street bands are in perpetual evidence, more particularly in the eastern part of the city. Most they congregate in the vicinity of the rum shops, the owners of which provide liquor for the "Musicianers," as the common people call them. The shops themselves are gay with flags and bunting. . . . Here and there, about the streets, may be seen some buffoons with costumes *a la* circus clown, astride of stilts, for the people's amusement; and maskers with grotesque habiliments to teach the little ones excellence of beauty, by contrast.

6

Music, Dance, and Games

Musical and dance practices enter so strongly into the European stereotypes of the character of African and African-derived peoples that it should come as little surprise that there are so many notices of such performances. What this section offers us is some of the earliest accounts of the occasions which helped give rise to these stereotypes. Whatever else was going on in the minds of these observers, their aesthetics were under assault, a point they seldom hesitated to make. The detailed notes they took are invaluable, and in many cases better than the kinds of reports we get of these arts today. If they have limitations, they are the usual ones of trying to express in words what is going on in music or bodily movement.

The song texts included here are very important, as songs this old from the West Indies have not been available for study until now. Games, on the other hand, were only casually noted during the period of these observations, but a sample is included here to show that they can be connected to the fuller accounts which have become available in the twentieth century.

RICHARD LIGON, *A True and Exact History of the Island of Barbadoes* (London, 1673), 48.

In the afternoons on *Sundayes,* they have their Musick, which is of kettle drums, and those of several sizes; upon the smallest the best Musician playes, and the other come in as Chorasses: the drum all men know, has but one tone; and therefore variety of tunes have little to do in this musick; and yet so strangely they varie their time, as 'tis a pleasure to the most curious ears, and it was to me one of the strangest noises that ever I heard made of one tone; and if they had the va-

280

riety of tune, which gives the greater scope in Musick, as they have of time, they would do wonders in that Art. And if I had not faln sicke before my coming away, at least seven months in one sickness, I had given them some hints of tunes, which being understood, would have serv'd as a great addition to their harmony; for time without tune, is not an eighth part of the Science of Musick.

HANS SLOANE, A *Voyage to the Islands* (London, 1707), vol. I, xlviii–xlix, lii.

... The Negroes are much given to Venery, and although hard wrought, will at nights, or on Feast days Dance and Sing; their Songs are all bawdy, and leading that way. They have several sorts of Instruments in imitation of Lutes, made of small Gourds fitted with Necks, strung with Horse hairs, or the peeled stalks of climbing Plants or Withs. These Instruments are sometimes made of hollow'd Timber covered with Parchment or other Skin wetted, having a Bow for its Neck, tye Strings ty'd longer or shorter, as they would alter their sounds. The Figures of some of these Instruments are hereafter graved. They have likewise in their Dances Rattles ty'd to their Legs and Wrists, and in their Hands, with which they make a noise, keeping time with one who makes a sound answering it on the mouth of an empty Gourd or Jar with his Hand. Their Dances consist in great activity and strength of Body, and keeping time, if it can be. They very often tie Cows Tails to their Rumps, and add such other odd things to their Bodies in several places, as gives them a very extraordinary appearance.

■ ■ ■

They have *Saturdays* in the Afternoon, and *Sundays,* with *Christmas* holidays, *Easter* call'd little or *Pigganinny, Christmas,* and some other great Feasts allow'd them for the Culture of their own Plantations to feed themselves from Potatoes, Yams, and Plantanes, &c. which they Plant in Ground allow'd them by their Masters, besides a small Plantain Walk they have by themselves.

They formerly on their Festivals were allowed the use of Trumpets after their Fashion, and Drums made of a piece of a hollow tree, covered on one end with any green Skin, and stretched with Thouls or Pins. But making use of these in their Wars at home in *Africa,* it was thought too much inciting them to Rebellion, and so they were prohibited by the Customs of the Island.

CHARLES LESLIE, *A New and Exact Account of Jamaica*, 3d ed. (Edinburgh, 1740), 326–27.

Sunday Afternoon the Generality of them dance or wrestle, Men and Women promiscuously together. They have two musical Instruments, like Kettle-Drums, for each Company of Dancers, with which they make a very barbarous Melody. They have other musical Instruments, as a *Bangil*, not unlike our Lute in any Thing but the Musick, the *Rookaw*, which is two Sticks jagged, and a *Jenkgoving*, which is a Way of clapping their Hands on the Mouth of two Jars: These are all played together, accompanyed with Voices, which make a very terrible Kind of Harmony.

J. G. STEDMAN, *Narrative of a Five Years' Expedition against the Revolted Negroes of Surinam* (Amherst: University of Massachusetts Press, 1971 [1796]), 362, 375–78.

Their *vocal music* is like that of the birds, melodious, but without time, and in other respects not unlike that of a *clerk* performing to the congregation, one person constantly pronouncing a sentence extempore, which he next hums or whistles, and then all the others repeat the same in chorus; another sentence is then spoken, and the chorus is a second time renewed, &c.

This kind of singing is much practised by the barge rowers or boat negroes on the water, especially during the night in a clear moonshine; it is to them peculiarly animating, and may, together with the sound of their oars, be heard at a considerable distance.

As a specimen, I have tried to set the following words to music, supposing a ranger going to battle, and thus taking leave of his girl:

■ ■ ■

No people can more esteem or have a greater friendship for one another than the negro slaves; they appear to have unbounded enjoyment in each other's company, and are not destitute of social amusements, such as the *soesa,* which consists in footing opposite to each other, and clapping with their hands upon their sides to keep in time. So very eager are they at this animating play, in which sometimes six or eight couples are engaged at once, that the violent exercise having been known to kill some of the negroes, it is forbidden by the magistrates at Paramaribo. *Awaree* is an innocent amusement, consisting in pitching with a large kind of marbles, in defect of which they use the awaree nuts or large pebbles.

The men also cudgel and wrestle; yet at this I think them inferior to either those of Cornwall or Devon. Most negroes are strong and active.* But swimming is their favourite diversion, which they practise every day at least twice or thrice, promiscuously, in groups of boys and girls, like the Indians, when both sexes exhibit astonishing feats of courage, strength, and activity. I have not only seen a negro girl beat a hardy youth in swimming across the river Comewina (while I was one of the party) but on landing challenge him to run a two mile race, and beat him again, naked as they were; while all ideas of shame on the one side, and of insult on the other, are totally unknown.—I shall now say something of their instrumental music and dancing. I have already mentioned the singing and the dancing of the *Loango* tribe in particular; and will now describe that practised by the other negro nations in general.

Their instruments of music, which are not a little ingenious, are all made by themselves, and consist of those represented in the annexed plate; where

No. 1, which is called *qua-qua,* is a hard sounding-board, elevated on one side like a boot-jack, on which they beat time as on a drum, with two pieces of iron, or two bones.

No. 2, is the *kiemba-toetoe,* or hollow reed, which is blown through the nostrils, like the nasal flute of Otaheite: it has but two holes, one at each end, the one serving to sound it, the other to be touched by the finger.

No. 3, is the *Ansokko-bania,* which is a hard board, supported on both sides like a low seat, on which are placed small blocks of different sizes, which being struck with two small sticks like a dulcimer, give different sounds, that are not at all disagreeable.

*Witness *James Jackson,* the equestrian rider, London, &c.

No. 4, is the *great Creole drum,* being a hollow tree, open at one end, and covered at the other with a sheep-skin, on which they sit astride, and so beat time with the palms of their hands; answering the effect of the bass-viol to the *qua-qua* board.

No. 5, is the *great Loango drum,* being covered at both ends, and serves the same purpose as a bass drum.

No. 6, is the *Papa drum,* beaten as the others.

No. 7, is the *small Loango drum,* beaten together with the great one.

No. 8, the *small Creole drum,* for the same use.

No. 9, is called *coeroema;* this is a wooden cup, ingeniously made, covered also with a sheep-skin, and beaten with two small rods or drum-sticks, after the manner of the *qua-qua* board.

No. 10, is the *Loango-bania.* This I thought exceedingly curious, being a dry board, on which are laced, and kept down by a transverse bar, different sized elastic splinters of the palm-tree, like pieces of whalebone, in such a manner that both ends are elevated to two other bars that are fixed under them; and the above apparatus being placed on

No. 11, which is a large empty *callebash* to promote the sound; the extremities of the splinters are snapt by the fingers, something in the manner of a piano-forte, when the music has a soft and very pleasing effect.

No. 12, is called by the negroes *saka-saka,* being a hollow gourd, with a stick and handle fixed through it, and filled with small pebbles and pease, not unlike the magic shell of the Indians. This they hold above their heads, and while they dance rattle it to measure.

No. 13, is a *conch,* or sea shell, which by blowing they sound, for pleasure, or to cause an alarm, &c. but is not used as an accompaniment to dancing.

No. 14, is called *benta,* being a branch bent like a bow by means of a slip of dry reed or warimbo; which cord, when held to the teeth, is beaten with a short stick, and by being shifted backwards and forwards sounds not unlike a jew's-harp.

No. 15, is the *Creole-bania,* this is like a mandoline or guitar, being made of a half gourd covered with a sheep-skin, to which is fixed a very long neck or handle. This instrument has but four strings, three long and one short, which is thick, and serves for a bass; it is played by the fingers, and has a very agreeable sound, but more so when accompanied by a song.

No. 16, is the *trumpet of war,* to command advancing, retreating, &c. and is called by the negroes the *too-too.*

No. 17, is a *horn* used to supply the place of the other, or on the plantations to call the slaves to work.

No. 18, is the *Loango too-too,* or flute, which they blow as the Europeans do, after the common way. It has but four holes for the fingers, and yet they make it produce a variety of sounds.—Such are the musical instruments of our African brethren, to which they dance with more spirit than we do to the best band in Europe.

To what I have stated, I will only add, that they always use full or half measure, but never triple time, in their dancing music, which is not unlike that of a baker's bunt, when he separates the flour from the bran, sounding *tuckety-tuck* and *tuckety-tuck* ad perpetuum. To this noise they dance with uncommon pleasure, and most times foot it away with great art and dexterity.

Saltantes Satyros imitabitur Alphesiboeus.

Every Saturday evening, the slaves who are well treated close the week with an entertainment of this kind, and generally once a quarter are indulged with a grand ball, to which the neighboring slaves are invited; the master often contributing to their happiness by his presence, or at least by sending them a present of a few jugs of new rum.

At these grand balls the slaves are remarkably neat, the women appearing in their best chintz petticoats, and many of the men in fine Holland trowsers. So indefatigable are they at this diversion, that I have known the drums continue beating without intermission from six o'clock on Saturday night till the sun made its appearance on the Monday morning; thus had passed six-and-thirty hours in dancing, cheering, hallooing, and clapping of hands. The negroes dance always in couples, the men figuring and footing, while the women turn round like a top, their petticoats expanding like an umbrella; and this they call *waey-cotto.* During this, the by-standing youths fill about the liquor, while the girls encourage the performance, and wipe the sweat from the brows and sides of the unwearied musicians.

It is indeed upon the whole astonishing to see with what good-nature and even good manners these dancing societies are kept up, of which I repeat it they are so fond, that I have known a newly-imported negro, for want of a partner, figure and foot it for nearly the space of two hours, to his shadow against the wall.

If to what I have stated relative to negro slaves, when under a candid and humane master, we further add, their never being separated from each other; parents seeing their children around them, sometimes till the third or fourth generation, besides the confidence that they are all provided for to the end of their lives;—then if we draw the comparison between this class of people, and the numberless wretched objects that disgrace the streets of *Europe,* we can assuredly not call those Africans who fall under the above description— *unhappy.*

JOHN LUFFMAN, *A Brief Account of the Island of Antigua* (London, 1789), 135–37.

LETTER XXX

To ———————————

St. John's, Antigua,
March 14, 1788.

Dear Sir,

Negroes are very fond of the discordant notes of the banjar, and the hollow sound of the toombah. The banjar is somewhat similar to the guittar, the bottom, or under part, is formed of one half of a large calabash, to which is prefixed a wooden neck, and it is strung with cat-gut and wire. This instrument is the invention of, and was brought here by the African negroes, who are most expert in the performances thereon, which are principally their own country tunes, indeed I do not remember ever to have heard any thing like European numbers from its touch. The toombah is similar to the tabor, and has gingles of tin or shells; to this music (if it deserves the name), I have seen a hundred or more dancing at a time, their gestures are extravagant, but not more so than the principal dancers at your Operahouse, and, I believe, were some of their steps and motions introduced into the public amusements at home, by French or Italian dancers, they would be well received; I do not mean, by the bye, to indicate that the movements of these fables are altogether graceful, but their agility and the surprising command of their limbs, is astonishing; this can be accounted for only by their being habituated to a warm climate, where elasticity is more general than in the colder latitudes: The principal dancing time is on Sunday afternoons, when the great market is over (the nature and utility of which I propose to give you in my next), in fact Sunday is their day of trade, their day of relaxation, their day of pleasure, and may, in the strictest sense of the words, be called the negroes holiday.

WILLIAM BECKFORD, *A Descriptive Account of the Island of Jamaica* (London, 1790), vol. II, 120–21, 216–19, 387.

When the mill is at work at night, there is something affecting in the songs of the women who feed it; and it appears somewhat singular, that all their tunes, if tunes they can be called, are of a plaintive cast. Sometimes you may hear one soft, complaining voice; and now a second and a third chime in; and presently, as if inspired by the solemn impressions of night, and by the gloomy objects that are supposed to dwell around, a full chorus is heard to swell upon the ear, and then to die away again to the first original tone.

The style of singing among the negroes, is uniform: and this is confined to the women; for the men very seldom, excepting upon extraordinary occasions, are ever heard to join in chorus. One person begins first, and continues to sing alone; but at particular periods the others join: there is not, indeed, much variety in their songs; but their intonation is not less perfect than their time.

■ ■ ■

The bender is an instrument upon which the Whydaw negroes, I believe, in particular, excel. It is made of a bent stick, the ends of which are restrained in this direction by a slip of dried grass; the upper part of which is gently compressed between the lips, and to which the breath gives a soft and pleasing vibration; and the other end is graduated by a slender stick that beats upon the nerve, if I may so express it, and confines the natural acuteness of the sound, and thus together produce a trembling, a querulous, and a delightful harmony.

I had a watchman very near my house, whose hut was close to the entrance of a bamboo-walk of considerable length, and which was surrounded by plantain-trees and other shrubs, through the former of which the midnight winds were heard to sigh; and on the latter, the nightingales seemed to contend in strength and sweetness of song; and when they paused, the bender took up, with its wild and various modulation, the rural strain, or joined in chorus the melancholy notes that were poured around. The combined effects of these impressions upon the mind, when the body has been long confined to sickness, and when langour and resignation almost make the patient indifferent to life, can hardly be experienced, excepting by those who have been in the situation above described.

The Caramantee-flutes are made from the porous branches of the trumpet-tree, are about a yard in length, and of nearly the thickness of the upper part of a bassoon: they have generally three holes at the bottom; are held, in point of direction, like the hautboy; and while the right hand stops the holes, in the left is shaken, by one of the party, a hollow ball that is filled with pebbles: but this instrument falls very far short of the other in modulation. I have frequently heard these flutes played in parts; and I think the sounds they produce are the most affecting, as they are the most melancholy, that I ever remember to have heard. The high notes are uncommonly wild, but yet are sweet; and the lower tones are deep, majestic, and impressive. Upon the dejected mind, and particularly at night, they have a very tender and affecting influence, insomuch that hypochrondriac dispositions will be sensibly softened, if not entirely overcome, by their intonations.

The notes of the bender might, I think, be introduced in solo parts, into some of our lighter symphonies and airs, or might perhaps have a pleasing effect, if played behind the scenes, and to fill up some of the pauses of the accompanied recitatives: and the Caramantee-flutes might, in solemn strains, particularly in choruses, be made to produce a most tender and sublime expression. No sounds can be more pathetically sweet, more sentimentally elevated, or more exquisitely deep; and I cannot help thinking that, in point of tone, it surpasses any single instrument with which I am acquainted.

I have often wished that my friend Parsons had heard, and could have instructed musicians in the execution of these different instruments, as his superior, though modest talents (and hence a pleasing commendation) would have made them valuable, if not in the chaste and spirited accompaniments of his airs, at least in the pathetic episodes, if I may so express it, of his sentimental and learned choruses; and in which he has displayed a taste and judgment, upon which professors, unprejudiced by country or by name, have bestowed the most warm and just encomiums. How enviable must be the character of him, whose music is not more soft than his manners, and whose talents, as a musician, must lose, when compared to his virtues as a man! This inadequate oblation to friendship, I am proud, in this public manner, to pay: but how shall I ever be able to discharge that unwearied attention and unremitting kindness, which have been, since my arrival in England, the principal support, as the most soothing consolation.

■   ■   ■

They are extremely fond of music and dancing; they have good ears and preserve the most perfect tune and time. Their musical instruments indeed (the Caramantee flutes and the bender excepted . . . with an omission however of a slender stick which the player of the last-mentioned instrument presses to the string a little below his mouth, to graduate the vibration), their musical instruments, if such they may be called, consist of a bonjour, originally taken, perhaps from a French word, as many have found their way by corruption among the negroes; a kind of Spanish guitar; a cotter, upon which they beat with sticks; a gomba, which they strike with their hands; a drum; a box filled with pebbles, which they shake with their wrists; and, to close the account, the jaw-bone of an animal, from which is produced a harsh and disagreeable sound: and it may easily be imagined, when these all together join in chorus, and are accompanied by a number of voices, what kind of music must assail, and fill the ear.

Their style of dancing is by no means ungraceful; and the different groups in which they assemble themselves upon these occasions, would make very picturesque subjects for a painter. They generally meet before their houses, and sometimes in the pastures under the shade of trees, where, if allowed, they continue their favourite diversions from night to morning.

J. B. MORETON, *Manners and Customs in the West India Islands* (London, 1790), 152–53, 155–58.

When working, though at the hardest labour, they are commonly singing; and though their songs have neither rhime nor measure, yet many are witty and pathetic. I have often laughed heartily, and have been as often struck with deep melancholy at their songs:—for instance, when singing of the overseer's barbarity to them:

> Tink dere is a God in a top,
> No use we ill, Obisha!
> Me no horse, me no mare, me no mule,
> No use me ill, Obisha.

Or, thus:

> If we want for go in a Ebo*
> Me can't go there!
> Since dem tief me from a Guinea,
> Me can't go there!

> If me want to go in a Congo*
> Me can't go there!

*Countries in Africa.

Since dem tief me from my tatta
Me can't go there!

If me want to go in a Kingstown
Me can't go there!
Since massa go in a England
Me can't go there!

•   •   •

Notwithstanding all their hardships, they are fond of play and merriment; and if not prevented by whites, according to a law of the island, they will meet on Saturday-nights, hundreds of them in gangs, and dance and sing till morning; nay, sometimes they continue their balls without intermission till Monday-morning. I have often gone, out of curiosity, to such meetings, and was highly diverted: their music is composed of anything that makes a tinkling sound; a hollow cane, or bamboo, with hides on it, in imitation of a fife; an herring-barrel, or tub, with sheep-skins substituted for the heads, in imitation of a drum, called a gumbay; but sometimes more "grandy balls," as they are called, are honored with a tabret and violin; . . . in which case, they are visited by the better sort of the neighboring plantation negroes, and suppers and strong liquors are prepared by a few of the knowing-ones. They prepare a number of pots, some of which are good and savory; chiefly their swine, poultry, salt beef, pork, herrings, and vegetables with roasted, barbecued, and fricasseed rats, etc. etc.; all which they divide in small quantities, in calabashes (bitts and half-bitts worth) on which those who are able to purchase regale themselves. Their funerals and weddings are celebrated in this manner: indeed, I think I never saw anything that so nearly resembled the amusements, particularly the patrons held on Sundays, by the vulgar peasantry in Ireland; where, to the music of a rotten bagpipe, or crazy fiddle, they dance to "tire each other down"; where they court, laugh, and sing at once; and cry, pipe and play at once; and where they gormandize and guzzle, fight and quarrel at once.

When dancing, they form themselves into a circular position, adjoining some of their huts, and continue all in motion, singing so loud, that of a calm night they may be heard about two miles distance—thus:

Hipsaw! my deaa! You no do like a-me!
You no jig like a-me! You no twist like a-me.
Hipsaw! my deaa! You no shake like a-me!

You no wind like a-me! Go, yondaa!
Hipsaw! my deaa! You no jig like a-me
You no work like a-me! You no sweet him like a-me!

Or thus:

Tajo, tajo, tajo! tajo, my mackey massa!
O! land, O! tajo, tajo, tajo!
You work him, mackey massa!
You sweet me, mackey massa!
A little more, my mackey massa!

Tajo, tajo, tajo! my mackey massa!
O! land O! tajo, tajo, tajo!
I'll please my mackey massa!
I'll jig to mackey massa!
I'll sweet my mackey massa!

Thus they go on; so that it would be almost impossible for a stoic to look on without laughing. The droll capers, and wanton gestures and attitudes—the languishing glances and grimaces, so consequential and serious, of those flat-nosed damsels, timed to admiration by their jetty beau partners, are truly curious. It is very amazing to think with what agility they twist and move their joints:—I sometimes imagined they were on springs or hinges from the hips downwards; whoever is most active and expert at wriggling is reputed the best dancer; you will find among them many beautiful young creatures; so that you can not possibly look on umoved: they have too many alluring tricks to seduce and lead men astray. Perseus was moved to war by the beauty of a black woman; the great Mark Antony, once lord of the empire, could not withstand Cleapatra's jetty charms; whilst roses and lillies fade, true black, like the yew that never sheds its leaves, is still the same.

BRYAN EDWARDS, *The History, Civil and Commercial, of the British Colonies in the West Indies* (Dublin, 1793), vol. II, 79–82.

. . . An opinion prevails in Europe that they possess organs peculiarly adapted to the science of musick; but this is an ill-founded idea. In vocal harmony they display neither variety nor compass. Nature seems in this respect to have dealt more penuriously by them than towards the rest of the human race. As practical musicians, some of them by great labour and careful instruction, become sufficiently expert to bear an under-part in a publick concert; but I do not recollect ever to have seen or heard of a Negro who could truly be called a fine performer on any capital instrument. In general they prefer a loud and long-continued noise to the finest harmony, and frequently consume the whole night in beating on a board with a stick. This is in fact one of their chief musical instruments; besides which, they have the Banjo or Merriwong, the Dundo, and the Goombay, all of African origin. The first is an imperfect kind of violin cello; except that it is played on by the finger like the guitar; producing a dismal monotony of four notes. The Dundo is precisely a tabor; and the Goombay is a rustick drum; being formed of the trunk of a hollow tree, one end of which is covered with a sheepskin. From such instruments nothing like a regular tune can be expected, nor is it attempted.

Their songs are commonly impromptu, and there are among them individuals who remember the improvisatore, or extempore bards, of Italy; but I cannot say much for their poetry. Their tunes in general are characteristick of their national manners; those of the Eboes being soft and languishing; of the Koromantyns heroick and martial. At the same time, there is observable, in most of them, a predominant melancholy, which to a man of feeling, is sometimes very affecting.

At their merry meetings, and midnight festivals, they are not without ballads of another kind, adapted to such occasions; and here they give full scope to a talent of ridicule and derision, which is exercised not only against each other, but also, not unfrequently, at the expence of their owner or employer; but most part of their songs at these places are fraught with obscene ribaldry, and accompanied with dances in the highest degree licentious and wanton.

At other times, more specifically at the burial of such among them as were respected in life, or venerable through age, they exhibit a sort of Pyrrhick or warlike dance, in which their bodies are strongly agitated by running, leaping, and jumping, with many violent and frantic gestures and contortions. Their funeral songs too are all of the heroick or martial cast; affording some colour to the prevalent notion, that the Negroes consider death not only as a welcome and happy release from the calamities of their condition, but also as a passport to the place of their nativity; a deliverance which, while it frees them from bondage, restores them to the society of their dearest long-lost and lamented relatives in Africa. But I am afraid that this, like other European notions concerning the Negroes, is the dream of poetry; the sympathetick effusion of a fanciful or too credulous an imagination. The Negroes in general, are so far from courting death, that, among such of them as have resided any length of time in the West Indies, suicide is much less frequent than among the free born, happy and civilized inhabitants of Great Britain.

ANONYMOUS, "Characteristic Traits of the Creolian and African Negroes in Jamaica, &c, &c," *Colombian Magazine*, April––October 1797 (Reprinted in 1976, Barry Higman, ed. [Mona, Jamaica: Caldwell Press, 1976], pp. 20–21).

African Music
The song and dance are always united when they associate to amuse themselves; it is on these occasions the Negroes of each tribe or nation assemble in distinct groups with their several instruments. Excellence in dancing is thought to depend on a due performance of certain gestures peculiar to each class.—For the persons deemed qualified to exhibit, the others form a circle, observing the time by antic motions of the body, clapping their hands, singing and rattling with their calabashes fixed to sticks; the instruments keeping up a continued sound.

When any dancer gives particular satisfaction to the audience, many of them make presents of ryals which they thrust into their mouths or bosoms, some officious negro going around the circle to keep back intruders. All who please dance in succession, without any formality, introduction, or invitation.

The Coromantines far excel the others in music, whose tunes are sung in canto fermo; while the Coromantines perform their airs in different parts not unlike our glees.

GEORGE PINCKARD, *Notes on the West Indies* (London, 1806), vol. I, 263–68.

Sunday is a day of festivity among the slaves. They are passionately fond of dancing, and the sabbath offering them an interval from toil, is, generally, devoted to their favorite amusement; and, instead of remaining in tranquil rest, they undergo more fatigue, or at least more personal exertion, during their gala hours of Saturday night and Sunday, than is demanded from them, in labor, during any four days of the week.

They assemble, in crowds, upon the open green, or in any square or corner of the town, and, forming a ring in the centre of the throng, dance to the sound of their beloved music, and the singing of their favorite African yell. Both music and dance are of a savage nature. I have wished myself a musician that I might take down for you the notes of their songs; which are very simple, but harsh and wholly deficient in softness and melody. . . .

The instrumental parts of the band consist of a species of drum, a kind of rattle, and their ever-delighting Banjar. The first is a long hollow piece of wood, with a dried sheep-skin tied over the end; the second is a calabash containing a number of small stones, fixed to a short stick which serves as the handle; and the third is a coarse and rough kind of guitar. While one negro strikes the Banjar, another shakes the rattle with great force of arm, and a third sitting across the body of the drum, as it lies lengthwise upon the ground, beats and kicks the sheep skin at the end, in violent exertion with his hands and heels, and a fourth sitting upon the ground at the other end, behind the man upon the drum, beats upon the wooden sides of it with two sticks. Together with these noisy sounds, numbers of the party of both sexes bawl forth their dear delighting song with all possible force of lungs; and from the combination, and *tout ensemble* of the scene, a spectator would require only a slight aid from fancy to transport him to the savage wilds of Africa. On great occasions the band is increased by an additional number of drums, rattles, and voices.

The dance consists of stamping of the feet, twistings of the body, and a number of strange indecent attitudes. It is a severe bodily exertion—more bodily indeed than you can well imagine, for the limbs have little to do in it. The head is held erect, or, occasionally, inclined a little forward—the hands nearly meet before—the elbows are fixed, pointing from the sides—and the lower extremities being held rigid, the whole person is moved without lifting the feet from the ground. Making the head and limbs fixed points, they writhe and turn the body upon its own axis, slowly advancing towards each other, or retreating to the outer parts of the ring. Their approaches, with the figure of the dance, and the attitudes and inflexions in which they are made, are highly indecent; but of this they seem to be wholly unconscious, for the gravity—I might say the solemnity of countenance, under which all this passes, is peculiarly striking, indeed almost ridiculous. Not a smile—not a significant glance, nor an immodest look escapes from either sex; but they meet, in very indecent attitudes, under the most settled, and unmeaning gravity of countenance. Occasionally they change the figure by stamping upon the feet, or making a more general movement of the person, but these are only temporary variations; the twistings and turnings of the body seeming to constitute the supreme excellence of the dance.

For the most part only two enter the ring at a time, but, occasionally, as many as three or four! each making a small contribution to the band at the time of stepping into the circle. They circle, violently, together until one is tired, and when this escapes from the circle another assumes the place, thus continuing to follow, one by one, in succession, so as frequently to keep up the dance, without any interval, for several hours.

Both musicians and dancers seem, equally, to delight in the amusement. They exert themselves until their naked skin pours off copious streams. The band seem to be quite insensible to fatigue, for, in proportion as the fluid distils from their pores, they increase their efforts, raising their voices, and beating the drum and the rattle, with additional violence: and such of the spectators whose olfactories have no relish for African odours, are sadly annoyed by the high essenced exhalation which spreads itself around.

Matthew Gregory Lewis, *Journal of a West India Proprietor* (London, 1834), 79–81, 226–28, 232–33, 322–24.

January 6 [1816]

The dances performed to-night seldom admitted more than three persons at a time: to me they appeared to be movements entirely dictated by the caprice of the moment; but I am told that there is a regular figure, and that the least mistake, or a single false step, is immediately noticed by the rest. I could indeed sometimes fancy, that one story represented an old duenna guarding a girl from a lover; and another, the pursuit of a young woman by two suitors, the one young and the other old; but this might be only fancy. However, I am told, that they have dances which not only represent courtship and marriage, but being brought to bed. Their music consisted of nothing but Gambys (Eboe drums), Shaky-shekies, and Kitty-katties: the latter is nothing but any flat piece of board beat upon with two sticks, and the former is a bladder with a parcel of pebbles in it. But the principal part of the music to which they dance is vocal; one girl generally singing two lines by herself, and being answered by a chorus. To make out either the rhyme of the air, or meaning of the words, was out of

the question. But one very long song was about the Duke of Wellington, every stanza being chorussed with,

> "Ay! hey-day! Waterloo!
> Waterloo! ho! ho! ho!"

I too had a great deal to do in the business, for every third word was
"massa"; though how I came there, I have no more idea than the
Duke.

The singing began about six o'clock, and lasted without a moment's pause till two in the morning; and such a noise never did I
hear till then. The whole of the floor which was not taken up by the
dancers was, through every part of the house except the bed-rooms,
occupied by men, women, and children, fast asleep. But although
they were allowed rum and sugar by whole pailfuls, and were most of
them *merry* in consequence, there was not one of them drunk; except
indeed, one person, and that was an old woman, who sang, and
shouted, and tossed herself about in an elbow chair, till she tumbled
it over, and rolled about the room in a manner which shocked the delicacy of even the least prudish part of the company. At twelve, my
agent wanted to dismiss them; but I would not suffer them to be interrupted on the first holiday that I had given them; so they continued
to dance and shout till two; when human nature could bear no more,
and they left me to my bed, and a violent headache.

■   ■   ■

March 22 [1816]

Mr. Plummer came over from St. James's to-day, and told me,
that the "insidious practices and dangerous doctrines" in Mr. Stewart's speech were intended for the Methodists, and that only the
charge to the grand jury respecting "additional vigilance" was in allusion to myself; but he added that it was the report at Montego Bay,
that, in consequence of my over-indulgence to my negroes, a song had
been made at Cornwall, declaring that I was come over to set them all
free, and that this was now circulating through the neighbouring parishes. If there be any such song (which I do not believe), I certainly
never heard it. However, my agent here says, that he has reason to
believe that my negroes really have spread the report that I intend
to set *them* free in a few years; and this merely out of vanity, in order
to give themselves and their master the greater credit upon other estates. As to the truth of an assertion, that is a point which never enters
into negro consideration.

The two ringleaders of the proposed rebellion have been condemned at Black River, the one to be hanged, the other to transportation. The plot was discovered by the overseer of Lyndhurst Penn (a Frenchman from St. Domingo) observing an uncommon concourse of stranger negroes to a child's funeral, on which occasion a hog was roasted by the father. He stole softly down to the feasting hut, and listened behind a hedge to the conversation of the supposed mourners; when he heard the whole conspiracy detailed. It appears that above two hundred and fifty had been sworn in regularly, all of them Africans; not a Creole was among them. But there was a *black* ascertained to have stolen over into the island from St. Domingo, and a *brown* Anabaptist missionary, both of whom had been very active in promoting the plot. They had elected a King of the Eboes, who had two Captains under him; and their intention was to effect a complete massacre of all the whites on the island; for which laudable design His Majesty thought Christmas the very fittest season in the year, but his Captains were more impatient, and were for striking the blow immediately. The next morning information was given against them; one of the Captains escaped to the woods; but the other, and the King of the Eboes, were seized and brought to justice. On their trial they were perfectly cool and unconcerned, and did not even profess to deny the facts with which they were charged. Indeed, proofs were too strong to admit of denial; among others, a copy of the following song was found upon the King, which the overseer had heard him sing at the funeral feast, while the other negroes joined in the chorus:—

SONG OF THE KING OF THE EBOES

Oh me good friend, Mr. Wilberforce, make we free!
God Almighty thank ye! God Almighty thank ye!
God Almighty, make we free!
Buckra in this country no make we free:
What Negro for to do? What Negro for to do?
Take force by force! Take force by force!

Chorus.

To be sure! to be sure! to be sure!

The Eboe King said, that he certainly had made use of this song, and what harm was there in his doing so? He had sung no songs but such as his brown priest had assured him were approved of by John the Baptist. "And who, then, was John the Baptist?" He did not very well know; only he had been told by his brown priest, that John the Baptist was a friend to the negroes, and had got his head in a pan!

March 26 [1816]

Young Hill was told at the Bay this morning, that I make a part of the Eboe King's song! According to this report, "good King George and good Mr. Wilberforce" are stated to have "given me a paper" to set the negroes free (i.e., an order), but that the white people of Jamaica will not suffer me to show the paper, and I am now going home to say so, and "to resume my chair, which I have left during my absence to be filled by the Regent."

Since I heard the report of a rebellious song issuing from Cornwall, I have listened more attentively to the negro chaunts; but they seem, as far as I can make out, to relate entirely to their own private situation, and to have nothing to do with the negro state in general. Their favourite, "We varry well off," is still screamed about the estate by the children; but among the grown people its nose has been put out of joint by the following stanzas, which were explained to me this morning. For several days past they had been dinned into my ears so incessantly, that at length I became quite curious to know their import, which I learned from Phillis, who is the family minstrel. It will be evident from this specimen, that the Cornwall bards are greatly inferior to those of Black River, who have actually advanced so far as to make an attempt at rhyme and metre.

NEGRO SONG AT CORNWALL

Hey-ho-day! me no care a dammee! (i.e. a damn)
Me acquire a house, (i.e. I have a solid foundation
      to build on)
Since massa come see we—oh!

Hey-ho-day! neger now quite eerie, (i.e. hearty,)
For once me see massa—hey-ho-day!
When massa go, me no care a dammee,
For how them usy we—hey-ho-day!

■   ■   ■

January 29 [1818]

There is a popular negro song, the burden of which is,—

"Take him to the Gulley! Take him to the Gulley!
But bringee back the frock and board."—
"Oh! massa, massa! me no deadee yet!"—
"Take him to the Gulley! Take him to the Gulley!"
      "Carry him along!"

This alludes to a transaction which took place some thirty years ago, on an estate in this neighbourhood, called Spring-Garden; the

owner of which (I think the name was Bedward) is quoted as the
cruellest proprietor that ever disgraced Jamaica. It was his constant
practice, whenever a sick negro was pronounced incurable, to order
the poor wretch to be carried to a solitary vale upon his estate, called
the Gulley, where he was thrown down, and abandoned to his fate;
which fate was generally to be half devoured by the john-crows, before death had put an end to his sufferings. By the proceeding the av-
aricious owner avoided the expence of maintaining the slave during
his last illness; and in order that he might be as little a loser as possible, he always enjoined the negro bearers of the dying man to strip
him naked before leaving the Gulley, and not to forget to bring back
his frock and the board on which he had been carried down. One poor
creature, while in the act of being removed, screamed out most pit-
eously "that he was not dead yet"; and implored not to be left to perish in the Gulley in a manner so horrible. His cries had no effect upon
his master, but operated so forcibly on the less marble hearts of his
fellow-slaves, that in the night some of them removed him back to the
negro village privately, and nursed him there with so much care, that
he recovered, and left the estate unquestioned and undiscovered. Unluckily, one day the master was passing through Kingston, when, on
turning the corner of a street suddenly, he found himself face to face
with the negro, whom he had supposed long ago to have been picked
to the bones in the Gulley of Spring-Garden. He immediately seized
him, claimed him as his slave, and ordered his attendants to convey
him to his house, but the fellow's cries attracted a crowd round them,
before he could be dragged away. He related his melancholy story,
and the singular manner in which he had recovered his life and liberty; and the public indignation was so forcibly excited by the shocking tale, that Mr. Bedward was glad to save himself from Kingston,
and never ventured to advance his claim to the negro a second time.

JAMES STEWART, *A View of the Past and Present State of the Island
of Jamaica* (Edinburgh, 1823), 269–73.

The slaves have little time to devote to amusement, but such occasions as offer they eagerly embrace. Plays, as they call them, are their
principal and favourite one. This is an assemblage of both sexes,
dressed out for the occasion, who form a ring round a male and female
dancer, who perform to the music of drums and the songs of the other
females of the party, one alternately going over the song, while her
companions repeat in chorus. Both the singers and dancers show the

exactest precision as to time and measure. This rude music is usually accompanied by a kind of rattles, being small calibashes filled with the seed of a plant called by the negroes *Indian shot*. Near at hand this music is harsh and clamourous, but at a distance it has not an unpleasant sound. When two dancers have fatigued themselves, another couple enter the ring, and thus the amusement continues. So fond are the negroes of this amusement, that they will continue for nights and days enjoying it, when permitted. But their owners find it prudent and necessary to restrain them from it, excepting at Christmas, when they have three days allowed them. This and harvest-home may be considered as their two annual festivals. Little do they consider, and as little do they care, about the origin and occasion of the former of those festivals; suffice it to say, that *Buckra* gives them their three days—though, by the bye, the law allows only two, in consideration of the injury they may sustain by three successive days of unbounded dissipation, and of the danger, at such a time of unrestrained licentiousness, of riots and disorder.

On these occasions the slaves appear an altered race of beings. They show themselves off to the greatest advantage, by fine clothes and a profusion of trinkets; they affect a more polished behaviour and mode of speech; they address the whites with greater familiarity; they come into their masters' houses, and drink with them; the distance between them appears to be annihilated for the moment, like the familiar footing on which the Roman slaves were with their masters at the feast of the Saturnalia. Pleasure throws a temporary oblivion over their cares and their toils; they seem a people without the consciousness of inferiority or suffering.

Many of them, however, but especially the men, give themselves up to excessive intemperance, which with their nocturnal dances, often produces sickness, and sometimes even death. Such is the violent exercise they undergo in these dancings, such the heedless manner in which they abandon themselves for successive nights and days to this favourite amusement, even in the open air, during the Christmas holidays, that were this unrestrained indulgence permitted for two or three weeks, instead of as many days, it would probably destroy a great number of these thoughtless people. After their riotous festivity, they experience a degree of lassitude and languor which for some days incapacitates them for much exertion or labour.

Plays, or dances, very frequently take place on Saturday nights, when the slaves on the neighbouring plantations assemble together to enjoy this amusement. It is contrary to the law for the slaves to beat their drums after ten o'clock at night; but this law they pay little regard to. Their music is very rude; it consists of the *goombay* or drum, several rattles, and the voices of the female slaves, which, by the bye, is the best part of the music, though altogether it is very rude. The drums of the Africans vary in shape, size, &c. according to the different countries, as does also their vocal music. In a few years it is probable that the rude music here described will be altogether exploded among the creole negroes, who show a decided preference for European music. Its instruments, its tunes, its dances, are now pretty generally adopted by the young creoles, who indeed sedulously copy their masters and mistresses in every thing. A sort of subscription balls are set on foot, and parties of both sexes assemble and dance country dances to the music of a violin, tambarine, &c. But this improvement of taste is in a great measure confined to those who are, or have been, domestics about the houses of the whites, and have in consequence imbibed a fondness for their amusements, and some skill in the performance. They affect, too, the language, manners, and conversation of the whites: those who have it in their power have at times their convivial parties, when they will endeavour to mimic their masters in their drinking, their songs, and their toasts; and it is laughable to see with what awkward minuteness they aim at such imitations. They have also caught a spirit of gambling from their masters, and often assemble and play at games of hazard with the dice, though there is a law against such species of gambling, and such slaves as are found assembled for this purpose are liable to punishment.

H. T. DE LA BECHE, *Notes on the Present Conditions of the Negroes in Jamaica* (London, 1825), 40–41.

Negroes in giving dances or plays sometimes go to great expense. I was present at a dance given by my black doctor, as the head negro who attends the hospital is called, which must have cost him more than two doubloons (thirty-two dollars). There was madeira wine, with liquors of various kinds, and an abundance of meat, poultry, fruits, &c. The only money expended on this occasion by the guests was a small trifle each to the fiddlers. Most frequently the host expects remuneration for his trouble and viands, and is paid a certain sum each by his guests.

The following is a literal copy of a negro ball ticket, which came into my possession; the ladies and gentlemen mentioned in it are the slaves upon an estate adjoining my own, and the person giving the dance a free man:—

> Vere, Hayses, 1824.
>   Wm. Gottshalk beg leave to inform the Ladies and Gentlemen at Dunkleys, that he intends giving a May Pole dance on the 3rd Saturday in May, wherein every attention shall be paid, and good accomodation, &c. &c.
>
>   TICKET—5 Shilling Each.

When a negro wishes to give a dance, he applies for leave to the overseer, who as a matter of course grants it; the day fixed upon is almost always Saturday, in order that they may keep it up during that night and the next day; the dance, or play, as it is sometimes called, commences about eight o'clock in the evening, and although contrary to law, continues to day-break with scarcely any intermission, those of the old school preferring the goombay and African dances, and those of the new, fiddles, reels, &c. The dance is discontinued at day-break in the morning, and the guests are then feasted; there is generally also a dinner and supper. The dance recommences the second evening, but does not continue through the night.

CAPTAIN J. E. ALEXANDER, *Transatlantic Sketches,* . . . (London, 1833), vol. I, 16, 130–31, 157–58, 95–97, 191–92.

There were no sounds but those of merriment; the song and chorus of a group of young negresses, the salutations and jokes of friends meeting, and the incessant gabbing of the old women, who when they can get no one to converse with, carry on a conversation (aloud) with their own sweet selves, like negroes at the balls, sometimes dancing to their own shadows on the wall for want of a partner.

                              ■   ■   ■

. . . I again proceeded into the bush, to visit an Indian settlement and the Tappacooma lake, 8 miles in length, formed by a dam between two sand hills, and intended to irrigate the Morocco estate in the event of a scarcity of rain. The negroes merrily plied the paddles, and we brushed past the overhanging trees to their favorite song of "Velly well, yankee, velly well oh!"

> De bottley oh! de bottley oh!
> Ne neger like the de bottley oh!
> Right early in de morning, de neger like de bottley oh!

> A bottle o'rum, loaf a bread,
> Make de neger dandy oh!
> Right early in de morning, de neger like de bottley oh!

∎ ∎ ∎

One Evening whilst sitting on the marble verandah at Ermore (Barbados), and listening to the ceaseless hum of the insects and the gentle rustling of the trees, and thinking of again venturing on the treacherous deep, I heard the lively sound of a drum at some distance, and immediately repaired to where the negroes were amusing themselves under the mild rays of the Cythian queen. On a level spot, surrounded by small houses of coloured and black people, was a bench, on which seated two negro fiddlers and a thin fellow beating a drum; behind stood a man shaking violently a calabash filled with small stones and reeds, and singing with contortions an African air. The crowd formed a ring, and those who wished to dance the Joan-Johnny stepped forward, presented the leader of the band with a bit, and he

> "Bid the fiddle to the banjar speak,
> The banjar to the calabash without,"

and a couple would twist their bodies, thump the ground with their heels, and circle round one another to the inspiring strains. The little black urchins, as usual, were sitting to one another on the outskirts of the admiring crowd, or kneeling down behind their elders, who would be pushed over admist shouts of laughter, or mimicking the actions of the white lookers on.

∎ ∎ ∎

It was a holiday, and Quashee and Quasheba were lounging about in their gala dresses, and waiting impatiently for evening, to commence their festivities in the "Great House." The men were dressed in white vests and trowsers, and cloth jackets; and the women in printed gowns, with straw hats or handkerchiefs on their heads. Everywhere as we passed through the different groups in the garden, the white teeth were displayed in a smile, and "How de massa? ready for dance massa!" was heard. The piccaninnies, black and mischievous as monkeys, were "scurrying" about, running between their parents' legs, laughing loud, and tumbling one another head over heels on the grass.

At last a drum is heard in the gallery, and the negroes take possession of the house; two or three musicians then seat themselves in chairs, and with fiddle, tambourine, and drum, strike up some lively jigs, at the same time thumping the floor vigorously with their heels.

Every one is alive; short cries of mirth are uttered by the men as they hand out their sable partners; and they lead one another up and down the lane of the country dance, with as much enjoyment as I have ever witnessed at a Highland wedding.

The little black urchins, boys and girls, are not idle round the room, whilst their parents are "tripping it" in the centre, but copying their elders, they "cut and shuffle" at a great rate; the mothers, with children at their breasts, alone quietly enjoy the scene. A worthless fellow who rushed in his chemise into the room, and attempted to join the well-dressed figurantes, was instantly expelled. Santa (sweet punch) and cakes, were handed round from time to time. Mulatta ladies looked in at the windows at the mirthful scene, but declined to join the negroes; and a few overseers and book-keepers "whispered soft nonsense" in their ears.

Outside the house, in the moonlight, a musician seated himself with his drum on the grass, and commenced singing an African air, when a circle of men and women, linked hand in hand, danced round him with rattling seeds on their legs, and joined in the chorus.

Oh! how I wished that some of the kind ladies of Peckham could have contemplated for five minutes this scene of mirth! could have beheld what they are pleased to call "the naked, starved, and oppressed negroes," well clothed, plump, and full of glee: instead of shrieks of misery, could have heard shouts of laughter: and instead of the clang of the whip, could have heard the lively music of the fiddles, and the gladsome songs of the creole dancers. Surely, then, their feeling hearts would prompt them to look for more distressed objects nearer home on which to exercise their benevolence, would induce them to leave emancipation to be wrought out by slow and rational means, and not cruelly insist, that since the planters have had for so long a time the use of their slaves, they should now give them liberty,—forgetting that to the suddenly emancipated slave this boon immediately opens the door to licentiousness and misery.

．　．　．

On Saturday night a negro wench balancing an empty bottle on her head, and rattling a calabash filled with small pebbles, advances with a dancing step to the music, and sings:

> "Ax de bottle what be da want,
> Massa full him, mass full him,"

Whilst Tim makes a triangle out of a stirrup and a rusty key, and Jack vigorously thumps a skin stretched across a barrel, throws back his wooly head, and shouts with delight at his own rude music.

F. W. N. BAYLEY, *Four Years' Residence in the West Indies*, 3d ed. (London, 1833), 69–71, 437–38.

In Barbados, however, as well as in other islands, masters are greatly plundered by their servants, of such things as poultry, porter, wine and sometimes even money; for the purpose of carrying them to entertainments, which the negroes give among themselves. These parties are carried on in the following manner: the members assemble at a certain hour, at the appointed place of rendezvous, which is usually a negro hut belonging to one of the party: tea and coffee are first handed around, after which, the musicians, consisting of perhaps three fiddlers, a tambourine player, and a man who beats an instrument called a triangle, commence playing, and the dancing continues for a while in the most lively and spirited manner.... After dancing, the group sits down to the supper table, the contents of which have all been stolen from the masters or mistresses of the different guests. One has brought a fowl, another a turkey; a third a ham; a fourth, a pie, pudding, or tartlet; a fifth a bottle of champagne; a sixth a bottle of madeira; a seventh a bottle of port; and eighth, a bottle of claret; a ninth a bottle or perhaps ½ a dozen of porter; and a tenth, pine apples, mangoes, oranges, shaddocks, plumbs, almonds and raisins, with a few *French* preserves, for which the donor had taken *french* leave; and a tempting water dessert: so that for the dessert they got more than they deserve; and the whole supper, even if it be not arranged upon the table according to the strictest rules of etiquette and may not be called elegant, is nevertheless a very substantial meal. After supper the parties separate, and each returns to his home; the masters know nothing of the matter....

■   ■   ■

I believe in one or two of the Leeward Islands it is more usual for the august assembly of sable revellers to carry on the gaieties on the green lawn before the dwelling of the proprietor, than to take possession of one of the rooms in the house. The music also is sometimes of wonderful variety. An empty barrel, "par exemple," with a large piece of parchment over the top, a kettledrum, a tambourine, a pipe, a *gumbay* or *bonja*, with sundry other instruments, and these aided by vocal efforts of men and women, boys and girls, do verily emit sounds of most terrific merriment and might frighten and amuse an unaccustomed bystander, more than any wot of. I must not, however, charge the slaves with a crime of which, if we except their young ones, they are seldom guilty, namely that of producing inharmonious and non-accordant sounds; on the contrary, they have, generally a good ear for music, they sing or whistle with wonderful correctness any tune they may have heard, they dance in excellent time, and are altogether very intelligent persons in anything connected with music. I remember when Mr. Thomas Haynes Bagby's song of

> I'd be a butterfly, born in a bower
> Where roses, and lilies, and violets meet, &c.

first came to Grenada it had not been a week in the island before every black scamp in Georgetown was singing the air to the following parody:

I

> Me a nigger boy, born in de hovel,
>> What plantain da shade from de sun wha da shine;
> Me learn to dig with de spade and de shovel,
>> Me learn to hoe up·de cane in a line.
> Me drink my rum, in de calabash oval,
>> Me neber sigh for de brandy and wine;
> Me be a nigger boy, born in de hovel,
>> What plantain de shade from de sun wha da shine.
>>> Me a nigger boy.
>>> Me a nigger boy,
>> When me live happy, wha for me repine?

II

> Me neber run from my massa' plantation.
>> Wha for me run? me no want for get lick;
> He gib me house, and me no pay taxation,
>> Food when me famish, and nurse when me sick.
> Willy force (free) nigger, he belly da empty,
>> He hab de freedom, dat no good for me.
> My massa good man, he gib me plenty,
>> Me no lobe Willy-force better than he.
>>> Me a nigger boy.
>>> Me a nigger boy.
>> Me happy fellow, den why want me free.

MRS. CARMICHAEL, *Domestic Manners and Social Customs of the White, Coloured, and Negro Population of the West Indies* (London, 1833), vol. II, 301–02; vol. I, 292; vol. II, 288.

> Fire in da mountain
> Nobody for out him,
> Take me daddy's bo tick (DANDY STICK)
> And make a monkey out of him.

Chorus.
Poor John! Nobody for out him, etc.

Go to de king's gaol,
You'll find a doubloon dey;
Go to de king's gaol,
You'll find a doubloon dey.
Chorus.
Poor John! Nobody for out him, etc.

The explanation of this song is, that when the bad negroes wanted to do evil, they made for a sign, a fire on the hill-sides, to burn down the canes. There is nobody up there, to put out the fire; but as a sort of satire, the song goes on to say, "take me daddy's bo tick," (daddy is a mere term of civility), take some one's dandy stick, and tell the monkeys to help to put out the fire among the canes for John; (meaning John Bull). The chorus means, that poor John has nobody to put out the fire in the canes for him. Then when the canes are burning, go to the gaol, and seize the money. . . .

■ ■ ■

. . . The amusements of the native African are much of the same kind as those of the creole negro; but they dance their own African dances to the drum, while the creole negroes consider a fiddle genteeler; though of an evening among themselves, they will often sing, dance, and beat the drum, yet they would not produce this instrument at a grand party. Fiddles and tamborines, with triangles, are essential there.

■ ■ ■

The children, besides dancing, have many games; some of which have a resemblance to those of Britain. "Through-the-needle-eye, boy" I found very common; also "French and English," and a game resembling "The hounds and the hare,' which all little masters and misses in Trinidad know by the name of "I'm fishing, I'm fishing all night, and what did I catch but a groupper";—a handkerchief is dropt at the word groupper, and the chase begins.

TRELAWNY WENTWORTH, *The West India Sketch Book* (London, 1834), vol. I, 65–67, 228–30; vol. II, 240–42, 282.

It would be difficult to convey an adequate idea of the very lively and imposing character of a West Indian harvest, combined with all the sublimity and loveliness of tropical scenery, and a tropical atmosphere: even slavery appears divested of its obnoxious and complicated character amidst the festivity and mirth which prevail; and such is the nourishing property of the sugar-cane, that the negroes, who consume great quantities of it, never appear so healthy and animated as at this particular season; it has a wonderful and immediate effect upon their whole system, frequently restoring the weak and sickly to the enjoyment of health and spirits.

The dwelling of the proprietor, or his attorney, is usually situated on an elevation to windward, in the vicinity of the works, to afford a commanding view over the estate, and to facilitate communication with the stores and hospital, as well as more immediate control over the labour carried on at the mill and boiling house. From this point, during the season of which we are speaking, is witnessed a scene of animation and cheerfulness, corresponding in character with that which is passing in the field; and we have often been constrained to listen to the light-hearted hilarity of the negroes, and to watch, with infinite satisfaction, the gambols of the rising generation, pelting each other with a macerated cane, which they are employed to strew in the sun to dry for fuel, after it has passed through the mill. The carts passing and repassing in conveying the bundles of canes from the field, the negroes transporting the canes to the mill, the mill vanes rustling in their revolution, and the confused clamour of voices in dialogue and song, present a singular contrast to that calm repose which nature seems to claim for herself in these clear and ardent climes, manifesting only at intervals her indignant wrath in hurricanes and earthquakes, as if impatient of the presence of man. Here is a song, or rather a *chorus*, which the negroes sing on such occasions, being a fair sample of their poetry and music; kept up, perhaps, by a few of them working together, whilst the others at the same time sing some popular English tune, recently imported, forming together, something like that delectable compound of harmony and discord, a "Dutch medley."

Shat - te - ray nite aw   cung la town,   Chaun fine my   dea-ry hun-ney.

Aw run roun da lemon tree,
Chaun fine my deary hunney.
Aw look behine da guaba bush,
Chaun fine my deary hunney.
Aw wash my pot, aw wash um clean,
Chaun fine my deary hunney.
Aw put in pease, aw put in poke.
Chaun fine my deary hunney.

Aw boil my pot, aw boil um sweet,
  Chaun fine my deary hunney.
Aw sweep my house, aw sweep um clean,
  Chaun fine my deary hunney.
Aw clean my nife, aw clean um shine,
  Chaun fine my deary hunney.
Aw mek my bed, aw mek um soff,
  Chaun fine my deary hunney.
Aw mak um up, aw shek um up,
  Chaun fine my deary hunney.

■ ■ ■

For some distance they had pulled at an easy rate and in silence, as if made unconscious of the work they were engaged in, by the absorbing interest of the passing scenes, but at length they were roused to activity by the word of preparation for a song having been passed among them, and the negro pulling the oar nearest to us, began a singular prelude which sounded between a grunt and a groan, like a paviour's accompaniment to his labour, or the exordium of a Quaker, when "the spirit" begins to move. He became more energetic with each succeeding stroke of the oar, which produced a corresponding ardour, and the greater precision in pulling among the other rowers, and when this was effected, another negro, whose countenance bore the stamp of much covert humour and sagacity, and who appeared to be a sort of *improvisatore* among them, commenced a lively strain which accorded exactly in time with the motion of pulling, each line of the song accompanying the impetus given to the boat, and the whole crew joining in chorus in the intervals between every stroke of the oars. The subject matter of the song was as discursive and lengthy as Chevy Chase; and it showed an aptitude at invention on the part of the leader, as well as a tolerable acquaintance with the weak side of human nature, on the score of flattery: a small portion of it will suffice. The words in italics form the chorus.

Hur - ra my jol-ly boys Fine time o' day We pull for Sam Thomas boys Fine time o' day.

Sam Thomas hab de fine girl,
  Fine time o' day.
Nancy Gibbs and Betsy Braid,
  Fine time o' day.
Massa cum from London town,
  Fine time o' day,

Massa is a hansome man,
  Fine time o' day.
Massa is a dandy man,
  Fine time o' day.
Him hab de dollar, plenty too,
  Fine time o' day.
Massa lub' a pretty girl,
  Fine time o' day.
Him lub' 'em much, him lub 'em true,
  Fine time o' day.
Him hunt 'em round de guaba bush,
  Fine time o' day.
Him catch 'em in de cane piece,
  Fine time o' day. etc.

■ ■ ■

"Mr. John Christian will Be happy for the ladies company on Saturday week to spend the evening at Gordon's.

"Mr. Christian is unacquainted with the ladies names so begs to be excused.

"To Madamoiselles at Bodkins."

So runs, verbatim, the original circular, written in a very tolerable hand, issued by Mr. John Christian, to invite the *polished* ebony damsels of the district in which he lived, to a *soiree* at an estate called Gordon's; and although we were not present to report progress of the entertainment, we doubt not it was as felicitous in all its details as music, mirth, and dancing could make it. These formal invitations are by no means uncommon; some of them printed on cards, in which, probably, the orthography is amended by the compositor at the printing-office in town. Very few of the slaves can write, but there are few, if any estates, that have not coloured people who have acquired some proficiency in the art, who are applied to on such occasions by the negroes, and among this class it is that the etiquette of sending cards is principally observed. Music and dancing, the negroes love to their heart's core, although of late years, they have been taught by the missionaries to believe that they are inconsistent with morality. At the time to which we are referring, dancing was frequent in the negro-houses in an evening, and once a week, a more general assemblage took place under the auspices of one negro, who invited people from the neighbouring estates. On such occasions, it was customary to ask leave of their master, to ensure a license for a greater duration of their obstreperous mirth, which, from the usual vicinity of his dwelling to the negro-houses, he must necessarily hear; and, as these entertainments were profitable to the negro providing them, it was expedient to admit of them according to the character of the applicant, and to regulate them in turns to avoid monopoly. Each negro coming to the assembly paid half a bit, or a bit, in order, partly, to meet the expense of a fiddler, who commonly charged as much as four and five dollars; and who, if not to be found among themselves, was always to be engaged from among the slaves upon some other estate. If it happened, that the negro giving the entertainment has inferior accommodation, he would borrow a more eligible spot from another, the dancing taking place in the house, and in the adjoining plot of ground: the profusion of beauty and ornament displayed by the tall luxuriant foliage, which usually over-canopies their dwellings, and the fresh fragrance of fruit and flowers so predominant in the night-season in the tropics, conspiring to cheer and gladden the hearts of the festive throng.

Often have we walked in amongst them, without interrupting in the least, their joyous gambols, or receiving any further notice, than the simple salutation of "How you do, Massa?" from all their voices at the same moment, unless, perchance, one of the bystanders whould pull a form towards us for a seat, or, if standing at the door, say, "Massa, you no come in?"

■   ■   ■

Barbadoes has not one harbour; Carlisle Bay, in front of Bridge-town, is an open roadstead, with not the best holding ground.

"And who in the name of fun and devilry is Mr. Cunningham?"

We put the question to a pretty Mulatto wench who was whiling away time at her needle, and singing *con multo sentimento* at the door of *Miss* Betsy Austin's hostelry, where we took shelter with a parched palate that would have done credit to the dipsas, a serpent whose bite is celebrated for causing inveterate thirst. All the information we could gain was, that Mr. Cunningham was a hero of other days who

An-te Nanny,   Open da door,   Pa-ter want da   sour-sop soup, Run, Mr. Cunningham,

run for you life,   run Mr. Cunningham,   run for you life,   run Mr. Cunningham,

Pa-ter da come   wid a load-ed   gun!

had been immortalized in song, and while Miss Betsy prepared us some beverage, we prevailed on Miss Julia to sing it again, that we might commit piracy upon the composition.

What motive caused Aunt Nanny to close her door,—whether Mr. Cunningham had forestalled Peter in his soursop soup, which is probable enough—or whether the culprit runaway escaped with his life, is a point which derives all its interest, like a mummy, from the mysterious folds in which time has enveloped it.

JAMES SMITH, *The Winter of 1840 in St. Croix, with an Excursion to Tortola and St. Thomas* (New York, 1840), 19–21.

. . . on Christmas Day we visited the house of an eminent physician, who is the proprietor of one or two plantations, and whose slaves, according to custom, on that day visited their master in a body, shook hands with him, and received an entertainment given by him, after which they danced for his amusement, or that of his friends, for several hours. We were much entertained, as well by the music as the dancing of these people. This gentleman is the proprietor of one or two hundred slaves, and it was no inconsiderable task to greet so many; it occupied much of the morning. Their instruments of music were rude drums, upon which they made a loud noise by tatooing with their hands, the women at the same time singing somewhat like the Shaking Quakers; after this music they danced without much order. They did not exhibit much hilarity in this exercise, for the most part their countenances were rather sad; probably they were restrained by the presence of their master. Christmas day and the day thereafter, are days of recreation for the slaves. Our boarding-house was visited by several hundreds, who danced for our amusement, and who introduced their queen to our inmates. She was a very good looking girl, and was dressed in satins, with decorations of flowers, jewels, etc. etc. She was preceded by two waiting-maids, bearing on staffs some insignia of office. These girls danced quite well, after which, a large circle being formed, the queen herself appeared in the centre of it, and after many graceful courtesies she commenced to dance alone, and continued to amuse us for twenty minutes or more, when she retired. This queen is herself a slave to a colored woman. She is chosen for life, and her decorations are furnished by contribution of the slaves. It is said this custom of having a queen is traceable back to Africa. I know a planter from Demarara, who, upon one occasion, purchased a lot of Africans from on board a slave ship; for some considerable time they were observed to pay great deference to one of the females of their number, and to endeavor, upon every occasion, to screen her from severe labor. Upon inquiry, it was found that she was the queen of their nation, and had been taken prisoner and enslaved with the rest of them. And what is remarkable, this deference is said to have continued until her death.

CHARLES WILLIAM DAY, *Five Years' Residence in the West Indies* (London, 1852), vol. I, 46–48, 52–53; vol. II, 297; vol. I, 85–86; vol. II, 121–22.

The Christmas holidays were such thoroughly drenching days, that negro splendour was for the time annihilated, but on the first fine day the festivities commenced. Hearing that a "Joe and Johnny" was to be held at a place called Cullumore Rock, a short distance from Bridgetown, I resolved to attend it. I found the locality, however, with some difficulty, having been directed toward the Roebuck, a place where dancing *a la mode* was to be carried on in a house; whereas a "Joe and Johnny," being a real negro dance, is always held in the open air.

The "Tum-tum" was an old familiar sound, and guided by its spirit-stirring thump, I found a numerous assemblage of ladies of colour, forming a ring in the unenclosed "back-yard" of a negro hut, being in fact a plot of ground behind the house. The ladies were provided with seats, though the negro gentlemen present were permitted to stand; but as it is an understood thing that a buckra gentleman will pay twice the usual charge, I was quickly accomodated on a sofa, where I was jammed in with two very dark chocolate ladies, highly scented with eau de cologne and musk, a very desirable precaution.

Our music consisted of fiddles, with a rude African-looking tambourine, savouring much of the savage; a 'tum-tum' or "tump," a piece of parchment stretched over what seemed to be a small iron-looped pail, a utensil which I religiously believe it to have been; and "de shot," a small gourd, as large as an orange, filled I understood with shot, and having a handle. This was the property of the "funny man" who rattled it against his hand, and screamed a sort of song, which gave the initiated much delight, but was quite unintelligible to me. The tum-tum was played by an alternate thump of the open-handed knuckles in the parchment, and then a slap of the palm on the wood. The object of the dance was to show the faces of the ladies to the admiring beaux, and a couple of dark beauties paid their "quaarter dollah" each and commenced. The first movement was *en avant* by both, the feet close together toeing and heeling it very gently, the *retirez* the same; then the feet were straddled in a somewhat indecorous manner for ladies, moving along and round à *la fandango*, with a motion similar to that exceedingly droll one used by tragic actors in a booth, "bent on deeds of blood," who sidle up to their victims by an alternate action of the heels and ball of the foot, without lifting their pedal extremities off the ground. Here, however, the ladies turned down the outer ankles as near the earth as possible, meanwhile advancing and retiring together, and then "shoeing around" each other, holding up their frocks à *la minuet de la cour*, with their heads looking down at their feet. These were the grand postures of the dance—an indispensable requisite which also seemed to be a solemn cast of countenance occasionally varied by a sentimental inclination of the head, as doleful in face, however, as if the parties were to be hanged the next minute. The dance was short enough for the money: the music stopped abruptly, and in a minute or two another pair of aspirants for public approbation went through the same evolutions. I must not omit to remark that the feet did *not* take the most active part in the dance, as that was executed by a prominent part of the person, commonly understood to be that peculiarly African development on which "Honour holds her seat."

.　　.　　.

I went on New Year's Day, in the evening, to another "Joe and Johnny." When I arrived, the rays of a sickly moon were gleaming on the broad-leaved plantain which waved over the heads of the dancers; . . . no fine madams—no jewelry—no eau de cologne—but negro girls, few of whom boasted shoes or stockings—most of them in their everyday rags, and everyday smell. This was the "real thing." How the band did work!—how they stamped, and wagged their heads in all the ecstacies of intense excitement, feeling full as much delight as the dancers. The figure of the dance was perhaps more apparent than before—*en avant deux*, the *retirez*, and what we should call a "set" to each other, the arms (holding the frock) wagging up and down, much as we see done in the negro dances on the stage. No one within the witchery of the music could keep still. Black nymphs, sleek as moles, showed by their contortions, how impossible it was. Arms involuntarily went up and down, and dark feet writhed like eels, whilst outside the legitimate circle a dozen couples were clandestinely profiting by the music to gratify their genuine negro propensities. This was dancing with *the soul* in it, and even the little black boys improved the occasion. I never could have imagined any thing so universal. St.

Vitus seemed to pervade the whole company. With respect to the music, a triangle was added to the instruments of the preceding "Joe and Johnny," and the "tump" was different in form to the first.

． ． ．

Christmas time is the grand saturnalia of the negroes of Barbuda. No work is done, and nothing goes on but dancing to the tum-tum from ten o'clock in the morning until nine at night.

． ． ．

One evening in Kingston (St. Vincent) I witnessed a "Willy" or jumbee dance, got up as an exhibition by an African Ebo negro. "De jumbee" was of course an imitation of the genuine. The spectators were chiefly negroes, as the majority of the whites, being hucksters, are interested in nothing beyond peddling. "De Jumpsa-man" was assisted by some of the Ebo soldiers of the negro regiment stationed here; two tum-tums, beating the dum call alloo, and five or six negro wenches from the Granadines singing an African chorus, and clapping their hands as an accompaniment. The Jumpsa-man was brought out of a negro hut on the shoulders of the soldiers, and being on stilts six feet high, fastened to his feet, was unable to assist himself, and was therefore placed upright by the wall. He was dressed in a guernsey-frock and a long striped trousers, made very wide, which concealed his feet. His face was covered with a mask of scarlet cloth, ornamented with cowrie shells; and having a huge wig and beard, with a grenadier's hairy cap on his head, he looked unearthly enough. The dance consisted of various contortions of the body sufficiently droll; for as the stilts had no supports of any sort, it was impossible for him to control his movements beyond preserving a perfect balance, which he maintained with great precision.

After having alternately amused and frightened the women for twenty minutes the Jumpsa-man was carried back to his hut: and then came the grand feat of the evening, which was to test his supernatural powers. A stout stick, about six feet long, held by four of the strongest men in the company, was, at a word from the Jumpsa-man, to fly out of their hands in spite of all their efforts. The stick was, with a great affectation of absence of all concealment paraded about amongst the spectators, with the offer that any one in the company might hold it. This two or three mulattoes volunteered to do, but somehow or other their evasions were made, and the *bâton* was finally intrusted to four stout confederates. The wizard, stripped of his mask, talked to the stick; the drums made a horrible noise, the singing ladies squalled to the top of their beut. Still the stick did not budge, and the magician looked non-plussed, and it was thought to be a dead failure, when suddenly din recommenced, the staff showed symptoms of yielding, and the men began to heave with their exertions to hold it. The struggle soon grew furious, the enchanted shillelah dragging its sable captors all over the yard; until at length, in spite of their efforts, it flew out of their hands and the powers of the magician were established. The sable spectators began to scratch their heads and look profound, convinced that there was evidently more in the thing than met the eye.

• • •

As we have heard something lately of negro melodies, I subjoin a genuine St. Kitts negro song, by Sam Matthews:

"Las' Saturday night, man,
A'cum na mi house, man,
A'no tink ponnoton (nothing),
As it down so softly,
Hungry da bang me (bang—vex)
I look 'pon de shelf, man.
I look for de ninyam (ninyam—food)
Sal'fish. Corn wangoo (cooked with boiled Indian corn)
Corn wangoo and callaloo (c—a sort of spinach)
Ya me da eat away;
I eat way 'pon ninyam—
Ninyam so sweet now—Eye, eye, a-a-ay!
Massa da calla me (call me),
He call me na great house (na—to). Ey-ey-a-a, etc.
I put by de ninyam,
Ya, me da go now;
He tell me: 'Mi boy now,
Cubenna, mi boy now (C.—his name)
You taka dis paper,
I go to mi massa
You run na Bastarre man (na—to; Bastarre (sic)—the capital of St. Kitts)
You gie Dactar Thompson,
Tomarrar morning you bring cum de hanswer!
Heart bin so vex now. Ey-ey-a-a-etc.
I taka de paper; I run na de great road,
I meet Dactar Thompson,
I meet um 'pon hos-back.
He redee de papar; he tell me; 'Mi boy now
Go 'lang you' homo (home);
Tomarrar morning, I send cum de hanswer:

Heart bin so glad now. Ey-ey-a-a-eye.
Yamee da run, man, yameedig, man (yamee—now here I am running)
I run na mi house, man!
I call 'pon mi wife, man!
I push-um—I shove um:
He won't gie no hanswer;
I wake um at las', man,
I tell um 'bout someting',
Someting da waalk de (de—there)
He walk na mi chamber.
He tell me: 'he b'lieve say de Jumbee. Ey-ey-a-a-etc.
I look for me bow-'tick (club or heavy stick)
Ya mi da lick wi' (which I beat with)
I lick 'way 'pon Jumbee,
Jumbee da bawl de'—Ey-ey-a-a-eye.
He jump na de back-door;
I meet Uncle Quacoo,
I tell um 'bout Jumbee;
Jumbee bin waalk de',
He waalk de' wi' shoe on!
He tell me, since he bin barn now,
He never bin hearee,
Jumbee could waalk de, and walk wi' de shoe on.
He tell me, he b'lieve say: 'Da, Massa!'
Ey-ey-a-a-eye.
Massa go killa me—oh!

ANONYMOUS, "Sketches in the West Indies," *Dublin University Magazine*, vol. 61 (1860), 613–14.

I have often been struck with the wild and picturesque appearance of the African and negro women who attend the drums and fife at tatoo. In the distance is heard the lonely surging of the sea; and in the pale moonlight approaches a band which, in its indistinctness, recalls the classical groups of Poussin. There is the clash of cymbals, the roll of the drum, the clear fifes; and in front of them all, with gestures of the most thorough *abandon*, and threading the endless maizes of their strange and graceful dance, with admirable regard to time, appears a company of bacchantes, whose light cloud-like flounces float about their somewhat luxuriant forms, and strange ringing laughter mingles with the clash of instruments, and the procession is again lost in the dim distance. . . .

On the occasion of the "John Canoe" these untaught danseuses acquit themselves to my taste, in a style infinitely more elegant than that of the Nautch girls of India. . . .

GREVILLE JOHN CHESTER, *Transatlantic Sketches* . . . (London, 1869), 80, 81–82.

The labouring classes in Barbados are badly off for amusements. Tops and marbles seem almost the only sports of the school-children, but when encouraged they take kindly to cricket. But it is hard to find places to play in, and parochial cricket clubs are either above or below the notice of the local clergy. Thus dancing is almost the only amusement, and the people dance well and gracefully. The low dancing-rooms, which may be opened by any profligate vagabond, are the disgrace and curse of the island; but *"Let ill alone"* is the motto in this as in other matters, and the local legislature is little likely to interfere. Sometimes a cottager in want of money will give a tea, charging a shilling entrance and the entertainment lasts till sunrise next morning. These teas lead to a great deal of immorality, and the evil is rather increased than lessened by the vociferous singing of the most sacred hymns throughout the whole night.

•   ■   •

A kind of harvest-home generally takes place at the end of the crop-gathering upon each estate. A cart laden with the last canes is drawn by mules decorated with ribbons, and attended by a crowd of labourers; the principal women being attired in white muslin. The mill and other estate buildings are gay with coloured kerchiefs which do duty as flags. Some ancient negro is put forward to make a speech to the planter, which he often does with considerable humour and address. Then the planter replies, and a glass of "falernum"—a beverage compounded of rum, lime-juice, and syrup—is handed round to each. Then dancing begins, and is carried on to a late hour to the sound of fiddles and a tambourine. Sometimes the proceedings are varied by the introduction of a "trash man," a figure, *i.e.* stuffed with cane trash and tied upon the back of a mule, which, being finally let loose, gallops about with his incongruous burden, to the great delight of the spectators.

HENRY G. MURRAY, *Manners and Customs of the Country a Generation Ago: Tom Kittle's Wake* (Kingston, Jamaica, 1877), 17.

It would take more time than we can afford here to go into a description of all the diversions with which the assembled mourners amused themselves, and pass off the night. "Hide and seek," "Hot bean well battered," "Thread the needle," "Beg you little water," &c., were played in their turns amidst much boisterous merriment. The notabilities to whom I am to introduce you did not arrive till late; and nobody would venture on a "Nancy Story" till "Red Head Thomas" came. In the meantime the fishermen who were there, after indulging in a good deal of "tall talk" on the perils incidental to their profession, struck up the song of their craft, while one man who sat astride an empty barrel—by beating the head of it with his hands—afforded instrumental accompaniment to the vocalists. This "John Joe," of whom they sang, was a sort of "Lightfingered Jack" among the fishermen, for his name survives in more ballads than one. But here goes (Sing)—

> "Me len him my canoe,
>   Him broke my paddle,
> John Joe widdle waddle.

> "Me len him my fish pot,
>   Him tief my net,
> John Joe, &c.

> "Me len him my harpoon,
>   Him tief my line,
> John Joe &c.

> "John Joe no hab
>   None hat pon him head,
> John Joe &c.

> "John Joe no hab
>   No shut pon him back,
> John Joe, &c.

> "Ef I catch John Joe
>   I wi broke him neck,
> John Joe &c."

L. D. POWLES, *The Land of the Pink Pearl or Recollections of Life in the Bahamas* (London, 1888), 147–49, 158–65.

... The darkies are fond of processions, and never miss an opportunity of getting one up.

About Christmas time they seem to march about day and night with lanterns and bands of music, and they fire off crackers. This is a terrible nuisance, but the custom has the sanction of antiquity, though no doubt it would have been put down long ago if the white young gentlemen had not exhibited a taste for the same amusement.

They are very fond of dancing, and I am afraid no amount of preaching or singing hymns will ever be able to put down the dance-houses, which are terrible thorns in the side of both magistrate and inspector of police.

A form of open-air dancing has also a great hold upon them. It is called a "fire-dance," and is, no doubt, a relic of savage life. I had heard so much about these fire-dances that I arranged with the sergeant of police to have one got up for my especial benefit. . . . The people formed a circle, and a fire was lighted in their midst. The music consisted of two drums that would not work unless frequently warmed at the fire. The company clapped their hands without ceasing all through the dance, chanting all the while in a sort of dreary monotone, "Oh kindoiah! kindoiah! (two African words) Mary come along!" When the dance was about half through, the refrain was suddenly changed to "Come down, come down," repeated over and over again with the same dreary monotone. Every now and then a man or a woman, or a couple together would rush into the centre of the circle and dance wildly about. There appeared to be no step or idea of figure about the performance, the aim and object of the dancers, as far as one could make it out, being to execute as many extravagant capers in and over, and around, and about the fire as they could without burning themselves. It was, in short, a savage African dance in European dress. Another evening Mr. James C. Smith and myself came suddenly upon one of these "fire dances"; on this occasion the refrain they sang was, "Go along, Yankee, poor old man."

• • •

The Africans rescued from the slave-ships brought with them from Africa the secret of making the genuine African thatch. I have been told that either they cannot or will not impart this secret, so that it will become a lost art when they die out. Some of the houses in Grant's Town, and one church are roofed with this thatch. Mr. Drysdale calls the latter "the handsomest roof on the inside that I ever saw, not even excepting one of our own church buildings." I never saw it myself.

This church belongs to a sect popularly known as "The Shouters," but whose proper title, so my orderly, Carey, informed me, was "The African Methodist Episcopal Church." I never got as far as the Shouters myself, but it is a favourite amusement among the winter visitors at the hotel to get up parties to go to the Shouter church on a Sunday evening.

Hymn-singing is the great feature of their service, and some of their hymns are of the most extraordinary description. The following collection I got partly from my boys whilst sailing on circuit, partly from my cook, Mrs. Malvina Whitehead. The first three are called "antems" as distinguished from hymns. I have already given Mr. Carey's definition of the two, but as far as I can make out the difference between them consists in that in the case of the antem the refrain is repeated after every line.

> "Hail, King ob de Jews!
> Oh, yes, it is Jesus, my Lord!
> I come to worship Thee!
> Oh yes, etc.
> Look ober yonder what I see!
> Oh, yes, etc.
> See dem children rise and fall!
> Oh, yes, etc.
> If de Lord Jesus gib to we!
> Oh, yes, etc.
> De wings ob an eagle, I fly way!
> Oh, yes, etc.
> De tallest tree in Paradise!
> Oh, yes, etc.
> Christian, call it tree ob life!
> Oh, yes, etc.
> Lot's wife turn to pillar ob salt!
> Oh, yes, etc.
> Run along Moses, don't get late!
> Oh, yes, etc.
> Before Lord Jesus, shut de gate,
> Oh, yes, etc."

■   ■   ■

> "You may talk, talk, talk, you may talk deceitful talk!
> When de general roll is called may I be dar!
> Yes, I'll be dar!
> Yes, I'll be dar!
> When de general roll is called may I be dar!
> You may laugh, laugh, laugh, you may laugh deceitful laugh.
> When de general roll, etc. etc.
> You may tink, tink, tink, you may tink deceitful things!
> When de general roll, etc. etc.
> Fine trees grow, grow, grow, dey grow in Paradise!
> When de general roll, etc. etc.
> King Jesus, tell, tell, tell, He tell me once before,
> When de general roll, etc. etc.
> To go, go, go in peace and sin no more!
> When de general roll, etc. etc."

■ ■ ■

"Unbeliever, don't you hear de hammer ring!
De hammer ring! De hammer ring!
Unbeliever, don't you hear de hammer ring!
Dat nail Him to de tree!"

Every succeeding verse is exactly the same, substituting "Blasphemer," "Backbiter," "Liar," "Slanderer," "Drunkard," and so on, for the first word.

It must not be imagined that the above are complete editions of these *"antems,"* for the singers improvise as they go along, and never stop until they are fairly exhausted.

A favorite amusement is to sit in a circle and sing the following chorus, taking the company's names all round. If the name is popular, he is "always ready when de bridegroom come." If the reverse, then he is "nebber ready when de bridegroom come." Sometimes opinions differ, and a certain amount of feeling is excited.

"Brudder _____ he always ready when de Bridegroom come!
Brudder _____ he always ready when de Bridegroom come!
Brudder _____ he always ready when de Bridegroom come!
Oh, my! dars no <u>sighing</u>
When de Bridegroom come."

I never was able to make out whether the word in italics (underlined here) was "sighing," "saying," or "Zion." I have distinctly heard all three, but though I have often asked which it was, I never could get an answer. For some reason or other, probably because they think you are making fun of them, they will not tell you anything about these hymns, for which they seem to rely entirely upon oral tradition. They will sing for you as long as you please, but you cannot induce them to repeat the words. The only way I could get hold of a great part of my collection was by constantly standing by, note-book in hand, whilst they were singing.*

The following is a favorite chorus:

"Oh, what'll I do when de lamp go out?
When de lamp go out? When de lamp go out?
Oh, what'll I do when de lamp go out?
What will I do dat day?
Oh, I want to see my Jesus when de lamp go out!
When de lamp go out, when de lamp go out!
So I'll send for my elder when de lamp go out!
Dat what I'll do dat day!

*That is whilst sailing on circuit.

Mr. Willshere, the superintendent minister of Baptist Missions, is deservedly a great favourite among them. For some reason he is always called "Fader Willshere"—a somewhat peculiar title for a Baptist clergyman—and it is very common to substitute his name as the doctor of souls who is to be called in "When the lamp goes out."

The following hymn contains about twenty-five verses. It was a great favourite with Theophilus Rolle, mate of the *Eastern Queen* during my first voyage. Often as I have heard him sing it, I could never catch more than the first verse.

> "When I go down to de wood for to pray,
>   Ole Satan, he say to me,
> You Jesus dead, and de Lord, he gone away,
>   And he no hear you pray!
> Oh, Lord, remember me! oh, Lord, remember me!
>   Remember me as de year roll round!
> Oh, Lord, remember me' "

The following also pass for hymns:

> "I am climbing Jacob's ladder;
> I am going higher and higher!
> I am climbing higher and higher,
>   Soldier ob de Cross."
>
> Chorus.
> "D'you tink I'se climbing higher and higher!
>   Soldier ob de Cross!"
>
> "Day star is arising!
> Tell de Lord I'se coming!
> Gabriel, blow de trumpet!
> Soldier ob de Cross."
>
> Repeat Chorus.
>
> "I'd rather pray my life away!
>   Oh! oh! oh!
> Dan go to hell and burn away!"
>
> Chorus.
>
> "Save me, Lord, from sinking down!
>   Oh! oh! oh!
> Save me, Lord, from sinking down!
>
> I had a book, 'twas gib to me!
>   Save me, Lord, from sinking down!
> And every line convicted me!"

Repeat Chorus.

"Ole Satan make a catch at me!
  Oh! oh! oh!
He miss my soul and catch my sins."

Repeat Chorus.

"I had a book, 'twas gib to me!
  Save me, Lord, from sinking down!
In every line was victory!"

Repeat Chorus.

"Tell me, Lord, shall I be dar now?
  To sit on Zion Hill,
Wrestle wid de angels,
  Till de break ob day?
Tell me, Lord, shall I be dar?
  Sit on Zion Hill all night,
And take a wrestle wid de angels?
  All night! All night!
Till de break ob day!
Oh, tell me, God, shall I be dar now?
Oh, tell me, God, shall I be dar now?
Oh, tell me, God, shall I be dar now?
Sit on Zion Hill!
  Wrestle wid de angels!
All night! All night!
  Till de break ob day!

Ole Satan say he no go way;
He hab my soul de judgment day!
I rather pray my life away!
Dan go to hell and spend one day!
  Carry de news! carry de news!
Sister, carry, carry the news!
  I'se bound to glory.
Go, carry de news!
Go, carry de news!
Go, carry de news!
  I'se bound to glory!

Come along, my sister, come along!
Come along, my sister, come along!
  De angels say dars noting to do
    But ring dat charming bell.
We'se almost gone, we'se almost gone,

But de angels say dars noting to do
But ring that charming bell!
Come, my sister, etc."[†]

ANONYMOUS, *A Short Journey to the West Indies, in which are Interspersed, Curious Anecdotes and Characters* (London, 1890), 87–91.

Philantropos was beginning to grow warm in delivering his sentiments when the overseer came to tell me that the negroes were dancing in honor of my arrival, and we went to enliven them with our presence.

A ring is formed in front of which they who wish to dance, place themselves—a woman is singled out by a beau-man, who exhibit all their powers of grace and activity—sometimes there are two men [who] dance with one woman; they follow, fan her with their handkerchiefs, court her and leave her alternately, and make you understand as perfectly as any ballet-master in Europe, what they mean.

The beau-men and beau-girls who are the chief dancers, are usually very finely dressed; they are but a small number, in comparison with the others, who keep back and join to sing for them. I was much surprised at the extravagance of some of their dresses, when I was let into the secret by Philanthropos:—"These beau-girls, said he, are the

---

[†]These shouting hymns are sometimes performed in the court of the hotel for the amusement of the visitors. Amongst the performers on these occasions, two boys, nicknamed "Moody" and "Sankey," were especially famous for a sort of sacro-comic duet and dance. "Moody" had disappeared before my time, but "Sankey" still survived. This hopeful, whose real name is Thaddeus de Warsaw Toot, is one of the cleverest young rascals I ever met. He is about fourteen years of age, and might be trained to anything, and I feel convinced if the enterprising Augustus Harris could see him, he would at once import him for Drury Lane. He has now gone out of the sacro-comic duet and dance line of business, and does odd jobs—good or bad is all the same to Sankey—for any one who will employ him. His best quality is fidelity to his employer for the time being, for when he lets himself out to any one he sells himself body and soul, and is incorruptible. As soon as he passes into another employment he transfers his fidelity, and would have no scruple about robbing his old master on behalf of his new one. He was once done whilst I was in Nassau, and the way he revenged himself was characteristic. Being sent with five shillings to buy sponges, he purchased a boxful from a man who sold him a lot of old pieces covered over with a layer of good sponges. Sankey was terribly crestfallen, but to retrieve his character he followed that man about till he saw him in the act of receiving five shillings. Sankey cut in like a knife, collared the money, with which he refused to part on any terms until he received the balance of sponges due to him. In a civilized country he would probably rise to a good position, or go for a long term of penal servitude. In earlier times he might have concluded a short, but brilliant, career upon the gallows!

mistresses of the overseers, and other white men, who think they can not be too lavish in adorning their persons—the beau-men are the favorites of the beau-girls, who secretly furnish them at the expense of their keepers." The music of these poor creatures has a wildness that finds a way to the heart—none of their rude instruments could produce any very pleasing effect, without the assistance of their voices, but so supported, the Banjaw, the Goombay, the Jawpone, inspire mirth and alacrity.

The Negroes are famous for the justness of their ear:—at their dances a few of them sing the tune first in a slender tone, and then the others join in chorus to repeat it loudly.

The moments appeared to glide away in forgetfulness, the approaching labour of the morning did not seem to interrupt their mirth, and I left them still dancing at two o'clock.

J. VAN SERTIMA, *Scenes and Sketches of Demarara Life*
(Georgetown, Demerara, 1899), 99–102.

When the great festal day does not fall on a Sunday, the slumberer is awakened by some music and much noise on the streets at any time between midnight and four o'clock in the morning, and small chance is there for him to dose off again in quietude, for the drum-beaters are nothing if not energetic and the musicians are nothing if not merry. There is a law here, I believe, for the suppression of the drum, but on such a joyous day as this, custom and inclination rule, and our policemen are forgiving. The street band is accompanied by a motley procession of people whose especial business, it seems is to arouse the whole city, and make grand acclaim touching the advent of the illustrious annual visitor. Sometimes in concert, oft times in confusion, drum and flute, cornet and clarionet, shac-shac and steel, tom-tom and tambourine proclaim the happy morn, while high above all, in dismal diapason, *vox humana* dins into your ear such proclamation as this:

> Chris'mas ma'nin' come again,
> An' I ent get no cawfee wata.

On such a day as this "cawfee wata," or even coffee, is taboo. The people's "wanity" (to use a Wallerism) is much stronger, and in the plenitude of their patriotism they revel in rum,—rum of colonial manufacture. . . . These merry-makers go by, and anon other merry makers, equally high-spirited come forward, all stir and sound signifying a season of frolic and festivity and rejoicing. Guitars and other stringed instruments also.

■   ■   ■

Meanwhile, throughout the day, the street bands are in perpetual evidence, more particularly in the eastern part of the city. Most they congregate in the vicinity of the rum shops, the owners of which provide liquor for the "Musicianers" as the common people call them. The shops themselves are gay with flags and bunting. . . . Here and there, about the streets, may be seen some buffoons with costumes *a la* circus clown, astride of stilts, for the people's amusement; and maskers with grotesque habiliments to teach the little ones excellence of beauty, by contrast.

SIR G. WILLIAM DES VOEUX, *Experiences of a Demerara Magistrate* (Georgetown: Argosy, 1948), (reprint of first 9 chapters of *My Colonial Service* [London, 1903]), 4–5.

As I was destined to spend a large proportion of the next four years in them, it may be as well to give here a short description of the boats used for travelling in Guiana by Europeans and the upper class of coloured people. Constructed usually of silverballi (one of the few woods of the country at once hard, durable, and light), they have four to six oars, and are undecked, a space of from seven to eight feet towards the stern being covered by a "tent" of wood. Side awnings protect from sun and rain, while for sleeping removable planks are fitted level with the seats, under which are the lockers for stores. Behind the tent a length of about three feet is uncovered in which sits the "cox." In his absence the boat can be steered from the tent. The rowers were usually negroes or "coloured men," who, when they got away from town and drink, showed marvellous endurance. I have known them of their own accord labour steadily at the oars for sixteen to eighteen hours, with scarcely any intermission, when they had any special desire to reach their destination quickly. At first when they began to tire I used to give them spirit, but I soon found by experience that this was worse than useless. It put some additional life into the stroke for a short time, but always caused a very quick collapse afterwards. At night the pace was increased when they sang in chorus. The songs, usually led by a Barbadian negro, were much of a kind described in Marryat's *Peter Simple,* remarkable neither for sense nor tune. Only one of the songs, as far as I remember, had in it anything approaching to melody. That was the Union battle-song of "John Brown," with the refrain of "Glory, hallelujah, as we go marching on." And even that reiterated many times, became, to say the least, monotonous; especially during the night hours when sleep in view of the next day's work was desirable. But however wanting in other respects, this singing was always in good time and no doubt lightened the labour, as it seemed absolutely essential to good going; . . .

7

Miscellaneous: Domestic Life, Work Conditions, Dress, Housing, Body Modifications, Weddings, Medicine, Rebellions, Discipline

CHARLES LESLIE, *A New and Exact Account of Jamaica*, 3d ed. (London, 1740), 322–23.

Their Owners set aside for each a small Parcel of Ground, and allow them the *Sundays* to manure it: In it they generally plant Maiz, *Guiney* Corn, Plantanes, Yams, Cocoes, Potatoes, &c. This is the Food which supports them, unless some of them who are more industrious than others, happen to raise a Stock of Fowls, which they carry to Markets on the *Sundays* (which is the only Market-day in *Jamaica*) and sell for a little Money, with which they purchase Salt-Beef or Pork to make their *Oglios* or Pepper-Pot. 'Tis surprising to see the mean Shifts to which these poor Creatures are reduced: You'll see them daily about 12 o'Clock, when they turn in from Work, till Two, scraping the Dung-hills at every Gentleman's Door for Bones, which, if they are so happy as to find, they break extremely small, boil them, and eat the Broth. The most of the Slaves are brought from the Coast of *Guiney;* when they first arrive, 'tis observed they are simple and very innocent Creatures, but they soon turn to be roguish enough: And when they come to be whipt, urge the Example of the Whites for an Excuse.

J. G. STEDMAN, *Narrative of a Five Years' Expedition against the Revolted Negroes of Surinam* (Amherst: University of Massachusetts Press, 1971 [1796]), 360–61.

I have formerly mentioned the names of more than a dozen of negro tribes; all these know each other by the different marks and incisions made on their bodies—for instance, the Coromantyn negroes, who are

most esteemed, cut three or four long gashes on each of their cheeks,
. . .

The *Loango* negroes, who are reckoned the worst, distinguish themselves by puncturing or marking the skin of their sides, arms, and thighs with square elevated figures, something like dice. These also cut their fore-teeth to a sharp point, which gives them a frightful appearance, resembling in some degree those of a shark: and all their males are circumcised, after the manner of the Jews.

Among the strange productions of nature, a species of people known by the name of *Accorees* deserves to be particularly noticed.— The *Accorees*, or Two-fingers, live amongst the Seramaca negroes, in the very upper parts of the river of that name. This heterogeneous tribe are so deformed in their hands and feet, that while some have three or four fingers and toes on each hand and foot, others have only two, which resemble the claws of a lobster, or rather limbs that have been cured after mutilation by fire, or some other accident. This deformity in one person would cause but small admiration; but that a whole community should be afflicted with this singularity, is certainly a most wonderful phenomenon. Having seen but *two* myself, and that at too great a distance to take a drawing of them, I cannot pretend to vouch for the truth of what I have only heard; but an engraving of one of these figures was positively sent to the Society of Arts and Sciences at *Haerlem;* while I beg leave to introduce, as a further voucher, the following extract from an old book of surgery and anatomy, procured me by the ingenious and learned *Owen Cambridge,* Esquire, of *Twickenham.*

> After Michaelmas term, in the year 1629, a body was brought from the place of execution to the College of Physicians, to be cut up for an anatomy; and by chance the officer of the college brought the body of a cruel wretch, who had murdered the son of one Master Scot, a surgeon of good note in this city. This wretch was of a very truculent countenance and aspect; his hair was black and curled, not very long, but thick and bushy; his forehead little above an inch high; his brows great and prominent; his eyes set deep in their sockets, his nose crooked, with a round knob or button at the end, which also somewhat turned upwards; on his upper lip he had some quantity of black hair, on his chin very few, straggling, black, and stiff; and his nether lip was as big as three lips. Such was his face; but the greatest deformity was his feet, and that almost to admiration; for they were both cloven, but not alike. One foot was equally divided between four and five inches deep into two toes, jointed like other men's toes, but as large each of them as half the foot could make them, with nails proportionable. The left foot was divided

likewise in the middle, but the division was not above three inches deep, or scarce so much; the one half which was towards the body, made one large toe, with a nail proportionable, like the inward half of the right foot; but the outward half was compounded of two toes, yet growing close and fast together. This monstrous shape of a man I have thought good to give this relation of, from certain knowledge, for there were a thousand witnesses of it present.

JOHN LUFFMAN, *A Brief Account of the Island of Antigua* (London, 1789), 94–97, 99–100, 102–05, 107, 114–16.

The weekly allowance of a field negro, is from three to five quarts of horse beans, rice, or Indian corn, with three or four salt herrings, or a piece of salted beef or pork, of about two pounds weight; but when the estates have such provisions as yams, eddas, guinea corn, sweet potatoes, plantains, and bananas, they are served in lieu of the former, and as nearly as possible in the same proportion. In addition to this allowance, every slave on a plantation, whether male or female, when they have attained their 14th or 15th year, has a piece of ground, from twenty five, to thirty feet square, allotted to them, which by some is industriously and advantageously cultivated, and by others totally neglected. These patches are found to be of material benefit to the country, their produce principally supplying the Sunday market (which is the greatest throughout the week, from being the negroes holiday) with vegetables. They are also allowed to raise pigs, goats, and fowls, and it is by their attention to these articles, that the whites are prevented from starving, during such times of the year as vessels cannot come to these coasts with safety.

The clothing of a field slave consists of a blanket, which serves them not only to sleep upon (tho' some have beds of dried plantain leaves), but to fasten about their bodies in damp weather, also a piece of woolen cloth, called a babbaw, which goes round the waist, a blue woollen jacket, and a party colored cap, of the same material. Their drink, as per allowance, is water. When sick they are attended by young doctors, whose principals contract with the owners of estates, or their attorney's, by the year, and the common price is six-shillings currency, equal to three-shillings and nine-pence sterling, per head. It is the business of these assistants to visit the estates, thus put under the care of their employers, twice a week, and on every plantation is an hospital or sick-house, where the slaves, as soon as infected with disorder, or having received hurt (the latter of which frequently happens in crop time) are sent. These places, at least such as have come within my observation, are as bad as you can well suppose, being not only destitute of almost every convenience, but filthy in the extreme, and the attendants generally such negroes as are nearly superannuated or unfit for active employment. I am much surprised how the medical gentlemen, even in the manner this business is performed, can make it pay the expenses attending thereon, at so small a premium, and indeed, I think it is impossible for them to get the keep of one of their horses out of these undertakings although they should make use of the very cheapest drugs that can be procured, or, if even only of medicinal simples, the growth of the island.

■   ■   ■

LETTER XXIII

To _____

St. John's, Antigua,
Oct. 3, 1787.

Dear Sir,

The negroes are turned out at sun rise, and employed in gangs from twenty to sixty, or upwards, under the inspection of white overseers, generally poor Scotch lads, who, by their assiduity and industry, frequently become masters of the plantations, to which they came out as indentured servants: subordinate to these overseers, are drivers, commonly called dog-drivers, who are mostly black or mulatto fellows, of the worst dispositions; these men are furnished with whips, which, while on duty, they are obliged, on pain of severe punishment, to have with them, and are authorized to flog wherever they see the least relaxation from labor; nor is it a consideration with them, whether it proceeds from idleness or inability, paying, at the same time, little or no regard to age or sex. At twelve they are turned in (that is, leave off work) to get what they can to refresh nature with; at half past one the bell rings, when they turn out and resume their labor until sun set; for the last hour they are chiefly employed in picking grass for the cattle, belonging to the estate, and when a sufficiency is collected for that purpose, they gather what they can for themselves, pack it up in bundles, which they carry to Saint John's, on their heads, and sell for one or more dogs, according to the quantity or demand for it.

■   ■   ■

LETTER XXIV

To _____

St. John's, Antigua,
Nov. 9, 1787.

Dear Sir,

The punishments inflicted on slaves, in this island, are various and tormenting. The picket, is the most severe, but as its consequences are well known in Europe, particularly among the military, I shall speak no further upon it, than to say it is seldom made use of here, but many other cruelties equally destructive to life, though slower in their operations, are practiced by the unfeeling, among which is the thumb-screw, a barbarous invention to fasten the thumbs together, which appears to cause excruciating pain. The iron necklace, is a ring, locked or rivetted about the neck; to these collars are frequently added what are here termed pot-hooks, additions, resembling the hooks or handles of a porridge pot, fixed perpendicularly, the bent or hooked parts turning outwards, which prevents the wearers from laying down their heads with any degree of comfort. The boots are strong iron rings, full four inches in circumference, closed just above the ankles, to these some owners prefix a chain, which the miserable sufferers, if able to work, must manage as well as they can, and it is not unfrequent to see in the streets of this town, at mid-day, negroes chained together by these necklaces as well as by the boots, when let out of their dungeon for a short time to breath the fresh air, whose crime has been endeavoring to gain that liberty by running away, which they well knew could never be otherwise obtained from their owners. The spurs are rings of iron, similar to the boots, to which are added spikes from three to four inches long, placed horizontally. A chain fastened about the body with a padlock, is another mode of tormenting this oppressed race of beings. A boy who has not yet seen his fourteenth year, passes by my house several times in a day, and has done so for these six months past, with no other cloathing, he also lays upon his chains, and although they are as much in point of weight as he ought reasonably to carry, yet he is obliged, through the day to fetch water from the country pond at the distance of half a mile from the house of his mistress, who is an old widow-woman. To the chains thus put on, a fifty pounds weight is sometimes added, as an appendage; this is undoubtedly a prudent measure, and admirably well calculated to keep the slave at home, as it must of course prevent the object thus secured, from escaping the rigor of his destiny. The bilboes, severe floggings, and sundry other methods of torturing these unhappy people, as best suits the caprice or inventive cruelty of their owners or employers, are here inflicted. The public whipper is a white man, who executes his office by a negro deputy, and the price for every flogging is two bits.

■ ■ ■

Slaves, for criminal offences, have within these few years, been admitted to a trial by a jury of six white men, at which proceedings two justices preside as judges. They are seldom hanged, unless for murder, it being the interest of the owners of such as are convicted, to get them off, the country allowing the masters but half the appraised value of such as are executed; they are therefore in mitigation generally flogged under the gallows, and sometimes sent off the island to be sold.

I remain, &c. &c.

■ ■ ■

LETTER XXVI

To _____

St. John's, Antigua,
Jan. 1, 1788.

Dear Sir,

The general idea of Europeans, that blacks only are slaves, is very erroneous, for slavery extends to every descendant of negroes (slaves) by white men, such as mulattoes, mestees and quarteroons, and the two latter mentioned, are frequently as fair as Englishmen, at least such of them as have been habituated to a sea-faring life, or to tropical countries. I have seen persons sold here, having blue eyes and flaxen-hair, and complexioned equal almost to any on your side the water, but such people fetch a lower price than blacks, unless they are tradesmen, because the purchasers cannot employ them in the drudgeries to which negros are put too; the colored men, are therefore mostly brought up to trades or employed as house slaves, and the women of this description are generally prostitutes. When taken into keeping by white men, they dress in a very ridiculous manner, assuming the name of their keeper for the time being, and laying it aside when turned off. There are persons in this island who let out their female slaves for the particular purpose of fornication, and that, as well as publickly cohabiting with them, is considered here merely as a venial error. These women are much more subservient to the will of their enamoratos, from a dread of punishment than a white would be, or even the laws of the country suffer, for it is not uncommon for some men to beat, and otherwise severely correct their colored mistresses. This connexion strikes at the root of honorable engagements with the fair, prevents marriages, and is, thereby, detrimental to the increase of legitimate population.

WILLIAM BECKFORD, *A Descriptive Account of the Island of Jamaica* (London, 1790), vol. I, 227–33, 254–57.

There is a pleasing bustle among the negroes, when they prepare to leave their huts, and to visit their grounds in the morning; when their different families, of various ages, sizes, and complexions (white excepted), put their little caravans, if I may so call them, into motion; and anticipate, with hoes, bills, and baskets, their approaching labour, or the loads of plenty with which they are to return.

The stir and impatience that is observed among their houses, with their picturesque appearance among the trees and shrubs with which they are surrounded, (and which mark with penquins, or other productions, the extent of their bounds) may be carried from nature to the easel, and produce a variety of features and of attitudes, and with such corresponding accompaniments, as would not have disgraced the pencil of Teniers, or the accurate imitation of Du Sart.

A negro village is full of those picturesque beauties in which the Dutch painters have so much excelled; and is very particularly adapted to the expression of those situations, upon which the scenes of rural dance and merriment may be supposed with the greatest conveniency to have happened. The forms and appearances of the houses admit of every variety which this particular species of rural imagery requires; and the surrounding objects of confined landscape, with the vulgar adjuncts of hogs, poultry, cats, baskets, chairs, and stools, are always at hand to fill up the canvas, and to give sense to nature, and truth and novelty to the representation of the scene.

Some of the villages of the negroes are built in strait lines, and some are confusedly huddled together; but those are infinitely the most picturesque that are surrounded, as many are (particularly those which have not been visited and destroyed by the late storms), by plantain, coco-nut trees, and shrubs. The houses consist of a hall in the middle, to which there are generally two doors, one opposite the other: and in this hall they cook their victuals, sit, chat, and smoak; nor do they hardly ever leave it without a fire. The sleeping-rooms have a communication with this general apartment; and are in number, according to the consequence of the inhabitant, either two, three, or four; one of which is sometimes floored, and sometimes adorned with a Venetian window. In the garden behind them is often another hut, which serves for buttery, store-house, stock-house, or a general repository: and, independently of these, they have pigsties enclosed, and hogs in proportion to their credit and condition.

The negro-houses are situated as near as possible to a river, or a spring; as it is of consequence to the comforts and necessities of those who inhabit them, that they should have the easy convenience of clean and wholesome water; and that of Jamaica is not surpassed, particularly near or at no great distance from the source, by this element, for pureness, coolness, and spirit, in any part of the habitable world.

Upon the banks of these rivers a great variety of picturesque groups is occasionally observed. Some negroes are seen diving into the springs, some washing themselves, and some their clothes. Some, the children in particular, are seen to dive like fish under the arches, over which is conducted the water that turns the mill; some stand upon the edges of the wooden bridge (which is scarcely elevated above the current), and receive the splashes of those below. They sometimes take a circuit upon the banks, and then plunge one after another into the running stream: and these gambols of the children I have often looked upon with perseverance and delight; and they are such as Pollenberg might have imitated without any degradation of his taste or art.

Those negroes that are born upon estates abundant in water, very soon become almost amphibious; and it is astonishing to see to what depths they will dive, from what cataracts descend, and for how long a time they will continue submerged without the necessity of aspiration: and of this I shall give some remarkable instances, when I come to treat of their river-fishing.

The negro children of both sexes very soon become expert divers, and able swimmers; and if it be considered at what a very tender age they venture into danger, it is astonishing to think how seldom an accident is known to happen. Sometimes, indeed, in the rainy seasons, and when the rivers are on a sudden rise, they are carried away, if they be too far distant from the mother's eye and out of other protection, by the swell and impetuosity of the torrents; and for this reason I think they should not be suffered to attend them, when they are obliged to go from home to wash, or to attend to other avocations.

Two or three coco-nut or orange trees adjoining to a negro's hut, are a little fortune; and I think it a pity that they are not encouraged in, rather than discouraged from, the plantation of different fruits. Some people have an idea, that, if the negro-houses be surrounded with clumps of vegetation, they may carry on every species of villainy without reserve; and to counteract which, they are in many places entirely exposed: nor do I find that this practice has ever removed the evils complained of; for the negroes are not better now, than when it was the custom to have their habitations entirely concealed. The houses are not now so picturesque as they formerly were; nor do I believe that they are more healthy; for the more the negroes are defended from air, the better will they, in general, be in health and spirits: for when they go to their grounds, or turn out to work in the morning, they very sensibly feel the alteration of the chilly air, when opposed to the warmth of their fires; and you see them tremble admist the dews and shiver to the breeze, with as much feeling as you observe represented in the tremors of the peasantry in colder climates.

As many of the negro-grounds are at a considerable distance from the plantation, in their journey thither may be observed many very pleasing and romantic situations, alternately varied by mountains and by dells, by water and by trees, and by many other enchanting varieties of rural imagery, that are peculiarly observable in the sequestered and the silent spots of that romantic region.

You now perceive a string of negroes in their matin march, while the vapours smoak around (having the first with deliberate caution bound up their clothes), one after the other wade through the head of a spring, part of which is fordable, though deep; and the depth of which is in other parts unfathomable; and the waters of which are as pellucid as crystal, and as cool as ice.

■　■　■

I suppose the negroes to be now arrived in their grounds, and to spread themselves, according to their connexions, over the face of the mountains, the trees of which have been recently felled for copperwood and lime, and selecting such spots, upon the elevations and bottoms, as are best adapted to their provisions; and a description of which, with their peculiar manner of planting, and the system and period of cultivation, will be minutely noticed, when I come to consider those productions which are only inferior to the sugar-cane in profit and use.

Where they collect themselves into groups upon some retired spot, from which the wood has not been cleared, and have to work their way amongst the withes, the bushes, and the rocks, they sometimes throw themselves into picturesque and various attitudes; and as the different clumps of vegetation begin to fall around them, the light is gradually induced, and shines in playful reflections upon their naked bodies and their clothes; and which oppositions of black and white make a very singular, and very far from an unpleasing, appearance. Their different instruments of husbandry, particularly their gleaming hoes, when uplifted to the sun, and which, particularly when they are digging cane-holes, they frequently raise all together, and in as exact time as can be observed, in a well-conducted orchestra, in the bowing of the fiddles, occasion the light to break in momentary flashes around them.

Some of their grounds are adjoining to roads and paths, and some are buried in the bosoms of the most sequestered dells; in many of which are seen to arise majestic trees of an amazing height and thickness, and which are not, excepting by strength and too often by bodily danger, to be levelled to the ground. This tedious occupation is left to the men, who very frequently fall a sacrifice to their exertions: indeed I have heard instances quoted, where several at a time have been crushed to death by the fall of a single tree.

When a tract of negro-provisions is regularly planted, is well cultivated, and kept clean, it makes a very husbandlike and beautiful appearance; and it is astonishing what quantities of the common necessaries of life it will produce. A quarter of an acre of this description will be fully sufficient for the supply of a moderate family, and may enable the proprietor to carry some to market besides; but then the land must be of a productive quality, be in a situation that cannot fail of seasons, be sheltered from the wind, and protected from the trespass of cattle, and the theft of negroes.

If a small portion of land of this description will give such returns, a very considerable number of acres, if not attended to, will, on the contrary, yield but little: and those negroes will hardly ever have good grounds, and of consequence a plenty of provisions, who are not allowed to make for themselves a choice of situation, and who are not well assured that it will be guarded and protected.

MATTHEW GREGORY LEWIS, *Journal of a West India Proprietor*
(London, 1834), 96–97, 100–02, 115–16, 119–20, 164–65, 181–83,
215–17.

January 13 [1816]
I have just had an instance strikingly convincing of the extreme
nicety required in rearing negro children. Two have been born since
my arrival. My housekeeper was hardly ever out of the lying-in apartment; I always visited it myself once a day, and sometimes twice, in
order that I might be certain of the women being well taken care of;
not a day passed without the inspection of a physician; nothing of indulgence, that was proper for them, was denied; and, besides their
ordinary food, the mothers received every day the most nourishing
and palatable dish that was brought to my own table. Add to this, that
the women themselves were kindhearted creatures, and particularly
anxious to rear these children, because I had promised to be their
godfather myself. Yet, in spite of all this attention and indulgence, one
of the mothers, during the nurse's absence for ten minutes, grew
alarmed at her infant's apparent sleepiness. To rouse it, she began
dancing and shaking it till it was in a strong perspiration, and then she
stood with it for some minutes at an open window, while a strong
north wind was blowing. In consequence, it caught cold, and the next
morning symptoms of a locked jaw showed itself. The poor woman
was the image of grief itself: she sat on her bed, looking at the child
which lay by her side with its little hands clasped, its teeth clenched,
and its eyes fixed, writhing in the agony of the spasm, while she was
herself quite motionless and speechless, although the tears trickled
down her cheeks incessantly. All assistance was fruitless: her thought-
lessness for five minutes had killed the infant, and at noon to-day it
expired.

This woman was a tender mother, had borne ten children, and
yet has now but one alive: another, at present in the hospital, has
borne seven, and but one has lived to puberty; and the instances of
those who have had four, five, six children, without succeeding in
bringing up one, in spite of the utmost attention and indulgence, are
very numerous; so heedless and inattentive are the best-intentioned
mothers, and so subject in this climate are infants to dangerous complaints. The locked jaw is the common and most fatal one; so fatal,
indeed, that the midwife (the *graundee* is her negro appellation) told
me, the other day, "Oh, massa, till nine days over, we *no hope* of
them." Certainly care and kindness are not adequate to save the chil-

dren, for the son of a sovereign could not have been more anxiously well treated than was the poor little negro, who died this morning.

.   .   .

The Africans (as is well known) generally believe, that there is a life beyond this world, and that they shall enjoy it by returning to their own country; and this idea used frequently to induce them, soon after their landing in the colonies, to commit suicide; but this was never known to take place except among fresh negroes, and since the execrable slave-trade has been abolished, such an illusion is unheard of. As to those who had once got over the dreadful period of "seasoning," they were generally soon sensible enough of the amelioration of their condition, to make the idea of returning to Africa the most painful that could be presented to them. But, to be sure, poor creatures! what with the terrors and sufferings of the voyage, and the unavoidable hardships of the seasoning, those advantages were purchased more dearly than any in this life can possibly be worth. God be thanked, all that is now at an end; and certainly, as far as I can as yet judge, if I were now standing on the banks of Virgil's Lethe, with a goblet of the waters of oblivion in my hand, and asked whether I chose to enter life anew as an English labourer or a Jamaica negro, I should have no hesitation in preferring the latter. For myself, it appears to be almost worth surrendering the luxuries and pleasures of Great Britain, for the single pleasure of being surrounded with beings who are always laughing and singing, and who seem to perform their work with so much *nonchalance,* taking up their baskets as if it were perfectly optional whether they took them up or left them there; sauntering along with their hands dangling; stopping to chat with every one they meet; or if they meet no one, standing still to look round, and examine whether there is nothing to be seen that can amuse them, so that I can hardly persuade myself that it is really *work* that they are about. The negro might well say, on his arrival in England— "Massa, in England every thing work!" for here nobody appears to work at all.

I am told that there is one part of their business very laborious, the digging holes for receiving the cane-plants, and which I have not as yet seen; but this does not occupy above a month (I believe) at the utmost, at two periods of the year; and on my estate this service is chiefly performed by extra negroes, hired for the purpose; which, although equally hard on the hired negroes (called a jobbing gang), at least relieves my own, and after all, puts even the former on much the same footing with English day-labourers.

.   .   .

January 19 [1816]

A young mulatto carpenter, belonging to Horace Beckford's estate of Shrewsbury, came to beg my intercession with his overseer. He had been absent for two days without leave, and on these occasions it is customary for the slaves to apply to some neighbouring gentleman for a note in their behalf, which, as I am told, never fails to obtain the pardon required, as the managers of estates are in general but too happy to find an excuse for passing over without punishment any offences which are not very heinous; indeed, what with the excellent laws already enacted for the protection of the slaves, and which every year are still further ameliorated, and what with the difficulty of procuring more negroes—(which can now only be done by purchasing them from other estates),—which makes it absolutely necessary for the managers to preserve the slaves, if they mean to preserve their own situations,—I am fully persuaded that instances of tyranny to negroes are now very rare, at least in this island. But I must still acknowledge, from my own sad experience, since my arrival, that unless a West-Indian proprietor occasionally visit his estates himself, it is utterly impossible for him to be *certain* that his deputed authority is not abused, however good may be his intentions, and however vigilant his anxiety.

■ ■ ■

I am indeed assured by every one about me, that to manage a West-Indian estate without the occasional use of the cart-whip, however rarely, is impossible; and they insist upon it, that it is absurd in me to call my slaves ill-treated, because, when they act grossly wrong, they are treated like English soldiers and sailors. All this may be very true; but there is something to me so shocking in the idea of this execrable cartwhip, that I have positively forbidden the use of it on Cornwall; and if the estate must go to rack and ruin without its use, to rack and ruin the estate must go. Probably I should care less about this punishment, if I had not been living among those on whom it may be inflicted; but now, when I am accustomed to see every face that looks upon me, grinning from ear to ear with pleasure at my notice, and hear every voice cry "God bless you, massa," as I pass, one must be an absolute brute not to feel unwilling to leave them subject to the lash; besides, they are excellent cajolers, and lay it on with a trowel. Nicholas and John Fuller came to me this morning to beg a favour, "and beg massa hard, quite hard!" It was, that when massa went away, he would leave his picture for the negroes; "that they might talk to it, all just as they did to massa."

■ ■ ■

February 6 [1816]

One of the most intelligent of the negroes with whom I have yet conversed, was the coxswain of my Port Royal canoe. I asked him whether he had been christened? He answered, no; he did not yet think himself good enough, but he hoped to be so in time. Nor was he married; for he was still young, and afraid that he could not break off his bad habits, and be contented to live with no other woman than his wife; and so he thought it better not to become a Christian till he could feel certain of performing the duties of it. However, he said, he had at least cured himself of one bad custom, and never worked upon Sundays, except on some very urgent necessity. I asked what he did on Sundays instead: did he go to church?—No. Or employ himself in learning to read?—Oh, no; though he thought being able to read *was a great virtue;* (which was his constant expression for any thing right, pleasant, or profitable;) but he had no leisure to learn on week days, and as he had heard the parson say that Sunday ought to be a day of rest, he made a point of doing nothing at all on that day. He praised his former master, of whose son he was now the property, and said that neither of them had ever occasion to lay a finger on him. He worked as a waterman, and paid his master ten shillings a week, the rest of his earnings being his own profit; and when he owed wages for three months, if he brought two his master would always give him time for the remainder, and that in so kind a manner, that he always fretted himself to think that so kind a master should wait for his rights, and worked twice as hard till the debt was discharged. He said that kindness was the only way to make good negroes, and that, if *that* failed, flogging would never succeed; and he advised me, when I found my negro worthless, "to sell him at once, and not stay to flog him, and so, by spoiling his appearance, make him sell for less; for blacks must not be treated now, massa, as they used to be; they can think, and hear, and see, as well as white people: blacks are wiser, massa, than they were, and will soon be still wiser." I thought the fellow himself was a good proof of his assertion.

.   ▪   ▪

February 21 [1816]

There are so many pleasing and amusing parts of the character of negroes, that it seems to me scarcely possible not to like them. But when they are once disposed to evil, they seem to set no bounds to the indulgence of their bad passions. A poor girl came into the hospital today, who had had some trifling dispute with two of her companions; on which the two friends seized her together, and each fixing her teeth on one of the girl's hands, bit her so severely, that we greatly fear her losing the use of both of them. I happened also to ask, this morning, to whom a skull belonged, which I had observed fixed on a pole by the roadside, when returning last from Montego Bay. I was told, that about five years ago a Mr. Dunbar had given some discontent to his negroes in the article of clothing them, although, in other respects, he was by no means a severe master. However, this was sufficient to induce his head driver, who had been brought up in his own house from infancy, to form a plot among his slaves to assassinate him; and he was assisted in this laudable design by two young men from a neighbouring property, who barely knew Mr. Dunbar by sight, had no enmity against him whatever, and only joined in the conspiracy in compliment to their worthy friend the driver. During several months a variety of attempts were made for effecting their purpose; but accident defeated them; till at length they were made certain of his intention to dine out at some distance, and of his being absolutely obliged to return in the evening. An ambuscade was therefore laid to intercept him; and on his passing a clump of trees, the assassins sprang upon him, the driver knocked him from his horse, and in a few moments their clubs despatched him. No one suspected the driver; but in the course of enquiry, his house as well as the other was searched, and not only Mr. Dunbar's watch was found concealed there, but with it one of his ears, which the villain had carried away, from a negro belief that, as long as the murderer possesses one of the ears of his victim, he will never be haunted by his spectre. The stranger-youths, two of Dunbar's negroes, and driver, were tried, confessed the crime, and were all executed; the head of the latter being fixed upon a pole *in terrorem*. But while the offenders were still in prison, the overseer upon a neighbouring property had occasion to find fault in the field with a woman belonging to a gang hired to perform some particular work; upon which she flew upon him with the greatest fury, grasped him by the throat, cried to her fellows—"Come here! come here! Let us Dunbar him!" and through her strength and the suddenness of her attack had nearly accomplished her purpose, before his own slaves could come to his assistance. This woman was also executed.

This happened about five years ago, when the mountains were in a very rebellious state. Every thing there is at present quiet. But only last year a book-keeper belonging to the next estate to me was found with his skull fractured in one of my own cane-pieces; nor have any enquiries been able to discover the murderer.

* * *

March 12 [1816]

The most general of the negro infirmities appears to be that of lameness. It is chiefly occasioned by the *chiga,* a diminutive fly which works itself into the feet to lay its eggs, and, if it be not carefully extracted in time, the flesh around it corrupts, and a sore ensues not easily to be cured. No vigilance can prevent the attacks of the chiga; and not only soldiers, but the very cleanest persons of the highest rank in society, are obliged to have their feet examined regularly. The negroes are all provided with small knives for the purpose of extracting them: but as no pain is felt till the sore is produced, their extreme laziness frequently makes them neglect that precaution, till all kinds of dirt getting into the wound, increases the difficulty of a cure; and sometimes the consequence is lameness for life.

There is another disease, which commits great ravages among them; for although in this climate its quality is far from virulent, and it is easy to be cured in its beginning, the negro will most carefully conceal his having such a complaint till it has made so great a progress that its effects are perceived by others. Even then, they will never acknowledge the way in which they have contracted it; but men and women, whose noses almost shake while speaking to you, will still insist upon it that their illness arises from catching cold, or from a strain in lifting a weight, or, in short, from any cause except the true one. Yet why they act thus it is difficult to imagine; for certainly it does not arise from shame.

Indeed, it is one of their singular obstinacies, that, however ill they may be, they scarcely ever will confess to the physician what is really the matter with them on their first coming into the hospital, but will rather assign some other cause for their being unwell than the true one; and it is only by cross-questioning, that their superintendents are able to understand the true nature of their case. Perhaps this duplicity is occasioned by fear; for in any bodily pain it is not possible to be more cowardly than the negro; and I have heard strong young men, while the tears were running down their cheeks, scream and roar as if a limb was amputating, although the doctoress was only applying a poultice to a whitlow on the finger. I suppose, therefore, that the dread of the pain of some unknown mode of treatment makes them conceal their real disease, and name some other, of which they know the cure to be unattended with bodily suffering or long restraint. In the disease I allude to, such a motive would operate with peculiar force, as one of their chief aversions is the necessarily being long confined to one certainly not fragrant room.

RICHARD WATSON, *A Defense of the Wesleyan Methodist Missions in the West Indies* (London, 1817), 59–60.

Mr. Fish, who spent many years in Jamaica, says,—

Sunday is chiefly spent by the field negroes in working their own grounds, which is the source from whence they derive their food; or in bringing what little spare produce they may have to market; for Sunday is the grand public market-day throughout the West Indies. The mechanics may work for their own profit and support, if any one chooses to employ them. The household negroes have to mind the house affairs, &c. Many who do not fear God, find a little time to play; and the pious, as far as permitted, spend their leisure Sabbath time in Christian duties.

Mr. Gilgrass, who also speaks of Jamaica, states,

The Sabbaths are spent generally as follows:—The slaves turn out to pick grass for the horses, mules, oxen, sheep, &c. There is no hay made in the islands, the grass they pick any where upon the estate, both morning and night throughout the year. After breakfast, a driver, with an overseer, accompanies the slaves to the negro grounds, given to them in lieu of allowance from the master; here they spend the blessed Sabbath toiling hard all day. This is their rest. The second Sabbath, these slaves carry to market their provisions to sell, &c. In Jamaica, some of them travel with heavy loads upon their heads, five, ten, fifteen, or twenty miles. To accomplish this journey in time to pick grass on the Sabbath night, they travelled all the preceding Saturday night; if they were not in time to pick the grass, no allowance was made, but many stripes were laid upon them. Those that neither work, nor go to the market, will sleep, smoak segars, and dance to a tomtom. The most pious slaves in the islands have to do the same work on the Sabbath as the others, when the master will not give the Saturday to do it in for that purpose. The slaves come to market in the forenoon, and from thence to the chapel; frequently the chapel yard was covered with market baskets whilst the slaves were at divine worship. The Sabbath is the chief market-day in all the islands.

ALEXANDER BARCLAY, *A Practical View of the Present State of Slavery in the West Indies* . . . (London, 1826), 303–10.

Houses and Gardens of the Negroes, their Mode of Life, &c.

The most common size of the negro houses is 28 feet long by 14 broad. Posts of hard wood about 9 feet long, or 7 above ground, are placed at the distance of two feet from one another, and the space between is closely wattled up and plastered. The roof is covered with the long mountain-thatch, palmeto-thatch, or dried guinea-grass, either of which is more durable than the straw thatch used in this country. Cane tops are also used for the purpose, but are not so lasting. To throw off the rain the thatch is brought down a considerable distance over the wall, which in consequence look low, and the roof high. The house is divided into three, and sometimes four apartments. The room in the middle occupying the whole breadth of the house, has a door on each side, to admit a circulation of air. This is the sitting apartment, and here the poorer class make fire and cook their victuals; the more wealthy have a separate kitchen at a little distance. The smaller houses have the sitting room in one end, and two sleeping apartments in the other.

Behind the house is the garden, filled with plantains, ochras, and other vegetables, which are produced at all seasons. It abounds also with cocoa-nut and calabash trees. A good cocoa-nut will be a meal to a man, and boiled among the sugar (which the negroes frequently do), would be feast to an epicure. It contains also about a pint of delicious juice, called, 'cocoa-nut milk;' the leaves which are thick, and twelve or fifteen feet long, are shed occasionally all the year round, and not only make excellent fuel, but are sometimes used for thatch. The nut also yields oil for lamps, and the shell is made into cups. Thus one tree affords meat, drink, fuel, thatch, oil for lamps, and cups to drink out of! No wonder it is so great a favourite that every negro village looks at a distance like a cocoa-nut grove. Nor are these the only uses of this singularly beautiful native of the tropics; for, besides that the fibry part of it is in the East Indies manufactured into ropes and clothing, the cultivation of it is attended with yet another advantage: from its great height, and perhaps in some degree from the pointed form of its leaves, it is very liable to be struck with lightning, and it affords near a house the same protection as a metallic conductor. Many a headless trunk stands a memento of violent thunderstorms. But though thus liable to be blasted and occasionally rent by the electric fluid, it is never shivered or thrown down; and its slim elastic stem bids defiance to the utmost fury of the hurricane. Blossoms, ripe fruit, and green, are to be seen upon it at all seasons of the year, and it thrives in the most indifferent soils.

The calabash tree produces a large fruit, not eatable, but nevertheless valuable, as the skin of it is a hard and solid substance, like the shell of a nut, and when scooped out, answers the purpose of holding water, or cut across the middle, makes two cups or dishes. Every negro has his calabash, and many have them carved with figures like those which are tattooed on the skins of the Africans. They are used to carry out their breakfast to them when at work in the field; and from their lightness and strength, are preferable for this purpose to almost any other kind of dish. Tin pans, however, are sometimes used. In the garden too, and commonly under the shade of the low outbranching calabash tree, are the graves of the family, covered with brick tombs.

Every family has a hogsty: poultry houses are not wanted; the chickens are carefully gathered at night, and hung up in baskets, to preserve them from the rats. The fowls lodge at all seasons in the trees about the houses. The premises belonging to each family are commonly surrounded with a fence; their provision grounds are generally at some distance.

The furniture in the negro houses of course varies very much according to the industry or indolence of the family. Some of the Africans have no idea of domestic comfort, and are so improvident that it is utterly impossible to make them comfortable. They will sell their very clothes to buy rum, nay, the pot given them to cook their victuals in; and I have known several instances of their pulling down and burning the very wattling of the houses provided for them, rather than take the trouble to collect firewood, although in abundance almost at their doors. With these nothing can be done; but their number is now small. The ordinary class of negroes have fixed beds, covered with deal boards and mats, on which they sleep under a single blanket or sheet, which is all that the climate requires. The rest of their furniture consists of a trunk or chest to hold their clothes, a small cupboard for their cups and dishes, iron pots and tin pans for cooking, a plain deal table, bench, and a few chairs. The more wealthy, of which the number has increased much during the last ten years, sleep on beds filled with the dried leaves of the plantain tree, used also by the free people of colour: and the whole of their furniture, as I have before observed, is such as would astonish an English visitor, who, seeing it, would not easily believe himself in the house of a slave.

The longest and shortest day differ only about two hours in Jamaica, and the negroes are always home between six and seven o'clock in the evening, except those detained in their turn at the work during crop time. The evening is their time of enjoyment, and they sit up late, visiting and entertaining one another. About half-past eleven is the hour at which they generally go to bed, and they rise about half-past five, taking only six hours of sleep; but many of them take also a short sleep between twelve and two, their resting hours in the middle of the day. They designate the hours of the night by the crowing of the cocks—"before cock crow," signifies before two o'clock; then follows "second cock crow"—then "cock crow fast"—and, lastly, "day cut," or dawn. The noise which some hundreds of cocks make about day-dawn in a negro village, amidst the usual stillness of a tropical morning, cannot easily be imagined by those who have not heard it.

Regularly when the work of the day is over, the driver goes to the overseer, to give an account of what has been done, and receive instructions for the following day. These instructions he communicates to the people under him, that they may know where to meet at work the following morning. When they get up at day dawn, the first thing each does is to take his breakfast to the cook. It consists of plantains, edoes, or yams, or a few of each, with a little fresh or salted fish, or crabs, which are very abundant. These articles are sometimes boiled plain, sometimes made into a soup with some other vegetables, according to the various tastes and means of individuals. Women having young children generally cook their husbands' breakfast, and take it out to them when they go to work, or, if not going to the same field, give it to the cook to take out. Any of the people that feel unwell, instead of going to work, are in attendance at the overseer's door in the morning, to obtain admission to the hospital, and although there may be nothing the matter with some of the applicants (for, like sailors and others, they like *"to skulk"* occasionally), they are readily indulged with a dose of medicine and a day or two to rest. Few days, indeed, pass on any estate but some solicit and obtain this indulgence.

Pregnant women and people advanced in life are employed with the young people at light work. For three months before lying in, and two months after, a woman does no work whatever. When the child is about a couple of months old she takes it out to the field. All the *"pickeninny mummas"* go to the same work, and the children are put down together in some shade near the field: one half of the mothers go to work, and the others sit with the children, nursing and doing needle work for themselves, and changing with the others every two hours or so. If it should rain they go home; or if a child should be fretful or apparently unwell, they either take it home or to the hospital.

When a child is weaned, its mother carries it to the nursery in the morning, where it is attended to during the day, and she calls at night to take it home to her own house.

Breakfast, as has already been stated, is carried out to the field about nine o'clock. The driver or head man sits down by himself; the others form into little groups, according to the intimacies and attachments; and although each has his own dish (except that a man and his wife have but one for both), it is not uncommon for the whole group to mess together, and finish first one dish, and then another. After breakfast they have generally, and in wet weather (the only time perhaps that it is of any use) always, an allowance of rum given them. Some drink it off immediately—others club and make up a bottle, which they take in turn and carry home to use or sell as they think proper. In very wet weather they do not go out to work at all; or if, after they are gone to the field, the day turns out very bad, they are called in. At twelve o'clock noon the shell is blown, and they disperse to enjoy two hours of rest, or to employ the time at their own concerns—mending their fences or hogsties, fishing, bathing, washing, carrying home fire-wood, cane-tops, or hog-meat, &c. A few roasted plantains, with a little fish, is all they seem to care about eating in the middle of the day; breakfast and supper being their chief meals. At half-past one o'clock the shell is blown again, and they re-assemble in the field at two.

The plantations have been very happily termed sugar gardens, and the general labour performed by the negroes may be compared to the cleaning and weeding of gardens in this country. The hardest work on them, as already noticed, is the turning up of a small portion of the field every year to be replanted. This is most commonly done by jobbing negroes, who become so much accustomed to this description of labour, that they will sometimes grumble at being sent to what is considered lighter work.

As to the overworking of the negroes, how is the belief of it to be reconciled with the well known fact, that they sit up amusing themselves for nearly one half of the night, and take only six hours of sleep? Let the man in this country accustomed to hard labour, say, if he finds six hours of sleep sufficient to restore exhausted nature? or if, when the toils of the day are over, he finds any enjoyment equal to repose? The negroes perform willingly and cheerfully their regular and accustomed quantity of work, but any attempt of an overseer to exact more is determinedly resisted and resented, and as I have already had occasion to notice, the sure consequence is, that every thing on the estate goes wrong.

MAJOR ALAN CHAMBRE, *Recollections of the West End Life in London* . . . (London, 1858), vol. II, 147–49.

Marriage, which in the days of slavery was of rare occurrence amongst the blacks, has of late years not only increased, but has become quite fashionable. How far the couples fulfill the relative duties of man and wife, I am unable to say. Marriage has been much encouraged by the missionaries, and must ultimately tend to their acquiring regular habits, and probably induce them to remain stationary wherever they may establish themselves.

We constantly saw them pass our house on their way to church, and always with the same ceremonial. The bridegroom comes first, attended by the bridesmaid of his *fiancée,* and a male friend escorts the latter! They are invariably dressed in the extreme of fashion, in expensive materials, such as white satin dresses, and bonnets trimmed with lace and flowers, not always in the best taste, nor are the colours becomingly assorted.

I remember being very much amused at seeing a party dressed as I have described on a very wet day, when the ladies were obliged to lift up their petticoats to avoid the mud. The bride showed a black calf above a pair of short cotton socks, which contrasted rather ludicrously with an elegant dress and satin shoes. Each of the gentlemen carried a new silk umbrella, parasol, or marquise, which appear to be quite a *sine quâ non* on such occasions, having no reference to use;— but it is esteemed, I suppose, an emblem of honour, as among Asiatics.

After the ceremony was over in the church, they paraded the town, without ever exchanging a word, looking very dignified, and followed by a numerous company of idlers. The rector of Montego Bay told me that he once married a couple in his church, when, at that part of the service where the man places the ring on the woman's finger, her hand having swelled, he could not get it on, and by some mismanagement it fell under the communion-table. He could hardly refrain from laughter when he saw the whole party down on all-fours searching for it under the altar. Although no carriage-and-four awaits the happy couple to convey them to their residence, they celebrate their marriage by a grand supper, where a seven-story cake invariably figures, and to partake of which they invite all their friends and relations. The evening is spent in copious libations and dancing to a late hour.

I mention particularly the seven-story cake, because, appearing as it does on these occasions, I cannot but think that it is a vestige of some traditional belief in the sanctity of the number, derived from the commandment of the Almighty to keep the seventh day holy.

GREVILLE JOHN CHESTER, *Transatlantic Sketches in the West Indies, South America, Canada, and the United States* (London, 1869), 80–81.

Marriages—rare events—are occasions of great festivity. Several weeks beforehand the betrothed issue cards of invitation, of which the following (names only excepted) is a verbatim specimen. It is printed on mauve-tinted paper:—

HYMENEAL.

"Mr. Quacco B. Pitt and Miss Quasheba Bispum's complements are respectfully offered, and will be happy of your company at St. _____'s Chapel, on Thursday, 24th, at 11 o'clock A.M., to participate in the celebration of their nuptals. An early answer will oblige."

The parties in this instance were a young cobbler and a washer-girl. However near the house is to the church, it is a point of honour to drive. Generally not less than five or six carriages are employed, a foolish and often ruinous expense. The dresses are most elaborate, and, as already specified, in very good taste. The Legislature have deprived the clergy of their marriage fees; but, on the day following the wedding, the officiating priest is waited on by a smiling black bridesmaid in white muslin and blue ribbons, with a large tray on her head covered with a white cloth, which being removed, displays a miniature wedding-cake and two or three sponge biscuits much befrosted with sugar. After the wedding the company return to the house of the bride, where a lunch is provided, and the evening generally closes with a dance. The display and consequent expense upon these occasions is a great obstacle to marriage; but in this matter the poor folks only ape the rich.

JOHN AMPHLETT, *Under a Tropical Sky* . . . (London, 1873), 57–59.

The peasantry of Barbadoes is nearly entirely black, though there are some few poor whites. They are civil, industrious, and contented; and since the island is so thickly inhabited, they are obliged to work; for though they generally own their own huts, and get a good deal out of the little patches of land attached to them, still it is not sufficient to keep them without working. They have the credit of being in a measure immoral, but since the females very largely outnumber the males, it is so accounted for. They are, as a rule, very honest, and no great crimes prevail amongst them. Offences against the person, as assaults and suchlike, are rare. The greatest temptation placed in their way, and one to which they seem not unfrequently to fall victims, is the facility for stealing sugar-cane from the cane-fields, which are totally unprotected except by watchmen, who of course cannot be in many places at one time. The negro is very fond of cane, and practically lives upon it during the crop-time—that is, while sugar is being made. The punishment for a first offence of stealing cane is three months' imprisonment; on a second conviction, six months, which term is also the punishment for all after offences of the same nature. Fowl-stealing is not very prevalent, though one sometimes hears of it; but for that also there is great facility because of the quantity of poultry kept at the various estates. Children abound, and the boys run about clothed in nothing till they are eight or ten, but the girls are invariably decently dressed.

The negroes are very religious on Sundays, and flock to church and chapel dressed in the most wondrous manner; but they do not carry their religion with them every day in the week, nor does it penetrate very deep. A negro one day, after hearing a powerful and uprousing sermon, announced to his friends that he was quite ready to die that night. One of his friends then, while the negro in question was going to bed by the light of a candle, approached his front door and knocked three times in a most sepulchral manner. "Who dere?" asked the negro. No answer, but three more knocks. "Who dere?" again he shouted. In a deep bass voice his friend answered, "I am Michael, the angel of death." "What you want here?" parleyed the negro inside. "I am come for the soul of Thomas Jones." A scuffle inside, and "O Lor'! O Lor'!" in a smothered voice. Out went the candle, and carefully peeping through the window of the hut, he said, "You come for Tom Jones, eh? Well, him just gone out;" and off he bolted as fast as he could through the back door. Another tale much to the same purpose, is the following: A nigger hut had a pumpkin-vine growing over the roof, and a fellow once climbed up to steal the pumpkins, when, to his horror, the vine gave way, and he was let through the roof, and came down between the owner and his wife, who were in bed. At his wit's end for an answer to the indignant com-

plaint and question of the disturbed sleeper, "Who dere?" his disturb-
er answered, "I am de debil himself, come to take you away." Away
went the man and his wife, one one way, another another, leaving the
thief in possession of the house and his stolen pumpkins, which had
fallen through with him, and with which he decamped in peace.

JAMES ANTHONY FROUDE, *The English in the West Indies* . . .
(London, 1888), 155–56.

From the market I stepped back upon the quay, where I had the luck
to witness a novel form of fishing, the most singular that I have ever
fallen in with. I have mentioned the herring-sized white fish which
come in upon the shore of the island. They travel, as most small fish
do, in enormous shoals, and keep, I suppose, in the shallow waters to
avoid the kingfish and bonitos, who are good judges in their way, and
find these small creatures exceptionally excellent. The wooden pier
ran out perhaps a hundred and fifty feet into the sea. It was a platform
standing on piles, with openings in several places from which stairs
led down to landing stages. The depth at the extremity was about five
fathoms. There is little or no tide, the difference between high water
and low being not more than a couple of feet. Looking down the stair-
cases, I saw among the piles in the brilliantly clear water unnum-
bered thousands of the fish which I have described. The fishermen
had carried a long net round the platform from shore to shore, completely inclosing it. The fish were shut in, and had no means of escape
except at the shore end, where boys were busy driving them back
with stones; but how the net was to be drawn among the piles, or
what was to be done next, I was curious to learn. I was not left long
to conjecture. A circular bag net was produced, made of fine strong
thread, coloured a light green, and almost invisible in the sea. When
it was spread, one side could be left open and could be closed at will
by a running line from above. This net was let carefully down between the piles, and was immediately swollen out by the current
which runs along the coast into a deep bay. Two young blacks then
dived; one saw them swimming about under water like sharks, hunting the fish before them as a dog would hunt a flock of sheep. Their
companions, who were watching from the platform, waited till they
saw as many driven into the purse of the inner net as they could trust
the meshes to bear the weight of. The cord was then drawn. The net
was closed. Net and all that it contained were hoisted into a boat, carried ashore and emptied. The net itself was then brought back and

spread again for a fresh haul. In this way I saw as many fish caught as
would have filled a large cart. The contrivance, I believe, is one more
inheritance from the Caribs, whom Labat describes as doing something of a similar kind.

X. BEKE, *West Indian Yarns* (Demerara and London, 1890), 260–61.

HARD SKULL

The thickness of a negro's skull is proverbial, and in former
times was, we fear, often made a subject of experiment. There was
once a merchant who used to bet that one of his porters would run his
head through a cheese, and this feat was frequently performed to the
amusement of a delighted audience of loafers. On one occasion, after
the "sangaree" had been passed round rather freely, the owner of the
hard-headed porter had a grindstone wrapped in canvas so as to imitate a "Double Gloster," and Mercury was desired to repeat the feat.
The grindstone was set up on edge and the poor fellow sent his head
with a bang at its centre; with a howl he fell back amid the laughter
of the unfeeling fellows around. But he raised himself, remarking
"Dat cheese well hard, 'spose he come last year; I think tho' he been
bruck." And on removing the covering the stone was indeed found to
be "bruck" or cracked through.

A few years ago at a county jail in England, a negro sailor who
was undergoing imprisonment there, attempted to commit suicide by
getting over the balusters at the top of the storey and throwing himself
down the "well" of the staircase, a very considerable height. He was
picked up senseless, but, strange to say, recovered in a few minutes
and did not appear to have received any injury. Some weeks after,
however, he effected his object by "butting" his head once against a
wall with comparative little force, but the injury was fatal.

The "Black Caribs" of St. Vincent, who are the descendants of
Carib and African ancestors, used to flatten the heads of their infants
by means of a board strapped across the forehead to distinguish them
from the African slaves imported as labourers, these lords of the soil
having an aversion to work. But this practice of distorting the shape of
the skull exists, or existed, among other Indian races.

BESSIE PULLEN-BURRY, *Jamaica As It Is, 1903* (London, 1903), 141.

A very usual complaint amongst the black women in Jamaica is the
information that they have a pain. "Missus, I'se got a pain!" has been

said to me in my walks in the country, the tone of voice being sepulchrally solemn.

They have a patent treatment for fever, called the "bush bath." This consists of equal proportions of the leaves of the following plants: akee, sour sop, jointwood, pimento, cowfoot, elder, lime-leaf and liquorice. The patient is plunged into the bath when it is very hot, and is covered with a sheet. When the steam has penetrated the skin, the patient is removed from the bath, and covered with warm blankets, leaving the skin undried. A refreshing sleep is invariably the consequence, and a very perceptible fall in temperature.

There is a native disease called "yaw," which the natives treat in their own fashion. The patient's feet are held in boiling water; this, however, is not so successful a treatment as the former, for I was told it generally results in sending the chill inward, and often pneumonia is the result.

Appendix:
A Sampler of Accounts of the
Slaves of the United States

WAYS OF SPEAKING:
SPEECH, NAMES, AND LETTERS

JOSEPH H. INGRAHAM, *The Sunny South; or, The Southerner at Home* (Philadelphia, 1860), 115–17.

On my way home, I called at a neat hut, built under a shady catalpa tree. A clean, broad stone was the doorstep; white half-curtains were visible at the small windows, and an air of neatness pervaded the whole. Before it was a small yard, in which grew two "Pride of China" trees, for shade, and a cabbage and gourd plant were on either side of the doorway. In the door sat old Aunt Phillisy, a negress withered to parchment by extreme age.

She says she is over a hundred years old, of which I have no doubt. She is African born, and still retains many words of her native dialect, with a strong gibberish of broken English. She was smoking a pipe, made of corn-cob, and rocking her body to and fro in the sunshine, in pure animal enjoyment. Her husband, old Daddy Cusha, who was nearly as old as his wife, was seated on a low stool in the room, but where the sun fell upon him. He was the most venerable object I ever beheld, in his way. He was stone blind, his head bald, and shining like burnished copper, and his beard white as fleeces of wool. His hands were folded upon his knees, and he seemed to be in silent communication with the depths of his own spirit. These two persons had not labored for years, and their master was providing for them in their old age. On every plantation you will find one or more old couples thus passing their declining years, in calm repose, after the toils of life, awaiting their transfer to another state of being. The care taken of the aged servants in this country is honorable both to master and slave.

I had often seen Mammy Phillisy and old Daddy Cusha—as Isabel, who was attached to them, almost every day brings them, with her own hand, "something nice" from the table. The first day I took dinner at the Park, I noticed this noble girl setting aside several dainties, and directing the servant in attendance, in a whisper, to place them on a side table; and I was led from it to believe some person, some very dear friend in the house, was an invalid. But I soon found that they were for Aunt Phillisy, Aunt Daphny, and Father Jack, and other venerable Africans of the estate, whose age and helplessness were thus tenderly regarded by the children of the master they had once faithfully served.

"Good morning, Aunt Phillisy," I said.

"Eh, goo' mornee, Mishy Katawinee," answered the old slave, with a brightening expression, "howee do, Mishy?"

"Very well, Aunt Phillisy," replied I, "I hope you and old Cusha are doing well."

"Yeesha, Mishy, we welly wellee. Takee seatee, Mishy," she said, rising and handing me a wicker chair. So I sat down and had a long chat with them. Old Cusha could recollect when he was taken prisoner in Africa. He said his people and another tribe fought together, that his tribe was beaten, and he, and his mother, and brothers, and sisters were all taken by "de oder brackee men for gold backshee; den dey put me board de leety ship," continued Cusha, "and, by'm by, we come to land, and dey sellee me in Wirginny. Oh, it long time 'go, Missee!"

Aunt Phillisy's memory traveled no farther back than "the big blue sea." Her life in a slaver seemed to have made such an indelible impression upon her that it had become the *era* of her memory. Before it, she remembered nothing. He face, breast, and arms were tattooed with scars of gashes, as were those also of her husband. While I was talking with them, one of their great-grandchildren came into the cabin. It was as black, as thick of lip, as white of eye, as long of heel, as thick of skull, as its genuine Afric forebears; which proved to me that the African loses none of his primal characteristics by change of climate and circumstances, nor by the progress of generations. The reflection was then forced upon my mind that these familiar looking negroes, which we see every day about us, are indelibly *foreigners!* Yet what Southerner looks upon his slave as a barbarian, from a strange, barbarous land, domesticated in his own house, his attendant at table, the nurse of his children? Yet no alien in America is so much a foreigner as the negro!

SIDNEY ANDREWS, *The South Since the War* (Boston, 1866), 227–29.

The language of the common people of the State [South Carolina] is a curious mixture of English and African. There is so little communication between the various sections that the speech of the northern part is in many particulars quite unlike that of the southern part. The language of the negroes is even more marked than that of the lower classes of the whites, and their isolation is such that each district of the State has a dialect of its own. To show how speech is corrupted, I may mention that I have met many negroes whose jargon was so utterly unintelligible that I could scarcely comprehend the ideas they tried to convey.

The negroes almost invariably drop the final *g* in words of two or more syllables that end in *ing*, as *comin'* for *coming, meetin'* for meeting &c. They also drop the final *d* in words of all syllables, as *an'* for *and*, and, *fin'* for *find, aroun'* for *around, behin'* for *behind*, &c. The final *t* is usually, but not always dropped, as *fas'* for *fast mos'* for *most;* though by a change of vowel it is sometimes retained, as *fut* for *foot, fust* for *first*, &c. The *f* in *of* is, I believe, always dropped, as *o' corn* for *of corn*, and *o' my cabin* for *of my cabin*. For the letter thus dropped *b* is sometimes substituted, as *chil' ob Pete* for *child of Peter, ob life* for *of life*, &c.

Exceptions to this general rule in regard to final letters are numerous enough: thus *going* becomes gwine, child becomes *chile* or *cheel, set* becomes *sette*, &c.

The letters *w* and *v* are frequently interchanged: thus *very* becomes *werry*, and *well* becomes *vell*, &c. On the other hand, *ve* is often changed into *b, forgib* for *forgive, lib* for *live*, &c. The letters *th* are never heard; their place in short words is filled by *d*, as *de* for *the, dis* for *this, dat* for *that*, &c; while in longer words the *h* is lost and the *t* retained, as *tree* for *three, trow* for *throw, tings* for *things*, &c.

From dropping letters the way is short to dropping syllables, and *gentleman* becomes *gen'l'man, little* becomes *leel, government* becomes *gov'ment, plantation* becomes *plan'shun, tabacco* becomes *bacca*, &c.

From a change of syllables the way is short to change of words and *us* becomes *we, she* becomes *her,* and *he* becomes *him;* thus *all of us* is *all we, she runs* is *her runs, he has got a whip,* is *him's got whip,* &c.

By a still more curious trick of words the pronoun *them* is used in the objective for any gender or number, but undergoes, among the low-country negroes especially, such a change itself as to be hardly recognizable. Tell me the meaning of the unique word *shum?* Yet it is in very common usage among the negroes of this class, and is their corruption of the words *see them.*

The term applied by the negroes to their owners or employers is not, as generally printed, *massa* or *mass'r.* They use the long *a,* and the word is really, out of the cities, *mawssa,* and sometimes even *mawrssa,* though this last pronunciation is rarely heard.

The terms *cousin* and *brother* are in common use among the negroes, and seem to be expressive of equality. The older and more trusted blacks of a plantation never speak of a field hand as *cousin;* but the field-hands designate each other as *Bro' Bob, Bro' John, Co'n Sally, Co' Pete,* &c.

Of words whose pronunciation is without rule, so far as I can discover, take the following instances: *shut* is *shet, such* is *sich, drove* is *druv, catch* is *ketch, there* is *thar, car* is *kear, steady* is *studdy, another* is *nudder, hear* is *hare, sure* is *sho, both* is *boff,* &c., &c.

The particle *da* is curiously used; thus, for *John is coming,* we have *John da come;* for *he runs in the road,* we have *he da run,* &c. Is the word a corruption of *do,* and is it indicative of present action? I am unable to suggest any other explanation, and that this is the true one I am not at all certain.

The salutation *how do you do* is never anything more than *how-dy,* and with the lower class of negroes is simply *huddy.* The words *dun gone* are in very common use, as, "We's jus' dun gone broke de co'n," "He's dun gone to town," "Her's done gone steal my gr'un'-nut," "All we gang o'nigger dun gone an' lef um," &c. The word *both* is not generally used, the phrase *all-two* taking its place.

The language of the lower classes of the whites is so much like that of the negroes that it is difficult to say where the English ends and the African begins. Very many of the strange words and phrases which I have mentioned as in use among the negroes I have also heard among the back-country whites. There are other instances, however, of a corruption of language in which the negroes have no part.

ELIZABETH HYDE BOTUME, *First Days Amongst the Contrabands* (Boston, 1893), 45–49.

... I soon discovered my words were like an unknown tongue to them. I must first know something of their dialect in order that we might understand each other.

Now I wished to take down the names of these children; so I turned to the girl nearest me and said, "What is your name?"

"It is Phyllis, ma'am."

"But what is your other name?"

"Only Phyllis, Ma'am."

I then explained that we all have two names; but she still replied, "Nothing but Phyllis, ma'am."

Upon this an older girl started up and exclaimed, "Pshaw, gal! What's you'm title?" whereupon she gave the name of her old master.

After this each child gave two names, most of them funny combinations. Sometimes they would tell me one thing, and when asked to repeat it, would say something quite different. The older children would frequently correct and contradict the younger ones. I know now that they manifested much ingenuity in invention or selection of names and titles. One boy gave his name as Middleton Heywood, shouting it out as if it were something he had caught and might lose. Whereupon another boy started up, saying angrily, "Not so, boy. You ain't Massa Middie's boy. I is."

All were now busily studying up their cognomens, and two or three would try to speak together before being called upon. One boy was "Pumpkin," another "Squash," and another "Cornhouse." The girls were "Honey," and "Baby," and "Missy," and "Tay," with an indiscriminate adoption of Rhetts, Barnwells, Elliots, Stuarts, and Middletons, for titles.

I thought of Adam's naming the animals, and wondered if he had been as much puzzled as I. Certainly he gave out the names at first hand, and had no conflicting incongruities to puzzle him. In time I enrolled fifteen names, the number present.

The next morning, I called the roll, but no one answered, so I was obliged to go around again and make out a new list. I could not distinguish one from another. They looked like so many peas in a pod. The woolly heads of the girls and boys looked just alike. All wore indiscriminately any cast-off garments given them, so it was not easy to tell "which was which." Were there twenty-five new scholars, or only ten?

The third morning it was the same work over again. There were forty children present, many of them large boys and girls. I had already a list of over forty names. Amongst these were most of the months of the year and days of the week, besides a number of Pompeys, Cudjos, Sambos, and Rhinas, and Rosas and Floras. I now wrote down forty new names, and I began to despair of ever getting regulated. Fortunately, the day before, I had given out two dozen paper primers with colored pictures, and had written a name on each. So I called these names, but only two or three children came forward to claim their books. So I laid the rest one side. Then half a dozen little heads were lifted up, and one boy said, "Please, ma'am, us wants one o'dem."

"I have no more, and these are given away already," I said.

"You'na done give dem to we!" they exclaimed. I asked the first boy what was his name. Then I looked over the books. No name had been put down like the one he gave. It was the same with all the rest. But as I turned the books over, one girl exclaimed, "Dar, da him!" And coming forward, she pointed to one of the primers with evident delight, saying, "Him's mine." I looked at the written name. It was Lucy Barnwell. I asked her name. It was Fanny Osborne. "Pshaw, gal!" exclaimed an older girl, "Dat's youn'a mammy's name."

Now the others came forward and picked out their own books. What marks they had to distinguish their property I have never been able to discover. But the children, and the older people too, rarely ever make mistakes in these ways. I have taken up a pile of books all just alike, and called to the children sitting in their seats to tell me to whom they belonged. They not only knew their own property, but their neighbors also.

In time I began to get acquainted with some of their faces. I could remember that "Cornhouse" yesterday was "Primus" to-day. That "Quash" was "Bryan." He was already denying the old sobriquet, and threatening to "mash your mouf in," to any one who called him Quash. I reproved the boys for teasing him. "Oh, us jes' call him so," with a little chuckle, as if he ought to see the fun. The older people told me these were "basket names." "Nem'seys [namesakes] gives folks different names."

It was months before I learned their family relations. The terms "bubber" for brother, and "titty" for sister, with "manna" for mother, and "mother" for grandmother, and father for all leaders in church and society, were so generally used, I was forced to believe that all belonged to one immense family. It was hopeless trying to understand their titles. There were two half-brothers in school. One was called Dick, and the other Richard. In one family there were nine brothers and half-brothers, and each took a different title. One took Hamilton, and another Singleton, and another Baker, and others Smith, Simmons, etc. Their father was "Jimmy of the Battery," or "Jimmy Black." I asked why his title was Black.

"Oh, him look so. Him one very black man," they said.

These men are well settled, and have families growing up in honor and respectability who are as tenacious of their titles as any of the F.F.V.'s.

One boy gave the name of Middleton, but afterwards came to me, wishing to have it changed, saying, "That's my ole rebel master's title. Him's nothing to me now. I don't belong to he no longer, an' I don't see no use in being called for him." But when I asked what other name he would choose, the poor fellow was much puzzled. He evidently supposed I could supply a proper cognomen as I supplied new clothes, picking out something to fit. In time he decided upon Drayton, as "that was a good name in secesh times, and General Drayton was a friend to we, an' no mistake. He fight on our side 'gainst his own brother when the first gun shoot."

That was the beginning of time for these poor freed people, "when the first gun shoot."

ROSSA BELLE COOLEY, *School Acres: An Adventure in Rural Education* (New Haven: Yale University Press, 1930), 156.

I have spoken of the "basket-names" given the children. When I asked a mother the reason for this she said, "So the evil one can't know the real name." Most of the mothers today would not even know the foundation for the custom. And so we find Precious, Treasure, Stormy, Better Days, Golden Days, Worky, Husky, Handsome, Fortune, and other jolly good descriptive names, Nob, Morsel, and Nice, and the twins, Peas and Beans!

REV. I. E. LOWERY, *Life on the Old Plantation in Ante-Bellum Days* (Columbia, S.C.: State Co., 1911), 34–35.

It will be noticed that the word "old" precedes the names of these horses. This does not signify that they were naturally old, but it was simply a designation given to them by the slaves, and the white folks accepted it and so styled the horses also. The slaves were adepts at giving nicknames to animals, to each other and even to the white folks. But the white folks seldom caught on to the nicknames given to them.

ELIZABETH HYDE BOTUME, *First Days Amongst the Contrabands* (Boston, 1893), 145–49.

Later in the winter the first woman came again to get a letter written, complaining she could not hear from her "old man." I now discovered her direction was "Jupiter Jones, ma'am." Alas! her first effort was all wrong. I felt sure the "Gibberty Johnson" document never reached him.

I saw a party of young girls waiting on the piazza one Saturday morning; and, as each had paper and a "wellup," I concluded they came for letter-writing. To my question, if they had come to see me, they replied demurely,—

"Us wait on Miss Fannie. *You* come, Miss Fannie; you know best what to say!" they all exclaimed eagerly, as that young lady appeared. These were love-letters evidently, and they were all very merry over them.

So Miss Fannie seated herself at a little table on the open piazza.

"Well, now, Georgie, you come first," she said. "What shall I write?"

"Why, you know, Miss Fannie," surprised at the question.

"But how shall I begin? Who are you writing to?"

"Mr. Wm. Lee, Co. G Street."

"Very well. What next? Shall I say 'My dear friend'?"

"Now, Miss Fannie! What would you say? You mus' be write letters like 'a this."

"Oh! but I never wrote to Mr. Wm. Lee. Is he your husband?"

"Ye-es—no-o,"—hesitatingly.

"Oh, he is!" exclaimed all the girls. "You know he is."

"Well, I haven't got the tiffity [certificate] yet, an' so I sha'n't call him that. An' I don't want him to t'ink I care much ef he never come back. Only to know I 'member him sometimes. You mus' talk stiff, but kind'a easy too."

So the young lady did the best she could; and when she read the letter over to them, they all shouted with delight, and one exclaimed,—

"I tell you, writing-larning's a powerful thing."

The next girl, Jane, said,—

"Now, Miss Fannie, I want you to write jes' as if you is talking to your own luvyer [lover], an' you 'specs him to marry you'na w'en he gits home. You knows w'at to say."

The young lady disclaimed the knowledge and the implied lover, at which they all exclaimed, "Oh! you is, Miss Fannie. You is got a hundred tousand luvyers," clapping their hands with great glee.

All these girls were pure black,—a fine lot. Girl number three walked boldly to the table, and said,—

"Now I am going to talk my letter, an," turning to her companions, "you mus'n't gap a word. I know jes' w'at to say. This is to Mr. John Gardener, orderly sergeant. Tell him I can't forgit him, an' I 'specs him ain't forgit me. I stan' jes' where he lef' me, an' I shall stan' there 'till he gits back; and' ef he never comes back, I shall stan' there still as long as I live."

This is the couple Colonel Higginson speaks of in his "Black Regiment," as "John wants fur marry Venus." When the First South United States Colored Troops, was quartered at the Old Fort Plantation, the wedding was arranged, and John's company all invited. But just before the chaplain arrived to perform the ceremony, the soldiers were called to arms and marched off, and the bride and her friends were left standing, disconsolately watching their disappearance.

The next girl, Susannah, said she wanted to come last, and all the girls must go away, so "only Miss Fannie one" could hear what she had to say. The others good-naturedly jeered at this, saying, "Her 'fraid o' we," "Her shame," etc.; but she was firm, so they left.

"Now, Miss Fannie, I want yer to write strange to this gentleman. Yer mus' say, 'Sir,' fur I don't call him my friend. Tell him he needn't exscuse fer writing, for I is more'n sprise to get his letters, sence he ain't no cause for waiting. I ain't know w'at he t'inks of me. Does he t'ink I is an apple way down on de groun', under his foot, that he can stoop down [making a very low gesture], an' pick up wid his hans'? Tell him I isn't dat. I is an apple high up on de top branch ob de tree. I ain't fur drop in his mouth, an' he can't reach me wid his han's [stretching her arms high above her head]. Ef he jump an' jump, till he jump his head off, he can't reach up to me."

We never knew whether there was an answer returned to this decisive letter, or not; but in a few months Susannah was married to a bright young fellow, one of her schoolmates, and one of her own gang of refugees.

One day a strange woman came, and said, "Missis, I come for git letter write back to Savannah."

"What is your name, auntie?"

"Peggy Owens, ma'am. Don't you *know* me? Why, Miss Fannie do, for she talked to me one night by my door."

They are always surprised that we do not remember them as readily as they do us.

"Well, Peggy, I am going to school now. You will be obliged to wait."

"Oh! I can wait all day for you, ma'am."

When I returned from school at noon I heard her story, and wrote her letter, a copy of which lies before me. It was the same touching recital of a hard experience which we were so constantly hearing. Driven out of Savannah by a cruel master, she and her husband fled with Sherman's army, although she had a baby but a few days old. Of course they brought nothing with them.

From Beaufort they were sent to one of the most remote houses in our district, where they both grew sick and the baby died. All the contrabands, especially the last who "came in," were sickly for a time from so great exposure, change of climate, water, etc.

She wrote to the elder of her church,—

> "Father Cuffy Anderson, I beg you to have praise in the church for me. Ask all the friends to pray for me, for I have lost my husband,—am a lone woman. There is no one left for me now but God. I give my best love to all my fellow-servants. The morning before my husband, Caddy Owens, died, he called me to him and said, 'Peggy, I was in a house last night not made with hands,—a big white house. I am going to leave you, gal, but I ain't going to fret 'bout you, for we been fight together a long time, and you'll brush on till you come to me.'
>
> "The next morning he said, 'Peggy, if you please to get up and make me some gruel, we'll drink together once more, and that will be for communion, for I'm goin', gal.'"

FOLKTALES

Louise-Clarke Pyrnelle, *Diddie, Dumps, and Tot; or Plantation Child-Life* (New York, 1882), 112–18.

"Once pun er time," she began, "dar wuz er bird name' Nancy Jane O, an' she wuz guv up ter be de swif'es'-fly'n thing dar wuz in de a'r. Well, at dat time de king uv all de fishes an' birds, an' all de little beas'es, like snakes an' frogs an' wums an' tarrypins an' bugs, an' all sich ez dat, he wur er mole dat year! an' he wuz blin' in bof 'is eyes, jes same like any udder mole; an', somehow, he had hyearn some way dat dur wuz er little bit er stone name' de gol'-stone, way off fum dar, in er muddy crick, an' ef'n he could git dat stone, an' hol' it in his mouf, he could see same ez anybody.

"Den he 'gun ter steddy how wuz he fur ter git dat stone.

"He stedded an' *he stedded*, an' pyeard like de mo' he stedded de mo' he couldn' fix no way fur ter git it. He knowed he wuz blin', an' he knowed he trab'l so slow dat he 'lowed 'twould be years pun top er years befo' he'd git ter de crick, an' so he made up in 'is min' dat he'd let somebody git it fer 'im. Den, bein'ez he wuz de king, an' could grant any kin' er wush, he sont all roun' thru de kentry eb'ywhar, an' 'lowed dat any bird or fish, or any kin' er little beas' dat 'oud fotch 'im dat stone, he'd grant 'em de deares' wush er dey hearts.

"Well, mun, in er few days de whole yearth wuz er movin'; eb'ything dar wuz in de lan' wuz er gwine.

"Some wuz er hoppin' an' some wuz er crawlin' an' some wuz er flyin', jes 'cord'n to dey natur'; de birds dey 'lowed ter git dar fus', on 'count er fly'n so fas'; but den de little stone wuz in de water, an' dey'd hatter wait till de crick run down, so 'twuz jes 'bout broad ez 'twuz long.

"Well, wile dey wuz all er gwine, an' de birds wuz in de lead, one day dey hyeard sump'n gwine f-l-u-shsh—f-l-u-shsh—an' sump'n streaked by like lightnin', and dey look way erhead, dey did, an' dey seed Nancy Jane O. Den dey hearts 'gun ter sink, an' dey gin right up, caze dey knowed she'd outfly eb'ything on de road. An' by'mby de crow, wat wuz allers er cunnin' bird, sez, 'I tell yer wat we'll do; we'll all gin er feas', 'sezee, an' git Nancy Jane O ter come, an' den we'll all club togedder an' tie her, 'sezee.

"Dat took dey fancy, an' dey sont de lark on erhead fur ter cotch up wid Nancy Jane O, an' ter ax' er ter de feas'. Well, mun, de lark he nearly kill hese'f er flyin'. He flew an' he flew an' he flew, but pyear'd like de fas'er he went de furder erhead wuz Nancy Jane O.

"But Nancy Jane O, bein' so fur er start uv all de res', an' not er dreamin' 'bout no kin' er develment, she 'lowed she'd stop an' take er nap, an' so de lark he come up with wid 'er, wile she wuz er set'n on er sweet-gum lim', wid 'er head un'er 'er wing. Den de lark spoke up, an', sezee, 'Sis Nancy Jane O,' sezee, 'we birds is gwinter gin er big feas', caze we'll be sho'ter win de race any how, an' bein' ez we've flew'd so long an' so fur, wy we're gwine ter stop an' res' er spell, an' gin er feas'. An' Brer Crow he 'lowed 'twouldn't be no feas' 'tall les'n you could be dar; so dey son me ter tell yer to hol' up tell dey come:

dey's done got seeds an' bugs an' wums, an' Brer Crow he's gwine ter furnish de corn.'

"Nancy Jane O she 'lowed ter herse'f she could soon git erhead uv 'em ergin, so she 'greed ter wait; an' by'mby hyear dey come er flyin'. An' de nex day dey gin de feas'; an' wile Nancy Jane O wuz er eatin' an' er stuffin' herse'f wid wums an' seeds, an' one thing er nudder, de blue jay he slope up behin' 'er, an' tied 'er fas' ter er little bush. An' dey all laft an' flopped dey wings; an' sez dey, 'Good-bye ter yer, Sis Nancy Jane O. I hope yer'll enjoy yerse'f,' sez dey; an' den dey riz up an' stretched out dey wings, an' away dey flewed.

"Wen Po' Nancy Jane O seed de trick wat dey played her, she couldn' hardly stan' still, she wuz so mad; an' she pulled an' she jerked an' she stretched ter git er loose, but de string wuz so strong, an' de bush wuz so fum, she wuz jes er was'en 'er strengt'. An' den she sot down, an' she 'gun ter cry ter herse'f, an' ter sing,

" 'Please on-tie, please on-tie Po' Nancy Jane O!
Please on-tie, please on-tie Po' Nancy Jane O!'

"An' atter er wile hyear some de ole bullfrog Pigunawaya. He sez ter hisse'f, sezee, "Wat's dat I hyear?' Den he lis'en, an' he hyear sump'n gwine,

" 'Please on-tie, please on-tie Po' Nancy Jane O!'

an' he went whar he hyeard de soun', an' dar wuz de po' bird layin' down all tied ter de bush.

" 'Umph!' says Pigunawaya, sezee, 'Ain't dis Nancy Jane O, de swif'es-flyin' bird dey is?' sezee; 'wat ail 'long yer chile? wat yer cryin' 'bout?' An' atter Nancy Jane O she up an' tol' 'im, den de frog sez:

" 'Now look er yer; I wuz er gwine myse'f ter see ef'n I could'n git dat gol'-stone; hit's true I don't stan' much showin' 'long o' *birds*, but den ef'n eber I gits dar, wy I kin jes jump right in an' fotch up de stone wile de birds is er waitin' fur de crick ter run down. An' now, s'posin' I wuz ter ontie yer, Nancy Jane O, could yer tuck me on yer back an' cyar mer ter de crick? an' den we'd hab de sho' thing on de gol'stone, caze soon's eber we git dar, I'll get it, an' we'll cyar it bof tergedder ter de king, an' den we'll bof git de deares' wush uv our hearts. Now wat yer say? speak yer min'. Ef'n yer able an' willin' ter tote me fum hyear ter de crick, I'll ontie yer; efn yer ain't, den far yer well, caze I mus' be er gittin' erlong.'

"Well, Nancy O, she stedded an' stedded in her min', an'

by'mby she sez, 'Brer Frog,' sez she, 'I b'lieve I'll try yer; ontie me,' sez she, 'an git on, an' I'll tuck yer ter de crick.' Den de frog he clum on her back an' ontied her, an' she flopped her wings an' started off. Hit wuz mighty hard flyin' wid dat big frog on her back; but Nancy Jane O wuz er flyer, mun, yer hyeard me! an' she jes lit right out, an' she flew an' she flew, an' atter er wile she got in sight er de birds, an' dey looked, an' dey see her comin', an' den dey 'gun ter holler,

"" 'Who on-tied, who on-tied Po' Nancy Jane O?'

An' de frog he holler back,

"" 'Pig-un-a-wa-ya, Pig-un-a-wa-ya, hooo-hooo!'

"Den, gemmun, yer oughten seed dat race; dem birds dey done dey leb'l bes', but Nancy Jane O, spite er all dey could do, she gaint on 'em, an' ole Pigunawaya he sot up dar, an' he kep' urg'n an' er urg'n Nancy Jane O.

"" 'Dat's you!' sezee; 'git herhead!' sezee. 'Now we're gwine to it!' sezee; an' pres'nly Nancy Jane O shot erhead clean befo' all de res'; an' wen de birds dey seed dat de race wuz los', den dey all 'gun ter holler,

"" 'Who on-tied, who on-tied Po' Nancy Jane O?'

An' de frog, he turn't roun', he did, an' he wave his han' roun' his head, an' he holler back,

"" 'Pig-un-a-wa-ya, Pig-un-a-wa-ya, hooo-hooo!'

"Atter Nancy Jane O got erhead er de birds, den de hardes' flyin' wuz thu wid; so she jes went 'long, an' went 'long, kin' er easy like, tell she got ter de stone; an' she lit on er' 'simmon-bush close ter de crick, an' Pigunawaya he slipt off, he did, an' he hist up his feet, an' he gin er jump, kerchug he went down inter de water; an' by'mby hyear he come wid de stone in his mouf. Den he mount on Nancy Jane O, he did; an', mun, she wuz so proud, she an' de frog bof, tell dey flew all roun' an' roun', an' Nancy Jane O, she 'gun ter sing,

"" 'Who on-tied, who on-tied Po' Nancy Jane O?'

"An' de frog he ans'er back,

"" 'Pig-un-a-wa-ya, Pig-un-a-wa-ya, hooo-hooo!'

"An wile dey wuz er singin' an' er j'yin' uv deyselves, hyear come de birds; an' de frog he folt so big, caze he'd got de stone, tell he stood up on Nancy Jane O's back, he did, an' he tuck'n shuck de stone at de birds, an' he holler at 'em,

" 'O Pig-un-a-wa-ya, Pig-un-a-wa-ya, hooo-hooo!'

"An' jes ez he said dat, he felt hisse'f slippin', an' dat made him clutch on ter Po' Nancy Jane O, an' down dey bof' went tergedder kersplash, right inter de crick.

"De frog he fell slap on ter er big rock, an' bust his head all ter pieces; an' Po' Nancy Jane O sunk down in de water an' got drownded; and' dat's de een'."

HOODOO AND FUNERALS

BENJAMIN HENRY LATROBE, *The Journals of Benjamin Henry Latrobe*, ed. Edward C. Carter II, John C. Van Horne, and Lee W. Formwalt, vol. 3, *1799–1820: From Philadelphia to New Orleans* (New Haven: Yale University Press, 1980), pp. 301–02.

MAY 4TH, 1819.

In going home to my lodgings this evening about Sunset, I encountered a croud of at least 200 Negroes men and women who were following a corpse to the cemetery. Of the women one half at least carried candles, and as the evening began to be dark the effect was very striking, for all the women and many of the Men were dressed in pure White. The funerals are so numerous here, or rather occupy so much of every afternoon in consequence of these being, almost all of them performed by the same set of priests proceeding from the same parish Church, that they excite hardly any attention. But this was so numerously attended, that I was tempted to follow it, and getting just in a line with the priests, I entered the Church Yard with them and placed myself close to the grave. The grave was about three feet deep, of which 18 inches were filled with water. It had been dug in a Mass of earth and bones, which formed a little hillock by its side. 10 or 12 Sculls were piled up upon the heap, which looked more like a heap of Sticks, so numerous were the ribs and thigh bones that partly composed it. As soon as the Priests who were 5 in number had entered the Cemetery preceded by three boys carrying the usual pair of urns and Crucifix on silver staves they began their chant, lazily enough, and continued it till they arrived at the Grave. The Coffin was then brought and immediately let down. It swam like a boat in the Water. The Priest began his prayers. In the mean* a great croud of women pressed close to the grave making very loud lamentations. At a partic-

*Obsolete phrase meaning "in the meantime." [Carter, Van Horne, and Formwalt, as is note†]

ular passage the Grave digger who was a little gray headed Negro, naked, excepting as to a pair of ragged short breeches, threw a shovel
full of earth upon the Coffin: and at the same instant one of the Negro
women who seemed more particularly affected threw herself into the
grave upon the Coffin and partly fell into the Water as the Coffin
swam to one side. The grave digger, with very little ceremony thrust
his shovel under her and then seized her with both hands round the
throat and pulled her up while others took hold of her legs and arms,
and she was presently removed. On the heap of bones stood a number
of boys who then began to amuse themselves by throwing in the
sculls, which made a loud report on the hollow Coffin, and the whole
became a sort of farce after the tragedy, the boys throwing about the
legs and thighs and hunting up the sculls for balls to pelt each other.
The noise and laughter was general by the time the service was over.
The women near the grave each plucked up a little grass before they
retired.

I went out in the midst of the confusion, and asked one of the
mourners in white, who was talking intelligible french to her companions, who the person was who seemed to be so much honored and lamented by her own color. She told me that she was a very old African
(Congo) Negress belonging to Madam Fitzgerald, and that most of
those who followed her to the grave were her Children, Grand children, great grand children, their husbands, wives and connexions. I
asked if her Grand daughter who threw herself into the grave could
possibly have felt such excessive distress at the death of an old
woman who before her death was almost childish and was supposed
to be above 100 Years Old—as to be tired of her own life. She
shrugged her shoulders two or three times, and then said, *"Je n'en
sçais rien, cela est une maniere."*[†]

This assemblage of negroes was an instance of the light in which
the Quadroons view themselves. There were none that I observed,
but pitch black faces.

FREDERICK LAW OLMSTED, *The Cotton Kingdom* (New York, 1861),
vol. I, 43–45.

Richmond.—On a Sunday afternoon I met a negro funeral procession
and followed after it to the place of burial. There was a decent hearse,
of the usual style, drawn by two horses; six hackney coaches followed

---

†Trans.: I don't know about that, that's the way it's done.

it, and six well-dressed men, mounted on handsome saddle-horses, and riding them well, rode in the rear of these. Twenty or thirty men and women were also walking together with the procession, on the side walk. Among all there was not a white person.

Passing out into the country, a little beyond the principal cemetery of the city (a neat, rural ground, well filled with monuments and evergreens), the hearse halted at a desolate place, where a dozen coloured people were already engaged heaping the earth over the grave of a child, and singing a wild kind of chant. Another grave was already dug immediately adjoining that of the child, both being near the foot of a hill, in a crumbling bank—the ground below being already occupied, and the graves advancing in irregular terraces up the hill-side—an arrangement which facilitated labour.

The new comers, setting the coffin—which was neatly made of stained pine—upon the ground, joined in the labour and the singing, with the preceding party, until a small mound of earth was made over the grave of the child. When this was completed, one of those who had been handling a spade, sighed deeply and said—

"Lord Jesus, have marcy on us—now! you Jim—you! see yar! you jes lay dat yar shovel cross dat grave—so fash—dah—yes, dat's right."

A shovel and a hoe-handle having been laid across the unfilled grave, the coffin was brought and laid upon them, on a trestle; after which, lines were passed under it, by which it was lowered to the bottom.

Most of the company were of a very poor appearance, rude and unintelligent, but there were several neatly-dressed and very good-looking men. One of these now stepped to the head of the grave, and, after a few sentences of prayer, held a handkerchief before him as if it were a book, and pronounced a short exhortation, as if he were reading from it. His manner was earnest, and the tone of his voice solemn and impressive, except that, occasionally, it would break into a shout or kind of howl at the close of a long sentence. I noticed several women near him, weeping, and one sobbing intensely. I was deeply influenced myself by the unaffected feeling, in connection with the simplicity, natural, rude truthfulness, and absence of all attempt at formal decorum in the crowd.

I never in my life, however, heard such ludicrous language as was sometimes uttered by the speaker. Frequently I could not guess the idea he was intending to express. Sometimes it was evident that he was trying to repeat phrases that he had heard used before, on similar occasions, but which he made absurd by some interpolation or distortion of a word, thus: "We do not see the end here! oh no, my friends! there will be a *putrification* of this body!" the context failing to indicate whether he meant purification or putrefaction, and leaving it doubtful if he attached any definite meaning to the word himself. He quoted from the Bible several times, several times from hymns, always introducing the latter with "In the words of the poet, my brethren;" he once used the same form, before a verse from the New Testament, and once qualified his citation by saying, "I believe the Bible says that."

He concluded by throwing a handful of earth on the coffin, repeating the usual words, slightly disarranged, and then took a shovel, and, with the aid of six or seven others, proceeded very rapidly to fill the grave. Another man had in the meantime, stepped into the place he had first occupied at the head of the grave; an old negro, with a very singularly distorted face, who raised a hymn, which soon became a confused chant—the leader singing a few words alone, and the company then either repeating them after him or making a response to them, in the manner of sailors heaving at the windlass. I could understand but very few of the words. The music was wild and barbarous, but not without a plaintive melody. A new leader took the place of the old man, when his breath gave out (he had sung very hard, with much bending of the body and gesticulation), and continued until the grave was filled, and a mound raised over it.

A man had, in the mean time, gone into a ravine near by, and now returned with two small branches, hung with withered leaves, that he had broken off a beech tree: these were placed upright, one at the head, the other at the foot of the grave. A few sentences of prayer were then repeated in a low voice by one of the company, and all dispersed. No one seemed to notice my presence at all. There were about fifty coloured people in the assembly, and but one other white man besides myself. This man lounged against the fence, outside the crowd, an apparently indifferent spectator, and I judged he was a police officer, or some one procured to witness the funeral, in compliance with the law which requires that a white man shall always be present at any meeting, for religious exercises, of the negroes.

W. H. COUNCILL, *Synopsis of Three Addresses* . . . (Normal, Alabama, 1900), no pagination.

The work of elevating the children of the South will be better appreciated when we look at one of them. In 1862 I was sent to live on a small plantation with "Aunt Phillis." All except Aunt Phillis and I were sent farther South to keep out of the way of the "Yankees." Aunt Phillis was a noted "Conjure woman." She exercised complete control over me—soul and body. I believed in her. I feared and worshipped her. She made me gather ratsbane, cut off snake heads, lizard legs, and capture toad frogs for her. I ventured once to peep into the "loft" over the beds in the little log cabin. Such a sight! Scores of heads of snakes, lizard feet and frog legs were drying to be powdered, and together with human hair, and road dust, to be made into voo-doo bags and sold as charms. She kept about her the "father and mother" of all other bags. Many a night have I looked with one eye through the hole in the torn quilt at Aunt Phillis, by the ghostly glare of dying embers down on her knees talking to her two little red bags, and reading future events by their movements to and fro, or whirl in a circle.

LAFCADIO HEARN, "The Last of the Voudoos," *Harper's Weekly,* vol. 29 (November 7, 1885), 726–27.

In the death of Jean Montanet, at the age of nearly a hundred years old, New Orleans lost, at the end of August, the most extraordinary African character that ever obtained celebrity within her limits. Jean Montanet, or Jean La Ficelle, or Jean Latanié, or Jean Racine, or Jean Grisgris, or Jean Macaque, or Jean Bayou, or "Voudoo John," or "Bayou John" or "Doctor John," might well have been termed "The Last of the Voudoos"; not that the strange association with which he was affiliated has ceased to exist with his death, but that he was the last really important figure of a long line of wizards or witches whose African titles were recognized, and who exercised an influence over the colored population. Swarthy occultists will doubtless continue to elect their "queens" and high-priests through years to come, but the influence of the public school is gradually dissipating all faith in witchcraft, and no black hierophant now remains capable of manifesting such mystic knowledge or of inspiring such respect as Voudoo John exhibited and compelled. There will never be another "Rose," another "Marie," much less another Jean Bayou.

It may reasonably be doubted whether any other negro of African birth who lived in the South had a more extraordinary career than that of Jean Montanet. He was a native of Senegal, and claimed to have been a prince's son, in proof of which he was wont to call attention to a number of parallel scars on his cheek, extending in curves from the edge of either temple to the corner of the lips. This fact seems to me partly confirmatory of his statement, as Berenger-Feraud dwells at some length on the fact that the Bambaras, who are probably the finest negro race in Senegal, all wear such disfigurations. The scars are made by gashing the cheeks during infancy, and are considered a sign of race. Three parallel scars mark the freemen of the tribe; four distinguish their captives or slaves. Now Jean's face had, I am told, three scars, which would prove him a free-born Bambara, or at least a member of some free tribe allied to the Bambaras, and living upon their territory. At all events, Jean possessed physical characteristics answering to those by which the French ethnologists in Senegal distinguish the Bambaras. He was of middle height, very strong built, with broad shoulders, well-developed muscles, inky black skin, retreating forehead, small bright eyes, very flat nose, woolly beard, grey only during the last few years of his long life. He had a resonant voice and a very authoritative manner.

At an early age he was kidnapped by Spanish slavers, who sold him at some Spanish port, whence he was ultimately shipped to Cuba. His West-Indian master taught him to be an excellent cook, ultimately became attached to him, and made him a present of his freedom. Jean soon afterward engaged on some Spanish vessel as ship's cook, and in the exercise of this calling voyaged considerably in both hemispheres. Finally tiring of the sea, he left his ship at New Orleans, and began life on shore as a cotton-roller. His physical strength gave him considerable advantage above his fellow-blacks; and his employers also discovered that he wielded some peculiar occult influence over the negroes, which made him valuable as an overseer or gang leader. Jean, in short, possessed the mysterious obi power, the existence of which has been recognized in most slave-holding communities, and with which many a West-Indian planter has been compelled by force of circumstances to effect a compromise. Accordingly Jean was permitted many liberties which other blacks, although free, would never have presumed to take. Soon it became rumored that he was a seer of no small powers, and that he could tell the future by the marks upon bales of cotton. I have never been able to learn the details of this queer method of telling fortunes; but Jean became so successful in the exercise of it that thousands of colored people flocked to him for predictions and counsel, and even white people, moved by curiosity or by doubt, paid him to prophesy for them. Finally he became wealthy enough to abandon the levee and purchase a large tract of property on the Bayou Road, where he built a house. His land extended from Prieur Street on the Bayou Road as far as Roman, covering the greater portion of an extensive square, now well built up. In those days it was a marshy green plain, with a few scattered habitations.

At his new home Jean continued the practice of fortune-telling, but combined it with the profession of creole medicine, and of arts still more mysterious. By-and-by his reputation became so great that he was able to demand and obtain immense fees. People of both races and both sexes thronged to see him—many coming even from far-away creole towns in the parishes, and well-dressed women, closely veiled, often knocked at his door. Parties paid from ten to twenty dollars for advice, for herb medicines, for recipes to make the hair grow, for cataplasms supposed to possess mysterious virtues, but really made with scraps of shoe-leather triturated into paste, for advice what ticket to buy in the Havana Lottery, for aid to recover stolen goods, for love powders, for counsel in family troubles, for charms by which to obtain revenge upon an enemy. Once Jean received a fee of fifty dollars for a potion. "It was water," he said to a creole confidant, "with some common herbs boiled in it. I hurt nobody; but if folks want to give me fifty dollars, I take the fifty dollars every time!" His office furniture consisted of a table, a chair, a picture of the Virgin Mary, an elephant's tusk, some shells which he said were African shells and enabled him to read the future, and a pack of cards in each of which a small hole had been burned. About his person he always carried two small bones wrapped around with a black string, which bones he really appeared to revere as fetiches. Wax candles were burned during his performances; and as he bought a whole box of them every few days during "flush times," one can imagine how large the number of his clients must have been. They poured money into his hands so generously that he became worth at least $50,000!

Then, indeed, did this possible son of a Bambara prince begin to live more grandly than any black potentate of Senegal. He had his carriage and pair, worthy of a planter, and his blooded saddle-horse, which he rode well, attired in a gaudy Spanish costume, and seated upon an elaborately decorated Mexican saddle. At home, where he ate and drank only the best—scorning claret worth less than a dollar the *litre*—he continued to find his simple furniture good enough for him; but he had at least fifteen wives—a harem worthy of Boubakar-Segou. White folks might have called them by a less honorific name, but Jean declared them his legitimate spouses according to African ritual. One of the curious features in modern slavery was the ownership of blacks by freedmen of their own color, and these negro slave-holders were usually savage and merciless masters. Jean was not; but it was by right of slave purchase that he obtained most of his wives, who bore him children in great multitude. Finally he managed to woo and win a white woman of the lowest class, who might have been, after a fashion, the Sultana-Validé of this Seraglio. On grand occasions Jean used to distribute largess among the colored population of his neighborhood in the shape of food—bowls of *gombo* or dishes of *jimbalaya*. He did it for popularity's sake in those days, perhaps; but in after-years, during the great epidemics, he did it for charity, even when so much reduced in circumstances that he was himself obliged to cook the food to be given away.

But Jean's greatness did not fail to entail certain cares. He did not know what to do with his money. He had no faith in banks, and had seen too much of the darker side of life to have much faith in human nature. For many years he kept his money under-ground, burying or taking it up at night only, occasionally concealing large sums so well that he could never find them again himself; and now, after many years, people still believe there are treasures entombed somewhere in the neighborhood of Prieur Street and Bayou Road. All business negotiations of serious character caused him worry, and as many took advantage of his ignorance, he felt small remorse for his own questionable actions. He was a notoriously bad pay, and part of his property was seized at last to cover a debt. Then, in an evil hour, he asked a man without scruples to teach him how to write, believing that financial misfortunes were mostly due to ignorance of the alphabet. After he had learned to write his name, he was innocent enough one day to place his signature by request at the bottom of a blank sheet of paper, and, lo! his real estate passed from his possession in some horribly mysterious way. Still he had some money left, and made heroic efforts to retrieve his fortunes. He bought other property, and he invested desperately in lottery tickets. The lottery craze finally came upon him, and had far more to do with his ultimate ruin than his losses in the grocery, the shoemaker's shop, and other establishments into which he had put several thousand dollars as the silent partner of people who cheated him. He might certainly have continued to make a good living, since people still sent for him to cure them with his herbs, or went to see him to have their fortunes told; but all his earnings were wasted in tempting fortune. After a score of seizures and a long succession of evictions, he was at last obliged to seek hospitality from some of his numerous children; and of all he had once owned nothing remained to him but his African shells, his elephant's tusk, and the sewing-machine table that had served him to tell fortunes and to burn wax candles upon. Even these, I think, were attached a day or two before his death, which occurred at the house of his daughter by the white wife, an intelligent mulatto with many children of her own.

Jean's ideas of religion were primitive in the extreme. The conversion of the chief tribes of Senegal to Islam occurred in recent years, and it is probable that at the time he was captured by slavers his people were still in a condition little above gross fetichism. If during his years of servitude in a Catholic colony he had imbibed some notions of Romish Christianity, it is certain at least that the Christian ideas were always subordinated to the African—just as the image of the Virgin Mary was used by him merely as an auxiliary fetich in his witchcraft, and was considered as possessing much less power than the elephant's toof." He was in many respects a humbug; but he may have sincerely believed in the efficacy of certain superstitious rites of his own. He stated that he had a Master whom he was bound to obey; that he could read the will of this Master in the twinkling of the stars; and often of clear nights the neighbors used to watch him standing alone at some street corner staring at the welkin, pulling his woolly beard, and talking in an unknown language to some imaginary being. Whenever Jean indulged in this freak, people knew that he needed money badly, and would probably try to borrow a dollar or two from some one in the vicinity next day.

Testimony to his remarkable skill in the use of herbs could be gathered from nearly every one now living who became well acquainted with him. During the epidemic of 1878, which uprooted the old belief in the total immunity of negroes and colored people from yellow fever, two of Jean's children were "taken down." "I have no money," he said, "but I can cure my children," which he proceeded to do with the aid of some weeds plucked from the edge of the Prieur Street gutters. One of the herbs, I am told, was what our creoles call the "parasol." "The children were playing on the *banquette* next day," said my informant.

Montanet, even in the most unlucky part of his career, retained the superstitious reverence of colored people in all parts of the city. When he made his appearance even on the American side of Canal Street to doctor some sick person, there was always much subdued excitement among the colored folks, who whispered and stared a great deal, but were careful not to raise their voices when they said, "Dar's Hoodoo John!" That an unlettered African slave should have been able to achieve what Jean Bayou achieved in a civilized city, and to earn the wealth and the reputation that he enjoyed during many years of his life, might be cited as a singular evidence of modern popular credulity, but it is also proof that Jean was not an ordinary man in point of natural intelligence.

FESTIVALS

JAMES EIGHTS, "Pinkster Festivities in Albany Sixty Years Ago," *Collections on the History of Albany* (Albany, 1867), vol. II, 323–27.

[This great festival of the negroes when slavery existed in the state, and when every family of wealth or distinction possessed one or more slaves, took place usually in May, and continued an entire week. It began on the Monday following the Whitsunday or Pentecost of the Catholic and Episcopal churches, and was the carnival of the African race, in which they indulged in unrestrained merriment and revelry. The excesses which attended these occasions were so great that in 1811 the common council was forced to prohibit the erection of booths and stalls, the parades, dances, gaming and drunkenness, with which they were attended, under penalty of fine or imprisonment; and being thereby deprived of their principal incitements and attractions, the anniversary soon fell into disuse, and is therefore unknown to the present generation. The following account of the Pinkster jubilee is taken from the *Cultivator,* for which it was written by Dr. James Eights, as the recollections of what he witnessed in his youth, when the custom was at its zenith. Pinkster hill, the scene of these celebrations, was the site of the Capitol, before the hand of man was stretched forth to pull down that eminence. Afterwards it was held at various places, but on the death of King Charles, it was observed with less enthusiasm, and finally sank into such a low nuisance as to fall under the ban of the authorities.]

Bright and beautifully broke the morning that ushered in the first great day of the Pinkster jubilee. The air was filled with melody, and the purple hued martins, from their well provided shelter against the walls, or from the far-projecting eaves of many antiquated mansions, were chattering with noisy garrulity, as if in thankfulness for having been brought safely through the night to witness the light of this new born day. The lilacs in the garden around were everywhere redolent with sweet smelling odors, while the pink blossomed azalias from the neighboring plains fairly saturated the bright morning air with their very-delicious fragrance. But, within doors, all was bustling commotion, nor did the overjoyous little ones, with their merry, gleesome mirth-ringing music to the ear, contribute greatly to quell these conflicting tumults within, and bring peace and order to this bewildering scene; but at every turn, where'er you went, you would be sure to encounter some one or more of these juvenile prattlers, frisking about with various garments on their arms and sometimes strewing them in wild dismay, all over the chamber floor, calling lustily for aid to adjust them in their befitting position; nor could a frown or even a scolding tongue for a moment quiet them in their noisy vociferations and frolicsome glee.

Quiet in some degree was at length restored to the household. The young members of the family—both white and colored—had peacefully submitted to the process of cleansing, and were now tastefully adorned in all their varied finery, with numberless small coins merrily jingling in their ample pockets, seemingly keeping time to their sprightly movements, as well as to the silvery music of their mirthful voices. To witness this scene of innocent delight was a pleasing sight to all, and caused the bright eye of the mother to sparkle with pride, and her affectionate heart to expand within her bosom.

Under the careful guidance of a trusty slave, forth we were ushered into the densely thronged streets, and never shall we forget the scene of gayety and merriment that there prevailed—joyous groups of children, all under the protecting care of some favorite old dame or damsel, gayley decorated with ribbons and flowers of every description, blithely wending their way along the different avenues that led to the far-famed Pinkster hill—and long before we reached the appointed place of rejoicing, were our ears greeted with the murmuring sound of many voices, harmoniously intermingled with the occasional shouts of boisterous mirth, and when we arrived on the field we found the green sward already darkened by the gathering multitude, consisting chiefly of individuals of almost every description of feature, form and color, from the sable sons of Africa, neatly attired and scrupulously clean in all their holiday habiliments, to the half clad and blanketed children of the forest, accompanied by their squaws, these latter being heavily burdened with all their different wares, such as baskets, moccasins, birch-bark, nick-nacks, and many other things much too numerous for us even here to mention, and boys and girls of every age and condition were everywhere seen gliding to and fro amid this motley group.

The Pinkster grounds, where we now found ourselves comfortably provided for in a friendly booth or tent, securely protected from the pressure of the swaying multitude without, gave us a most convenient opportunity to inspect the place, and witness at our leisure the entire proceedings of this tumultuous mass of human beings, as they passed in disorderly review before our eyes. The grounds were quaintly laid out in the form of an oblong square, and closely hemmed in with the rude buildings on every side save one, and this was left free, so as to give entrance and freely to admit the crowd. Beyond this square, and in the rear of all the tents, were to be found the spaces appropriated to the various exhibitions, such as of wild animals, rope dancing, circus-riding and the playing ground of all simple gaming sports. Here might be seen for a moderate pittance, the royal tiger of Bengal, and the lordly lion from Africa, with a monkey perched over the entrance door, profusely provided for by the youth and children of the white population; and much did these little ones enjoy themselves in witnessing the wonderful agility with which this diminutive satire on man caught the numerous cakes and other good things thrown within his reach; and then there was Mademoiselle Some-one, with a hard, unpronounceable name, to perform amazing wonders on the slack rope; and in the next enclosure was Monsieur Gutta Percha, to ride the famous horse Selim, and throw a somerset through a blazing hoop, attended by the great Rickett, the celebrated clown of the day, to display his stock of buffoonery on horseback, and break his neck, if necessary, to afford the amplest satisfaction to the assembled auditors.

Thus passed the first day of the festival, merry enough, no doubt, but, being considered vastly ungenteel for the colored nobility to make their appearance on the commencing day, we must defer our more minute details of the ceremonies until the approaching morrow.

The morning sun rose again as beautifully over the smiling landscape as on the preceding day, and cast a cheerful glow of animation over everything around; the excited youngsters, too, were all awake at the early chirping of the birds, and with their silver-toned voices gave a lively chorus to the surrounding scene. After the preliminary preparation, as on the previous day, each was again attired in an appropriate manner to revisit the festal meeting at the usual hour. Early again the crowd were assembled, fully prepared to enter with pleasurable feelings into all the exciting events, as they from time to time should transpire; but far more circumspect were they, and orderly in their demeanor, as all the more respectable members of their community were there to witness any discreditable act, and ever afterward be sure to reward the transgressors with their most severe indignation and contempt.

The master of ceremonies, on this occasion—the Beau Brummel of the day—was Adam Blake, then body servant to the old patroon, and a young man in all the grace and elegance of manner, which so eminently characterized his progress through life until his dying day; to him was unanimously entrusted the arduous duty of reducing to some kind of order this vast mass of incongruent material, which his superior ability soon enabled him to accomplish with complete success.

The hour of ten having now arrived, and the assembled multitude being considered most complete, a deputation was then selected to wait upon their venerable sovereign king, "Charley of the Pinkster hill," with the intelligence that his respectful subjects were congregated, and were anxiously desirous to pay all proper homage to his majesty their king. Charles originally came from Africa, having, in his infant days, been brought from Angola, in the Guinea gulf; and soon after his arrival became the purchased slave of one of the most ancient and respectable merchant princes of the olden time, then residing on the opposite bank of the Hudson. He was tall, thin and athletic; and although the frost of nearly seventy winters had settled on his brow, its chilling influence had not yet extended to his bosom, and he still retained all the vigor and agility of his younger years. Such were his manly attributes at this present time.

Loud rang the sound of many voices from the neighboring street, shoutingly proclaiming the arrival of the master of the revels, and soon the opening crowd admitted him within their presence, and never, if our memory serve us, shall we forget the mingled sensations of awe and grandeur that were impressed on our youthful minds, when first we beheld his stately form and dignified aspect, slowly moving before us and approaching the centre of the ring. His costume on this memorable occasion was graphic and unique to the greatest degree, being that worn by a British brigadier of the olden time. Ample broad cloth scarlet coat, with wide flaps almost reaching to his heels, and gayly ornamented everywhere with broad tracings of bright golden lace; his small clothes were of yellow buckskin, fresh and new, with stockings blue, and burnished silver buckles to all his well-blacked shoe; when we add to these the tricornered cocked hat trimmed also with lace of gold, and which so gracefully set upon his noble, globular pate, we nearly complete the rude sketch of the Pinkster king.

The greetings were at length over, and the hour of twelve having arrived, peace and tranquility had once more been partially restored to the multitude; his majesty, the king, was in the midst of his assembled friends and subjects, and the accomplished master of the ceremonies with his efficient aids were busily employed in making the necessary arrangements to commence the festivities with zeal and earnestness; partners were then selected and led out upon the green, and the dancing was about to commence.

The dance had its peculiarities, as well as everything else connected with this august celebration. It consisted chiefly of couples joining in the performances at varying times, and continuing it with their utmost energy until extreme fatigue or weariness compelled them to retire and give space to a less exhausted set; and in this successive manner was the excitement kept up with unabated vigor, until the shades of night began to fall slowly over the land, and at length deepen into the silent gloom of midnight.

The music made use of on this occasion, was likewise singular in the extreme. The principal instrument selected to furnish this important portion of the ceremony was a symmetrically formed wooden article usually denominated an *eel-pot*, with a cleanly dressed sheep skin drawn tightly over its wide and open extremity—no doubt obtained expressly for the occasion from the celebrated *Fish slip*, at the foot of the Maiden's lane. Astride this rude utensil sat Jackey Quackenboss, then in his prime of life and well known energy, beating lustily with his naked hands upon its loudly sounding head, successively repeating the ever wild, though euphonic cry of *Hi-a-bomba, bomba, bomba,* in full harmony with the thumping sounds. These vocal sounds were readily taken up and as oft repeated by the female portion of the spectators not otherwise engaged in the exercises of the scene, accompanied by the beating of time with their ungloved hands, in strict accordance with the eel-pot melody.

Merrily now the dance moved on, and briskly twirled the lads and lasses over the well trampled green sward; loud and more quickly swelled the sounds of music to the ear, as the excited movements increased in energy and action; rapid and furious became their motions, as the manifold stimulating potions, they from time to time imbibed, vibrated along their brains, and gave a strengthening influence to all their nerves and muscular powers; copiously flowed the perspiration, in frequent streams, from brow to heel, and still the dance went on with all its accustomed energy and might; but the eye at length, becoming weary in gazing on this wild and intricate maze, would oft-times turn and seek relief by searching for the king, amid the dingy mass; and there, enclosed within their midst, was his stately form beheld, moving along with all the simple grace and elastic action of his youthful days, now with a partner here, and then with another there, and sometimes displaying some of his many amusing antics, to the delight and wonderment of the surrounding crowd, and which, as frequently, kept the faces of this joyous multitude broadly expanded in boisterous mirth and jollity. And thus the scene continued until the shades of night and morning almost mingled together, when the wearied revelers slowly returned to their resting places, and quickly sought their nightly repose.

Morning again returned with all its renovating influence, when most of the sable throng were seen loitering along the streets toward the accustomed field of sports; and the bright day moved merrily onward to its close, with all the happy enjoyments of that which had preceded it; and long ere the night had again arrived, the upper class of revelers had left the ground to seek entertainment elsewhere, or spend the evening in tea-party gossip, among their numerous friends and visitors. And thus terminated the third day of the Pinkster festival.

On the succeeding fourth and fifth days, the grounds were left to the free enjoyment of the humbler classes, as well did they improve the time in joyous merriment until near the close of the latter, when, instigated by the more potent draughts they swallowed, speedily brought on wrangling discord, quickly succeeded by rounds of fighting, bruised eyes, and bloody noses unnumerated, big Jack Van Patten, the city bully, being unanimously declared the champion of the lists, having successfully overthrown all his numerous opponents.

The last day of the week, and also of the Pinkster revels, was chiefly occupied in removing the unpurchased materials from the field, and also in the distribution of the remaining vestiges of the broken meats and pastries to the poorer classes of individuals who still lingered about the now almost abandoned ground of rejoicing. Some few liquoring establishments still continued their traffic, being amply patronized by the more rude and belligerent number that yet remained, as if loth to leave the endearing spot as long as a stimulating drop could there be procured.

The following sabbath was literally considered by them as really a day of rest, and mid-day's sun was at its height e'er many awoke from their refreshing slumbers, and the succeeding day found the numerous visitors joyfully journeying toward their respective homes. Our ancient city was at length again left to its usual quietude, and all things within its confines soon became properly restored to its accustomed routine of duty and order. And thus ended the Pinkster holidays, with all its rolicking festivities.

HENRY B. WHIPPLE, *Bishop Whipple's Southern Diary, 1843–1844* (Minneapolis: University of Minnesota Press, 1937), 51.

Dec. 27 [1843]. This is with the negroes the last day of the feast and with them the "great day." The negroes are out in great numbers arrayed in their best and their ebony faces shine with joy and happiness. Already have they paraded, with a corps of staff officers with red sashes, mock epaulettes & goose quill feathers, and a band of music composed of 3 fiddles, 1 tenor & 1 bass drum, 2 triangles & 2 tambourines and they are marching up & down the streets in great style. They are followed by others, some dancing, some walking & some hopping, others singing, all as lively as lively can be. If any negro refuses to join them they seize him & have a mock trial & sentence him to a flogging which is well laid on. Already have they had several such court martials. Here they come again with flags flying and music enough to deafen one & they have now two fifes to increase their noise. Whatever others may think, I am satisfied that these seasons of joyous mirth have a happy effect upon the negro population. They levy contributions on all the whites they see & thus find themselves in pocket money. I am really sore I have laughed so long and so heartily. . . .

CAPTAIN GREGORY SEAWORTHY (GEORGE HIGBY THROOP), *Bertie: or, Life in the Old Field, . . .* (Philadelphia, 1851), 217–19.

"Is this 'ere house haunted?" asked the professor, as he met me on Christmas morning.

"I hope not."

"Wal, I hope so tew. I was pretty well tuckered aout last night after so long a ride, an' so I s'posed I sh'u'l git a good night's rest, but, Lord bless ye! sech noises I never heerd!"

"Perhaps it was the 'John Kooner'!"

"The John what?"

"I will explain. The Negroes have a custom here of dressing one of their number at Christmas in as many rags as he can well carry. He wears a mask, too, and sometimes a stuffed coon-skin above it, so arranged as to give him the appearance of being some seven or eight feet high. He goes through a variety of pranks, which you will have an opportunity to see by and by, and he is accompanied by a crowd of Negroes, who make all the noise and music for His Worship the John Kooner."

"Wal, what's all this 'ere firin' and shutin' we heerd 'beout daylight?"

"A part of the celebration of Christmas, as essential to the ceremonies as the hanging up of stockings by the little folk."

The family were soon astir. "Christmas gift! Christmas gift! Wish you merry Christmas!" shouted Molly, as she came to the door.

The morning was beautiful. The air was "frosty, but kindly." A huge fire was blazing in the parlor, and an enormous bowl of egg-nogg was already in preparation. The Negroes were lounging about in holiday attire, awaiting the customary Christmas dram. This was duly given them by little Molly, who distributed the whisky with the air of a queen. The colonel came into the piazza rubbing his hands, and caught her in his arms in a genuine doting hug.

Breakfast was announced, and we had barely left the table when a loud shout betokened the arrival of the hero of the Christmas frolic. We hastened to the door. As the Negroes approached, one of the number was singing a quaint song, the only words of which that I could distinguish were those belonging to the chorus,

Blow dat horn ag'in!

One of them carried a rude deal box, over which a dried sheepskin had been drawn and nailed, and on this, as if his salvation depended on it, the man was thumping with ear-splitting din. Beside him was another, who kept up a fierce rattle of castanets; another beat a jaw-bone of some horse departed this life; and still another had a clevis, which he beat with an iron bolt, thereby making a very tolerable substitute for a triangle. The chief mummer, or John Kooner, kept up, in the meantime, all conceivable distortions of body and limbs, while his followers pretended to provoke his ire by thrusting sticks between his legs. One of the party seemed to officiate as bear-leader, to direct the motions of the unknown chief mummer. They approached the piazza, knelt on the ground, and continued to sing, one of them improvising the words while the rest sang in chorus,

O! dear maussa!
O! dear missus!
Wish ye merry Christmas!

The expected dram was given them. A few pieces of silver were thrown from the piazza, and they left us, singing a roisterly song, the chorus of which was

By on de row!

MUSIC AND DANCE

JOHN F. WATSON, *Annals of Philadelphia, and Pennsylvania, in the Olden Time; . . .* , ed. Willis P. Hazard, enlarged ed. (Philadelphia, 1927), vol. II, 265 (1st ed., 1830).

Many can still remember when the slaves were allowed the last days of the fairs for their jubilee, which they employed ("light hearted wretch!") in dancing the whole afternoon in the present Washington square, then a general burying ground—the blacks joyful above, while the sleeping dead reposed below! In that field could be seen at once more than one thousand of both sexes, divided into numerous little squads, dancing, and singing, "each in their own tongue," after the customs of their several nations of Africa.

BENJAMIN HENRY LATROBE, *The Journals of Benjamin Henry Latrobe,* ed. Edward C. Carter II, John C. Van Horne, and Lee W. Formwalt, vol. 3, *1799–1820: From Philadelphia to New Orleans* (New Haven: Yale University Press, 1980), pp. 203–05.

FEBY. 21ST, 1819.

.   .   .

This long dissertation has been suggested by my accidentally stumbling upon the Assembly of Negroes which I am told every Sunday afternoon meets on the Common in the rear of the city.* My ob-

*This was Congo Square, at Ramparts and Orleans streets, originally known as Circus Square, and today called Beauregard Square. An 1817 law restricted Negro dancing to Sundays before sundown and only in areas approved by the mayor. Mayor Augustin Macarty directed that dancing could take place only at Congo Square under police supervision. The city directory for 1822 noted: "The Circus *public square* is planted with trees, and inclosed, and is very noted on account of its being the place where the Congo, and other negroes, *dance, carouse and debauch on the Sabbath,* to the great injury of the morals of the rising generation; it is a foolish custom, that elicits the ridicule of most respectable persons who visit the city." Paxton, *Directory,* p. 40; Henry A. Kmen, *Music in New Orleans: The Formative Years, 1791–1841* (Baton Rouge: Louisiana State University Press, 1966), p. 227. [Carter, Van Horne, and Formwalt, as are notes †–‖]

ject was to take a walk with Mr. Coulter on the Bank of the Canal Carondelet as far as the Bayou St. John.[†] In going up St. Peters Street and approaching the common I heard a most extraordinary noise, which I supposed to proceed from some horse Mill, the horses trampling on a wooden floor. I found however on emerging from the houses, onto the common, that it proceeded from a croud of 5 or 600 persons assembled in an open space or public square. I went to the spot and crouded near enough to see the performance. All those who were engaged in the business seemed to be *blacks*. I did not observe a dozen yellow faces.[‡] They were formed into circular groupes in the midst of four of which, which I examined (but there were more of them) was a ring, the largest not 10 feet in diameter. In the first were two women dancing. They held each a coarse handkerchief extended by the corners in their hands, and *set* to each other in a miserably dull and slow figure, hardly moving their feet or bodies. The music consisted of two drums and a stringed instrument. An old man sat astride of a Cylindrical drum about a foot in diameter, and beat it with incredible quickness with the edge of his hand and fingers. The other drum was an open staved thing held between the knees and beaten in the same manner. They made an incredible noise. The most curious instrument however was a stringed instrument which no doubt was imported from Africa. On the top of the finger board was the rude figure of a Man in a sitting posture, and two pegs behind him to which the strings were fastened. The body was a Calabash. It was played upon by a very little old man, apparently 80 or 90 Years old. The women squalled out a burthen to the playing, at intervals, consisting of two notes, as the Negroes working in our cities respond to the Song of their leader. Most of the circles contained the same sort of dancers. One was larger, in which a ring of a dozen women walked, by way of dancing, round the music in the Center. But the instruments were of different construction. One, which from the color of the wood seemed

†Andrew S. Coulter, an engineer, left Baltimore in May 1818 to set up the engines of the New Orleans Waterworks, and he remained in charge of the works after BHL's death. BHL noted that Coulter had "the fullest instruction on every part of the work, and his personal character as a skillful Mechanic, and for probity is too fully established, not to entitle him to confidence." BHL to Mayor and Council of New Orleans, 17 September 1819, Benjamin Henry Latrobe Papers, Tulane University Library, *PBHL, microfiche ed.*, 239/F5.

Canal Carondelet, which connected the city with Lake Pontchartrain, was begun by Spanish Gov. Francisco Louis Hector, Baron de Carondelet in 1794. Clark, *New Orleans*, p. 291.

‡I.e., mulattoes.

new, consisted of a block cut into something of the form of a cricket bat with a long and deep mortice down the Center. This thing made a considerable noise, being beaten lustily on the side by a short stick. In the same Orchestra was a square drum looking like a stool, which made an abominably loud noise: also a Calabash with a round hole in it, the hole studded with brass nails which were beaten by a woman with two short sticks.

A Man sung an uncouth song to the dancing which I suppose was in some African language, for it was not french,§ and the Women screamed a detestable burthen on one single note. The allowed amusements of Sunday, have, it seems, perpetuated here, those of Africa among its inhabitants. I have never seen any thing more brutally savage, and at the same time dull and stupid than this whole exhibition. Continuing my walk about a mile along the Canal, and returning after Sunset near the same spot, the noise was still heard. There was not the least disorder among the croud, nor do I learn, on enquiry, that these weekly meetings of the negroes have ever produced any mischief.‖

J. Finch, *Travels in the United States of America and Canada* (London, 1833), 237–38.

Almost every night parties take place among the slaves on the plantations; they assemble from a great distance, and have a number of

§Many Louisiana slaves spoke a Creole patois that retained African phrases and speech patterns. In 1833 Thomas Hamilton noted that the slaves of southern Louisiana "jabber a sort of *patois* unlike any thing I ever heard in France, though my intercourse with the French peasantry has been tolerably extensive." [Hamilton], *Man and Manners in America*, 2 vols. (Philadelphia, 1833), 2:105. See also Robin, *Voyages dans l'Interieur de la Louisiane*, 3:185–89; Henry Edward Krehbiel, *Afro-American Folksongs: A Study in Racial and National Music* (New York: G. Schirmer, 1914), p. 134; Bernard Katz, ed., *The Social Implications of Early Negro Music in the United States* (New York: Arno Press and the New York Times, 1969), pp. 47–48.
‖BHL's considerable musical experience, which was entirely within the European tradition, did not prepare him for his first exposure to African music and dancing in New Orleans. To music lovers trained to appreciate Italian *bel canto,* the strained vocal style admired by Africans seemed harsh and ugly. Like many of his white contemporaries, BHL was very critical of the alien strong rhythms, polyrhythms, and repeated short phrases that characterized black American music. In particular, the blacks of New Orleans were less acculturated than those BHL had observed elsewhere in the U.S. because that city's close ties with the Caribbean islands and its Franco-Spanish traditions encouraged the persistence of African cultural patterns. See Dena J. Epstein, *Sinful Tunes and Spirituals: Black Folk Music to the Civil War* (Urbana: University of Illinois Press, 1977) and Roger Bastide, *African Civilizations in the New World,* trans. Peter Green (London: C. Hurst, 1971).

amusements. These vary in different States: the slaves follow the example set by their masters. In Maryland dancing is fashionable; the slaves frequently dance all night. In Virginia musical parties are more frequent; every negro is a musician from his birth. A black boy will make an excellent fiddle out of a gourd and some string. In autumn they play tunes on the dried stalks of Indian corn, when it is still standing in the field. By striking it near the ground or at the top, they make it discourse most excellent music. The banjo is another instrument they are fond of, but the supreme ambition of every negro is to procure a real violin. By saving the few pence which are given them, selling chickens, and robbing a little, if necessary, they generally contrive to make up the sum. An instrument of music seems necessary to their existence.

WILLIAM B. SMITH, "The Persimmon Tree and the Beer Dance," *Farmer's Register*, 6 (April 1839), 59–61.

Some years ago, I rode in the night to visit a patient, and as I passed the house of Mr. Samuel Poe, in the lower end of Prince Edward, I heard the tones of a banjor, and was told by the old gentleman, (Mr. Poe,) that his servants had brewed a barrel of persimmon beer, and he gave them the privilege of having what they called a "beer dance." Curiosity induced me to ride to the door, accompanied by Mr. Poe, and the other gentlemen. And here we saw rare sport! "an unco sight!" Not, however, such a sight as Tam O'Shanter saw when he peeped into "Kirk-Alloway," for the dancers there were *"warlocks and witches"*; here they were Virginia slaves, dancing jigs and clapping "juber," over a barrel of persimmon beer. It occurred to me, that if Tam could have made his appearance about this time on his gray mare *Meg*, the scene would have frightened *Maggie* more than the *"bleeze"* of "Kirk-Alloway"; and Tam might have roared out, "weel done Cutty Sark!" a thousand times, and the torch-lights would not have been extinguished.

The ball was opened with great ceremony by singing a song known to our Virginia slaves by the name of "who-zen-John, who-za."

> Old Black bull come down de hollow,
> He shake hi'tail, you hear him bellow;
> When he bellow, he jar de river,
> He paw de yearth, he make it quiver.
> Who-zen-John, who-za.

This was a sky-rocket thrown out, as a prelude to the grand exhibition, and will give the reader some idea of what is to follow. Those who could not get seats in the house, took their stand outside, peeping in the door and through the logs, making remarks on the dancers; and here I will observe, that there was a complete Babel jargon, a confusion of tongues!

"Down the road, come show me de motion." "Set to your partner, Dolly."—"Cut him out, Gabe."—"Sal, *does* put her foot good."—"Yonder come de coal-black horse."—"The yellow roan's up! hear how he lumbers! he's a *rael* stormer, ring clipper, snow-belcher and *drag out*."—"Congo is a *scrouger*; he's up a gum, and no bug-eater I tell you; he carries a broad row, weeds out every thing—hoes de corn, and digs de taters,"—"Molly look like kildee; she move like handsaw—see how she shake herself."—"Hello! in there, I wish you all sen' us out some simmon beer." "Lor! *see* how Aggy shake her foot! she *ken* pull the whip-saw down."—"Nick? come here and see Ben cross hi' bow-legs! look at hi' mouf! when he grin, hi' mouf and teeth like hen-ness full o' eggs."—"Nick? I reckon if Tamar's cat stay in there much longer, they will mash her guts out; her skin 'ont hold peas."—"Come here, Gabe; come, if you please; Jackson's Dick is dancing with Ellington's Nance! see how she quivers! *Now*, Nance!—*Try*, Nance!—She does but look pretty.—When she sets and turns, she is like a *picter*—and she is fine form, back. Dick shan't have Nance; I'll kick him high as the meat house first." (Sings.) "She *bin* to the North, she *bin* to the south, she *bin* to the east, she *bin* to the west, she *bin* so far *beyond* the sun, and she is the *gal* for me."—"Dick had'n't no business dancing with Nance; he ain't a man of *gumption*. I tried him, and he can't be made to understand the *duramatical* part of the function, the function of the fundamental, and the *imperality* of ditrimental things. Gabe? Dick's a fool, and you may tell him Sambo says so: he is knock-knee'd, and ugly enough to eat *Gumbo*." "Well, I know that; sing on Sambo."

> I went from the great-house, down to the kitchen,
> To get a knot of light-wood to see to go fishing,
>   To treat granny Dinah;
>
> I went to the stable, I cotch master gray horse,
> I clap the saddle *pon* him and he trot like *do'nk* care.
>   He *do'nk* care, he *do'nk* care.

Having become tired of this out of door conversation, we concluded to view the group in the house. Here the banjor-man, was seated on the beer barrel, in an old chair. A long white cowtail, queued with a red ribbon, ornamented his head, and hung gracefully down his back; over this he wore a three-cocked hat, decorated with peacock feathers, a rose cockade, a bunch of ripe persimmons, and to cap the climax, three pods of red pepper as a top-knot. *Tumming* his banjor, grinning with ludicrous gesticulations and playing off his wild notes to the company. Before him stood two athletic blacks, with open mouth and pearl white teeth, clapping "Juber" to the notes of the banjor; the fourth black man held in his right hand a jug gourd of persimmon beer, and in his left, a dipper or water-gourd, to serve the company; while two black women were employed in filling the fire-place, six feet square, with larded persimmon dough. The rest of the company, male and female, were dancers, except a little squat wench, who held the torch light. I had never seen Juber clapped to the banjor before, and you may suppose I looked upon such a novel scene, with some degree of surprise. Indeed I contemplated the dancing group, with sensations of wonder and astonishment! The clappers rested the right foot on the heel, and its clap on the floor was in perfect unison with the notes of the banjor, and palms of the hands on the corre-sponding extremities; while the dancers were all jigging it away in the merriest possible gaiety of heart, having the most ludicrous twists, wry jerks, and flexible contortions of the body and limbs, that human imagination can divine.

> The whole world is a ball we find,
> The water dances to the wind;
> The sea itself, at night and noon,
> Rises and dances to the moon.
>
> The earth and planets round the sun,
> Still dance; nor will their dances be done,
> Till nature in one blast is blended;
> Then may we say the ball is ended.

The rude ballad set to Juber, corresponds admirably with the music and actors in this wild fantastic dance. While the clappers were laboring in the performance of their office, they responded at the same to the notes of the banjor.

> Juber up and Juber down,
> Juber all around de town,
> Juber dis, and Juber dat,
> And Juber rou' the simmon vat.
>   Hoe corn, hill tobacco,
>   Get over double trouble, Juber boys, Juber.

Uncle Phil, he went to mill,
He suck de sow, he starve de pig,
Eat the *simmon,* gi 'me de seed,
I told him, I was not in need.
  Hoe corn! hill tobacco!
  Get over double trouble, Juber boys, Juber.

Aunt Kate? look on the high shelf,
Take down the husky dumplin,
I'll eat it wi' my *simmon* cake.
To cure the rotten belly-ache.
  Hoe corn! hill tobacco!
  Get over double trouble, Juber boys, Juber.

Racoon went to *simmon* town,
To choose the rotten from de soun',
Dare he *sot* upon a sill,
Eating of a whip-poor-will.
  Hoe corn! hill tobacco!
  Get over double trouble, Juber boys, Juber.

When supper was announced, the banjor-man, was first served; then the clappers and beer bearer, and lastly, the beaux and their partners. Each had a huge loaf of larded persimmon bread with a gourd of beer.

FRANCES ANN KEMBLE, *Journal of a Residence on a Georgian Plantation in 1838–39* (London, 1863), 127–29.

The boat he went in was a large, broad, rather heavy, though well-built craft, by no means as swift or elegant as the narrow eight-oared long-boat in which he generally takes his walks on the water, but well adapted for the traffic between the two plantations, where it serves the purpose of a sort of omnibus or stage-coach for the transfer of the people from one to the other, and of a baggage-wagon or cart for conveyance of all sorts of house-hold goods, chattels, and necessaries. Mr. _____ sat in the middle of a perfect chaos of such freight; and as the boat pushed off, and the steersman took her into the stream, the men at the oars set up a chorus, which they continued to chant in unison with each other, and in time with their stroke, till the voices and oars were heard no more from the distance. I believe I have mentioned to you before the peculiar characteristics of this vertible negro minstrelsy—how they sing in unison, having never, it appears, attempted or heard any thing like part-singing. Their voices seem of-

tener tenor than any other quality, and the tune and time they keep
something quite wonderful; such truth of intonation and accent would
make almost any music agreeable. That which I have heard these people sing is often plaintive and pretty, but almost always has some resemblance to tunes with which they must have become acquainted
through the instrumentality of white men; their overseers or masters
whistling Scotch or Irish airs, of which they have produced by ear
these *rifacciamenti*. The note for note reproduction of "Ah! vous di-
rai-je, maman?" in one of the most popular of the so-called negro melodies with which all America and England are familiar, is an example
of this very transparent plagiarism; and the tune with which Mr.
_____'s rowers started him down the Altamaha, as I stood at the steps
to see him off, was a very distinct descendant of "Coming through the
Rye." The words, however, were astonishingly primitive, especially
the first line, which, when it burst from their eight throats in high
unison, sent me into fits of laughter.

> "Jenny shake her toe at me,
>   Jenny gone away;
> Jenny shake her toe at me,
>   Jenny gone away.
> Hurrah! Miss Susy, oh!
>   Jenny gone away;
> Hurrah! Miss Susy, oh!
>   Jenny gone away."

What the obnoxious Jenny meant by shaking her toe, whether defiance or mere departure, I never could ascertain, but her going away
was an unmistakable subject of satisfaction; and the pause made on
the last "oh!" before the final announcement of her departure, had
really a good deal of dramatic and musical effect. Except the extem-
poraneous chants in our honor, of which I have written to you before,
I have never heard the negroes on Mr. _____'s plantation sing any
words that could be said to have any sense. To one, an extremely
pretty, plaintive, and original air, there was but one line, which was
repeated with a sort of wailing chorus—

> "Oh! my massa told me, there's no grass in Georgia."

Upon inquiring the meaning of which, I was told it was supposed to
be the lamentation of a slave from one of the more northerly states,
Virginia or Carolina, where the labor of hoeing the weeds, or grass as
they call it, is not nearly so severe as here, in the rice and cotton lands

of Georgia. Another very pretty and pathetic tune began with words that seemed to promise something sentimental—

> "Fare you well, and goody-by, oh, oh!
> I'm goin' away to leave you, oh, oh!"

but immediately went off into nonsense verses about gentlemen in the parlor drinking wine and cordial, and ladies in the drawing-room drinking tea and coffee, etc. I have heard that many of the masters and overseers on these plantations prohibit melancholy tunes or words, and encourage nothing but cheerful music and senseless words, deprecating the effect of sadder strains upon the slaves, whose peculiar musical sensibility might be expected to make them especially excitable by any songs of a plaintive character, and having any reference to their particular hardships. If it is true, I think it a judicious precaution enough—these poor slaves are just the sort of people over whom a popular musical appeal to their feelings and passions would have an immense power.

FREDERICK LAW OLMSTED, A *Journey in the Seaboard Slave States, with Remarks on Their Economy* (New York, 1856), 394–95, 554, 607–10.

Negro Jodling. "The Carolina Yell."

I strolled off until I reached an opening in the woods, in which was a cotton-field and some negro-cabins, and beyond it large girdled trees, among which were two negroes with dogs, barking, yelping, hacking, shouting, and whistling, after 'coons and 'possums. Returning to the rail-road, I found a comfortable, warm passenger-car, and, wrapped in my blanket, went to sleep. At midnight I was awakened by loud laughter, and, looking out, saw that the loading gang of negroes had made a fire, and were enjoying a right merry repast. Suddenly, one raised such a sound as I never heard before; a long, loud, musical shout, rising, and falling, and breaking into falsetto, his voice ringing through the woods in the clear, frosty night air, like a bugle-call. As he finished, the melody was caught up by another, and then, another, and then, by several in chorus. When there was silence again, one of them cried out, as if bursting with amusement: "Did yer see de dog?—when I began echoing, he turn roun' an' look me straight into der face: ha! ha! ha!" and the whole party broke into the loudest peals of laughter, as if it was the very best joke they had ever heard.

After a few minutes I could hear one urging the rest to come to work again, and soon he stepped towards the cotton bales, saying, "Come, brederen, come: let's go at it; come now, coho! roll away! eeoho-eeoho-weeioho-i!"—and the rest taking it up as before, in a few moments they all had their shoulders to a bale of cotton, and were rolling it up the embankment.

· · ·

Slave High Life

He was a good violinist and dancer, and, two nights a week, taught a negro dancing-school, from which he received two dollars a night, which, of course, he spent for his own pleasure. During the winter, the negroes, in Montgomery, have their "assemblies," or dress balls, which are got up "regardless of expense," in very grand style. Tickets are advertised to these balls, "admitting one gentleman and two ladies, $1;" and "Ladies are assured that they may rely on the strictest order and propriety being observed." Cards of invitation, finely engraved with handsome vignettes, are sent, not only to the fashionable slaves, but to some of the more esteemed white people, who, however, take no part, except as lookers-on. All the fashionable dances are executed; no one is admitted, except in full dress: there are the regular masters of ceremonies, floor committees, etc.; and a grand supper always forms a part of the entertainment.

· · ·

We backed out, winded round head up, and as we began to breast the current, a dozen of the negro boat-hands, standing on the freight, piled up on the low forecastle, began to sing, waving hats and handkerchiefs, and shirts lashed to poles, towards the people who stood on the sterns of the steam-boats at the levee. After losing a few lines, I copied literally into my note-book:

"Ye see dem boat way dah ahead.
    Chorus.—Oahoiohieu.
De San Charles is arter 'em, dey mus go behine.
    Cho.—Oahoiohieu.
So stir up dah, my livelies, stir her up; (pointing to the furnaces).
    Cho.—Oahoiohieu.
Dey's burnin' not'n but fat and rosum.
    Cho.—Oahoiohieu.
Oh, we is gwine up de Red River. oh!
    Cho.—Oahoiohieu.
Oh, we must part from you dah asho'.
    Cho.—Oahoiohieu.

Give my lub to Dinah, oh!
   Cho.—Oahoiohieu.
For we is gwine up de Red River.
   Cho.—Oahoiohieu.
Yes, we is gwine up de Red River.
   Cho.—Oahoiohieu.
Oh we must part from you dah oh.
   Cho.—Oahoiohieu."

(The wit introduced into these songs has, I suspect, been rather over-estimated. On another occasion I took down the following:

"John come down in de holler,
  Oh, work and talk and holler,
  Oh, John, come down in de holler,
Ime 'gwine away to-morrow.
   Oh, John, &c.
Ime gwine away to marry,
   Oh, John, &c.
Get my cloves in order,
   Oh, John, &c.
I'se gwine away to-morrow,
   Oh, John, &c.
Oh, work and talk and holler,
   Oh, John, &c.
Massa guv me dollar,
   Oh, John, &c.
Don't cry your eyes out, honey,
   Oh, John, &c.
I'm gwine to get some money,
   Oh, John, &c.
But I'll come back to-morrow,
   Oh, John, &c.
So work and talk, and holler,
   Oh, John, &c.
Work all day and Sunday,
   Oh, John, &c.
Massa get de money,
   Oh, John, &c."

After the conclusion of this song, and after the negroes had left the bows, and were coming aft along the guards, we passed two or three colored nurses, walking with children on the river bank; as we did so the singers jumped on some cotton bales, bowed very low to

them, took off their hats, and swung and waved them, and renewed
their song:

> "God bless you all, dah! ladies!
> Oh, John come down in de holler.
> Farwell, de Lord be wid you, honey.
> Oh, John come down, &c.
> Done cry yerself to def,
> Oh, John, &c.
> I'm gwine down to New Orleans,
> Oh, John, &c.
> I'll come back, dough, bime-by,
> Oh, John, &c.
> So far-you-well, my honey,
> Oh, John, &c.
> Far-you-well, all you dah, shore,
> Oh, John, &c.
> And save your cotton for de Dalmo!
> Oh, John, &c."

JOSEPH H. INGRAHAM, *The Sunny South; or, The Southerner at
Home* (Philadelphia, 1860), 104–08.

We had just risen from the tea-table, last evening, when old George
made his appearance at the steps of the gallery, and, baring his bald
head, he bowed with a politeness that Lord Chesterfield would have
envied, and made us this speech:

"Young Missises and Massa colonel; old George take de liberty
to 'vite you to come to de dance out door by de ol' elm. Massa hab
giv' me new fiddle, and I takes pleasure to gi' de white folks a consart,
and show de young ladieses how my scholars dance."

We accepted George's polite invitation, and as the moon was full
we went over to the village. We were guided to the tree by the bright
light shed from half a dozen pine torches, held in the hands of as
many African animated statues, whom George had conspicuously stationed to throw light upon the scene.

As I approached the spot, I was struck with its novelty, for I have
not yet been long enough here to become familiar with all plantation
customs. I have told you that the negro village of the estate is pictur-
esquely disposed on the borders of a pretty *mere,* a few hundred yards
from the house. We crossed the water, by a wicker bridge, and had
most of the dwellings of the slaves in full view, occupying two streets

and three sides of a square. The lights of pine-wood flung a red and wild glare upon their fronts, and upon the lake, and upon a group of more than a hundred Africans of both sexes, who were assembled about the tree. It revealed, also, here and there an old man or woman, helpless through age, seated in their hut-doors, in order to enjoy as much of what was going on as they could.

We already found the dignified George seated upon his bench, fiddle in hand. On his right stood a short, fat negro, holding a banjo, and on his left was another slave, with eyes like the bottoms of China cups, holding two hollow sticks in his hand. Behind George was a toothless negress, having before her a section of a hollow tree, shaped like a drum, with a dried deer-skin drawn tightly over it; in her shining fist she grasped a sort of mallet. Chairs, assiduously provided, were placed for us, and the buzzing of pleasure, occasioned among the numerous company of Ham's posterity, having subsided, at a majestic wave of George's fiddle-bow, the concert began! The first time was a solo, and new to me, and so beautiful and simple that I made old George play it for me to-day in the house, and I copied the music as he did so. He says his father taught it to him. Certainly the negroes have striking native airs, characterized by delightful surprises and touching simplicity. Their chief peculiarity is cheerfulness.

George having first played a soft strain, the banjo struck in a second; then came the hollow sticks, like castanets, but five times as large, hollow, and more musical; and, lastly, the old negress thumped in a base on her hollow drum. The perfect time, the sweet harmony, the novelty of the strange sounds, the singular combination enchanted me. I must confess that I have never heard true music before; but then I should acknowledge I have not heard any operatic music in an opera-house. But do not smile if I say that I believe George and his three aiders and abettors would be listened to with pleasurable surprise, if they should play as I heard them play, by a Walnut street audience. *Real* African concert-singers are not, however, in fashion. White men blacked are only *comme il faut*. Is it not odd that a city audience will listen to *imitation* negroes, and yet despise a concerto composed of the Simon pures? After George had played several pieces, one of which was "Lucy Long," as I had never heard it before, and had received our praises, he said, always speaking with the dignity of an oracle:

"Now, if massa and de young ladieses please, we had de small-fry show demselve! Come, tand out here, you litty niggers! Show de white folk how you dance de corn dance!"

Thereupon a score of little darkies, from five years of age to a dozen years, girls and boys together, sprang from the crowd, and placed themselves in the space in front of us. Half of them were demi-clad, those that had shirts not being troubled with any superfluous apparel, and those that had trousers being shirtless; in a word, not a black skin was covered with but one species of garment, and this was generally a very short and very dirty, coarse *camisa*.

"Now make de dirt fly!" shouted George, as he struck up a brisk air alone—banjo, hollow sticks, and drum being silent.

The younglings obeyed the command to the letter. They danced like mad! The short-skirt flaps flew up and down, the black legs were as thickly mixed up as those of a centipede waltzing; woolly heads, white eyes, glittering teeth, yells and whoops, yah-yahs, and wou-wous, all united, created a scene that my shocked pen refuses to describe. The little negroes did full credit to old George's skill, and he evidently felt it. He sawed away desperately till the sweat rained from his furrowed brow. He writhed, and rose, and bent over, and stood up, and did every thing but lie down, playing all the while without cessation, and in a sort of rapturous ecstasy. Banjo caught the inspiration, and hollow sticks started after, while drum pounded away like young thunder, yelling a chant all the while, that, had her grandmother sung it to Mungo Park, would have driven him from the shelter of her hut to the less horrible howls of the desert. The little Africans danced harder and harder. Their parents caught the spirit of the moment, and this one, dashing his old cap down, sprang into the arena, and that one, uttering a whoop, followed, till full fifty were engaged at once. I never enjoyed any thing so much! I could fancy myself witnessing some heathen incantation dance in the groves of Africa! The moonlight shining through the trees, the red glare of the torches upon them, their wild movements, their strange and not unmusical cries, as they kept time with their voices to their quick tramping feet, their dark forms, their contortions, and perfect *abandon*, constituted a *tout ensemble* that must be witnessed to be appreciated.

THOMAS WENTWORTH HIGGINSON, *Army Life in a Black Regiment* (Boston, 1870), 131–34.

A regiment ordered on picket was expected to have reveille at daybreak, and to be in line for departure by sunrise. This delighted our men, who always took a childlike pleasure in being out of bed at any unreasonable hour; and by the time I had emerged, the tents were nearly all struck, and the great wagons were lumbering into camp to receive them, with whatever else was to be transported. The first rays of the sun must fall upon the line of these wagons, moving away across the wide parade-ground, followed by the column of men, who would soon outstrip them. But on the occasion which I especially describe the sun was shrouded, and, when once upon the sandy plain, neither camp nor town nor river could be seen in the dimness; and when I rode forward and looked back there was only visible the long, moving, shadowy column, seeming rather awful in its snake-like advance. There was a swaying of flags and multitudinous weapons that might have been camels' necks for all one could see, and the whole thing might have been a caravan upon the desert. Soon we debouched upon the "Shell Road," the wagon-train drew on one side into the fog, and by the time the sun appeared the music ceased, the men took the "route step," and the fun began.

The "route step" is an abandonment of all military strictness, and nothing is required of the men but to keep four abreast, and not lag behind. They are not required to keep step, though, with the rhythmical ear of our soldiers, they almost always instinctively did so; talking and singing are allowed, and of this privilege, at least, they eagerly availed themselves. On this day they were at the top of exhilaration. There was one broad grin from one end of the column to the other; it might soon have been a caravan of elephants instead of camels, for the ivory and the blackness; the chatter and the laughter almost drowned the tramp of feet and the clatter of equipments. At cross-roads and plantation gates the colored people thronged to see us pass; every one found a friend and a greeting. "How you do, aunty?" "Huddy (how d'ye), Budder Benjamin?" "How you find yourself dis mornin', Tittawisa (Sister Louisa)?" Such salutations rang out to everybody, known or unknown. In return, venerable, kerchiefed matrons courtesied laboriously to every one, with an unfailing "Bress de Lord, budder." Grave little boys, blacker than ink, shook hands with our laughing and utterly unmanageable drummers, who greeted them with this sure word of prophecy, "Dem's de drummers for de nex' war!" Pretty mulatto girls ogled and coquetted, and made eyes, as Thackeray would say, at half the young fellows in the battalion. Meantime the singing was brisk along the whole column, and when I sometimes reined up to see them pass, the chant of each company, entering my ear, drove out from the other ear the strain of the preceding. Such

an odd mixture of things, military and missionary, as the successive
waves of song drifted by! First, "John Brown," of course; then, "What
make old Satan for follow me so?" then, "Marching Along"; then,
"Hold your light on Canaan's shore"; then, "When this cruel war is
over" (a new favorite, sung by a few); yielding presently to a grand
burst of the favorite marching song among them all, and one at which
every step instinctively quickened, so light and jubilant its rhythm,—

> "All true children gwine in de wilderness,
> Gwine in de wilderness, gwine in de wilderness,
> True believers gwine in de wilderness,
> To take away de sins ob de world."—

ending in a "Hoigh!" after each verse,—a sort of Irish yell. For all the
songs, but especially for their own wild hymns, they constantly improvised simple verses, with the same odd mingling,—the little facts of
to-day's march being interwoven with the depths of theological
gloom, and the same jubilant chorus annexed to all; thus,—

> "We're gwin to de Ferry,
>   De bell done ringing;
> Gwine to de landing,
>   De bell done ringing;
> Trust, believer
>   O, de bell done ringing;
> Satan's behind me,
>   De bell done ringing;
> 'T is a misty morning,
>   De bell done ringing;
> O de road am sandy,
>   De bell done ringing;
> Hell been open,
>   De bell done ringing";—

and so on indefinitely.

The little drum-corps kept in advance, a jolly crew, their drums
slung on their backs, and the drum-sticks perhaps balanced on their
heads. With them went the officers' servant-boys, more uproarious
still, always ready to lend their shrill treble to any song. At the head
of the whole force there walked, by some self-imposed pre-eminence,
a respectable elderly female, one of the company laundresses, whose
vigorous stride we never could quite overtake, and who had an enormous bundle balanced on her head, while she waved in her hand,

like a sword, a long-handled tin dipper. Such a picturesque medley of fun, war, and music I believe no white regiment in the service could have shown; and yet there was no straggling, and a single tap of the drum would at any moment bring order out of this seeming chaos. . . .

BISHOP D. PAYNE, *Recollections of Seventy Years,* ed. C. S. Smith (Nashville, 1888), 253–55.

I have mentioned the "Praying and Singing Bands" elsewhere. The strange delusion that many ignorant but well-meaning people labor under leads me to speak particularly of them. About this time I attended a "bush meeting," where I went to please the pastor whose circuit I was visiting. After the sermon they formed a ring, and with coats off sung, clapped their hands and stamped their feet in a most ridiculous and heathenish way. I requested the pastor to go and stop their dancing. At his request they stopped their dancing and clapping of hands, but remained singing and rocking their bodies to and fro. This they did for about fifteen minutes. I then went, and taking their leader by the arm requested him to desist and to sit down and sing in a rational manner. I told him also that it was a heathenish way to worship and disgraceful to themselves, the race, and the Christian name. In that instance they broke up their ring; but would not sit down, and walked sullenly away. After the sermon in the afternoon, having another opportunity of speaking alone to this young leader of the singing and clapping ring, he said: "Sinners won't get converted unless there is a ring." Said I: "You might sing till you fell down dead, and you would fail to convert a single sinner, because nothing but the Spirit of God and the word of God can convert sinners." He replied: "The Spirit of God works upon people in different ways. At camp-meeting there must be a ring here, a ring there, a ring over yonder, or sinners will not get converted." This was his idea, and it is also that of many others. These "Bands" I have had to encounter in many places, and, as I have stated in regard to my early labors in Baltimore, I have been strongly censured because of my efforts to change the mode of worship or modify the extravagances indulged in by the people. In some cases all that I could do was to teach and preach the right, fit, and proper way of serving God. To the most thoughtful and intelligent I usually succeeded in making the "Band" disgusting; but by the ignorant masses, as in the case mentioned, it was regarded as the essence of religion. So much so was this the case that, like this man, they believed no conversion could occur without their agency, nor outside of their own ring could any be a genuine one. Among some of the songs of these "Rings," or "Fist and Heel Worshipers," as they have been called, I find a note or two in my journal, which were used in the instance mentioned. As will be seen, they consisted chiefly of what are known as "corn-field ditties:"

> "Ashes to ashes, dust to dust;
> If God won't have us, the devil must.
> "I was way over there where the coffin fell;
> I heard that sinner as he screamed in hell."

To indulge in such songs from eight to ten and half-past ten at night was the chief employment of these "Bands." Prayer was only a secondary thing, and this was rude and extravagant to the last degree. The man who had the most powerful pair of lungs was the one who made the best prayer, and he could be heard a square off. He who could sing loudest and longest led the "Band," having his loins girded and a handkerchief in hand with which he kept time, while his feet resounded on the floor like the drumsticks of a bass drum. In some places it was the custom to begin these dances after every night service and keep it up till midnight, sometimes singing and dancing alternately—a short prayer and a long dance. Some one has even called it the "Voudoo Dance."

GEORGE W. CABLE, "A Negro Folk-Song," *The Folk-Lorist*, vol. I, no. 1 (July 1892), 54.

There is a kind of folk-song in the Southern States which it might be found very interesting to consider, if only some one would give it some research. Doubtless there are educated negroes in the South who might do this, and who would have facilities for such a labor of love, which others would hardly command. I allude to the snatches and refrains which the negro slaves used to sing to the games they played, often by torchlight in groves of oaks or avenues of persimmons, hard by their "quarters," continuing them half through a summer night. Sometimes they were induced to play these games close by the master's own house, for the delight of his family as spectators. Two or three fragments still linger in my memory, and I offer one as a slight hint of what might be done.

O me! pit - y po' me!   I'm   in dem   la-dies'   gya'-din!

Oh me! pit - y po' me!   I'm   in dem   la-dies'   gya'-din!

Bow to de ladies,   Su-san Gay,   Bow to de gen-'le-men,   Su-san Gay.

Bow to de la-dies,   Su-san Gay,   Bow to de gen-'le-men,   Su-san Gay.

GEORGE MERRICK, *Old Times on the Upper Mississippi; . . .* (Cleveland, 1909), 157–60.

The cabin orchestra was the cheapest and most enduring, as well as the most popular drawing card. A band of six or eight colored men who could play the violin, banjo, and guitar, and in addition sing well, was always a good investment. These men were paid to do the work of waiters, barbers, and baggagemen, and in addition were given the privilege of passing the hat occasionally, and keeping all they caught. They made good wages by this combination, and it also pleased the passengers, who had no suspicion that the entire orchestra was hired with the understanding that they were to play as ordered by the captain or chief clerk, and that it was a strictly business engagement. They also played for dances in the cabin, and at landings sat on the guards and played to attract custom. It soon became advertised abroad which boats carried the best orchestras, and such lost nothing in the way of patronage.

Some of the older generation yet living, may have heard Ned Kendall play the cornet. If not, they may have heard of him, for his fame was at this time world-wide, as the greatest of all masters on his favorite instrument. Like many another genius, strong drink mastered him, and instead of holding vast audiences spellbound in Eastern theatres, as he had done, he sold his art to influence custom on an Alton Line boat. It was my good fortune to have heard him two or three times, and his music appeals to me yet, through all the years that lie between. The witchery and the pathos of "Home, Sweet Home," "Annie Laurie," the "White Squall," and selections from operas of which I had then never even heard the names, cast such a spell that the boat on which he travelled was crowded every trip. Pity 'tis that one so gifted should fall into a slavery from which there was no redemption. He died in St. Louis, poor and neglected, a wreck infinitely more pitiable than that of the finest steamboat ever cast away on the Great River.

One of the boats on which I served employed a sextet of negro firemen, whose duty, in addition to firing, was to sing to attract custom at the landings. This was not only a unique performance, but it was likewise good music—that is, good of its kind. There was nothing classic about it, but it was naturally artistic. They sang plantation melodies—real negro melodies, not the witless and unmusical inanities which under the name of "coon songs" pass with the present generation for negro minstrelsy. Of course these darkies were picked for their musical ability, and were paid extra wages for singing.

The leader, Sam Marshall, received more than the others, because he was an artist. This term does not do him justice. In addition to a voice of rare sweetness and power, Sam was a born improvisatore. It was his part of the entertainment to stand on the capstan-head, with his chorus gathered about him, as the boat neared the landing. If at night, the torch fed with fatwood and resin threw a red glow upon his shining black face, as he lifted up his strong, melodious voice, and lined out his improvised songs, which recited the speed and elegance of this particular boat, the suavity and skill of its captain, the dexterity of its pilots, the manfulness of its mate, and the loveliness of Chloe, its black chambermaid. This latter reference always "brought down the house," as Chloe usually placed herself in a conspicuous place on the guards to hear the music, and incidentally the flatteries of her coal-black lover. As each line was sung by the leader the chorus would take up the refrain:

> De captain stands on de upper deck;
> (Ah ha-a-a-ah! Oh ho-o-o-o-ho!)
> You nebber see 'nudder such gentlehem, I 'spec;
> (Ah ha-a-a-ah, Oh ho-o-ho.)

and then would follow, as an interlude, the refrain of some old plantation melody in the same key and meter, the six darkies singing their parts in perfect time and accord, and with a melody that cannot be bettered in all the world of music.

> De pilot he twisses he big roun' wheel;
> (Ah ha-a-a-ah, Oh ho-o-o-oh.)
>
> He sings, and he whissels, and he dance Virginia reel,
> (Ah ha-a-a-ah, Oh ho-o-o-ho),—

an undoubted reference to Tom Cushing, who, before his promotion to the pilot house was said to have been a tenor in grand opera in New York. He was a beautiful singer at any rate; could whistel like a New York newsboy, and dance like a coryphée. The "Old Man" would have been willing to take his oath that Cushing could and did do all three at the same time, in the most untimely hours of the morning watch, at the same time steering his steamboat in the most approved fashion.

The next stanza was:

> " 'Gineer in the engin' room listenn' fo' de bell;
> He boun' to beat dat oder boat or bus' 'em to—heb'n,"

was accepted as a distinct reference to Billy Hamilton, as the manner of stating his intention to win out in a race was peculiar to the junior engineer, and the proposition was accepted without debate.

> "De Debbel he come in the middle of de night;
> Sam, dere, he scairt so he tuhn mos' white—Jes like dat white man
> out dere on de lebbee,"

pointing at some one whom he deemed it safe to poke fun at, and of course raising a laugh at the expense of the individual so honored.

> "Des look at dem white fokses standin' on de sho';
> Dey la-a-a-aff, and dey la-a-aff, till dey cain't laff no mo'—ha-ha-
> ha-ha-ha,"

and Sam would throw back his head and laugh a regular contagion into the whole crowd—on the boat and "on de sho," opening a mouth which one of the darkies asserted was "de biggest mouf dis nigger ebber saw on any human bein' 'cept a aligator"; or, as the mate expressed it: "It was like the opening of navigation."

> "Dish yer nigger he fire middle do';
> Shake 'em up libely for to make de boat go,"

was a somewhat ornate description of Mr. Marshall's own duties on board the boat. As a matter of fact he did very little firing, personally, although when a race was on he could shovel coal or pitch four-foot wood into the middle door with the best of them, at the same time, singing at the top of his voice. Upon ordinary occasions he let the other darkies pitch the cord wood while he exercised a general supervision over them, as became an acknowledged leader.

To hear these darkies sing the real slave music, which was older than the singers, older than the plantation, as old as Africa itself, wherein the ancestors of some of them at least, might have been kings and princes as well as freemen, was better than the fo'c'sle comedies enacted for the amusement of the passengers. These minor chords carried a strain of heartbreak, as in the lines:

> "De night is dark, de day is long
> And we are far fum home,
> Weep, my brudders, weep!"

And the closing lines:

> "De night is past, de long day done,
> An' we are going home,
> Shout, my brudders, shout!"

were a prophecy of that day of freedom and rest, after centuries of toil and bondage, the dawn of which was even then discernible to those who, like Abraham Lincoln, were wise to read in the political heavens the signs of its coming.

MISCELLANEOUS

FREDERICK LAW OLMSTED, *A Journey in the Seaboard Slave States, With Remarks on Their Economy* (New York, 1856), 448–49.

Slave "Marriages" . . .

While watching the negroes in the field, Mr. X addressed a girl, who was vigorously plying a hoe near us.

"Is that Lucy?—Ah, Lucy, what's this I hear about you?"

The girl simpered; but did not answer nor discontinue her work.

"What is this I hear about you and Sam, eh?"

The girl grinned; and, still hoeing away with all her might, whispered "Yes, sir."

"Sam came to see me this morning."

"If master pleases."

"Very well; you may come up to the house Saturday night, and your mistress will have something for you."

Mr. X. does not absolutely refuse to allow his negroes to "marry off the place," as most large slave-owners do, but he discourages intercourse, as much as possible, between his negroes and those of other plantations; and they are usually satisfied to choose from among themselves.

When a man and woman wish to live with each other, they are

required to ask leave of their master; and, unless there are some very obvious objections, this is always granted: a cabin is allotted to them, and presents are made of dresses and housekeeping articles. A marriage ceremony, in the same form as that used by free people, is conducted by the negro preacher, and they are encouraged to make the occasion memorable and gratifying to all, by general festivity. The master and mistress, when on the plantation, usually honor the wedding by their attendance; and, if they are favorite servants, it is held in the house, and the ceremony performed by a white minister.

G. A. SALA, *America Revisited* (London, 1883), 350–52.

But it was not in turbans and plaid shawls that the coloured ladies of New Orleans commanded notice and extorted admiration during the Carnival. They appeared in the height of the fashion, as expounded by *Le Follet*, the *Gazette des Modes*, and *Myra's Journal*—but read generally, as witches' prayers are said to be, backwards. "Magnolious" and "spanglorious" are, perhaps, the most suitable epithets which hyperbole can supply to convey a notion of these astonishing *outre* rigs-out. The much-bustled crinoline of twenty years ago was now and then employed to distend the "princess" robe of to-day, and the result was a liberal display of white cotton stocking. In some cases the hose had been "pinked," like unto the hose of an impecunious ballet-girl; and these, with a pair of white taffety boots, with high heels, produced a very "pleasing" effect. Laced petticoats, sometimes decorated with a fringe of quack advertisement bills, which during the whole of the Carnival were sown broadcast on the pavement, were much noticed and sunshades of pink, yellow, and sky-blue alpaca were much in demand. As a rule, the toilet of the coloured ladies did not run so far as gloves; but they "took it out," as the saying is, in pocket-handkerchiefs edged with cheap lace and in enormous reticules. And, dear me, what a perfume of patchouli there was on the side-walk.

ELIZABETH H. BOTUME, *First Days Amongst the Contrabands* (Boston, 1893), 109–11, 236–37.

One day, early in the winter, I received a note from General and Mrs. Saxton, saying they were coming with a party to visit the school, and would be there by three o'clock p.m. This was when Sherman's army was moving through Georgia. Mrs. Saxton knew that in the chaotic condition of things I did not like to entertain visitors unaware.

I thought this a good time to urge upon the children to make themselves as clean and tidy as possible. To encourage them I gave out a large number of wooden pocket-combs which had been given me. Then I dismissed them, charging them to run home, but to be sure to come back before two o'clock, with clean faces and hands, and their heads brushed. They hurried off delighted.

Alas! How little I knew of these erratic beings! I was as ignorant of their powers of comprehension as they of my meaning. What did two o'clock or luncheon signify to them! Absolutely nothing. They have very little idea of what I meant.

"Teacher sen' we home, an' us is to go back." That was all, and any time would do.

I shall never forget those hours of anxious waiting all alone. Not a chick nor a child to be seen. A great stretch of rough cotton-fields on three sides of me, and the broad river on the fourth. In desperation I rang again and again my little cracked handbell,—this was before the arrival of my schoolhouse bell,—hoping to arouse some one.

Promptly at three o'clock the general and his party came in sight. There were General Saxton and his staff officers, and General O.O. Howard and his staff. Brave men on horseback, and fair ladies in carriages, and I stood alone to greet them, with no school for them to see.

I begged the general to drive on to Old Fort, which was one of the points of interest, whilst one of the party went back to order forward the children. He met the whole gang hurrying along. They had seen the general's party drive by, and concluded it was time for them to start. Their nonchalance as they marched into the schoolroom was exasperating after all the time I had spent in anxious waiting. In less than ten minutes the room was full of scholars seated in order, with clean and shining faces and well combed heads. Each child wore the wooden comb stuck on the top of the head like a top-knot, for ornament, and they evidently felt fine.

The variety and grotesqueness of their clothing defies description. No doubt each of them had assumed the best thing he could find, no matter to whom it belonged. Girls had on men's coats, some of which were so big they reached to the ground. Boys had entire suits made of bed-ticking and old horse blankets. The chief thing seemed to be to prove how little clothing could be made to cover them and keep them on the verge of decency.

On this occasion they had followed my directions to the letter. Some of the children looked as if they had ducked their head the last thing before they started. The water was trickling down their faces and into their necks.

One boy had half of his head shaved, while the other half was untouched. A girl had put on a long-sleeved apron I had given her, "hind side before," so as to wear it like a sack. I had written her name on a piece of white paper and pinned it on the sleeve, and she would not allow this to be taken off. Indeed, she wore this name as long as her apron lasted, having care enough to take it off when the apron was washed, and then pinning it on again.

. . .

The colored women seemed to delight more in an old garment than a new one. They felt at liberty to cut and alter and patch it *ad libitum;* besides it gave them excuse for asking for "one needle and a leetle bit o' thread," which they always got.

At one time we had thirty new plaid worsted dresses all cut and basted sent us for the sewing-school. The girls were delighted; but when they carried them home, the mothers considered them altogether too short. It was highly indecorous to have the feet and ankles show below the dress; so they pieced them out, often with most unsuitable material, putting old cloth with the new, and a cotton frill to a worsted skirt. One woman got new cloth, which she inlaid to widen and lengthen and enlarge her child's gown. It looked, when done, like a modern "crazy quilt." It was very odd, but really not ugly.

Biographical Notes on Authors Reprinted

THE WEST INDIES

NOTE: The location (in italics) preceding each entry is the site of the description.

ALEXANDER, CAPTAIN SIR JAMES EDWARD
(1803–85)

Tobago (p. 191) and Guyana
> British Army officer and explorer, served in India, Southern Asia, the Crimea, and New Zealand.

Selected Works
> *Transatlantic Sketches, Comprising Visits to the Most Interesting Scenes in North and South America, and the West Indies.* London, 1833.
> *Travels from India to England; Comprehending a Visit to the Burman Empire, and a Journey through Persia, Asia Minor, European Turkey, in the years 1825–26.* London, 1827.
> *Life of the Duke of Wellington; Embracing his Civil, Military, and Political Career.* 2 vols. London, 1840.
> *L'Acadie: or Seven Years' Explorations in British America.* 2 vols. London, 1849.
> *Cleopatra's Needle, the Obelisk of Alexandri, its Acquisition and Removal to England Described* . . . London, 1879.

AMPHLETT, JOHN
(1845–1918)

Barbados
> English writer and historian of Worcestershire.

411

Selected Works
> *Under a Tropical Sky: A Journal of First Impressions of the West Indies.* London, 1873.
> *Wornton Kings.* (A novel). London, 1875.
> *A Short History of Clent.* London and Oxford, 1890.
> *The Church Warden's Accounts of Saint Michaels in Bedwordine, Worcestershire.* 2 vols. Oxford, 1894–95.
> *The Botany of Worcestershire.* Birmingham, 1910.

ATWOOD, THOMAS
(died 1793)

Dominica
> Chief judge of Dominica and the Bahamas.

Selected Works
> *The History of the Island of Dominica.* London, 1791.
> *Observations on the True Method and Treatment and Usage of the Negro Slaves in the British West Indies Islands.* 1790.

BAIRD, ROBERT
(1798–1863)

Jamaica
> United States Minister, missionary preacher, educator, and reformer.

Selected Works
> *Impressions and Experiences of the West Indies and North America in 1849.* London, 1850.
> *A View of the Valley of the Mississippi.* 1832.
> *History of the Temperance Societies.* 1836.
> *Visit to Northern Europe.* 1841.
> *Protestantism in Italy.* 1848.

BARCLAY, ALEXANDER
(1785–1864)

Jamaica
> Commissioner of emigration, Jamaica.

Selected Works
> *A Practical View of the Present State of Slavery in the West Indies, or an examination of Mr. Stephen's slavery of the British*

West Indian Colonies, containing more particularly an account of the actual condition of the negroes in Jamaica: with observation on the decrease of the slaves since the abolition of the slave trade, and the probable effects of legislative emancipation; also structures on the Edinburgh review, and the pamphlets of Mr. Cooper and Mr. Bickell. London, 1826, 1828.

Jamaica: Remarks on Emigration to Jamaica; Addressed to the Coloured Class of the United States. New York, 1840.

BAYLEY, FREDERICK WILLIAM NAYLOR
(1808–53)

Barbados
> Born in Ireland; writer, editor, journalist. Accompanied his father on army offices to Barbados in 1825 and remained until 1829. Drama and music critic, *Morning Post*, 1831; founded and edited the *National Omnibus*; first editor of *Illustrated London News*, 1842–48. Author of popular songs, including "The Newfoundland Dog."

Selected Works
> *Four Years' Residence in the West Indies.* London, 1830. 3d ed., 1833.
> *An Island (Grenada) Bagatelle.* 1829.
> *Scenes and Stories by a Clergyman in Debt.* 3 vols. 1835.
> *New Tale of a Tub.* 1841, 1847.
> *Comic Nursery Rhymes.* 1842.
> *Little Red Riding Hood.* 1843.
> *The Model of the Earth.* 1851.

BECKFORD, WILLIAM
(died 1799)

Jamaica
> English historian, resident planter in Jamaica.

Selected Works
> *Remarks on the Situation of the Negroes in Jamaica. Impartially made from a local experience of nearly thirteen years in that island.* London, 1790.
> *History of France from the Most Early Records to the Death of Louis XVI.* London, 1794.

A *Descriptive Account of the Island of Jamaica*. 2 vols. London, 1790.

BEKE, X.
(*See* Hawtayne, George)

BELISARIO I. M.

Sketches of Character in Illustration of the Habits, Occupations and Costume of the Negro Population in the Island of Jamaica. 3 parts. Kingston, 1837–38.

BREEN, HENRY HEGART
(1805–82)

St. Lucia
English writer and official, born in Kerry, Ireland, and educated in Paris. Government administration, St. Lucia, 1857–61.
Selected Works
St. Lucia: Historical, Statistical, and Descriptive. London, 1844.
Diamond Rock and other Poems. 1849.
Modern English Literature: Its Blemishes and Defects. London, 1858.
Warrowarra, the Carib Chief: A Tale of 1770. 2 vols. London, 1876.

BRONKHURST, REVEREND H. V. P.

Guyana
Methodist minister.
Selected Works
The Colony of British Guyana and its Labouring Population; containing a short account of the colony, and brief description of the Black Creole, Portuguese, East Indian, and Chinese cookies . . . collected . . . from sundry articles published . . . at different times, and arranged by Rev. H.V.P. Bronkhurst. London, 1883.
The Ancestry or Origin of our East Indian Immigrants . . . Georgetown, Demerara, 1886.
Among the Hindues and Creoles of British Guiana. London, 1888.

A Descriptive and Historical Geography of British Guiana and West Indian Islands. Demerara, 1890.

CAMPBELL, CHARLES
(1793–?)

Jamaica
Memoirs of Charles Campbell, at present prisoner in the Jail at Glasgow. Including his adventures as a seaman, and as an overseer in the West Indies. Written by himself to which is appended, an account of his trial before the circuit court of Justiciary at Glasgow, 27th April 1826. Glasgow, 1828.

CARMICHAEL, MRS. A. C.

St. Vincent (Vol. I) and Trinidad (Vol. II)
Selected Works
Domestic Manners and Social Conditions of the White, Coloured, and Negro Population of the West Indies. 2d ed., 1839. London, 1833.
Five Years in Trinidad and St. Vincent: A view of the social conditions of the White, Coloured, and Negro Population of the West Indies. 2 vols. London, 1834.

CHAMBRE, MAJOR ALAN

Jamaica
Recollections of West End Life in London: with Sketches of Society in Paris, India, and etc. 2 vols. London, 1858.

CHESTER, REVEREND GREVILLE JOHN
(1830–93)

Barbados
British clergyman.
Selected Works
Transatlantic Sketches in the West Indies, South America, Canada, and the United States. London, 1869.
Poems. London, 1856.
A Church Hymn-Book with Metrical Psalms. London, 1859.

*Catalogue of the Egyptian Antiquities in the Ashmolean Museum,
    Oxford.* Oxford, 1881.
*Notes on the Present and Future of the Archeological Collections
    of the University of Oxford.* Oxford, 1881.
Ella Cathullin, and other poems Old and New. London, 1883.
Evelyn Manworing: A Tale of Hampton Court Palace. London,
    1883.

DANCE, REVEREND CHARLES DANIEL

Guyana
    British missionary to Guyana and Venezuela.
Selected Works
    *Chapters from a Guianese Log-Book, or the folk-lore and scenes
        of sea-coast and riverlife in British Guiana. Company sketches
        of Indian, Boviander and Negro life, habits, customs, and leg-
        endary tales, with historic notes, political and natural . . .*
        Georgetown, Demerara, 1881.
    *Recollections of Four Years in Venezuela, a mission priest in the
        Diocese of Guiana.* London, 1876.

DAY, CHARLES WILLIAM

*Barbados (Vol I, 46–48, 52–53); St. Vincent (Vol. I, 85–86); Trinidad
(Vol. I, 313–16); St. Kitts (Vol. II, 121–22); British Virgin Islands (Vol.
II, 61–64; 111–14; and 297.)*
Selected Works
    Five Years' Residence in the West Indies. 2 vols. London, 1852.
    The Maxims, Experiences, and Observations of Agogos. Boston,
        1844.
    More Hints on Etiquette. London, 1838.
    *The American Ladies' and Gentlemen's Manual of Elegance,
        Fashion, and True Politeness.* Buffalo, 1849.

DE LA BECHE, SIR HENRY THOMAS
(1796–1855)

Jamaica
    British geologist.
Selected Works
    Notes on the Present Conditions of the Negroes in Jamaica. Lon-
        don, 1825.

Manual of Geology. 1831.
Researches in Theoretical Geology. 1834.
Report on its Geology of Cornwall, Devon, and West Somerset.
1839.

DES VOEUX, SIR GEORGE WILLIAM
(1834–1909)

Guyana
Selected Works
> *Experiences of a Demerara Magistrate 1863–1869; with an ap-
> pendix comprising the author's letter to the Secretary of State
> for the Colonies on the subject of the treatment of East Indian
> immigrants on Sugar Estates.* Georgetown, British Guiana,
> 1948. (Reprint of first 9 chapters of *My Colonial Service* [Lon-
> don, 1903]).
> *My Colonial Service in British Guiana, St. Lucia, Trinidad, Fiji,
> Australia, Newfoundland, and Hong Kong, with Interludes.*
> London, 1903.

EDWARDS, BRYAN
(1743–1800)

Jamaica
> British West India merchant. Born in Westbury, Wiltshire. Went
> to Jamaica in 1759 to live with an uncle; admitted to family busi-
> ness and became a successful merchant. Returned to England
> several times, permanently in 1792. Secretary of Association for
> Promoting the Discovery of the Interior Parts of Africa, 1797.
> Elected to Parliament in 1796; opposed abolition of the slave
> trade.
Selected Works
> *The History, Civil and Commercial, of the British Colonies in the
> West Indies.* 2 vols. Dublin, 1793.
> *An Historical Survey of the French Colony in the Island of Santo
> Domingo.* 1797.

FROUDE, JAMES ANTHONY
(1818–94)

Jamaica
> English historian and writer. Born in Darlington, Devonshire.
> Friend of Thomas Carlyle and Matthew Arnold. Editor of *Fraser's*

Magazine, 1860–74. Elected rector, University of St. Andrews, 1867. Visited Norway, 1881; Australian Colonies, 1884–85; West Indies, 1886–87. Froude was Regius Professor of Modern History, Oxford, 1892.

Selected Works

The English in the West Indies; or the Bow of Ulysses; with Nine Illustrations from Sketches by the Author. London, 1888.

The Book of Job. 1854.

History of England From the Fall of Wolsley to the Defeat of the Spanish Armada. 12 vols. London, 1856–70.

Thomas Carlyle: History of his Life in London. 7 vols. London, 1884.

Oceania, or, England and her Colonies. London, 1886.

GARDNER, WILLIAM JAMES
(1825–74)

Jamaica

English missionary to Jamaica. Founder of the Kingston Benefit Building Society and the Provident Benefit Society.

A History of Jamaica. London, 1873.

HAWTAYNE, GEORGE H. (X. BEKE pseud.)
(1832–1902)

Guyana

Educated at King's College, London. Corresponding member of the Zoological Society of London and of the Pharmaceutical Society of Great Britain. Private secretary to governor of the Windward Islands from 1869 to 1871. Acted as colonial secretary of St. Vincent, 1871–74. Administrator-general of British Guiana, 1881–99.

West Indian Yarns. Demerara and London, 1890.

KELLY, JAMES

Jamaica

Merchant of Jamaica.

Voyage to Jamaica, and Seventeen Years residence in that Island Chiefly written with a view to exhibit negro life and habits; with extracts from Strange and Harvey's "West Indies in 1837" . . . Belfast, 1838.

KIRKE, HENRY
(1842–1925)

Guyana
English barrister and colonial official. Acting court judge in British Guiana, 1874. Sheriff of Essequibo, 1877.
Selected Works
Twenty-five Years in British Guiana. London, 1898.
Thurston Meverell; or, The Forest of the Peak: a Romance. London, 1868.
The First English Conquest of Canada, with some account of the Earliest settlements in Nova Scotia and Newfoundland. London, 1871.

LANIGAN, MRS.

Antigua
Antigua and the Antiguans. London, 1844.

LESLIE, CHARLES

Jamaica
Selected Works
A New and Exact Account of Jamaica, wherein the ancient and present state of that colony, its importance to Great Britain, Laws, Trade, manners and religion, together with the most remarkable and curious animals, plants, trees, etc. are described: with a particular account of the sacrifices, libations, etc. at their day in use among the Negroes. Edinburgh, 1739. 3d ed., London, 1740.
A New History of Jamaica, from earliest accounts, to the taking of Porto Bello by Vice-Admiral Vernon. In thirteen letters from a gentleman to his friend . . . London, 1740.

LEWIS, MATTHEW GREGORY
(1775–1818)

Jamaica
Born in London. Author, poet, and playwright; best known for the gothic romance, *The Monk*, 1794; attaché to British Embassy at The Hague; M. P. for Hindon, Wiltshire, 1796–1802. Inherited

estates and slaves in Jamaica, 1812. In 1816–18 he visited the
West Indies to view the conditions of slaves on his land.
Selected Works
> *Journal of a West India Proprietor*. London, 1834.
> *Ambrosio, or the Monk*. 3 vols. London, 1795.
> *Village Virtues*. 1796.
> *Poems*. 1812.

LIGON, RICHARD

Barbados
> Seventeenth-century English traveler and merchant. After being
> ruined in political crises in 1647, he tried to recoup his fortunes
> in the West Indies. After purchasing horses and cattle in the
> Cape Verde Islands, Ligon landed in Barbados, where he re-
> mained 3 years, despite yellow fever and famine. Ligon worked
> the plantation purchased by Sir Thomas Mody Ford, although he
> repeatedly suffered from tropical diseases. When he returned to
> England in 1650 his creditors had him thrown in prison. He
> wrote the story of his experiences while in prison.
Selected Work
> *A True and Exact History of the Island of Barbadoes*. London,
> 1657, 1673.

LLOYD, WILLIAM.

Barbados
> *Letters from the West Indies, During a Visit in the Autumn of
> MDCCCXXXVI and the Spring of MDCCCXXXVIII* London,
> 1839.

LONG, EDWARD
(1734–1813)

Jamaica
> Born Cornwall, England; Jamaican judge.
Selected Works
> *The History of Jamaica*. 3 vols. London, 1774.
> *The Anti-Gallician, or the History and Adventures of Henry Cob-
> ham, Esq*. 1757.

Letter on the Colonies. 1775.
A Pamphlet on the Sugar Trade. 1782.

LUFFMAN, JOHN
(1776–1820)

Antigua

British geographer, publisher, engraver, and goldsmith. Luffman
visited Antigua, 1786–88, and engraved a map of the island, published by Faden in 1793. In addition to his own works, he engraved the plates for Lavater's *Physiognomical Sketches,* and
maps and plans for many other authors.

Selected Works

*A Brief Account of the Island of Antigua, together with the cus-
toms and manners of its inhabitants, white as well as black: as
also an accurate statement of the food, clothing, labour, and
punishment of slaves. In letters to a friend. Written in the years
1786, 1787, 1788.* London, 1789; 2d ed. 1790; German ed. 1790.
*Select Plans of the Principal Cities, Harbours, Ports, etc. in the
World.* 2 vols. London, 1801.
Elements of History and Chronology. 2 vols. London, 1805.
*Luffman's Geographic and Topographical Atlas, consisting of
maps of countries, plans of cities and forts, ports and harbours,
battles, etc.* London, 1815–16.

LYNCH, MRS. HENRY (NÉE THEODORA ELIZABETH FOULKS)
(1812–85)

Jamaica

British writer of poetry and prose. Born in Sussex to a daughter
of a Jamaica sugar planter. Wife of Jamaican barrister, Henry
Mark Lynch; after his death in 1845, she returned to England
and wrote fiction, some it for children, much of it set in the West
Indies.

Selected Works

The Wonders of the West Indies. London, 1856.
The Cotton Tree, or Emily, the Little West Indian. London, 1847.
The Family Sepulcher, a Tale of Jamaica. London, 1849.
Maude Effingham, A Tale of Jamaica. 1849.
Rose and Her Mission, a Tale of the West Indies. 1863.

*Years Ago, A Tale of West Indian Domestic Life of the Eighteenth
Century.* London, 1865.

MADDEN, RICHARD ROBERT
(1798–1886)

Jamaica
Irish surgeon, writer, and British colonial administrator. In
1833–34, special magistrate in Kingston, Jamaica, charged with
enactment of the statute abolishing slavery. In 1836–40, super-
intendent of liberated Africans and judge arbiter in the mixed
court of commission, Havana.
Selected Works
*A Twelve Month's Residence in the West Indies, during the tran-
sition from slavery to apprenticeship.* 2 vols. London, 1835.
Travels in the West Indies. London, 1838–40.
The Slave Trade. London, 1843.
*Egypt and Mohammed Ali, Illustrative of the Condition of His
Slaves and Subjects.* London, 1841.
The United Irishmen; Their Lives and Times. 7 vols. London,
1843–46.

MARSDEN, PETER

Jamaica
An Account of the Island of Jamaica. Newcastle, 1788.

MORETON, J. B.

Jamaica
Manners and Customs of the West India Island. London, 1790.

MURRAY, HENRY G.

Jamaica
Selected Works
*Manners and Customs of the Country a Generation Ago: Tom
Kittle's Wake.* Kingston, Jamaica, 1877.
*Manners and Customs of the Country a Generation Ago; Brown
Sammy Finds a Wife and Finds Trouble, or "Married hab Teet";*

the Sequel to Brown Sammy in Search of a Wife. Kingston, 1876.

Feedin Perrit: A Lecture Illustrative of Jamaican Mythology. Kingston, 1877.

NUGENT, LADY MARIA (SKINNER)
(1771?–1834)

Jamaica
Wife of Lieutenant-General George Nugent, governor of Jamaica, 1801–05.

A Journal of a Voyage to, and Residence in, the Island of Jamaica . . . London, 1839.

Lady Nugent's Journal. Edited by Frank Cundall. London, 1907. Reprint of the 1839 book.

PHILLPOTTS, EDEN
(1862–1960)

Bahamas
British playwright and novelist. Born in India, 1852, son of an Indian army officer; family returned to England after father's death. Assistant editor, *Black and White* weekly. Wrote an average of 3 or 4 books a year: poetry, plays, essays, mysteries, and retold classics. Wrote many plays in collaboration with Arnold Bennett and Jerome K. Jerome: with the latter he wrote the comedy *The Prude's Progress*, 1895.

Selected Works
In Sugar-Cane Land. London, 1894.
The Prude's Progress. 1895.
Lying Prophets. 1897.
Children of the Mist. 1898.
The Human Boy. 1899.
My Devon Year. 1904.

PINCKARD, GEORGE
(1768–1835)

Virgin Islands
British physician and army officer. Served in the West Indies, Guiana, and Ireland. Promoted to the rank of Deputy Inspector

General of Hospitals. Established Bloomsbury Dispensary, London, and was its physician for 30 years.
Notes on the West Indies. 3 vols. London, 1806.

POWLES, L. D.

Bahamas
    Land of the Pink Pearl. London, 1888.

PULLEN-BURRY, BESSIE
(born 1858)

Jamaica
Selected Works
    Ethiopia in Exile: Jamaica Revisited. London, 1905.
    Jamaica As It Is, 1903. London, 1903.

RAMPINI, CHARLES J. G.
(1840–?)

Jamaica
    Sheriff of Elgin.
Selected Works
    Letters from Jamaica, "The Land of Streams and Woods." Edinburgh, 1873.
    Shetland and the Shetlanders. Kirkwall, 1884.
    A History of Moray and Nairn. 1897.

SCHAW, JANET J.
(1731–1801)

Antigua
    The only known details of Janet Schaw are that she was a Scotswoman who traveled with her brother between 1774 and 1776 and kept a journal which went unpublished until 1921.
    Journal of a Lady of Quality. J. Schaw; being the narrative of a journey from Scotland to the West Indies, North Carolina, and Portugal in the years 1774 to 1776. Edited by Evangeline Walker Andrews in collaboration with Charles McLean Andrews. New Haven, 1927. Yale Historical Publication of Man-

uscripts and Edited Texts no. 6. 2d ed., Oxford University
Press, 1934, 1939.

SCOLES, REVEREND J. S. (INATIUS)

Guyana
  Sketches of African and Indian Life in British Guiana. Demerara,
  Georgetown, 1885.

SCOTT, MICHAEL
(1789–1835)

Jamaica
  Born near Glasgow, educated at Glasgow University, Scott set-
  tled in Jamaica and went into business. Although he returned to
  Scotland and married in 1818, he was back in Jamaica shortly,
  before entering permanently into the family trading firm in 1822.
  Tom Cringle's Log. First published anonymously in *Blackwood's
  Magazine,* September 1829–August 1833; first published in
  book form in Paris, 1836. Reprint. London: J. M. Dent, 1969.
  The Cruise of the 'Midge,' first published anonymously in *Blackwood's Magazine,* March 1834–June 1835; first published in
  book form in Paris and Edinburgh, 1836.

SEWELL, WILLIAM GRANT
(1829–62)

Jamaica
  Journalist and author, born in Quebec. Studied law but became
  a New York journalist, 1853. Went to the West Indies for his
  health in 1860.
  *The Ordeal of Free Labour in the British West Indies. Letters
  from Jamaica in 1860.* New York, 1861; London, 1862.

SLOANE, SIR HANS
(1660–1753)

Jamaica
  British physician and naturalist. Physician to the governor of Jamaica, 1687–88. President, College of Physicians, 1719–35. Cho-

sen president of the Royal Society on the death of Newton, 1727.
Physician-General to the Army, 1722. Baronet, 1716. First Physician to George III, 1727. Physician in Charge, Christ's Hospital, 1694–1730. Promoter of the Colony of Georgia, 1732. His be-
quest of biological collections (together with the Horleian MMS
and Collonian Collection) formed the basis of the British
Museum.

Selected Works

A *Voyage to the Islands of Madera, Barbadoes, Nieves, St. Christophers, and Jamaica, with the Natural History of the Same.*
London, vol. I, 1707; vol. II, 1725.

*Catalogus Plantarum quae in Insula Jamaica sponte provenciunt
aut vulgo coluntur.* London, 1696.

*An Account of Medicine for Sòreness, Weakness, and other Dis-
tempers of the Eyes.* London, 1745, 1750.

SMITH, JAMES

Virgin Islands

*The Winter of 1840 in St. Croix, with an Excursion to Tortola and
St. Thomas.* New York, 1840.

STEDMAN, JOHN GABRIEL
(1744–97)

Surinam

Officer commissioned in Stuart's Regiment of the Scots Brigade;
rose to rank of lieutenant-colonel. Born in Holland, son of an officer in the Scots Brigade in service for the States-General of
Holland. (Some of the illustrations in his book on Surinam were
engraved by William Blake.)

*Narrative of a Five Years' Expedition against the Revolted Ne-
groes of Surinam, in Guiana on the Wild Coast of South America, from the year 1772 to 1777: elucidating the History of that
country, and describing its Productions, viz., Quadrupedes,
Birds, Fishes, Reptiles, Trees, Shrubs, Fruits and Roots; with
an account of the Indians of Guiana and Negroes of Guinea.*
2 vols. London, 1796. 2d ed., 2 vols., 1806. Reprint. Amherst:
University of Massachusetts Press, 1971.

STEWART, JAMES

Jamaica
> A *View of the Past and Present State of the Island of Jamaica*
> . . . Edinburgh, 1823. Originally published anonymously as *An*
> *Account of Jamaica and its Inhabitants*. London, 1808.

VAN SERTIMA, J.

Guyana
Selected Works
> *Scenes and Sketches of Demarara Life*. Georgetown, Demerara,
> 1899.
> *Among the Common People of British Guiana*. Georgetown,
> Demerara, 1897.
> *The Creole Tongue of British Guiana*. New Amsterdam, Berbice,
> 1905.

VERNON, B. J.

Jamaica
> *Early Recollections of Jamaica* . . . *To which are added trifles*
> *from St. Helena relating to Napoleon and his suit*. London, 1848.

WATSON, RICHARD
(1781–1833)

> English Methodist preacher. President, Wesleyan Missionary
> Society, 1821, 1827, 1832. First editor, *Liverpool Courier*, 1808.
> Watson drafted the resolution in favor of gradual emancipation
> which was adopted by the Missionary Committee in 1825 and by
> the General Conference in 1830.

Selected Works
> *A Defense of Wesleyan Methodist Missions in the West Indies*.
> London, 1817.
> *Conversations for the Young, designed to Promote the Profitable*
> *Reading of the Holy Scriptures*. London, 1830.
> *Life of the Rev. John Wesley, Founder of the Methodist Society*.
> London, 1831.

WEED, THURLOW
(1797–1882)

Virgin Islands
     Journalist and political leader, New York State Whig and Repub-
     lican parties. Owner, *Rochester Telegraph;* publisher, *Anti-Ma-*
     sonic Enquirer; member, New York State Assembly; publisher,
     Albany *Evening Journal;* editor, New York *Commercial Advertiser.*
Selected Works
     Letters from Europe and the West Indies. Albany, 1866. Re-
          printed in *Virgin Island View* (St. Thomas, VI), vol. II, no. 7
          (December 1966), 32–38.
     Autobiography. Edited by his daughter, Harriet A. Weed. Bos-
          ton, 1883.

WENTWORTH, TRELAWNY

Barbados, Virgin Islands
     The West India Sketch Book. London, 1834.

WILLIAMS, CYNRIC R.
(born 1786)

Jamaica
     A Tour through the Island of Jamaica, from the Western to the
          Eastern End, in the Year 1823. London, 1826, 1827.

THE UNITED STATES

NOTE: The location (in italics) preceding each entry is the site of the
description.

ANDREWS, SIDNEY
(1837–80)

South Carolina (Inland)
     U.S. journalist born in Sheffield, Mass. Contributor to *Boston*
     Advertiser, Atlantic Monthly, Every Saturday. Editor, Alton, Ill.
     Daily Courier. Special correspondent to *Chicago Tribune* and

Boston Advertiser, 1864–69. Private secretary to Massachusetts governor, 1872. Secretary, Massachusetts Board of Charities, 1872–80.

The South Since the War, as shown by Fourteen Weeks of Travel Observation in Georgia and the Carolinas. By "Dixon." Boston, 1866.

BOTUME, ELIZABETH HYDE

South Carolina (Sea Islands)
U.S. Civil War patriot, teacher.
First Days Amongst the Contrabands. Boston, 1893.

CABLE, GEORGE WASHINGTON
(1844–1925)

Journalist and author. Born in New Orleans and educated at Washington and Lee, Bowdoin, and Yale; served in the Civil War, 1863–65; worked as a reporter for the *New Orleans Picayune,* 1865–79; wrote stories for *Scribner's Monthly* from 1879 forward, and devoted himself to literature. He founded the (Northampton, Mass.) People's Institute for Workers' Education and later lectured widely, for a time with Mark Twain.

Selected Works
"A Negro Folk-Song." *Folk-Lorist,* vol. I, no. 1 (July 1892), 54.
Old Creole Days. New York, 1879.
The Grandissimes. New York, 1880.
"Creole Slave Songs." *Century Magazine,* 31 (1886), 807–28.
"The Dance in Place Congo." *Century Magazine,* 31 (1886), 517–32.

COOLEY, ROSSA BELLE
(1873–1949)

South Carolina (Sea Islands)
Principal and teacher, born Albany, N.Y. A. B., Vassar, 1893. Taught in New York, 1893–97; Hampton Institute, Hampton, Va., 1897–1904; principal of Penn Normal Industrial and Agricultural School, St. Helena's Island, S.C.

Selected Works
Homes of the Freed. New York, 1926.

School Acres: An Adventure in Rural Education. New Haven,
1930–31.

Livestock Problems in Production, Marketing and Management.
By R. B. Cooley, C. Harper, and Frank G. King; ed. R. W.
Gregory. Chicago, 1939.

COUNCILL, WILLIAM HOOPER
(1848–1909)

Alabama

Born a slave, Fayetteville, S.C. Teacher and lawyer, Ph.D., Mor-
ris Brown College, 1867. Founder and president of Agricultural
and Mechanical College, at Normal, Ala. Contributor to *Arena,
Forum,* and other magazines. Active in the A.M.E. Church.

Selected Works

*Synopsis of Three Addresses Delivered at the Chatauqua Assem-
bly at Waterloo, Iowa, July 10, 14, 15; at Chatauqua Assembly
at Spirit Lake, Iowa, July 11–12; and at State Normal School
of Iowa at Cedar Falls, July 15, 1900* . . . (Normal, Ala., 1900).

Lamp of Wisdom, or Race History Illuminated. Nashville, 1898.

The Negro Laborer. Huntsville, Ala., 1887.

The Negro and the South: His Work and Progress. Normal, Ala.,
n.d.

The South and the Negro. Normal, Ala., 1900.

EIGHTS, DR. JAMES

Albany, New York

Reminiscences of the City of Albany. Albany, 1836.

"Pinkster Festivities in Albany Sixty Years Ago." *Collections on
the History of Albany* (Albany, 1867), vol. II, 323–27.

FINCH, JOHN

Virginia

Selected Works

*Travels in the United States of America and Canada; including
some account of their scientific institutions, and a few notices
of the geology and mineralogy of those countries, to which is
added an essay on the natural boundaries of empires.* London,
1833.

The Natural Boundaries of Empires; A New View of Colonization.
London, 1844.

HEARN, LAFCADIO
(1850–1904)

New Orleans
Born Santa Maura Island, Greece, of Rosa Tessima, and C. B.
Hearn, Surgeon-Major in the British army. He emigrated to New
York in 1869 and found regular work with the *Cincinnati Enquirer* and the *Cincinnati Commercial* from 1873 to 1877. In
New Orleans he wrote for the *Item* and *Times-Democrat.* His
writings and letters make him America's first systematic collector
of folklore and dialect. From 1887 to 1889 he lived in Martinique
and wrote *Two Years in the French West Indies* and *Youma.* In
1880 he moved to Japan and became a major literary figure
there.
Selected Works
"The Last of the Voudoos." *Harper's Weekly,* vol. 29 (Nov. 7,
1885), 726–27.
Ghombo Zhèbes. 1886.
Two Years in the French West Indies. 1890.
Youma. 1890.
Glimpses of Unfamiliar Japan. 1894.

HIGGINSON, THOMAS WENTWORTH
(1823–1911)

South Carolina
Born into a wealthy merchant's family in Cambridge, Mass., Higginson attended Harvard College and Divinity School and was
ordained a minister. He was active in antislavery and women's
suffrage movements. During the Civil War he was made colonel
and led an all-black regiment, the 1st South Carolina Volunteers,
from 1862 to 1864.
Selected Works
Army Life in a Black Regiment. Boston, 1870.
Atlantic Essays. 1971.
Malbone (a novel). 1969.

INGRAHAM, JOSEPH HOLT
(1809–1860)

Tennessee
> Born Portland, Me. Author of historical fiction; teacher; Episco-
> pal clergyman. A sailor in his youth, he later taught at Jefferson
> College, Washington, Miss., and published fiction in the 1840s
> (80 novels by 1840, 20 in 1845–46 alone; many of these were first
> published in weekly newspapers). After marrying the daughter
> of a Mississippi planter, he remained in the South.

Selected Works
> *The Sunny South; or, The Southerner at Home.* Philadelphia,
>   1860.
> *The Southwest, by a Yankee.* 2 vols. 1835.

KEMBLE, FRANCES ANNE
(1809–93)

Georgia
> English actor and author. A member of a famous acting family,
> Fanny Kemble made her debut as Juliet at Covent Garden
> in 1829. After 3 years of leading parts, she accompanied her
> father on a tour of the United States in 1832. She married Pierce
> Butler of Philadelphia in 1834 and was divorced from him in
> 1849.

Selected Works
> *Journal of a Residence on a Georgian Plantation in 1838–1839.*
>   London, 1863.
> *Francis the First: An Historical Drama.* London, 1832.
> *Journal of Frances Anne Butler.* 2 vols. Philadelphia, 1835.
> *The Star of Seville: A Drama.* 1837.
> *Poems.* Philadelphia, 1844.
> *A Year of Consolation.* 2 vols. 1847.

LATROBE, BENJAMIN HENRY
(1764–1820)

New Orleans
> Born in Fulneck, England, and educated in England and Ger-
> many. Coming to the United States as an architect, he designed
> the Richmond penitentiary in 1797, the Bank of Pennsylvania in

Philadelphia in 1801, the south wing of the U.S. Capitol in 1803, and many other government and private buildings. He died of yellow fever while building a city water supply for New Orleans.

The Journals of Benjamin Henry Latrobe. Edited by Edward C. Carter II, John C. Van Horne, and Lee W. Formwalt. Vol. 3, *1799–1820: From Philadelphia to New Orleans.* New Haven: Yale University Press, 1980.

LOWERY, REVEREND IRVING E.
(born 1850)

Selected Works

Life on the Old Plantation in Ante-Bellum Days; or a story based on facts. Columbia, S.C.: The State Co., 1911.

Consecrated Talent. Boston, 1887.

MERRICK, GEORGE BYRON
(1841–1931)

St. Louis

Old Times on the Upper Mississippi; The Recollections of a Steamboat Pilot from 1854–1863. Cleveland, 1909.

OLMSTED, FEDERICK LAW
(1822–1903)

South Carolina (Inland), 394–95; 448–49; Alabama, 554; New Orleans (Riverboat), 607–10.

American landscape architect, farmer, and writer. Educated at Yale, M.A.; Amherst; LL.D., Harvard. Secretary of U.S. Sanitary Commission 1861–63; appointed architect-in-chief and Superintendent of Central Park, N.Y.C., 1858. Designer of parks in Brooklyn, Boston, Bridgeport, Trenton, Montreal, Buffalo, Chicago, Milwaukee, Louisville, and of the U.S. Capitol grounds and terrace, the World's Fair in Chicago, and private estates. Traveled in the East Indies, Europe, and America.

Selected Works

The Cotton Kingdom. 2 vols. New York, 1861.

Walks and Talks of an American Farmer in England. New York, 1852.

A Journey in the Seaboard Slave States, With Remarks on Their Economy. New York, 1856.

A Journey in the Back Country. New York, 1860.

Journeys and Explorations in the Cotton Kingdom. 2 vols. London and New York, 1862.

PAYNE, REVEREND DANIEL ALEXANDER
(1811–93)

Baltimore, Philadelphia

A clergyman and college president, Daniel Payne was an Afro-American born in Charleston, S.C. As an educator, he taught slaves in Charleston until the practice was outlawed. In 1840 he moved to Philadelphia, where he taught school and entered the Lutheran ministry. In 1852 he was elected Bishop of the A.M.E. Church in New York. He then served as president of Wilberforce University in Ohio from 1865 to 1876. He established the Bethel Literary Association in Washington, D.C., and visited the White House to urge President Lincoln to sign the Emancipation Bill in 1862.

Selected Works

Recollections of Seventy Years. Edited by C. S. Smith. Nashville, 1888.

A History of the African Methodist Episcopal Church. 3 vols. Baltimore, 1805.

Bishop Payne's First Annual Address to the Philadelphia Annual Conference of the African Methodist Episcopal Church . . . 16 May 1853. Philadelphia, 1853.

Recollections of Men and Things. 1879.

Historical Sketch of Wilberforce University. Xenia, 1879.

PYRNELLE, LOUISE-CLARKE

Mississippi

Diddie, Dumps, and Tot; or Plantation Child-Life. New York, 1882.

SALA, GEORGE AUGUSTUS HENRY
(1828–96)

New Orleans

London journalist, son of an Italian father and a Demerara

planter's daughter; an associate of Dickens, he wrote numerous articles on London low life, and in 1863–64 he served as *London Telegraph* correspondent in the United States.

Selected Works
> *America Revisited.* London, 1883.
> *The Life and Adventures of George Augustus Henry Sala.* 2 vols. 1895.

SEAWORTHY, CAPT. GREGORY
(*See* Throop, George Higby)

SMITH, WILLIAM B.

Virginia
> "The Persimmon Tree and the Beer Dance." *Farmer's Register,* 6 (April 1939), 59–61.

THROOP, GEORGE HIGBY (Capt. Gregory Seaworthy, pseud.)
(1818–96)

North Carolina
Selected Works
> *Bertie: or, Life in the Old Field, a humorous novel . . . with a letter to the author from Washington Irving.* Philadelphia, 1851.
> *Nag's Head, or Two Months Among "The Bankers." A Story of Seashore Life and Mariners.* 1850.

WATSON, JOHN FANNING
(1779–1860)

Philadelphia
> Philadelphia banker and historian who co-founded the Historical Society of Pennsylvania in 1824. Led movements for the proper markings of graves of historic personages; became secretary and treasurer of the Philadelphia, Germantown, and Norristown Railroad in 1847. Author of select reviews of foreign literature and historical chronicles of Philadelphia and New York.
> *Annals of Philadelphia, and Pennsylvania, in the Olden Time; being a collection of memoirs, anecdotes, and incidents of the city and its inhabitants, and of the earliest settlements of the inland part of Pennsylvania . . .* Philadelphia, 1830. 2d edition

expanded to 3 vols. with revisions by Willis Hazard, published by Edwin S. Stuart, 1927.

WHIPPLE, HENRY BENJAMIN
(1822–1901)

Georgia

An Episcopal bishop, Whipple was born in Adams, N.Y. In 1859 he was consecrated the first Episcopal bishop of Minnesota and in 1860 established a mission among the Sioux, where he worked for federal Indian policy reform. Whipple was a trustee for the Peabody Fund for educational work in the South.

Selected Works

Bishop Whipple's Southern Diary, 1843–1844. Minneapolis: University of Minnesota Press, 1937.

Lights and Shadows of a Long Episcopate. 1899.

Taopi and His Friends, or Indian Wrongs and Projects. By Bishop Whipple of Minnesota; Rev. S. D. Hiaman, Missionary to the Santee Sioux Indians; and Mr. Wm. Welsh of Philadelphia; including the celebrated report of the Indian Peace Commissioners, and Letters on Indian Civilization by various authorities. Philadelphia, 1869.

Index

Entries in italics (except for periodicals) are native terms. Entries in quotation marks are key lines of songs.